Hollywood Plateau

By

Robert Crane

Also by Robert Crane

Two Friends Over Drinks (with John Cerney)

Boom! The Baby Boomer Album

Crane: Sex, Celebrity, and My Father's Unsolved Murder (with Christopher Fryer)

My Life as a Mankiewicz (with Tom Mankiewicz)

Bruce Dern: A Memoir (with Bruce Dern and Christopher Fryer)

Jack Nicholson: The Early Years (with Christopher Fryer)

SCTV: Behind the Scenes (with Dave Thomas and Susan Carney)

Burn the Ice (with Kirk Driscoll, Steve DeWinter, Leslie Bertram, Deborah S. Hildebrand)

No Stone Unturned (with Kell O'Connell)

To Leslie Bertram Crane, Grace Kono-Wells, Chloe
and John Rezek

Interviews and articles originally appeared in *Playboy*, *Oui*, *Good Housekeeping*, *Los Angeles Times*, *KCET* Magazine, *USA Today*, *Hwy 111*, *Ventura Blvd.*, *Genesis*, *Playgirl*, *Palm Springs Life*, *Valley Scene* Magazine, *L.A. Style*, *Los Angeles*, *Seven*, The *Rotarian*, *Auto Focus* website, and *Cheech and Chong's Comedy Film Festival* Magazine.

Editors included John Rezek, Stewart Weiner, Patrick McGilligan, Dian Hanson, Stephen Randall, Ed Dwyer, Jan Golab, Toy Gibson, Richard Cramer, Linda Grasso, Pat Button, Irv Letofsky, and Patricia Bradford Rambo II.

Co-writers on selected pieces were Phil Hartman, David Diamond, Christopher Fryer, Leslie Bertram, Carl Spihek, B.J. Wilkom, and Kell O'Connell.

Many of the interviews were transcribed and typed by Keystrokes in Santa Monica, California.

Thanks to Meagan Bejar, Ricky Bejar, Janet Spiegel/Spiegelmedia, Suzy Friendly, Niki Dantine, Jill Cartter, Andy Erish, David Arnoff, Joe Coyle and Kill Fee Productions.

Special thanks to Kari Hildebrand.

Contents

Introduction

This collection of interviews and articles covers the years 1974-2013. I was young. The performers and artists seemed more mysterious. There weren't weekly award shows yet or dozens of chat programs. The thrill was in the mining and exposure of nuggets of wisdom, experience, and observation formed during the creative person's rise to notoriety. The offered quotes were colorful with many flavors. There was an air of nonchalance. The subjects were individuals tied only to their own constitutions.

When celebrity publicists evolved into more than hand-holders and demanded the interview questions in advance while social media became a revolution, I knew the art of the conversation with notables was dead and short puff pieces were coming up fast on the horizon.

The celebrity was now one with the medium. There were no middlemen. There was no longer a waiting period. The new outlets were instant and 24/7. Branding became more important than talent. *How* one said it was more memorable than *what* one said. Magazines died and the remaining publishing business transformed into a receptacle of "famous" people sharing dubious or non-existent talents.

On the downside, some of the pieces herein contain crude questions and answers. There was no political correctness. Enlightenment was a seldom-used word. Women wore "The Little Black Dress" because of figure considerations. But, on the upside, there were still elements of surprise and discovery found in creative individuals who were not afraid to make the reader work for the drama and laughter. We, the audience, felt as though the famous person was sharing secrets with us and he or she was our best friend for a few moments.

--Robert Crane

ACTRESSES

Robert Crane

Rachel Weisz

The mummy's lust object wants a potion to make her invisible. We think that's a very bad idea.

1

PLAYBOY: Please explain your intense interest in Harry Houdini.

WEISZ: He was one of the earliest socially acceptable images of S&M—bound and chained—standing there in pain but with a triumphant look on his face. That's not why I'm drawn to him. I just love the showmanship, that no prison, no chain could hold him. The art of illusion and, in general, escapology is fascinating. Houdini's last name originally was Weisz and he was Hungarian. My dad is Hungarian—my secret fantasy has always been that I'm related to Houdini.

2

PLAYBOY: Your mom is a psychotherapist. Does that mean there's a greater likelihood you'll end up on a couch?

WEISZ: A casting couch or a psychoanalyst's couch? I just avoid couches in general. Best to stay off the couch.

3

PLAYBOY: You spent some of your childhood in Austria. Could psychoanalysis have been invented anywhere else?

WEISZ: I can't think of anywhere else it could have happened. Turn-of-the-century Vienna was completely wild culturally. It was Victorian, but it had these amazing double standards. So while it was very Catholic, very moral, there was this fiery counterculture going on. There were masked orgies in the Vienna woods. There was incredible sexual liberation at the time that gave birth to psychoanalysis, which was all about what was really going on underneath. Freud had plenty to work with in Austria.

4

PLAYBOY: What's the greatest psychological insight that your mother ever gave you?

WEISZ: Never trust a man in a bow tie. It's not true actually, because my dad is in his 70s now and he's taken to wearing bow ties. But my mom is slightly tongue-in-cheek about it. She's just full of balls of wisdom.

5

PLAYBOY: You did a nice job capturing the classic lace-bloused, heaving-bosom allure of a librarian in *The Mummy*. Did you take that look home with you?

WEISZ: I got a letter from a librarian in England who said she felt I totally misrepresented librarians. She was really angry. I kept the letter. In the movie my character was kind of clumsy, a bit forgetful and a little ditsy, and this librarian wondered why a librarian would be so ditsy. She wrote me that librarians come in all different shapes, sizes and styles, which I guess is true.

6

PLAYBOY: In *Enemy at the Gates* you achieved the impossible—looking incredibly sexy while being filthy dirty. Did you realize you were paving new cinematic ground?

WEISZ: Wow, no. I don't think so. But we definitely got into the mud and the dirt. It was quite refreshing because normally in a movie you're made to look good all the time. The worse we looked, the better. The more mud on our face, the more dust in our hair, the better. It's quite liberating. It's like being a kid in a sandpit. Kits love to get dirty, climb trees, get messy. It's a good feeling. I was lucky I had a hot bath every night. I didn't sleep in the mud.

7

PLAYBOY: Your father is an inventor. What did you wish he would have invented?

WEISZ: Probably a potion that you can drink and be invisible. That would be great. It would be fascinating to be able to watch people and they wouldn't be able to see you. It would be useful to me as an actor because part of your job is to watch people. But it would be useful for other reasons, too. I'd go to the White House, find out what Bush is up to—what's really going on in there.

8

PLAYBOY: What things have you done while listening to *Stairway to Heaven*?

WEISZ: I'm afraid nothing too exotic. Driven a car. Definitely gone jogging. It makes me run if I listen to it on a Walkman. I've danced. Really boring things. I've cooked. Well, that's a lie. I have boiled eggs, I should say. Gotten ready to go out.

9

PLAYBOY: How come actors want to be rock-and-roll stars and rock-and-roll stars want to be actors?

WEISZ: Hard to say, since very few people can do both. Jack Black is one of the few who can pull it off. He's a rock star, an actor, a comedian. Jack is the ultimate combo.

10

PLAYBOY: Your father called your lips "Mick Jagger lips." Did you work with that?

WEISZ: Mine aren't as big as Mick's. My younger sister's, Minnie's, are. I think they rival Jagger's lips. If I had said it to someone I would have meant it as a compliment, because I think he's got amazing lips. But from my dad, who's missed out on rock and roll, it was not a compliment. He was saying that I move my mouth too much. It wasn't like Greta Garbo—still enough. So it was not a compliment.

11

PLAYBOY: You own a Jaguar. Are you crazy?

WEISZ: No! I just sold it. It was my beautiful vintage car, one of the most beautiful cars ever. It was a Seventies model, a 4.2 Sovereign. It was a very big, powerful car, a four-door.

12

PLAYBOY: Did you have a special arrangement with your mechanic?

WEISZ: I wish. No, it just cost me lots of pounds. The final straw was—I'm not well versed mechanically—but the power-steering fluid container sprung a leak so all the fluid drained onto the ground, and I had to drive this huge car without power steering, which meant my muscles and arms were really challenged. It was like driving a truck. Everything that could go wrong went wrong with the car. I finally sold it for parts. The person who bought my Jag was just going to chuck it up. That's all it was good for.

13

PLAYBOY: We understand you are an Elvis fan. Do you accept everything about him or are there some parts of his life about which you're in denial?

WEISZ: Some Elvis fans have read all the biographies and know everything about him. I love the way he looked and I listen to his music, but I'm not a fanatic. I think I just fell in love with him when I was a little girl, watching his movies on TV on Saturday afternoons. I'm not in denial about any moment of Elvis' life. What's incredible to me is that at the end of his career when he was fat and drugged up and not himself, he could still sing. What's that famous recording where he bursts out laughing? He's drunk out of his mind. Even then, he sang like an angel, like nothing could steal his voice from him. It was effortless for him. So I loved him in all stages. I think he was cute even when he was fat and wasted.

14

PLAYBOY: Have you ever been tempted to try a deep-fried banana and peanut butter sandwich?

WEISZ: No, I haven't. I've hard that one sandwich is, like, 4000 calories. I think it's fascinating that Elvis and Brando—two of the most beautiful and lusted-after male icons ever—both said, "Fuck you, quit treating me like a sex object" and got fat. Interesting, isn't it?

15

PLAYBOY: You went to Cambridge. What is the title of your favorite paper?

WEISZ: I don't think you're going to want to print this. My favorite essay is "For the Etruscans" by the American feminist writer Rachel Blau DuPlessis. It's about wondering where, or if, there is a female language rather than a male language. Most things around us were created by men. The paper questions if behind the language or words there is something else. It's written in a nonlinear style—a way in which women might think. Like, if a man's telling a story and says, "I was walking down the street," the women asks, "What time was it?" "It doesn't matter what time it was. I was walking down the street." It's kind of all over the place.

16

PLAYBOY: What's the best paper you wrote?

WEISZ: I did a paper on Henry James that would have been published in the *Henry James Quarterly*. I was asked to edit it. I had to lose 1000 words, and I didn't bother. So I'm unpublished.

17

PLAYBOY: Could you date anyone less educated than you?

WEISZ: Sure. Definitely. There are different kinds of intelligence. I would like to believe that love transcends everything—that someone who is from America could flirt with someone who is from Japan. It's a completely different culture. Love should transcend all.

18

PLAYBOY: How do you flirt like a Brit?

WEISZ: I think that Americans are just as good. At the end of the day, flirting is a pretty universal language. Americans are more direct. British people are more indirect about everything. I'm making this up as I go along. How am I supposed to know? I like American men, let me just say that.

19

PLAYBOY: Can you explain the sorry state of British dentistry?

WEISZ: Well, I guess the real answer is because our health care has been free. You go to the dentist here and they will tell you that you have eight cavities when you really maybe have only one. In England they'll tell you that you haven't got any because dental care is free. Actually, that's not true. Now you have to pay for your dental work. It was free for a long time. We don't cap our teeth and try to make everything look perfect. You have pretty unattainable images of perfection that, to us, are sort of characterless. We like a bit of character—a little yellowing, a little rotting, a little wonky, coffee stains, cigarette stains. Irregular teeth—we like that.

20

PLAYBOY: Maybe the Brit medical community spent too much time developing those veterinary skills.

WEISZ: I'm sure! I don't have a pet, but I'm sure that we have the best vets in the world. As you know, the British love their pets more than their children.

Carrie Fisher

The feistiest woman in the universe talks about first dates, being rich...and why Darth Vader should be called Darthy.

Robert Crane caught up with the diminutive daughter of Debbie Reynolds and Eddie Fisher at her home in Laurel Canyon. He reports, "Carrie Fisher lives in a log cabin. Really. The only tip-off to her wealth is a Mercedes 450 SL parked in the driveway. Carrie talks fast and loud and doesn't forget the audience for a moment. She takes charge, like Princess Leia, but is much more attractive in person without that costume and the doughnuts on the side of her head."

1

PLAYBOY: Are you afraid of being known for the rest of your life as Princess Leia and not as Carrie Fisher?

FISHER: I'm resigned to the fact that I will be, in a very pleasant way. I thought I was going to end up as Tammy. So you can imagine it's some kind of relief. It's OK that I'm this gun-toting girl in the sky. I'm not afraid of that.

2

PLAYBOY: What do you want Princess Leia to do that she can't do?

FISHER: A hundred things. I asked George Lucas nicely if she could have a drinking problem or take soma or *anything*, because she's had a rough couple of films: She's been tortured by Darth Vader; she had a space boyfriend and he was frozen; she's been wounded; a planet was blown up with her parents on it—the whole shot. I thought she would have some kind of problem after that. I wanted another girl up in space with me, shopping, talking about guys—"The space suit really doesn't do him justice; he's really cute underneath all that plastic." Also, I have a costume I want to use that I think even *Playboy* would be proud of. Anyway, I don't take drugs or drink in space. Nobody does that.

3

PLAYBOY: If it were up to you, what would happen to Princess Leia?

FISHER: She'd get blown up. In midsentence: "And another thing; this aircraft is not—" Boom! She just gets a little testy. She's had two films to work it out and she hasn't done it. They blow people up well in these films.

4

PLAYBOY: Who is the lucky man who introduces you to full princesshood and under what circumstances?

FISHER: First of all, one has to assume that Han Solo's kiss is the first space kiss that Princess Leia has encountered. She's just a soldier and she never goes below barracks. I thought maybe he'd be a

7

robot. We'd cut to a fireplace and the embers would go down, and we'd cut back and I'd look exactly like Princess Di. But I guess it doesn't happen like that in space.

5

PLAYBOY: Can you foresee having a relationship with Vader?

FISHER: Yeah, but not of the kind that you're suggesting. He's not a real nice guy. Not your standard relationship. There are other styles of relationships that I don't like to imagine. He's just tortured me and everything. The guy's not attractive. He has funny hair. He's not black. He may be neuter. A lot of this is open to people's interpretations. Maybe he's gay. Vader is gay and he's embarrassed about some tattoos he had put on his face. He got drunk one night. No, he has some kind of problem with facial hair. What can I tell you? You'll find it out in the third film. You had a glimpse of him in *The Empire Strikes Back*. He looked like some vegetables gone bad.

6

PLAYBOY: We still remember your scenes from *Shampoo*. Princess Leia is a nun compared with that character. Which one do you have an easier time relating to?

FISHER: *Shampoo*—because it's a contemporary role. Princess Leia is very cartoon-like. In *Shampoo*, you could improvise. You can't improvise in space. Usually, in stressful situations, one would go, "Oh, my God; oh, shit!" You can't say, 'Oh, my God!' in space. You can't have any time references. It's more difficult to move within that dialog and have it sound natural. I've always found my character very stilted compared with the other ones, but it's a fairy tale. It's more difficult to play that, because you have to bring yourself to it. Leia has dry, almost parched humor. That stuff is difficult. I always felt as if I were a girl who was being led into this $10,000,000 boy's toy. *Shampoo* was easy. It had nothing to do with my character's promiscuity. It had to do with her reality. At the time I did *Shampoo*, I was a virgin. I knew nothing. They would kid me. Warren [Beatty], Hal [Ashby] and Robert [Towne] would all fall apart laughing and I would, too. My line to Warren was "Want to fuck?" and I was supposed to be hostile and mean and power-crazy. I would say that line and fall apart, because Warren had told the others that I didn't know what I was talking about and that was very funny to them. I knew about everything, which was probably why I didn't want to *do* anything. I was the last in my class. I was 17, almost 18.

7

PLAYBOY: Were you grounded when your mother saw your scenes in *Shampoo*?

FISHER: No. She helped me with my dialog and asked if I could, maybe, say screw instead of fuck. She wanted a five- as opposed to a four-letter word. I don't think my grandparents saw it. My grandmother has a pacemaker, so they don't see that kind of film. My father was fond of it. My mother liked it. She's not really Tammy, just as I'm not really Princess Leia. She's a regular human being. I've actually heard her say that word.

8

PLAYBOY: There is a rumor that you've made more money from the *Star Wars* films than your parents made during their entire careers.

FISHER: I think Andy Warhol started that rumor. People like it. It sounds good. I'd like it if I weren't me. I could call and get an accountant and figure it out. My mother made 53 films and did night-club work. They didn't get paid as much as we do now; but no, it's not true. I've been working for only eight years.

9

PLAYBOY: What are the net effects of being raised by show-business parents/

FISHER: Look at me; I'm a wreck. The worst. Don't ever do it. If you had grown up with my parents, it would have been real weird for you. I didn't grow up with both of them, but growing up with even one of them was not—I mean, I was on the movie-star map. When I was three hours old, I was photographed by *Modern Screen*. I don't like being photographed. My father is now publicly saying that he took a lot of drugs. I don't remember that. I spent my summers in Vegas. That was camp to me—sitting by the pool and hearing that weird music and having people paged.

10

PLAYBOY: Was there anything in your father's book that embarrassed you?

FISHER: I read some of it. He can't embarrass me. I don't own him. That's how he wanted to work out his life: to write about it and gain that perspective. I read it to see whether or not he talked badly about my mother. They're not on good terms.

11

PLAYBOY: Growing up with prominent breasts, were you made to feel any particular way about them?

FISHER: Breasts? Mine? I don't even think about myself like that. In *Shampoo*, it's true. For *Star Wars*, they had me tape down my breasts, because there are no breasts in space. Camera tape, gaffer tape. At the end of every day, I was going to draw a lottery and one of the crew could rip off the tape. I never did it, though. Actually, my mother is more famous for her breasts than I could ever be for mine. Groucho Marx, in front of Nate 'n Al's, once told me she had a great chest. He was going to visit her in the hospital to see if they were real. He also said that on the Cavett show. So I have some. I have two.

12

PLAYBOY: We have heard that you are financially set for life. What unexpected things has that allowed you to do?

FISHER: I have this house and I have an apartment in New York. And I can always pick up the check for dinner. I'm pretty comfortable financially, but you never are for very long. If you make a lot of money, taxes come screaming to your door and take most of it away. I've done well for somebody who's 26. Unfortunately, I was brought up real privileged. That allows you material comfort, which I always had. It allowed me not to be financially dependent on my mother at 18 and to live real comfortably and travel and do things. I don't do ridiculous things with money. My business manager has socked mine away so hard, I'm loath to buy a chair. One of my mother's biggest threats was always that she'd take away my Saks card. Now I don't even have one. Money is a nice thing to have. Everything you see here I own.

13

PLAYBOY: On what do you spend exorbitant amounts of money?

FISHER: I take a lot of lessons. I do a lot of intensive seminars. I travel a lot. I spend a lot on clothes and sexy lingerie, video tapes and books and furniture and primitive folk art. It's best to buy art if you really know what you're buying. I like Magritte and a guy named Donald Roller Wilson. I like surrealists. I have such anxiety about money.

14

PLAYBOY: Do you oversee your own investments and bills?

FISHER: Yeah, but they don't make that much sense to me. Just enough so I know I'm not being railroaded. I don't turn everything over to my business manager.

15

PLAYBOY: Are you a corporation?

FISHER: Yup. Deliquesce. Paul Simon named it for me. It means melting. He's into etymology, as am I, slightly. He knows all these real strange words. That's the strangest of them all.

16

PLAYBOY: Is there a social etiquette for being rich?

FISHER: Not that I'm aware of but probably so. I'm completely unconscious and underwater about it. If I want to do something that costs a lot of money and I want to do it with someone who doesn't have much money, I'll pay. Everybody contributes something. If all I contribute is money, I feel really terrible, because I would like my contribution to be more than that. But if I want to go somewhere and this particular person can't afford it, the etiquette on that is "I'll pay for you to come if you'll come." It all evens out, I think. It's never been a problem that I pick up more than my share of bar bills.

17

PLAYBOY: How can men impress you?

FISHER: Lifting weights. Saving people from drowning. Diving off a building. Setting themselves on fire. I'm totally impressed. They impress me if they can have a good time most of the time. When they don't struggle in their lives, that's impressive.

18

PLAYBOY: What won't you do on a first date?

FISHER: I won't marry the guy. I won't get engaged. I won't have anyone's child. I'm fond of kissing. It's part of my job. God sent me down to kiss a lot of people. I usually meet people in a group. Actually, I don't date, so I don't know what I would or wouldn't do. I'll date awhile this week and get back to you.

19

PLAYBOY: With whom would you want to spend your life, Yoda or E.T.?

FISHER: Yoda's a little better-looking. E.T. seems like a much more pleasant person. He seems real nice, but Yoda is a teacher, and I like learning things. At this point, let me say E.T., because he's so much more popular. I like Yoda. I like that he's smaller than I am. It's like *The Dating Game* with extraterrestrials: "Extraterrestrial Number One, how far would I have to go on our first date—Pluto or Uranus, so to speak?"

20

PLAYBOY: At its leanest, what does your purse contain?

FISHER: Oh, fuck. I've got everything in here. What do you want? I always feel as if I'm moving. I haven't lived in one place for about four years. I have my passport, my checkbook, my beeper for the phone, postcards; it's nuts. I carry books with me. It weighs four or five pounds. I have another purse in it. I have all this junk. I don't even know what it is. And that's lean. It's frightening. I don't know how to minimize those contents. It's like having a backpack everywhere I go. I think life is an eternal campground.

Julianna Margulies

ER's heart-stopping nurse on what we'd find underneath her scrubs and in her medicine cabinet, and why toast is nature's perfect food.

Born in New York City and raised in England and France, Julianna Margulies never intended to become an actress. Her love was art history and roaming through the world's great museums. However, during her first year at Sarah Lawrence College, she studied theater as a creative outlet and soon found herself cast in productions. After graduation, Margulies forged a successful theater career in New York (including a part in "The Substance of Fire"), which led to appearances on "Homicide" and "Law and Order." While visiting a friend in Los Angeles, Margulies auditioned for a guest role in the pilot episode of "ER." Impressed with her work, executive producers Steven Spielberg and Michael Crichton chose her for the role of nurse Carole Hathaway. "ER" is consistently among the top five programs in the Nielsen ratings and is the highest-rated drama series in more than 20 years. Members of the cast have been nominated for many acting awards, but Margulies is the sole recipient of an Emmy. She has also been nominated for Golden Globe and Screen Actors Guild awards. Her career has recently expanded to the big screen with co-starring roles in "Paradise Road" opposite Glenn Close and "Traveller" with Bill Paxton.

Robert Crane cornered the kinetic Margulies at a coffeehouse in Santa Monica. He reports: "Despite her hectic seven-day-a-week filming schedule (four spent on a movie in New York, three on "ER" in Los Angeles), Margulies is a nonstop energy source focused on her work. She loves what she does. She also has the most intense and groomed eyebrows I've ever stared at."

1

PLAYBOY: You have been dubbed Crash Cart—an apparent reference to your celebrated clumsiness. Under what circumstances are you more graceful?

MARGULIES: Probably when I'm in a beautiful dress, going out for the evening, when I try to have some sort of grace and walk with a little elegance. It doesn't seem to be my style for the most part. I'm kind of proud of my bruises. My extreme clumsiness happens when I'm not thinking very well. We were filming the show once and were running down the hallway with a gurney. We turned a corner, and I got stuck between a door and the gurney. It was one of the most painful things I've ever felt. The set doctor checked to see if I still had a pelvic region, and we did the shot over.

2

PLAYBOY: What actual nursing skill would you like to have?

MARGULIES: I worry that when someone is really choking, I'm not going to know how to do the Heimlich maneuver. And I'd love to be able to save a life. That is the ultimate, isn't it? I was at the gym when a girl fainted. Everyone turned to me, and I was on the treadmill going, "I play a nurse on TV. What am I going to do?" It's flattering, though, when they turn to me, because I must be doing by job right.

3

PLAYBOY: What's easier, putting a catheter in an attractive guy or in an unattractive guy?

MARGULIES: It would be easier to put a catheter in an attractive guy because at least you could stare at his face and get some relief. It's a disgusting job, but somebody's got to do it. If the guy is unattractive, you get the job done quicker. I have never put a catheter in anyone, so I'm bullshitting this whole thing.

4

PLAYBOY: Is it hard to feel attractive in scrubs? Do you keep your nurse's outfit at home for those special moments?

MARGULIES: It's hard, but I've come to terms with it. I just accept that I'm going to be a pink blob for the day, and I pray that I have a great T-shirt color underneath. I leave my uniform on the floor in my dressing room, hoping never to see it again. They're a thorn in my side, those pink scrubs.

5

PLAYBOY: We heard that Steven Spielberg said you remind him of his ex-wife, Amy Irving.

MARGULIES: He said to me the first year we were shooting, "You remind me of my ex-wife." I don't think that's why I was hired. NBC and Warner pretty much brought me on, and then Michael Crichton had to OK it. I met Amy Irving recently at a restaurant and she said, "So apparently we're twins." It was great. Personally, I think I look like George Clooney. There are more men I look like than women, but I've heard that I look like Nancy Kerrigan, Kirstie Alley, even a dark-haired Michelle Pfeiffer. I've heard Madonna—imagine that. I think I look like an eastern European Jew, quite frankly.

6

PLAYBOY: Among medical support people, which group is the hunkiest?

MARGULIES: No thought there. Firemen. I mean, they can swing you onto their shoulder with one arm and carry you down a ladder. Of course, you're going to want to end up with a doctor, because you'll have security for the rest of your life. But if it's just a matter of, you know, then you've got to go with the firemen.

7

PLAYBOY: Which characters on *ER* have not achieved their erotic potential?

MARGULIES: Laura Innes—Dr. Weaver. Man, I think she is so sexy, and that hasn't been explored at all. She walks with a crutch, but that's just her character. She is so beautiful and sexy, and I can't wait for her to get a love interest. That's going to be fun. And then, of course, there's Abe Benrubi, who plays Jerry, the really big guy. I want to see him have sex.

8

PLAYBOY: Rate your male co-stars' sexual heat.

MARGULIES: That would be like fucking your brother. These guys are the brothers I never had, and there is something so wrong with the idea of actually sleeping with any of them. Not that all four of them aren't desirable, they are, but it goes beyond that. It would be sick, unless of course we went back to Kentucky and tried it. I'm from New York, and in New York we don't do that.

9

PLAYBOY: What discipline best describes courtship and love—dance, opera or hydraulics?

MARGULIES: One of the most erotic things you can do is spend all night dancing with someone, I mean, like, beautiful dancing, you know, or even sexy dancing. With disco, there's a rhythm and a mood that stays with you forever. I've always wanted to tango, but I don't know how.

10

PLAYBOY: You once said that you would go back to waitressing rather than do a role you hate. Give us an example.

MARGULIES: There was one role I was supposed to do—the producers wanted me to cut my hair, straighten it, dye it red and play a vixen who gets into bed with a lot of stupid, ugly men. In order to live with myself, I decided it'd be better to sling hash for one more round. It was a TV show that aired once or twice. And I would have been stuck with short, red hair. Come on.

11

PLAYBOY: You've lived, traveled and studied in Europe. What can a young woman learn there that she can't learn in the United States?

MARGULIES: She can learn a lot about history, culture and art—just walking down a street in Paris you're surrounded by it. She can learn a lot about great food. She would learn how to enjoy life, because that's what Europeans do. In so doing she would become much more grounded. Bodies aren't an issue. Breasts aren't an issue. I grew up going to topless beaches and it was never an issue. Then I came here and suddenly I was being stared at and was told I was doing the wrong thing. All of a sudden it was bad to have breasts. If Americans relaxed and allowed the body to be what it is, then we wouldn't make such a big deal out of sex. Girls are much more mature in Europe. I was the skinny, scrawny, boy-body with no breasts, and my friends who were the same age—12 years old— had breasts and their periods already. They were so much more advanced. On the other hand, I was street-smart and could handle a conversation at a young age.

12

PLAYBOY: Have you received any letters from heartbroken men in Europe?

MARGULIES: Apparently, we're very big in France right now, and I'm getting all these French love letters. French was my first language, but I'm so rusty at it that I sit there for hours trying to translate. I'm sure the letters are really beautiful, French being the most beautiful language in the world. I also get a lot of prison letters. I am going to be a prison wife to four or five different guys in the next few years. But, hey, we all have our destiny.

13

PLAYBOY: What theme or homage show is *ER* ripe for?

MARGULIES: I would love to do a dream sequence so we could shoot in Hawaii for a week. I was trying to explain it to the producers. We work really hard, and it would be nice to go to Hawaii for ten days. You'd see Dr. Greene in a lei and a grass skirt, you know, doing that thing with his little glasses. Then you'd see this image of Laura without her cane, running in the sand, and Gloria sitting there with all these men around her, and nurse Hathaway playing the conga, feeling the rhythm. It really would be fun. And then we'd all wake up, like we were having our own little daydreams in different parts of the hospital. This is why I'm not a writer.

14

PLAYBOY: Your father is a successful ad executive who has written many famous jingles. Complete the couplet "Plop, plop, fizz, fizz…."

MARGULIES: My thing was, Dad, can you write for a car company so we can get BMWs or something? We have enough Alka-Seltzer in the house for a lifetime. As a kid, I wasn't allowed to watch television, so I never knew what a big deal that commercial was. When I got older and people asked me what my father did, I'd say, "Oh, he writes commercials. He wrote that Alka-Seltzer commercial." I never realized the impact it had. My father is a heavy-duty intellectual, so it's not his proudest moment. He finds it ironic that he spent four years studying philosophy and then wrote "Plop, plop, fizz, fizz" and got all of these accolades for it. My father said to me recently, "I watch you on *ER* and you're my little girl. I see you on *Letterman*, I can't relate. You come out in these glamorous things and look so different from what I'm used to seeing." When I'm acting it's fine, but he doesn't get all the publicity stuff. It's hard for him to relate to it as a father. I understand that. It's very odd. In *Traveler*, the movie I did with Bill Paxton, I do a little striptease number. I'm wearing boxers and a bad Sears bra—my choice—that never comes off. I don't want my dad to see it. It's like Hollywood forgets that you're someone's little girl, you know.

15

PLAYBOY: With all the Emmy nominations that *ER* has received, was it weird for you to be singled out the year that you won?

MARGULIES: Noah Wyle said to me the night that I won, "God, if that isn't poetic justice," because I wasn't really accepted in the beginning. It wasn't the cast—it was the publicity. I was kept out of everything, so I wasn't seen as part of the cast. They had spent the summer together doing publicity, and then I came on. They tried to keep me a secret. I didn't end up in any of the pictures, and no one knew who I was. The cast had already bonded, and I felt like an outsider. So when I won, it brought me into the loop. I was flattered, I was honored. It got me a raise.

16

PLAYBOY: Seinfeld is the king of cereal. Is it true you're the queen of toast?

MARGULIES: When you toast something, the smell that permeates the house is so beautiful. There's something so grounded about bread. You know, "Give us this day our daily bread." And toasted bread is best when the butter melts just right, and you put a little jam on it. Light toast doesn't do it for me. It's got to be toasted pretty well. Not burnt, but just right. For Christmas I was given the toaster I've been waiting for my whole life. It looks like a Fifties radio, and it has four big slots so you don't have to cut the bread too thin. It has a timer for when you are out of the room, because you have to bring the toast up manually. It will keep the toast warm for ten minutes. That's heaven. It's from Williams-Sonoma. And I couldn't buy it for myself because I was embarrassed that it was so expensive. It sits on my kitchen counter with pride.

17

PLAYBOY: Are you an organ donor?

MARGULIES: Yeah. All of them. Proud to be one.

18

PLAYBOY: What would we find in your medicine cabinet?

MARGULIES: You'd find Nyquil, which I just recently discovered. It's great. I had a slight cough and it put me out. That's my newest acquisition. You'd find a big bottle of Advil—I don't believe in suffering with cramps. You'd find old nail polish and nail polish remover, which I never use. You'd find old drugs, including Percodan and Percocet, that I never finished because they make me crazy. I've had friends say, "Listen, I'll buy those from you." For some reason I can't let go of them.

19

PLAYBOY: Under what circumstances would you not revive a date?

MARGULIES: I've had one blind date in my life. I was a freshman in college and my sister set me up with a guy from her office. He sounded great on the phone. He picked me up at her house and he had on a dog collar and one of those earrings with a chain that went from his nose to his ear so if he snapped his head too far his earlobe would rip. And he was about 6'8". The worst date I've ever had. If he had passed out in the middle of the street, I'm not sure I would have woken him up. I probably would have just said goodbye.

20

PLAYBOY: Will you stay with the show?

MARGULIES: If I can keep doing my two films a year, and do *ER*, yes. I love my character, but I have to be able to go off and do another character in order to keep her fresh. The producers are very understanding of that. I try to pick interesting projects. Ninety-eight percent of the Screen Actors Guild is unemployed. What am I going to do, complain? I don't think so.

Milla Jovovich

The power waif sets us straight about fake ID cards, French husbands and celebrity shoplifting.

At 26, Milla Jovovich has saved the world more often than anyone had any reason to expect. Jovovich's parents were a Russian actress and a Yugoslavian medical student who left the Soviet Union for California when their daughter was five years old. Milla, who was called a commie at school, started taking acting classes at the age of nine. Jovovich made her film debut on Disney Channel's The Night Train to Kathmandu. In 1988, at the age of 12, she made history as the youngest girl ever to appear on an American fashion magazine cover. Richard Avedon photographed her as one of Revlon's most unforgettable women. Jovovich graced 15 covers that year, and People magazine named her one of its 50 Most Beautiful People.

At 14, Jovovich earned her first major film role, in Return to the Blue Lagoon. She took on supporting roles, opposite Sherilyn Fenn in Two Moon Junction, and in Richard Linklater's Dazed and Confused (at 16, she wed her co-star Shawn Andrews, but the marriage was annulled months later). Roles in Bruce Evans' Kuffs and in Chaplin, starring Robert Downey Jr., followed. In addition to acting and modeling, Jovovich was developing her music and signed a deal with EMI Records, which released The Divine Comedy to critical acclaim.

Jovovich hit it big in films when director Luc Besson cast her in The Fifth Element opposite Bruce Willis. She appeared in Spike Lee's He Got Game and then she and Besson launched their dream project, The Messenger: The Story of Joan of Arc, placing her in the role once played by screen icons Ingrid Bergman and Jean Seberg. The impressive cast included John Malkovich, Dustin Hoffman and Faye Dunaway. Jovovich, meanwhile, had married Besson. After several tempestuous years they divorced.

Jovovich continues to model (she has a deal with L'Oreal) and has appeared in The Claim, Wim Wenders' The Million Dollar Hotel and Zoolander. This year she stars as Alice, the zombie killer, in boyfriend Paul Anderson's Resident Evil. Other projects include No Good Deed opposite Samuel L. Jackson, You Stupid Man, co-starring William Baldwin, and Dummy with Adrian Brody.

Robert Crane caught up with Jovovich at Château Marmont in Hollywood. He reports: "Milla is a tamperproof source of energy. She will be the one still standing at the end—despite the ex-husbands, failed relationships, film hits and misses. She is strong and embraces chaos. Jovovich brought her dog to the interview. Its name is Madness."

1

PLAYBOY: Comparisons between you and Brooke Shields are inevitable—young models, *Blue Lagoon* films. Tell us how you're different from her.

JOVOVICH: Brooke and I have completely different images. She's always been very much America's sweetheart, and I am not. I'm an alien. I'm Russian. When I was a teen I moved to Europe, started working in music, recorded an album and went on tour with my band. By the time that was all over, I was doing *The Fifth Element*. The similarities between us include our strong mothers. My mom always wanted me to be an actress and that was pretty much what she trained me for since I was little, which was kind of the same with Brooke. We were both the youngest girls to be on the cover of a fashion magazine. She was 13 or 14, and I was 12. And I hope when I'm in my 30s, I'll have a TV show like she did. I'm fine with modeling my career after Brooke Shields'—she's done great.

2

PLAYBOY: Which *Blue Lagoon* film was better?

JOVOVICH: Overall, hers was better, but I was a better actress.

3

PLAYBOY: What's most important: talent, ambition or a really good publicist?

JOVOVICH: All of them. The biggest mistake that a lot of actors and other artists make is to rely wholly on their talent. But talent without discipline means nothing. My mom attended film school in Russia, one of the most difficult film schools back in the Sixties. One of the things she always told me to make sure I stayed in line was, "Milla, the most-talented kids in film school in the first year (it was a four-year course) dropped out by the fourth year. And the least talented ones who worked their butts off were at the top of the class by the end." So what is talent? It's a natural-born thing, but if it's not refined and disciplined and channeled in the right way, it turns destructive. It turns into ego, and it turns into "I'm a genius, I don't need to do anything. I can drink and be rude…." I know a guy who's an amazing writer and works at a car wash. You know he's never going to do anything because he has no drive. And a publicist? I have a publicist.

4

PLAYBOY: Is the euro making your life any easier?

JOVOVICH: I have no clue about the euro. All I know is that England doesn't want anything to do with it, and if England doesn't want anything to do with it, neither do I. The English know they have got the strongest currency in the world. I trust them about money.

5

PLAYBOY: Is Milla short for something?

JOVOVICH: It is short for Milizta. Can you imagine, Milizta Jovovich? It's hard enough as it is. I curse my parents every day. Why didn't they change my name?

6

PLAYBOY: How important is it for a woman to have at least one French husband?

JOVOVICH: French men are great. They know how to treat a woman. I'd recommend them.

7

PLAYBOY: What is the most useful way to get through a fashion shoot?

JOVOVICH: The best way to get through a fashion shoot is to have as few thoughts as possible. In the end, people want to make you look a certain way, and the more you fight the longer it takes to get there. I do what they ask me to. I'm professional. Fashion shoots for me are pretty much automatic. I do my job, I'm nice and polite, and then I go home. Modeling does nothing for anybody, artistically speaking, unless you're the photographer or the stylist. The models are the lowest rung in the fashion industry. They are the least creative. There are some models who really know style and bring their own style to a shoot, but they're few and far between. Modeling is quick money, easy money and good money. It's not that big a deal.

8

PLAYBOY: Did you enjoy being a girl?

JOVOVICH: Yeah, I had a great time. I think I had a pretty special childhood because there was a balance of good and bad magic. I had a lot of problems on a personal level, family things, but on the other hand I was working and understanding things. I was very creative, took lots of classes, played guitar. I was hanging out with my friends and being bad, doing all the things a teenager wants to do. Thank God I'm here to tell the story. I had a chance to have an adult lifestyle at an early age and at the same time express myself and be a kid. Now I'm 26 and my life is pretty stable. It's not like I'm 26, straight out of college and saying, "What am I going to do?" I've got a lot of plans. I have my company, I just bought a house and I'm paying attention to make other sensible investments. I like being in my mid-20s and being on top of everything and not confused and crazy.

9

PLAYBOY: How proficient were you in disguising your age? Have you had to actually lie about it?

JOVOVICH: When I was 15, 16, and 17 and going out to clubs, my friends and I had fake IDs that looked nothing like us because they were from wallets we would find in rest rooms. I don't think people really care that much. As long as you're young and beautiful, they're like, "Come on in."

10

PLAYBOY: You've cut a wide path through available guy talent. Apparently it does not take much to pique your interest, but what does it take to sustain it?

JOVOVICH: It's hard to say because none of my relationships have lasted. I've mostly been in relationships of the two-to-four-year type since I was 17. When guys first meet me, they're mystified by my independence. They like the fact that I'm young and pretty, have money and stability and don't need anything from them. They don't know what to do to get me. Then they start resenting the things they loved about me in the first place. It's, "You're always working," or "You have to cancel this trip," or "You didn't call." I hate the phone. I have two cell phones, but I don't know where one of them is. I check my answering machine once a week. I'm really the worst person if you're trying to call me. I'll say, "Let's just make a date right now to see each other because I don't like talking on the phone." So if you're my boyfriend you're not going to talk to me on the phone that much. Maybe once a day I'll call to ask how are you, to say I love you, bye. But I'm not into having major conversations on the phone. That pisses some people off. It's this possessiveness people have. I'm guilty of it myself, but most of the time I wish guys would give me more space. My days are filled—with research, reading, playing guitar, making business calls, going on auditions. It seems as soon as your professional life is great, your personal life is a disaster. As soon as your personal life is wonderful, you know you haven't been working. But my boyfriend right now is amazing. We've been going out for almost a year. I've had a lot of things that have been emotionally trying, and he's stuck with me. So I don't know, maybe he's the one.

19

11

PLAYBOY: How do you protect a guy from feeling used?

JOVOVICH: I thought guys liked feeling used. I didn't know that was something you had to protect them from. Use me, baby, abuse me. Talk to me in a year, because I have to use this new information and see how it works.

12

PLAYBOY: Your ads for Donna Karan show you with Gary Oldman in Paris and Jeremy Irons in Vietnam. Can you explain?

JOVOVICH: We figured I would play an international, independent woman dating older, sophisticated men. I love them and leave them, then go to some exotic place with another one. At the end of the last shoot we did, I said the next one should be for Donna Karan maternity wear. I said, "Listen, she's going to look like a complete slut if she has a different guy on the next campaign." But they used another model anyway, so it's like the guy got a new girlfriend. I didn't know the relationship would end that way.

13

PLAYBOY: Where do you rank shoplifting on the spectrum of thrill seeking?

JOVOVICH: Pretty low. Free Winona!

14

PLAYBOY: Let's assume you've received a presidential pardon. What were your worst offenses?

JOVOVICH: Not bad enough for a presidential pardon, that's for sure. I don't really have any vices. Actually, I just got back from skiing, and, like an idiot, I went on the moguls and wiped out so hard I can't do anything. I'm so mad. Why did I do that? I could be skiing right now. But no, I had to take a crazy risk.

15

PLAYBOY: Models want to become actors and actors want to become rock stars. Which of these vocations is the most wholesome?

JOVOVICH: The entertainment business isn't wholesome. It just isn't. Maybe the Olsen twins are wholesome, but they just hit puberty, so I don't know. You have to be competitive as an actor. It screws up your principles. Actors would be much nicer to each other if there weren't so much pressure from agents and managers. If you want a wholesome career, don't get into the entertainment business. There are too many temptations. Saying that, I don't know a business that is wholesome. Capitalism is unwholesome. It's not about loving your brother; it's about looking out for number one. That's the American lifestyle, and there's nothing wrong with it.

16

PLAYBOY: Which career is the riskiest?

JOVOVICH: Modeling, because there are no laws. It's something the government has passed over. There are no child laws regarding how long you can work, or whether you're being schooled. At least with acting, you have to have a teacher on the set. In Milan there are a lot of 14-year-old girls doing shows with 15-, 16- and 17-year-old girls who are experimenting with things that are dangerous. A lot of these girls are not with their parents and they're confused. They've dropped out of school and they're just naïve little oysters waiting to be scooped up. Unfortunately, if your parents aren't around, or somebody who knows better, you'll get taken advantage of. In acting and music there are people behind the artists who got them to where they're disciplined enough. Modeling is not that way. Th work is boring, and it can take all day, but it's not hard. It's not mentally stimulating. It's like being a fifth grader in a first grade class. After a week, it gets really boring and you want something to challenge you. To be young, out of school, with no parents, a boring job—the only interesting part is after work when you go out to clubs and stuff. When I do a film, the work that goes into it is really difficult, so when I get home, all I want to do is sleep.,

17

PLAYBOY: Are soccer hooligans part of the fun or a necessary evil?

JOVOVICH: Both. My boyfriend, who's English, says part of the experience of going to a soccer game is the violence. He says the difference between American football and English soccer is that football is a family sport and soccer isn't. Only crazy people take their children to English soccer games because everyone throws things at the opposing fans. One guy ended up with a dart in his head. It's not a family sport.

18

PLAYBOY: All the famous Ukrainians we know are figure skaters, weight lifters or gymnasts. How did you escape?

JOVOVICH: If my mother had a been a ballerina or a figure skater, I would have been one, too. But my mother was an actress, and that inspired me when I was little. But trust me, if my mom had been a figure skater, I'd be the best figure skater in the world now.

19

PLAYBOY: What do you consider to be the worst interior design excesses of the rich and famous?

JOVOVICH: I'd have to say MTV's *Cribs*. There's something wrong with showing people your home, especially with the money these people make and the taste they have. To bring a TV crew to your home is kind of trashy. It makes people envious of you. I know I feel that way when I watch those shows, and I hate it. I thought Mariah Carey's lingerie closet was a bit much, but there are two couches in her house that are to die for.

20

PLAYBOY: You've described your character in *Resident Evil* as a hard-ass, and you've described yourself as a hard-ass. Do men ever get to see the soft side of Milla?

JOVOVICH: I'm a hard-ass when it comes to my work, and I'm not scared to take risks. On a social level, I'm not hard at all. Maybe with certain men, the ones who say, "Hey!" That kills me. Anyone who says hello by pointing a finger at me I will hate for life. There's no second chance.

Robert Crane

Karen Black
Lady with Soul

"I look at a man and notice a man and I watch a man and I listen to a man and find that I'm beginning to be violently turned on."

Not many people know that besides being an extraordinarily sensitive actress and mother, Karen Black has a great set of pipes. She exercised them for an appreciative audience on the old Saturday Night Live a few years back, and she is now on the verge of making a record deal. It was a welcome change of pace for her. After all, she's appeared in 24 films over the last eight years, many of them memorable: Five Easy Pieces, The Great Gatsby, Nashville, The Day of the Locust and the made-for-television classic Trilogy of Terror.

Born in Park Ridge, Illinois, Karen attended Northwestern University. She left before graduating to try her hand at acting in New York, although she could have easily pursued a modeling career instead of the stage. Her face is absolutely striking, particularly her large, wandering eyes that make her resemble a lioness at times.

Los Angeles and the Sunset Strip introduced themselves to her through the personages of Jack Nicholson, Bruce Dern and Peter Fonda, among others. Next came an Academy Award nomination for Five Easy Pieces, two Golden Globes for The Great Gatsby and Airport '75, a Grammy nomination for Nashville, then fame, fortune, two marriages, one child, and finally, eccentricity. Karen currently lives in a 70-year-old mansion in Los Angeles with her array of antiques and more than a dozen cats.

After taking a few years off to raise her son, Hunter, Karen is clearly back in the Hollywood mainstream, pursuing her creative impulses with inevitable interesting results. She has managed to survive fickle Hollywood as few have—avoiding the drugs, sex and sellout. She follows an eclectic and often contradictory pattern: loud and soft-spoken, ugly and beautiful. But two things do remain constant in this walking chameleon: two rather large, bony feet. That's right. Like models and dancers have.

OUI: The last interviewer from OUI Magazine, L.M. "Kit" Carson, eventually became your husband. What is it about interviewers from OUI that turns you on?

BLACK: Usually they're short and they don't make a pass, because they think you expect them to. This particular interviewer had a combination of being safe and dangerous as a personality—an irresistible combination for me. It's a challenge. It excites you, but you feel you'll find peace somewhere in all that excitement.

OUI: What made him dangerous?

BLACK: He just had an edge to the way he thought—something cold, mathematical and precise, though not particularly detailed.

OUI: How long was it before you knew you had fallen in love with him?

BLACK: I fell in love with him that night, terribly in love. We talked for five hours into the night. The next day, I could see nothing but his face. I couldn't think. I couldn't finish a thought. I began to have mild sexual fantasies. That went on for two or three days—it takes me a month to get their clothes off, even in my dreams.

OUI: What kinds of men turn you on?

BLACK: What really turns me on, incredibly, is the quality of kindness, the quality of compassion. I'm more turned on by seeing how a man treats his fellow man than by how he treats me. I think real compassion is something very hard to come by. I also like a very discerning mind, someone who's interested in what things mean, why people do what they do, the origins of impulses in life. So I tend to like writers, directors.

OUI: What about actors?

BLACK: No. Writers and directors. And the other thing that interests me is the people who can write music, which is a complete mystery to me. I go crazy over them. That kind of intelligence—very sensual, very feeling—makes me very excited. Usually, people who are doing that say real surprising and funny things. Someone who's interested in why things occur is usually being himself, and a person who's being himself has his own original thoughts. There's no way of penetrating something that's completely original. You can't enter that space. That's what I mean about him being dangerous. You can't enter, because it's private. It's the person's very own. You can't possibly predict what he'll say. He had an edge. I guess it's violence. I like men who are capable of violence. I think if a person can't get angry and can't put up with other people being angry, they're not good people.

OUI: What was it like being in love with Jack Nicholson?

BLACK: Ecstatic. We never went to bed. He's a very large being, and he used to give me lessons in humanity. I'd say, "That person doesn't exist. You can't find him. He's somewhere sunk deep in his skull, and there's no way of getting him out." He would say, "Blackie, you can find anybody if you look deep enough, and that's the way it is." He taught me that I am fine just the way I am. I was very new to Hollywood, you know, and I knew I had an appetite for life. But I didn't know these things equaled some kind of charm. He sort of taught me that they did, and he welcomed me to the community. It was a very great gift that I don't think he knows he gave me.

OUI: Was he the first person to call you "Blackie"?

BLACK: Yeah. He always has nicknames for everybody.

OUI: Do you like that name?

BLACK: Yeah, I love it.

OUI: Why didn't things work out with Nicholson?

BLACK: I think he likes very skinny girls who are 22 years old, and I was neither.

OUI: What was your worst relationship?

BLACK: I think my worst relationship was with my first husband. In a way, it was very wonderful because we would talk for hours and hours. I was just brimming with life. I must have had a white cloud around me. But he was never married, and I do like to get married when I get married. I mean, I thought that's what I had done, but he didn't really get married. It was extremely hard for me to keep running full steam into this wall of his—which was "I'm not married to you"—even though we were married. It was extremely painful. I would turn freezing cold and tremble all over while we were breaking up. I couldn't control myself; I'd fall off chairs and things. It was terrible. I really got rather ill.

OUI: What sort of fantasies do you have?

BLACK: Fantasies? Sexual fantasies?

OUI: Let's start with that.

BLACK: My sexual fantasies are a little bit aberrant. I like imagining men being tied up, and I, sort of, lick them all over and do everything to them.

OUI: How do men generally approach you?

BLACK: Men don't approach me.

OUI: Why?

BLACK: I don't know. I would have to have my own questionnaire for them.

OUI: How do you approach men?

BLACK: Well, I notice a man and I watch a man and I listen to a man and I find that I'm beginning to be violently turned on. So I just attack. I'm very faithful. I stay with one man for years and years. I refuse to be unfaithful. As long as I'm with one man, I can't be unfaithful. Even if I break up with them and we're still going to bed once in a while and they have other girlfriends, I don't look for another boyfriend. It's kind of an odd thing to be as flagrant in my affections and as bourgeois in my approach to love and marriage.

OUI: What flatters you?

BLACK: I like it very much when a man likes to look at me. Just look. I like that. It doesn't happen very often, or maybe they do it so covertly you can't tell. I like looking at men a lot. It's like eating. It's completely fulfilling and satisfying to just look, *look* into the face of the man you love.

OUI: Why do you like being in love?

BLACK: I like being in love because I like experiencing myself as a generous person. When you're in love, you're inspired to ultimate generosity. You just want to give the person anything they need. The part I don't like about love is that when you're really in love with someone, there's always a kind of nagging fear that you'll displease them. After a while, thank God, that goes away. I don't like that emotion very much. I think it's a part of life and the basic life-force to give and touch.

OUI: When do you know you're in love?

BLACK: When I'm in love.

OUI: A lot of women are into derrieres these days. What parts of men do you find attractive?

BLACK: I like necks a lot. Something about a neck...I always, sort of, want to get my mouth on it. I like chests, too. The front, just the front, right on the chest. I just love chests.

OUI: What do you think about men's clothing today? What turns you on? What turns you off?

BLACK: I'm very specific about that. I love short hair, depending on the man. It depends on the face. I like hair back, pushed back away from the face so that the cheekbones and nose and forehead come out. That's very hot. I like the relaxed style of clothing today. I like soft shirts that are open. I like them with a jacket. I like tweed and flannel and coarse, golden-blond kinds of colors on a man. I also like burgundy. I like black on a man tremendously. I like the casual but suave—I don't like that word—you know, kind of hot with an edge to it.

OUI: You have striking eyes.

BLACK: Me? I have terrible eyes. They're absolutely my worst feature. I hate my eyes. I hate them.

OUI: What do you think is your most interesting feature?

BLACK: My eyes. That doesn't mean they're pretty, but they're interesting. But that's everybody's most interesting feature. How can you call a nose *interesting*?

OUI: What is interesting about your eyes?

BLACK: Well, what probably makes my eyes interesting is that I love seeing. I just love seeing. I see like a person who's been blind for a century and has suddenly got his sight back. Colors drive me crazy. But my best feature is my mouth, because there's a lot of it.

OUI: The more the better?

BLACK: Don't put words in my mouth.

OUI: You've played women who are sexy, vulnerable, emotional, conniving. Are you like any of your characters?

BLACK: All of my characters are parts of me, but never the whole. When you play a character, what you do is: You just *don't be* certain things; then you've got *her* left over. And that's the truth. It's a negative reality. It should be. For example, if you're playing someone who's stupid, you simply don't think. You do what people do when they don't think, which is look, laugh, feel affectionate about things, withdraw from things. So now you have a full, whole person like people really are, but a person who doesn't seem to be very intelligent. But you don't *act* stupid, because nobody who is stupid is *acting* stupid. You see, you're not doing the particular quality, you're doing the things that are left over when a certain quality is absent. The part I'm doing now is not a negative reality. It's so very far from me, and I'm not sure my work is quite as good.

OUI: What kind of woman do you identify with most?

BLACK: I don't like the term *identify with*. I guess I don't like it because I don't really understand it. I can tell you want I like. I like people who do what they do when they're doing it. I had a girlfriend who would go with guys for 15 years and never marry them. She said, "When I go on the road, I like to have affairs, and if I'm married to someone, I can't do that. I'd feel guilty." She said this with no guilt, no self-recrimination of any kind. I really admire that. I like women who are free to go after what they want. I like women who are free to penetrate and move things and change things, women who don't equivocate about whether they're right or wrong. To them, it seems correct that such and such be so, and they try to move life around to make that forthcoming. I like that.

OUI: What is your favorite character that you've played?

BLACK: It was in a movie that nobody saw. The film was called *The Pyx*, and she was a girl I had to do quite a lot of studying on. She was a heroin addict, and I didn't like her as a person. But I liked playing her because I'm very effusive and unstoppable. I'm very outflowing as a personality. When I play someone who's defensive, someone who is trying to stop themselves from giving, trying to reject the flow of nature—to love, to find, to be and to see—then I think it's better, because it's the yin and the yang. It's well rounded. It may be more difficult, but I get more satisfaction in the long run. I mean, you can't pretend to laugh on film. You can pretend to know something and you can pretend to think something, but you can't pretend to be a free spirit if you're not really one.

OUI: What is your most embarrassing work?

BLACK: I'm not ever embarrassed. In the film I'm going now [*The Grass is Singing*], I haven't liked some of the rushes. Everyone else does, but I don't. Sometimes in dreams, I have to do a play—it's usually the second act of some play of Shakespeare's—and I haven't memorized a line of it and I'm terribly embarrassed. My most embarrassing work is on the set when I want and need something very much, but I'm afraid to ask for it, like I feel my hair should be a certain way and the girl won't do it that way. I get really embarrassed. Or if I can sense that a person would rather not pay attention to me, and if they don't pay attention to me, I'll fail in my work—that can present problems. I did this horrible film once. It's absolutely horrible. I did it in Florida, and I didn't know what was going on. As an actress, you have to figure out the line of a character. It's very hard work. You have to read the scene, and then the scene after, and then you have to read the whole part after that scene. You have to figure out where she is in the line of changes at any particular moment. Very often, you don't have to do that. But in this case, I had to do that, and I didn't, because I didn't recognize that it was necessary. When you see the movie, the character is here, there and everywhere. It just makes no sense at all. It was really embarrassing.

OUI: What do you think about nudity in magazines?

BLACK: I guess it's nice for 14-year-old boys. It's good for them.

OUI: What about male nudity?

BLACK: No. I think men should keep those parts of themselves for their lovers only. I really do.

OUI: How did you see yourself at 18, physically and mentally?

BLACK: Hip-heavy, flat-chested, absolutely beautiful face, terribly frizzy hair—which at that time, nobody wanted. Mentally, I was just thinking everything at every minute and just eating up all the books I could. I got A's in classes that other people didn't get A's in. I got into college without graduating from high school. I was very smart then. I was very dispersed. I was extremely, extremely vulnerable and very easy to overrun. If someone looked cross-eyed at me in a certain way, I could be depressed for a week. I was on a roller coaster. I was like a light anybody could turn on and off.

OUI: How does your present lifestyle differ from what you thought it would be like when you were 18?

BLACK: I never would have imagined that success could bring with it so many hassles. There are hundreds of parts to it: household, children, health, cooking, what you eat, how you stay thin, how you ingratiate yourself to people even though you already love them, making sure you get enough sleep so you can do your work, being in love and how that fits in, how that kills your career, how that ruins your life, how that helps, how you must have it, where you put it, how you do it. There are so many parts to it: How do you get movies? What movies do you take? Who helps you? Who is helping you? Who really isn't helping you? Who's pretending? Who really means what they say? It's very, very difficult. It's amazingly full and rich and desperate.

OUI: Who has come closest to being your ideal man?

BLACK: My current one, Michael [Michael Raeburn]. When he was in college, he decided that Portuguese was an interesting language because it was rough and strong. He just made that decision. So he learned Portuguese perfectly and went to Portugal and found out all about the natives and studied them and learned what it was like. He's a man who never behaves like a dilettante. If he fastens on to something, it has value to him. He totally commits himself. He just finished a book. He didn't know what he was writing to begin with, but he did it over and over until it was just the way he wanted it. He did it for a year, relentlessly. I guess relentless is a way of life. It never stops when someone is like that; they seem to be hooked into the native condition. He's brilliant. It's a little scary trying to keep up with him. He's very informed. I'm not. He's extremely interested in being close and the mechanism involved in becoming close to a woman. There are things that don't work. There are things that do work. He's gentle, sensitive and ravenous.

OUI: Where do you place the importance of your career now that you've been married and have a child?

BLACK: I would die for my child if it came to that. That's a real interesting question to ask yourself: Whom would I die for? I like that question.

OUI: What kind of impact has being a single mother had on your life?

BLACK: I haven't been a single parent long enough to experience the full impact.

OUI: Where do you place the importance of your career?

BLACK: I'm trying to sort it out. I'm wondering if I would die for my career. I probably wouldn't. I'd get a job as a governess. It seems to change all the time, the relationship between—I won't say my marriage, because that's over—between my child and my career. For example, at the beginning, I didn't want to do anything but be with my son, Hunter. I could have done other things, but I would much rather be with Hunter. You couldn't tear me away. That went on for about four years. Now, I may have thought that my career was more important than my child, if you were asking me intellectually. On the other hand, if you just looked at me moment by moment, you'd find that I preferred the child, I think. Now he's almost five, and I don't know where he is right now. That wouldn't have been true a year ago. I would have known exactly where he was. Until I was sure that he could do without me, that he was all right, that he has this self-assurance, self-esteem, that he can survive spiritually without me, I couldn't relinquish that necessity of his. Now I think he's like that, and I can go on with my career more easily.

OUI: What are the differences between East Coast men and West Coast men?

BLACK: I have no idea.

OUI: What about European men and American men?

BLACK: I've met two male chauvinists in my life; one was from England and the other from Egypt. I guess there are fewer chauvinists in America than practically any other country. I really don't think that it's the location, though. It's the male mind.

OUI: What has been your most romantic location?

BLACK: I guess Africa. [Laughs.]

OUI: What do you think about casual sex as opposed to the long-term relationship?

BLACK: I think casual sex is like too much pot: kind of decadent. You see, love is admiration. But what is it that you admire? Do you admire someone's soul or skin? Or all of it or a little of it? What part of the person do you admire? When it gets to that, you hook up with something that's profoundly important; the feelings of love and tenderness and generosity and wanting the well-being of another are hooked up with the admiration for somebody's skin and the curve of their back. In casual sex, I just think you're in trouble because you're degrading yourself.

OUI: What kind of role would you like to play that you haven't yet?

BLACK: I guess what they call wardrobe pieces: people who live in castles, royalty, Shakespeare. I've done Shakespeare, but never on the screen. Dostoevsky onscreen is great—things with an elegant but primal passion for life.

OUI: How do you perceive yourself? Beautiful? Sexy?

BLACK: I probably change more in my own eyes than I do in anyone else's. I'm certain that sometimes I'm completely ugly. I know it. Other times, I think I'm absolutely beautiful. I think I have one of the best mouths and a pretty unbeatable nose. I hate my eyes because they're all over my face. I like my waist and shoulders and neck. I think they're pretty wonderful. I think my legs are nice and long, but they get too heavy at the top. My breasts change size month to month because I lose and gain a lot of weight. I like my breasts when I'm fat. And they're all right when I'm thin, but I don't like them as well. I like my nipples. I think they're a nice color, nice and big and dark. I love some of the eccentricities about my body. I love my feet because they're bony. They look like a farm person's. I like my appendicitis scar—which is about eight inches long and three quarters of an inch thick and just like satin. It's a very pretty color.

OUI: Have you experimented with drugs?

BLACK: No. I'm against drugs.

OUI: You've never done drugs?

BLACK: I've done grass three times. That's about it.

OUI: You've donated a good deal of money to Scientology. Can you explain your affiliation with them?

BLACK: This is too personal and too controversial to comment on.

OUI: What do you think about when you want to exude an aura of sexiness?

BLACK: When you ask a question like that, there's another intrinsic question that's within it, which is: When do you *want* to exude that? I don't think about it. If you're mad about somebody, you respond in kind, and then, I suppose, you exude sex. If you're not mad about somebody, then why exude sex? If it's required in a character, well, I don't know, I suppose I just think of something sexual.

OUI: What are your views on younger men?

BLACK: I think that they're probably younger than older men. What do you mean?

OUI: Have you ever had any relationships similar to the one we saw in *In Praise of Older Women*?

BLACK: Well, I think there's something about women that's a little different from men. I hate to generalize, but women seem to get old early and stay young the rest of their lives. Men tend to get old late and stay that way. So, every often, I think you'll find the kind of fertile resonance to be very similar in older women and younger men. Because a woman seems to return to spring all the time. Maybe it's part of being something that makes babies. Women can never remember the hassle of birth. There's that spring that's part of womanhood. When a man is young, he's sort of seeking. He's got his head sticking out on his neck, and he's just wondering. He's looking for it. My first husband was younger than I. Not a whole lot, though.

OUI: Is there more romance today or less?

BLACK: Less.

OUI: What about for you personally?

BLACK: Today? There's plenty. I think the relationship between sex and love is a crucial and dangerous one. I think that if people were in their native state, they would want to have a child with everybody they went to bed with. That would mean a very different cultural and social setup than we have. I think it would make us love people very much. That's difficult. My way of dealing with that is to be willing to have a baby with every man I go to bed with. I go to bed with a new man once every five years.

Mariska Hargitay

Jayne Mansfield's daughter talks about bodybuilders, saddles and her dream man—Robert De Niro.

Being the daughter of Jayne Mansfield carries with it more baggage than Ivana Trump takes on vacation. But actress Mariska Hargitay, 37, has outdistanced critics' expectations and found distinction on her own terms. The star of NBC's critically acclaimed hit drama Law and Order: Special Victims Unit fills the TV screen with a unique energy.

Hargitay grew up in Beverly Hills, the daughter of the quintessential Fifties sexpot Mansfield and bodybuilder and former Mr. Universe Mickey Hargitay. Three years after her parents divorced, Mariska, just three, was in the backseat of the automobile during the accident that claimed Mansfield's life. Her father remarried. Mariska and her three brothers spent summers in Italy, where her father acted in spaghetti Westerns, and in Hungary, where Mariska and her brothers attended camp and learned the language. Back in Los Angeles, Hargitay attended a private Catholic grade school, then enrolled at Marymount High, a highly honored all-girls school. She became a jock, excelling in swimming and track. On a lark, she tried out for a school play, Salad Days, and won a part. Hargitay went on to study theater arts at UCLA, securing an agent and work before she graduated. A bit part in Bob Fosse's Star 80, an LA stage appearance in Women's Work and regular roles on the television series Falcon Crest, Can't Hurry Love and Prince Street followed. Hargitay was successfully forging her own identity as an actress. She made notable guest appearances on Seinfeld, Ellen, thirtysomething and Wiseguy, bringing her to the attention of ER's producers. In 1997 Hargitay joined NBC's top-rated series in the recurring role of Cynthia Hooper, Anthony Edwards' love interest. Producer Dick Wolf took notice and invited her to co-star as Detective Olivia Benson on his Law and Order spin-off, Special Victims Unit.

On the big screen, Hargitay has appeared as a hooker opposite Nicolas Cage in Leaving Las Vegas, in David Lynch's Hotel Room and in David E. Kelley's Lake Placid, co-starring Bridget Fonda.

Robert Crane caught up with Hargitay at Mercer Kitchen in New York. He reports: "Mariska is every bit as passionate, strong and sexy as her detective character on SVU. Her mother, of course, appeared in PLAYBOY many times, and, in her honor, Hargitay wore a tight black shirt with the Rabbit Head logo embossed in white. People stared. I lost interest in the menu."

1

PLAYBOY: What ingredients go into a good goulash?

HARGITAY: This is where I'm going to be untrue to my roots, because I haven't the faintest idea. Not a clue. I think it's stew with a little paprika. That's all I know. I'm more into Italian cuisine.

2

PLAYBOY: You're well-traveled. Americans don't know about middle European history after World War I. What are they missing out on?

HARGITAY: American children are so safe and fearless because they've never known war, they've never known tragedy or what it's like to be bombed, or to live in fear of being attacked at any minute. When you're a kid and you see that, your perspective of the world changes. I remember being in Hungary when I was little and being held by immigration or by the Hungarian police. They were messing with me because they said I didn't have the right papers, and I was a kid by myself going in and out of Hungary. They told me I was going to jail and that I'd never be able to go home. And they were laughing. They were older teenage boys. And I sat there crying, thinking I was never getting home, and then they gave me the OK and got me on the plane. You learn to survive. I was very fortunate when I was a kid. My parents sent me to private schools where kids for the most part were well-to-do and privileged. But they were missing something so beautiful—a connection that people have when there is trauma and disaster. They didn't understand how frail and precious life is.

3

PLAYBOY: Why has the former Austro-Hungarian Empire produced so many bodybuilders?

HARGITAY: I don't know, but I'm thrilled about it. I think the real answer is oppression and wanting to get over that. There are some amazingly strong human beings—these human spirits—who say, "I'm bigger than what happened to me, and no one will ever be bigger than me again." I met Arnold Schwarzenegger when I was 13 years old, with full braces—that weird age when you're just not cute. It was the time when *10* was out with Bo Derek and being called a "10" was the compliment of the minute. Arnold looked at me and said, "Ten—you're an 11!" And I was like, "Yes!" I was an awkward, gawky 13-year-old, and he made my teens—not just one year! It was really great.

4

PLAYBOY: Do you have a favorite picture of your mother?

HARGITAY: Absolutely. It's at home, the one picture in my house—a very dear picture of her. She's caught in thought. She didn't know that she was going to be photographed. And it's a window to her soul. There are certain photographs that capture something, that you can't stop staring at, and those are my favorites.

5

PLAYBOY: The most famous one is the Hollywood shot with Sophia Loren checking out your mother's cleavage.

HARGITAY: That picture has haunted me my whole life. I love it and I hate it. I hated it when I was little, but now I see it differently because my mother was such a celebrator of life, and she transcended fear and judgment. That's something to aspire to. So I love it now. It's so human. You could make a movie off that picture. There's part of me that looks at it like, Wow! That's awesome! That's so great! But there's another part of me that's like, That's my mom.

6

PLAYBOY: What is the proper shape for a pool?

HARGITAY: Olympic is the proper shape for a pool. I was on a swim team when I was a kid, and I was obsessed with the Olympics. I swam for four years on the varsity team, and I was always frustrated

31

that the pool wasn't long enough. I wanted to keep going without turning. My second choice would be heart shaped. But you couldn't swim laps, and I'm a bit of a fish, so that would be frustrating.

7

PLAYBOY: What did Louis L'Amour tell you about riding a horse?

HARGITAY: He wrote one of my book reports when I was in fifth grade. He taught me so much about writing and riding. He taught me to stay steady and hold on tight. Louis L'Amour was like a second father to me. And I have to tell you this story because his daughter, Angelique, was my very best friend, from the first day of kindergarten. I used to spend a lot of my weekends with her family. And so it was one of those Sunday nights. You know, at 7:30 you look at your homework and you're like, "Oh, I forgot this part. I forgot to read this book." I hadn't read the book and I was so scared. Louis and I wrote the whole report, based on questions he asked me about the book. And it was so genius. The teacher was like, "Oh my gosh." And I remember saying, "Thank you." And the next time I saw him I told him I got an A! It was really cool.

8

PLAYBOY: Tell us about getting comfy on a saddle.

HARGITAY: I love saddles. I started riding when I was five, so I feel so at home on a horse. It's all about trust, and totally letting go. And I'll just leave it at that. There's safety in letting go.

9

PLAYBOY: How do you tell who you're riding that you're the boss?

HARGITAY: Oh, they know. It's just like when you size people up—animals are better at it than we are. You let the horse know you want to play, and you're on the same team, but not to fuck with you.

10

PLAYBOY: Is Robert De Niro aware of your obsession with him?

HARGITAY: God, I hope so. I'm just waiting for him to come to me. I worship him. My favorite movie is *We're no Angels*. Sean Penn also rules. And Sean Penn doing Robert De Niro, as he did in *Casualties of War*, that's genius.

11

PLAYBOY: Name De Niro's best and worst roles.

HARGITAY: *Taxi Driver* and *Raging Bull* are what started it all for me and the rest of the world. I didn't like the one with Meryl Streep, *Falling in Love*. I just didn't care. *Midnight Run* with Charles Grodin—that's right up there. And that's what I'm saying: How do you go from *Raging Bull* to *Midnight Run*? How do you do that?

12

PLAYBOY: Can you characterize him in a sentence? What is it that clicks with you?

HARGITAY: He just has that thing that for decades people have been trying to put their finger on. The thing that makes you go, "Oh my God. I get you. I want that. I want to take that in. I want to be in it. I want to be around it. You touch me, you make me feel something different. Or you touch a place in me that I don't know how to access." He is so truthful and yet far out. Sometimes you think the truth would be more linear, and he goes another way. Even though you don't know where he's going to take you, you feel safe going. Wherever he goes, we trust him that it'll pay off. And that's the thing that's toughest about acting.

13

PLAYBOY: Do you consider yourself a De Niro stalker?

HARGITAY: No, I don't. I do hang out at Nobu [one of De Niro's restaurants in New York], but not for that reason. I mean, sure, I've had my moments—like stalking his apartment when people have pointed it out to me. I'm not going to lie to you. But if I saw him on the street, I'd probably look down, because I wouldn't know what to do.

14

PLAYBOY: Do you want to use this space for a message?

HARGITAY: I love you. Come and find me now! If you don't act with me in your next movie, you're missing something huge. I'm waiting, sweetheart! Sweetheart, why haven't you called? Time is a-ticking. I'm not going to wait forever. No. Yes, I will.

15

PLAYBOY: What's the best time to be in New York?

HARGITAY: Fall. One of my favorite things about being in New York is getting on a bike. There's such complete freedom. When I moved to New York, the first six months were so insane. Nothing in my life was constant. And then I met my boyfriend, who has a bike, and we started riding around on the bike, and my whole life changed. Last night we drove for an hour and a half to the north end of the city on the bike, and the smells were so palpable. They made my blood hot. They reminded me of when I was a kid in Italy. Burning leaves, different foods, trees and flowers that were so sensual and so healing. I felt like I was being tickled and sort of rubbed in the smells and in the weather and in the way the air felt on my skin. It's such a magical place in the fall. There is nowhere else like it. I am a person that any minute I have free I'm on a plane to Italy. That's where I go. It's my home away from home, my sanctuary. But in the fall, I want to be in New York. This hard city caresses you in the fall.

16

PLAYBOY: How effective is travel in getting rid of the taste of a bad boyfriend?

HARGITAY: Perfect. It's just what the doctor ordered.

17

PLAYBOY: What was your most grueling trip?

HARGITAY: I'm terrified of flying. I've held hands with strangers. I'll hold anyone's hand. I get really stressed and need to connect in fear, so I grab people. On my way to Africa recently, everyone was asleep—except for me, because I can't sleep on planes. This guy starts screaming and I thought the plane was going down. Everyone woke up screaming. Panic in first class on the way to Africa. The guy was having a nightmare and he freaked everyone out. You could feel the energy for 20 minutes and you couldn't calm down.

18

PLAYBOY: Would you rather have a cop or a doctor as a boyfriend?

HARGITAY: Doctor. I would never want to be with a cop. I don't mean to get teary on you, but I went to the Top Cops Awards—it's like the Academy Awards for cops. It was all these heroes telling their stories about the amazing things they'd done, and everyone in the audience was in tears. The number of cops who are killed in the line of duty is such an accepted thing. I have become very friendly with the New York City police departments in every borough. I know too many stories about killing and hate crimes. I know cops' wives, and it's like they give their husbands permission to leave them widowed. I'm not strong enough. I learned that at a young age—about losing somebody you love. I just couldn't function knowing my spouse was in jeopardy every day.

19

PLAYBOY: What are the rewards of doing a show about victims of sexual crimes?

HARGITAY: A woman came up to me on the subway. She was a violinist, and she told me that she had seen an episode about a piano teacher who was molesting his students. She told me she had been molested by her violin teacher, and she didn't know what to do. She told me our show was so resonant. When people tell you those kinds of stories, it reaffirms that you have a responsibility, because there are so many sexually abused people in this world. This is something people do not want to talk about, and they're so scared of it. Our show can be a forum for people who have been traumatized.

20

PLAYBOY: The truth: Do you know any girls like the ones who are portrayed on *Sex and the City*?

HARGITAY: I'm a big fan of Sarah Jessica Parker's, but I've never seen the show. So I can't comment.

Ashley Judd

Hollywood's Phi Beta Kappa wildcat on bourbon, French words and why she shuns underwear.

A Phi Beta Kappa French major from the University of Kentucky and one of the hottest young actors in Hollywood today, Ashley Judd has emerged with a wallop from the shadows of her country music superstar mother (Naomi) and older sister (Wynonna). Judd's parents divorced when she was young, and she divided her time between them—attending a dozen schools in 13 years.

After college, Judd made her major film debut in the acclaimed Ruby in Paradise, which some critics maintain is her best work. She took supporting roles in Heat opposite Al Pacino and Robert De Niro; A Time to Kill, co-starring Sandra Bullock and Matthew McConaughey; and Smoke, playing the daughter of Harvey Keitel. During the shooting of Smoke, Judd also starred on Broadway in William Inge's Picnic. She received Emmy and Golden Globe nominations for her portrayal of Norma Jean Baker in HBO's Norma Jean and Marilyn. But her breakthrough role was in the box office hit Kiss the Girls, co-starring Morgan Freeman. She also garnered good notices for her supporting role in last year's Simon Birch. Judd can be seen in two forthcoming films—Eye of the Beholder and Double Jeopardy, which co-stars Tommy Lee Jones.

Robert Crane caught up with Judd on the set of Double Jeopardy in Vancouver. He reports: "Judd grabbed two director's chairs and positioned them right out in the middle of the set and crew. With our knees touching, the interview began. She is fearless, has a razor-sharp wit, is totally into her craft and is drop-dead gorgeous. At one point she had to change pants for a scene. She dropped trou right in front of everyone so we could continue the interview and not keep director Bruce Beresford waiting. Now, that's dedication."

1

PLAYBOY: Describe the rides at your theme park Ashleywood.

JUDD: I don't know how well attended my theme park would be, because you'd have to think a lot. There would probably be some kind of dictionary at every turnstile, and I would have mazes designed like 16th century Italian gardens. Some rides would definitely involve lipstick and beautiful dresses. Riding horses would figure somehow, and there'd be a whole Kentucky Wildcats neighborhood.

2

PLAYBOY: You and William F. Buckley like to read dictionaries for fun. List three words you're dying to use in conversation. Extras points if you use them in the same sentence.

JUDD: His lack of perspicacity was revealed by the calumny with which he spoke. Hence, a debacle ensued. Debacle is not so fantastically challenging a word but it is wonderful in the mouth.

3

PLAYBOY: Dresses with slits: engineered for comfort or for showmanship?

JUDD: Showmanship. Engineered via satellite while attending Kentucky basketball games. Last-minute dressing stages observed by a roomful of people, none of whom observed any danger whatsoever. And the overbearing motherly types too. Engineered with the hazard unobserved. I'm talking about my Richard Tyler Oscars gown, as I presume you were. But obviously the design answer to your question is both. Not that a kick pleat wouldn't accomplish the same thing.

4

PLAYBOY: What gets lost in translation when you study French in Kentucky?

JUDD: Actually, I gained so much in the translation. I came to comprehend English grammar by studying French. It enhanced my native tongue. I took four years in high school and four at university, with multiple courses in any given semester. Accrued a lot of time.

5

PLAYBOY: L'Academie Francaise should lighten up, don't you think? What English words should be allowed in French?

JUDD: Oh, I disagree. [*Speaking French*] I congratulate them for being one of the last bastions of hard-assedness. I love the Academie. They're righteous in a great historic way. I'm thinking about slang—OK, blow job in French is *la pipe*. Who wants to say *la blow job* when you can say *la pipe*? The French Academy has a great point.

6

PLAYBOY: Were you ever benched at the University of Kentucky?

JUDD: No, but my seatmate, who was as spastic a fan as I, was once given a technical. The other team took its two shots and everything. Did I mention my seatmate is my family's attorney?

7

PLAYBOY: Matthew McConaughey, Michael Bolton and Lyle Lovett—we're not describing a straight line here. Account for quirks of the heart. What's it like riding on the back of Lyle's motorcycle?

JUDD: First of all, this is as appropriate a time as ever to disband the rumor that Lyle and I dated. We absolutely never did. I've never been on the back of his motorcycle. He rides those motocross things. He's into BMX or something. I'm not sure.

8

PLAYBOY: Is there any single insight that you've found always to be true?

JUDD: Yeah. The book is always better than the movie.

9

PLAYBOY: What haven't you done by 30 that you thought you would have?

JUDD: Absolutely nothing. I'm actually close to doing some things that I never thought I'd do. I don't own a Porsche yet, though.

10

PLAYBOY: When you use a Stair Master at a gym, are there more people behind you or in front of you?

JUDD: Usually in front, because that way they get the front and the reflection from the mirror behind me. Actually, they usually keep at least a 15-foot distance because I sweat so much they'd slip if they got too close. The Stair Master is an easy thing to have around on a set. It's not my end-all choice, but it's definitely a helpful apparatus.

11

PLAYBOY: Describe and contrast: cracker, redneck, white trash.

JUDD: That's an incomplete set—you didn't mention hillbilly. They're all very different. In the benign sense, a cracker would be someone who is a maverick and verbally wacky, perhaps says things that others would consider inappropriate. Maybe a little out of touch with reality. A redneck, I think, does not automatically denote a racist person. Being a redneck in the pure sense is about having a great love for the outdoors and living on lakes or rivers. White trash, to me, is a malevolent kind of ignorance, people who suffer from meanness, either innately or who have had meanness instilled in them. Hillbillies are something else. They're private and really living in an old-timey way.

12

PLAYBOY: Give us your overview of Kentucky bourbon.

JUDD: Blanton's, a small distillery in Frankfort. Beautiful handmade barrels, and every bottle has a parchment label indicating from which batch it's been poured. Very nice.

13

PLAYBOY: What is so bad about underwear?

JUDD: It's uncomfortable.

14

PLAYBOY: Aren't you putting underwear workers out of a job?

JUDD: It's also affecting the need for laundry detergent. My mother instigated all of this. She's a hazard, in the best sense of the word. She happened to remark in public that I don't wear underwear, and it's followed me ever since. I'd like for it to go away.

15

PLAYBOY: You have said, "Once you've kissed, you've kissed." Name the best on-screen kissers.

JUDD: I liked that Liv Tyler and Joaquin Phoenix kiss in a movie that isn't otherwise notable. It was so lovely because they were so pure and young and they had fallen in love in real life. I knew that when I went to the theater, and I saw the sweetest undercurrent. Rhett and Scarlett—I mean, it doesn't get much better than that in terms of a cantankerous kiss. Oh, *Maltese Falcon*, when Humphrey Bogart grabs that woman. Wow! That was out of hand. His hand kind of scrunches her cheek. Was there a kiss between Michelle Pfeiffer and Daniel Day-Lewis in *The Age of Innocence*? That's a great relationship. I'm sure there's a great one in *Porky's*.

16

PLAYBOY: Anybody you've worked with?

JUDD: No, I don't really kiss. It would be too hot.

17

PLAYBOY: Has Clinton exceeded all his genetic expectations?

JUDD: We don't know that much about his dad, do we? He has exceeded my patience. So has that Mr. David Kendall, his attorney, who comes out of the grand jury hearing excoriating Starr for invasion of privacy. This is a guy who represents the *National Enquirer* and has for years. The height of hypocrisy.

18

PLAYBOY: Clinton—an unconscionable sexual predator or just a good old boy?

JUDD: Well, if you're dumb, are you unconscionable?

19

PLAYBOY: Ever tried to educate any of your dates?

JUDD: No. They all managed to hang themselves before I had a chance.

20

PLAYBOY: In *The Locusts* your character is called a "come bucket." Have you been called worse?

JUDD: Careless. A dictionary at every turnstile. And if you want to go on the high-thrill rides, it's a thesaurus. Welcome to Ashleywood, synonym game to the stars.

Gina Gershon

The showgirls survivor on lap dances and cigars and how she got those snarling lips.

A few years ago, Gina Gershon played two different, aggressively sensual lesbians—first in the universally scorned Showgirls, then in the critically acclaimed Bound. It set her up for every actor's nightmare—typecasting.

But Gershon shifted gears and reinvented herself in the hit Face/Off, opposite John Travolta and Nicolas Cage; in Palmetto, co-starring Woody Harrelson; and now in Michael Mann's The Insider, with Al Pacino. She also appears on network television, playing a private investigator in David Kelley's Snoops for ABC.

Gershon was a troubled teenager growing up in Los Angeles when her parents persuaded her to attend Beverly Hills High School, where she immersed herself in drama classes. Upon graduation, she moved to New York and earned a Bachelor of Arts degree from New York University.

She studied acting with such prominent teachers as David Mamet and Sandra Seacat and appeared onstage in The Substance of Fire, Camille and Nanawatai. Gershon also became a founding member of the New York City-based theater company Naked Angels.

Robert Crane caught up with the closet comedian in Los Angeles. He reports: "Although Gershon doesn't do many interviews, it's not because she's slow with a remark. She's wonderfully funny. The exotically beautiful actress doesn't take the celebrity side of her career seriously, but when the mention of work comes up, she adjusts her hat and becomes the intense, studied actor. Either way, I couldn't keep my eyes off her."

1

PLAYBOY: We've noticed you love cigars. When is a cigar just a cigar?

GERSHON: When it's lit. I did the cover of *Cigar Aficionado*, so I'm supposed to talk about loving cigars. I've smoked them a couple of times. My father used to smoke cigars. I love the idea and the concept, and I love the smell of cigars.

2

PLAYBOY: Do you bite off the ends or do you use a cigar bris?

GERSHON: I have a *mohel* come over with a special clipper. I hold down the cigar and he clips it, and everyone cries.

3

PLAYBOY: Tell us, to what extent is size important?

GERSHON: Size counts. That's all.

4

PLAYBOY: Explain the enduring allure of Jennifer Tilly.

GERSHON: She's so damn girlie. It's her voice and her mannerisms. She's just fun to watch. I always find people who are unique very attractive. And I think she's really a character. She is who she is. In fact, she takes who she is to the next level, which I think is great.

5

PLAYBOY: If she were a cocktail, how would you make a Jennifer Tilly?

GERSHON: She'd be like a cosmopolitan but with rum; something kind of fruity and intoxicating. You don't quite know how drunk you are until all of a sudden you're on the floor.

6

PLAYBOY: What were the best things to come out of *Showgirls*?

GERSHON: Love and adoration from drag queens. Drag queens come up to me on the street and can show me the dance moves. RuPaul knew my lipstick color. I was flattered.

7

PLAYBOY: Do you recommend that a woman give her boyfriend or husband lap dances as presents?

GERSHON: Sure, on a regular basis. It doesn't have to be a present, though it makes a nice gift. It's a fun way to exercise and loosen up at the end of the day. It's the gift that goes on giving.

8

PLAYBOY: On *Snoops* you play a private investigator. Have you ever been investigated privately?

GERSHON: Not that I know of. The whole point is that you don't know.

9

PLAYBOY: Is it an honorable profession?

GERSHON: Sure. But in any profession, there's a sleazy side and an honorable side. I'm an honorable investigator. I make too much money for sleaze work. It's the type of operation that's 20 grand just to walk in the door. I don't think many sleazy people have that much money, or it must be really good sleaze if they do.

10

PLAYBOY: Is it a good idea to investigate the people you're emotionally involved with?

GERSHON: No. If you don't trust the person, there's a problem.

11

PLAYBOY: In one article you mentioned you'd like to frolic with friends in a Jacuzzi full of noodles. We can set that up, if you like.

GERSHON: That was a high school fantasy of mine. I had this dream of moving to New York and having a loft with a Jacuzzi in the middle of it. I would have parties where I would fill the Jacuzzi with noodles, people would sit in there and then put their bodies into paint—primary colors like really serious deep, deep blue and really pure red—and paint these huge murals. The noodles would kind of loosen everyone up to be free on the canvas. I thought that would be a really fun party. Unfortunately, I never got around to doing it. It reminds me of a Magritte painting, but it would be live-action. You could even make a video of people doing it. It's probably a lot more interesting to imagine, though.

12

PLAYBOY: Do you like to cook or just eat?

GERSHON: Both. I like to eat so much I'm actually a pretty good cook. But I cook mainly breakfast. At night I never get around to it, though I'd like to. I made excellent eggs in the morning.

13

PLAYBOY: Sexually speaking, can too many cooks spoil the sauce?

GERSHON: That depends what kind of sauce it is.

14

PLAYBOY: Describe how sexy food is.

GERSHON: It's oral. It's tasty. There are different textures to it. It's satisfying. I don't trust people who don't eat. And I would bet that if you don't love food or enjoy eating, you probably don't enjoy sex that much. I think there's a correlation, because it's just so sensual and primal. Eating, sleeping, fucking—those are primary needs. If you don't enjoy eating, there's a primal instinct that is being repressed, and I think it affects everything.

15

PLAYBOY: Is food sexier when you make it or order it?

GERSHON: Probably when you make it. It's good to get your hands dirty. Anything dirty is kind of sexy. I like the idea of starting off clean and then getting really dirty. There's something primal about that too, because there's an uninhibitedness that goes with it. It's like when you're a kid and you play football—you don't care how muddy you get because you're so involved in the moment. You just enjoy what you're doing. I think it's the same with sex and with cooking food.

16

PLAYBOY: You've described yourself as a roller coaster. Tell us about the ride. Do your boyfriends find it exhilarating or do they hurl?

GERSHON: Oh God, a nauseating ride. Just kidding. My favorite part of a roller-coaster ride is when you're going up and you're slightly scared and really excited. You don't know what's coming next but you know it's going to be good. My boyfriends find it terrifying and exhilarating. If they can't hang on, they get off the ride. You can't handle it, go on the carousel.

Robert Crane

17

PLAYBOY: Those snarling lips. Natural or acquired?

GERSHON: They must be natural, because I'm not aware of when I do it. Sometimes I'll watch a film and I'm like, Oh my God, I had no idea I was doing that crooked thing. I was obsessed with Elvis Presley when I was little. Maybe it's unconscious Elvis, wishing to be Elvis. I have no idea. Maybe it comes from watching my dog. Even when he growls he looks so cool.

18

PLAYBOY: Your family consists mainly of musicians. Which instrument best describes you? Do you finger it or blow into it?

GERSHON: Probably both. I like blowing instruments and fingering them. Actually, I love playing the Jew's harp, which you do both to. There are a lot of musicians in my family—composers, musicians, managers.

19

PLAYBOY: Your character in *Bound* was appealing for many reasons. Do you actually know how to fix plumbing?

GERSHON: Not at all. My mother told me she thought I was a very good actress because she believed the plumbing part. I'm clueless about plumbing. I can barely plug a light into a wall. I'm not proud of this, but I can pick locks now. I'm better at that stuff.

20

PLAYBOY: You have described yourself as chameleon-like. If we put you on your back and rub your stomach, will you fall asleep?

GERSHON: Depends on who's doing the rubbing. I think I said that in response to a specific question. Someone probably said to me, "You're very chameleon-like." It's one of those things that gets turned around and makes you sound like an asshole. I think I was probably talking about my eyes, because I blink like a lizard—I don't close my eyes all the way. The doctor once said, "That's very chameleon-like—very lizard-like." I blink like a lizard. Does that make me cold-blooded or just dry-eyed?

Lucy Liu

The best thing to happen to "Ally McBeal" expounds on hair jobs, chopsticks and being a moron in love.

Just when the hit series Ally McBeal was becoming predictable in its unpredictability, a litigious powerhouse named Ling Woo turned the show on its head. She's played by actor Lucy Liu.

The daughter of Chinese immigrants, Liu grew up in Queens. She attended NYU and later the University of Michigan, where she majored in Asian languages and cultures. During her senior year, Liu auditioned for a supporting role in Andre Gregory's stage adaptation of Alice in Wonderland. Instead, she won the lead, and her acting career was born.

Liu's work in theater productions, including M. Butterfly, led to guest appearances on NYPD Blue, The X-Files and LA Law. A role on ER brought her to the attention of Ally McBeal creator David Kelley, who was searching for new characters and story lines. He immediately cast Liu in a supporting role.

Liu has parlayed her exposure on the show into a growing movie career, including a memorable role as a dominatrix opposite Mel Gibson in Payback. "I read the script," she said, "and thought it was dark and interesting." She has also appeared in Clint Eastwood's True Crime and in Molly with Elisabeth Shue.

Liu still finds time for stage work as a member of Los Angeles' Met Theater Development Ensemble. And, she's an accomplished fine artist who has had solo shows in Soho and Venice, California.

Robert Crane caught up with the indefatigable Liu on the set of Ally McBeal in Los Angeles. He reports: "Liu changed into a skimpy leather ensemble for her role as Ling Woo and asked me to zip her up. It was my pleasure. While we sat in her dressing room, she constantly tugged at her skirt as she became more animated and vocal. The frequent interruptions by makeup artists, assistant directors, personal assistants and a boyfriend with two dogs didn't affect Liu's stream of thought. She's beautiful, determined and opinionated, and she has a great pair of legs, which she attributes to climbing—rock climbing."

1

PLAYBOY: Ling Woo, the character you play on *Ally McBeal*, has been responsible for some innovative TV moments, such as licking Richard Fish's lips. For what other breakthroughs do you want to be responsible?

LIU: Ling has done a lot of stuff. She's licked lips, she's sucked fingers and she's given hair jobs. I don't know how David Kelley comes up with these things. They are now the mark of Ling. She definitely has a lot of other things up her sleeve. She's trying to show Fish a little more about foreplay. I think there's also a power struggle between Ling and Fish: He wants to have intercourse and she doesn't want to—to the extent that she's trying to prove a point. She has to stand strong.

She might have a lot of other things in store before she gives it up to him. It makes it a little more interesting. I think the tension will build—at least for him.

2

PLAYBOY: You're a martial artist, fine artist, accordion player, rock climber. What do you have against being lazy?

LIU: Sometimes I'm lazy, but I always have something creative I want to do or work on. It's nice to lounge around the house. But if you're an artist, you got to have some fucking money. You work at McDonald's if you have to. You got to earn some money so you have confidence when you walk into a room and present yourself. Success is definitely a point of view, but success to me is just like, Hey, guess what? I'm paying my own rent. I went out and bought this food. I used to get up at three or four o'clock in the morning to make omelettes for people just so I could have some money. Believe me, I didn't want to do that. It wasn't a great job, but I did it. I'm a firm believer in not living off somebody else. I'm really independent that way, and I hope I remain that way. Get off your ass is what I would say.

3

PLAYBOY: What's the most enduring myth about Asian women?

LIU: That our vaginas are slit a different way. That's the major one. Mine is, however, and I'm proud of it. It's a nice discovery, but now that you're printing it, nobody will be curious anymore.

4

PLAYBOY: Defend that most maligned instrument—the accordion.

LIU: Defend it? There's nothing to defend! It's an instrument that breathes with you. You control the sound, you create the energy, you determine how loud it is. The emotional backing of the instrument is something you create also, depending on how much you pull and push and how much you breathe with it. Somebody can play one song completely flat, and someone else can play it with so much emotion you're on the verge of tears. It's something you create. It's like a part of you—as opposed to a guitar or a flute. Go blow on that!

5

PLAYBOY: Rock climbing: You climb like crazy, then you come down. Are we missing something?

LIU: I understand why people do extreme sports: They give you a feeling you can't match. It's close to death. It's so dangerous that you get a certain high from it. Once you get that high, there's nothing you can replace it with. I lived in New York all my life and was never athletic. I came out here and I started doing things I'd never done before, like hiking and roller-skating. Women are better climbers than men, generally, because men usually try to muscle their way up with their arms. By the time they're a quarter of the way up they are exhausted and they've blown themselves out. Women usually have stronger legs. It's called the four points—if your four points are even, then your energy is dispersed in a good way. It's a Zen way of working out. You feel like you're reaching a goal. You have to try it to understand it. It's actually a really safe sport if you do it right, because you're completely locked into the rock. If you do fall, you should be hanging—everything should be attached.

6

PLAYBOY: How good can a non-Asian get with chopsticks? Any tips?

LIU: Pretty good. There's a right way to use them and I don't use them properly. I have friends who are Canadian and Caucasian and American who use chopsticks much better than I do. I don't use them properly, but I get the food and that's the most important thing.

7

PLAYBOY: You're an artist. Do you understand the reviews in *Artforum*?

LIU: They reviewed a piece I saw in New York titled *White on White*. It was white canvas with white paint on it. They went into this whole breakdown of the idea behind it. After a while you start thinking, Wow, it was a really good idea for this person to paint white on white. It's revolutionary. In reality it was white on white—anyone could have done it. I think art is subjective. I applied for an NEA grant once. I submitted slides of my work along with an impassioned essay. They ended up giving the grant to somebody who was handing out dollar bills in Mexico. It was about the energy of giving the money out. I was really pissed off. I don't understand that or things that are really abstract. I'm a visual person. I understand that modern art is different. I can appreciate it to a certain degree, but it kind of pisses me off.

8

PLAYBOY: In *Payback*, did Mel Gibson come quietly or did you have to rough him up a bit?

LIU: Roughing up is always a good thing, never forget that. Everybody likes to be roughed up. And I don't think any man comes quietly. Mel is a great guy.

9

PLAYBOY: Are we condemned to choose one from column A and one from column B, or are we free to choose whatever we want from all over the menu?

LIU: In my life, I choose from every column. People grow and change. You learn about stuff, you get more experienced, you learn you were ignorant before. You can't expect to know everything. I wasn't allowed to watch *Three's Company* when I was growing up because it was about two women and a guy living together. We always sneaked in and watched it even though we weren't supposed to. When you start categorizing things, that's when people go crazy. You want column B because you're in column A. You want anything you don't have. But you shouldn't deny yourself anything.

10

PLAYBOY: Do you get off on the idea of having a love slave?

LIU: I get so off on it. It's great. I love it because he bows down to me and it's such a feeling of power. His weakness is something that's just delicious. Weakness can be delicious, but only when [*Ally McBeal* co-star] Greg Germann delivers it. Sometimes it's just like, Good Lord, get the spatula, get the jellyfish off me. But when Greg does it, it's like quivering. You just want to slap him, and when you do, he enjoys it. He eats it up. The more he enjoys it, the more you enjoy it. So we work off each other's energy. Plus, he's so powerful in his everyday life as a lawyer and a money fiend that it's nice to see him get down and quiver.

11

PLAYBOY: Is this real acting for you, or do you see where it comes from?

LIU: It's hard for me. I was so terrified the day I had to lick Fish's finger, because it was so phallic. I was on the verge of tears because it was like I was selling my soul on national television—licking this guy's cock, practically. If anything, it would get me a second job at the Pink Pussycat Theater. I was so terrified, and then I just did it. I wasn't sure how to feel about it. Then I had to do it again a few episodes later and it was easier. I guess it was easier because I'm accepting myself more as a woman people are attracted to. I'm seeing that I can be a leading lady doing these things.

12

PLAYBOY: If you thought Calista Flockhart were too thin, you'd tell her, right?

LIU: No, I wouldn't. I'm just not close enough to her to tell her something like that. I think she looks great. She is in great shape. If people thought I were too heavy, I'm not sure I'd want them to tell me. It's a personal issue.

13

PLAYBOY: Your character, Ling, describes men as horny toads. Is that so wrong?

LIU: It's not so much that it's wrong, because women are horny toads too a lot of the time. Sometimes women want to go out and screw and leave in the morning just like some guys do. I just happen to think that, as a whole, women are a lot more emotional and need a certain amount of security that men don't always have the ability to offer. It's a social issue, it's a gender issue, and it's something that gets in the way. But it's not particularly bad.

14

PLAYBOY: How can you avoid being a moron in love?

LIU: Can't. You have to be a moron in love. That's the fucked-up thing about love. I've done so many stupid things. When I'm really into something I'm in it all the way. I'll do almost anything without thinking about it until the relationship is over. Then I just think about what a fucking idiot I was. You give yourself 100 percent to the relationship or to the person and you can't think straight. Your mind is somewhere else. In fact, Hallmark should make a Valentine's Day card that says, "Thank you for being such a moron." Maybe I'll do it if this job doesn't work out.

15

PLAYBOY: What are the danger signs that a relationship is over the top?

LIU: When there's a lot of unnecessary drama in the relationship. When you walk in the door and he's got his penis hanging out of his pants. Normal stuff. He has gone and got a scrotum tuck—that's when you know something's gone wrong. You know, those telltale everyday things.

16

PLAYBOY: Asian sex secrets—myth, hype or just plain good sense?

LIU: The mystique should live on, baby. Everyone thinks what they do is really mysterious and wonderful and unique and that they're the best lover in the world. Everyone should have that mentality, or they should try to improve on it. The Asian mystique is that you don't talk and you look really small. That's the attraction. Keep your mouth shut and turn over! I don't know what the Asian sex secrets are—if somebody has them, let me know.

17

PLAYBOY: Can you envision an adult film based on *The Karate Kid?*

LIU: Yeah, *Whacks On, Whacks Off.* Enough said. No one's ever forgotten that phrase. There have been so many funny spoofs on films. I get a kick out of them, though I don't know if I would ever actually want to go to the theater to see them.

18

PLAYBOY: What is the best message you've received in a fortune cookie?

LIU: [*Pulling them out of her wallet*] "Be assertive and you will win." "You will be unusually successful in business." "Get away from home for a while to restore your energies." That's the best one. "Your talents are in fine shape, utilize them to their fullest."

19

PLAYBOY: Which of men's many shortcomings should they get over?

LIU: If you're working and they're not. If you have money and they don't have any, it's not a big deal. If he has a small penis, I don't give a shit. I don't want to hear about it. I don't want him constantly talking about it. It's so ridiculous, so silly. The more he emphasizes it, the more I'm going to focus on it. Shut up! I'm no expert on men's shortcomings, but I think there's a certain amount of ego involved with most men—that's what makes men men. I love men. They are extremely odd animals of prey. That's what makes them so wonderful. If anything, men are mysterious. If you try to break everything down and analyze it, you're going to have too much information on your hands. You're not going to know what to do with it. You have to experience it as it is. If it doesn't work out, move on to the next one.

20

PLAYBOY: What would you order in a bar to signal sexual readiness?

LIU: Listen, honey, if I order anything in a bar I'm ready. I'm not a heavy drinker. If I drink at all, I start getting loose and feeling pretty crazy. I think alcohol makes you feel immortal, like you can jump off a building or leap in front of a car. I love drinking sake, and sometimes I'll have an Absolut and cranberry with a lime or something like that. But I have to do it with somebody I'm really comfortable with and who I can eliminate the next day. Who won't be missed? I can put him out of his misery.

Lisa Kudrow

The thinking man's friend on the power of ditz, the truth about Vassar girls and the allure of frilly tennis underpants.

Graduating from Vassar College with a degree in biology, Lisa Kudrow intended to pursue a career in medical research and work with her father, a world-renowned headache specialist. But Kudrow's brother's good friend, actor and comedian Jon Lovitz, inspired her to audition for the Los Angeles improvisational group the Groundlings. She made the cut and, after appearing with the group for a few years, was offered guest roles on television's "Coach," "Cheers" and "Newhart." During the 1995 season, she was in two popular series, "Mad About You" and "Friends." Her "Friends" character, Phoebe, is a New Age ditz and arguably the funniest member of the cast. In support of the last point, she has garnered Emmy and Golden Globe award nominations as well as one for the American Comedy Awards.

Kudrow's career has recently expanded to the big screen, with co-starring roles in Albert Brooks' "Mother"; in "Romy and Michelle's High School Reunion," in which she plays opposite Mira Sorvino; and in the independently produced "Clockwatchers," with Parker Posey. In addition, Kudrow finds time to perform with the Groundlings and a new group, the Transformers.

Robert Crane caught up with Kudrow in West Hollywood. He reports: "Lisa is prettier and taller in person than on television, and her hair should be as popular as Jennifer Aniston's."

1

PLAYBOY: Ditz has a proud history—Judy Holiday and Marilyn Monroe, among others. Is exceptional intelligence a gift or a burden?

KUDROW: Mostly a burden. I never knew my IQ because my parents were liberal and refused to have me assessed. When I started playing stupid people, I allowed them to be in the rest of my life, too. So I'd go through life acting a little stupid or just not getting it. Life was so easy then. I did that up until *Friends,* when, for some reason, it bugged me. I wanted the rest of the cast to know that I wasn't really dumb. So I stopped and life got hard. We decide that someone is stupid when they're really nice and don't have that funny, sarcastic judgment that rips someone to shreds. If you don't have that quality, people assume you don't get it—that you're dumb. I had made a choice to be a nice person and not acknowledge the nasty stuff. But I had to stop if I wanted to be considered a person with a brain.

2

PLAYBOY: In playing a ditz, from whom do you take your inspiration?

KUDROW: I'm not patterning myself after any actor who played a dumb person. I admire Judy Holliday and Marilyn Monroe was very funny and played a really great dumb woman. I appreciate their work, but I don't have them in mind when I'm working. My dumb people aren't sexy dumb. Mine are regular dumb—and they're not even really dumb, I don't think. They are people who aren't focused on whatever it is the camera is focused on at the moment.

3

PLAYBOY: Who is the model for the bad folk songs your character sings on *Friends*—Leonard Cohen?

KUDROW: It depends on what I've been listening to when we're taping the show. For one song it was Alanis Morissette—that inappropriate, out-of-nowhere anger. *Smelly Cat* was kind of Chrissie Hynde. I write the melodies because I have to. I don't really play guitar. You can't show me a tune. I have to write it. I'm with BMI—I don't have my own publishing company yet. A collection of my songs would make a fun comedy album, but part of me would feel too bad for the real musicians and songwriters who are struggling to make a living at it. Then I show up.

4

PLAYBOY: Do people who have friends need to watch *Friends*?

KUDROW: If anyone needs to watch any TV show, they're in trouble. I don't think normal people actually let *Friends* replace their social life. Like, "I don't need friends anymore because every Thursday night I've got six actors I've never met who pretend to be other people." But it was fun when I would watch the show with Courteney [Cox] at her house and she would have people over.

5

PLAYBOY: Do friends have to be kooky to be interesting?

KUDROW: No. In fact, someone who is kooky is the most uninteresting person in the world, because kooky is not like a real anything. Anyone is interesting. The camera just happens to be turned on this group. You can do this with any group. As long as their hair and makeup are done well and they're well lit, you're going to go, "OK, I'm supposed to pay attention to them." I like *The Real World* on MTV. I'd like to know if it's real or not, because I've been told that the cast kind of knows the camera is there so they purposely do stuff. I think the first season was real because I know someone who edited it and who was in on the creation of it. I love *The Real World*.

6

PLAYBOY: When you shoot *Friends*, is it cold in the studio? Courteney and Jennifer look chilly sometimes.

KUDROW: Yep. Because of the lights and the cameras and stuff it's very cold in the studio. Thank God I wear a lot of vests and things.

7

PLAYBOY: Which companies have approached you for commercials? Martin or Gibson guitars, perhaps?

KUDROW: No, God, they haven't. A company that makes macaroni and cheese approached me. It was like, "Wouldn't it be fun if you didn't get what was going on and then you get it because you're eating a big plate of starch?" I've turned down requests because, sometimes, there really isn't enough money in the world.

8

PLAYBOY: Jennifer Aniston has the haircut of the Nineties. What does it say about us as a people?

KUDROW: That we're sheep. If something looks good, we want to try it. Heroin is really big now. How much more of a lemming can you be?

9

PLAYBOY: Of the things people say about Vassar girls, which are true?

KUDROW: That they overdress. Everything was a cocktail dress at Vassar. It wasn't very collegiate, in a good way. I purposely chose a school that doesn't have sororities or fraternities.

10

PLAYBOY: If you were to bequeath an endowment to Vassar, say, the Kudrow Building or the Kudrow Professorship, to which department would you give it?

KUDROW: I loved the biology department. I would help so they could do research without the pressure of securing grants from big corporations. All the research in that department was in obesity. If you were interested in anything else, you probably wouldn't get funding for it. The money was in obesity.

11

PLAYBOY: Your father is a well-known doctor who specializes in headaches. Did that disqualify you when you were single from using the phrase "I have a headache" to avoid further social obligations?

KUDROW: I never used the headache line. I was always too honest—"I'm really not attracted to you, so I can't" or "I never had any intention of sleeping with you, so I won't." Much more forward.

12

PLAYBOY: Which television ads for pain relief were appealing to your family, and which ones did you make fun of?

KUDROW: You mean were we like plumbers sitting around laughing at Drano commercials? We didn't do that. I asked one time, thinking I would get an in-the-know answer, "Is Excedrin really good? Which is the best aspirin?" The answer was, "It doesn't matter."

13

PLAYBOY: You and Conan O'Brien were an item—Vassar girl meets Harvard man. What went wrong?

KUDROW: We became fast friends after an improvisation class we had together. We were the only two who connected. A girl said to me once, "Hey, you went to Vassar and he went to Harvard. So, did you guys know each other before?" And I'm supposed to be the one who's stupid. Yeah, see, there's a tunnel between all the Ivy League and sister schools. Actually, I don't know what went wrong. The question is funnier than the answer.

14

PLAYBOY: Describe your first date with Conan.

KUDROW: There wasn't a date. It just happened. One night I told him I had a crush on him. I had been thinking about it for a while. He'd be perfect: We're best friends. He's smart. I respect him a lot and he's attractive. When it came time to tell him, I broke into a cold sweat and almost fainted.

15

PLAYBOY: Did you dump Conan when his ratings hit bottom?

KUDROW: What happened was, he took off to do his show and there wasn't room for filling David Letterman's shoes and having a long-distance relationship. So that ended that. But within a month or two of breaking up, we met the people we're with now. I've done his show three times. It's really fun. We talk all the time. My husband and I spent New Year's with Conan and his girlfriend. Conan is one of my husband's favorites. It's too good to be true.

16

PLAYBOY: Your husband is French. Who does the cooking?

KUDROW: I do. He doesn't cook at all. He'll open a can of soup. He's a French boy who was taken care of his whole life. There was a lot of pressure at first. We'd have friends over from France and he'd want me to make something like pommes de terre dauphinoise. You know what that is? Potatoes au gratin. But they have to call it that. Then it has to be hard to make. They judged it. French people judge. Make no bones about it. They judge away.

17

PLAYBOY: Some people contend that the aggressor in an argument can't lose if he conducts it in French. Does your husband revert to French to win arguments?

KUDROW: The argument would be over—but only because I wouldn't know what he was saying anymore. I could just leave the room, I guess. French expletives slip in. He says *merde*—piece of shit—a lot. Everything is *du merde*. Everything is "of shit." His parents were here and started laughing because everything he said was "of shit." They said they were "the father of shit, the mother of shit."

18

PLAYBOY: You're a serious tennis player. Did you letter at Vassar?

KUDROW: I was on the varsity tennis team, but it wasn't that hard to accomplish. I played first doubles. A couple of times I got to play singles. In high school, I was on the varsity team. I was pretty serious for a little while--I had a personal coach and was thinking about playing in tournaments. Whatever my brother David was doing, I was interested in. I was pretty good, too.

19

PLAYBOY: What's the deal with tennis skirts and those frilly underpants?

KUDROW: Skirts are so much cuter than shorts, and that A-line is flattering. The skirt is so short that you have to wear something. They make it frilly so you think it's not just underwear. It's really underwear.

20

PLAYBOY: If you had known Mira Sorvino in college, describe a road trip the two of you would have taken.

KUDROW: To the Smithsonian, so Mira could explain some things to me.

Juliette Lewis

The liquid-eyed actor speaks out on her prisoner fans, her bad-girl past and sucking De Niro's thumb.

At the age of six, Juliette Lewis was given a part in Clint Eastwood's Bronco Billy. In 1987, she had a leading role in the miniseries Home Fires. At 14, seeking exemption from child labor laws that restricted shooting schedules for minors, she petitioned the court to grant her legal majority. When she was 16, she played Chevy Chase's daughter in National Lampoon's Christmas Vacation and starred in the television film Too Young to Die. During that shooting she began an affair with older co-star Brad Pitt. At 18, Lewis was working with Robert De Niro in Cape Fear, for which she garnered Academy Award and Golden Globe nominations for best supporting actress.

Lewis became a sought-after actor and at the same time earned a reputation as a loose cannon. She next appeared with Woody Allen in Husbands and Wives, followed by memorable performances as a dysfunctional innocent opposite Brad Pitt in Kalifornia, as a waitress from Queens in Romeo Is Bleeding, co-starring Gary Oldman, and as a drifter hanging out with Johnny Depp and Leonardo DiCaprio in What's Eating Gilbert Grape. Then Oliver Stone cast Lewis alongside Woody Harrelson as two mass-murdering folk heroes in Natural Born Killers. Lewis avoided typecasting with turns opposite Steve Martin and Adam Sandler in Nora Ephron's comedy Mixed Nuts and Ralph Fiennes in the science-fiction action film Strange Days, followed by Quentin Tarantino's ode to vampires, From Dusk Till Dawn.

After a struggle with drugs and alcohol, Lewis came back strong with well-reviewed work in The Other Sister, an Emmy-nominated performance by Showtime's My Louisiana Sky and a co-starring role as Jennifer Lopez' best friend in Enough. Lewis carries a heavy workload this year with roles in the comedy Old School with Luke Wilson and Vince Vaughn, in Mike Figgis' The Devil's Throat opposite Dennis Quaid and Sharon Stone and in Blueberry with Michael Madsen and Vincent Cassel.

Robert Crane caught up with the reinvigorated actor at Chateau Marmont in Hollywood. He reports: "Lewis is way too bright and energetic. A relationship with her could never be boring or predictable. She does things her way. She's also much more attractive in person than on the screen. She kills, in a natural-born way."

1

PLAYBOY: Are girls who have tattoos promiscuous? And which is a better indicator of a woman's sexual heat—tattoos or piercing?

LEWIS: I think it's square to have tattoos. Go back to the basics and be really organic, kind of pure, un-inked, under-sexualized. I am so against piercing. I have a little tattoo of a heart on my neck, and I'm having a Hello Kitty removed from my wrist. If you find yourself getting pierced and tattooed, maybe you should look into doing something more creative with your time.

2

PLAYBOY: What's a creative use of your time? Do you throw good parties?

53

LEWIS: Yes, and choosing the right people is everything. My husband and I have an eclectic bunch because he's a pro skateboarder. We had a Christmas party that was pretty fun. He invited photographers, skateboarders, people who run skate magazines. I invited musicians, actors, designers. It was a real creative blend. Also parents. Being a parent is an interesting thing. Here's my party recommendation: The Cars anthology. It has the hits and then it has their cool music that didn't break out. It's upbeat but not too intrusive. It has just enough kick.

3

PLAYBOY: When some women have good sex, they tell everyone. Even their mothers. Do you?

LEWIS: No, because I'm not in fucking high school anymore. I just build on it for next time with my one and only and expand on whatever we were doing before. I've talked to my mom, but not too intimately. My mom is a good friend of mine. But we don't get overly explicit.

4

PLAYBOY: A woman's stomach is a sexy, powerful place. How do you use yours?

LEWIS: I'm an actress, so I should be into my looks and all that stuff, but I'm really not. This stomach thing is funny. The Turks invented belly dancing, but most men think it's a parking lot. I saw a girl in Beverly Hills wearing a half shirt. My sister and I have a little voice we use for a certain kind of woman. You can tell as she's walking down the street that all she's interested in is if her stomach looks OK. She's like, "Oh, I hope my stomach's cool. Does everybody see it?" I get to play one of those girls in *Old School*. I don't like half shirts, I like long shirts. When I want to feel sexy sometimes or show off a little bit, I'll usually wear a short skirt because I inherited dancer's legs from my parents. I've been told they look all right.

5

PLAYBOY: To a guy, the phrase, "Can I have a drawer?" is frightening. What is the equivalent phrase from a female's point of view?

LEWIS: "Could I borrow your car? I'm getting one next week—I gave them a down payment—but could I borrow yours now?" Borrow a woman's car? Not a good sign.

6

PLAYBOY: Do you think you have an especially appreciative fan base among the prison population?

LEWIS: People both in and out of prison are appreciative of my performances. My *Natural Born Killers* fans are not in prison. The ones who love *Natural Born Killers* are very intelligent. When I shot it in Joliet, we went on a tour of the facility. Coincidentally, *Cape Fear* had played the week before I toured the prison. They all seemed pretty happy about that film, especially the scene that would be stimulating to some inmates. It was brilliant timing. The thumb scene was still fresh in their minds, so prisoners heckled me, saying, "Put your thumb in your mouth, girl." Prisoners seem to like television, and TV fame is much scarier because it's intimate—the actor always plays the same character. That gets scary for people, so I've heard.

7

PLAYBOY: Tell us something that you once feared but feel comfortable doing now.

LEWIS: Going someplace where there is a large crowd. When I'm in crowds I feel like chaos is going to happen. Someone will get shot. But I went to a Rolling Stones concert in Dodger Stadium about four years ago that was therapeutic. I went with a friend, and we were on the grass. I did an exercise where I looked around and just embraced it. Once the concert started I was a complete fanatic, singing every song.

8

PLAYBOY: How can we help change your bad-girl image?

LEWIS: I don't want to change anything because I just played a psychopath and played it well. I think that's cool. In *Natural Born Killers*, a woman who was full of rage and anguish and being obnoxious was more shocking than a man would have been. Right after that I did a Nora Ephron-Steve Martin comedy called *Mixed Nuts*, but it didn't do well. I like to do the unpredictable in film. People have seen me as intense because of some of the movies I've been in, like Cape Fear and *Kalifornia* and *Natural Born Killers*. But those have been interspersed with movies that aren't intense.

9

PLAYBOY: Have we seen the demise of the bad girl?

LEWIS: What is a bad girl these days? It's almost become trite. I don't know the difference between bad and good. That's why I'm into the progressive girl. Are there bad girls anymore? There are stupid girls.

10

PLAYBOY: What's more dangerous to the general public, people having sex in an automobile or talking on a cell phone?

LEWIS: Talking on a cell phone. Unless I'm living a sheltered life, I don't see the sex part happening. Some people can't do two things at once. I, however, can.

11

PLAYBOY: Do you have any incantations that actually work?

LEWIS: I was big into spells when I was younger. If I felt wronged I would make up something like, "Your car is going to catch on fire." I wouldn't do anything about it. I said this once to a guy, "You just watch. Within a month you'll be in jail." I said that to a petty criminal, so it's not like I'm psychic. And yes, he went to jail.

12

PLAYBOY: We have to ask about *Cape Fear* and your scene with Robert De Niro. We have heard women value the size of a man's thumb. What can you tell by sucking a man's thumb?

LEWIS: That was one of my favorite movies of all time because of Robert De Niro, but as far as what you can tell by sucking a thumb, I have no clue. That's not what's going on when you're doing that kind of scene. There were all kinds of cat-and-mouse things that were going on that led up to the thumb infiltration.

13

PLAYBOY: What kind of lasting impression did you leave on De Niro?

LEWIS: I'm sure he was happy that I held my own in the scene—that I did a decent job. That's where inexperience works for you. You haven't developed notions on how to behave, which I think is good for an actor. That scene is so complicated because it's about a guy persuading a girl to trust him when she has no reason not to trust him other than that he hurt her mom's dog. She doesn't know what the audience knows. It's a little magical. When I was working with De Niro all the moments fell into place. The scene was something De Niro and Scorsese came up with. All I knew was that he was supposed to walk up to me and kiss me. The thumb thing was De Niro's idea—it was such a violation. They also came up with my wearing a retainer for the part. It's a puberty thing. They came up with those images to have an impact on the audience.

14

PLAYBOY: In *Natural Born Killers*, did Rodney Dangerfield's character influence your personal hygiene?

LEWIS: No. Rodney's such a sweet guy. It's good he was funny, because it was a sitcom spoof. I had to jump on his back. I wanted to make sure the emotion was there and that I looked enraged, but at the same time I was worrying about Rodney—I didn't want to put his back out. I didn't want to hurt him.

15

PLAYBOY: Does Oliver Stone have a vision of the corrupting violence on the edge of American culture, or is he just a nutty guy with a dirty mind?

LEWIS: He's definitely not the latter. Oliver is brilliant. Is he exploiting something or is he making a comment on violence? As with the snipers in Washington, any wack job now knows he'll be front-page news. That's what Oliver was commenting on. It's not that complicated, but he knew he was hitting the news media in the face—and, boy, they did not like it. I think he's wickedly brilliant and funny, too. A lot of people don't know he's funny.

16

PLAYBOY: Do most directors have a particular vision, or do they just want to see their star naked?

LEWIS: That's more of a question for the producer.

17

PLAYBOY: If you feel that it's appropriate, would you do a nude scene?

LEWIS: Yes. In *Blueberry*, I'm naked underwater. It's really beautiful. American films with nudity are only sexual. I think nudity is fine, but I would like to see it in a nonsexual context. Having a phone conversation naked or something. Reality stuff.

18

PLAYBOY: Does Woody Harrelson make more or less sense now that you're clean?

LEWIS: First of all, my little destructive youth stint was when I was 21, 22. It was not during that movie. Woody is Woody. He has some convictions. We just worked together, and he's funny. I'm OK with people as long as they have a sense of humor. Regarding his pro-hemp stance, I'm not down with the pot culture. It's like, get a day job, dudes, do something else. I understand when you're 14 how pot is the almighty, your guru. Now I don't get it.

19

PLAYBOY: If we were in a lingerie store now, toward what would you gravitate?

LEWIS: I like panties. I'm trying to be demure by saying panties. I usually say underwear. I've always gone braless, but now I'm into finding colorful bras, so I might look for those too.

20

PLAYBOY: You've worked with top-notch directors. Whose phone call would you immediately return?

LEWIS: I'd say pretty much everybody's, but Mike Figgis and I are like two peas in a pod. He's my new best pal. He's a great guy, and he's trying to push the envelope. We don't need to put out product and TV dinners all the time. I would immediately call back Martin Scorsese, Oliver Stone and Woody Allen. Isn't it funny I've worked with two Woodys? Do you know any other Woodys working in Hollywood?

Teri Garr

Our favorite dizzy blonde speaks out on great breasts, bad dates and how Letterman lured her into that shower.

Robert Crane caught up with the effervescent Teri Garr at her office in Los Angeles. He reports, "Teri is as pretty, funny and full of doubt in person as she is on the big screen. Angst could easily be her middle name. A dancer in nine Elvis Presley movies, Garr prominently displayed her fabulous legs while wearing a business suit straight out of 'Mr. Mom.' In case you were wondering, she doesn't enjoy being asked what it's like to be David Letterman's girlfriend."

1

PLAYBOY: If men were food, describe your favorite meal.

GARR: Burger and fries are very appealing, if you get my drift. Sometimes, gourmet food is good, too. Slow, nice gourmet food.

2

PLAYBOY: About what are you neurotic?

GARR: Relationships with men. I never shut up about them. What does he mean? Why can't I? Why can't he? Why doesn't he? Why don't I? It's the same shit over and over. It's endless. I don't know what's going to stop it. Maybe shock therapy.

3

PLAYBOY: Describe your recurring dreams.

GARR: Robert Redford is in my dreams a lot. I don't know why. I don't know what he represents. I don't take any notice of him. He's just another actor. All of a sudden, he'll be in a dream. I'll be working with him. I'll wake up in the morning and go, "Robert Redford. Why?" I like him very much, but it's not like Brando or De Niro. I'll dream that I walk off the stage and someone says, "You were fabulous The audience was crying." I go, "Me?" "You. We never knew that you had the capacity and depth. You were really beautiful and sexual and moving." I go, "Me?" I wake up feeling great in the morning. If dreams help you conquer your fears, then I'm in great shape.

4

PLAYBOY: What flatters you?

GARR: Good lighting. Pink lights. Vittorio Storaro, one of my favorite cameramen. Driving around L.A. in a fancy car and being recognized. You know, the construction-worker deal; you're walking down the street and they whistle at your ass. It feels good. When people come up to me and tell me they like my work as an actress, I say, "Thank you. Can I have a dollar? Is there some way I can turn this flattery into cold cash? Otherwise, it's not worth much to me, is it?"

5

PLAYBOY: If you could change one thing about yourself, what would it be?

GARR: I would have bigger breasts. I always thought that would be the answer. It's why everybody is popular. I'd be coping out if I had that surgery done, though. "What is essential is invisible to the eye," says the Little Prince.

6

PLAYBOY: David Letterman: the truth.

GARR: We're secretly married and have a couple of kids. But don't print it, please. He begged me, "Don't tell anybody." The relationship appears to be something that it isn't. I go on the show because I like David and I've known him for years. When I did *Young Frankenstein*, I went on a tour of ten cities in ten days. I thought that was the glamor part of show business. David Letterman had a radio show in Indianapolis that I appeared on and he asked the same stupid questions—"So, what's it like out there in Hollywood? What kind of car do you drive?" So, now, we have this relationship that has some time behind it. That's the only thing that makes it look so comfortable on TV. I guess we flirt with each other. We don't hang out. He's a very driven person. He's out to be at the top of the NBC peacock. He's clawing his way to the middle. He's good at talk-show stuff. He's funny. To do *The Tonight Show* is harder, because Johnny Carson always asks, "Who are you dating? When are you getting married? Who are you living with?" It's all about dating and personal life. I like Johnny a lot, but he's like a father. "It's none of your damn business, Johnny." You can go on *Letterman* and talk about how stupid beauty pageants are. David's funny, and, of course, we're married.

7

PLAYBOY: How did Letterman lure you into his shower?

GARR: I've done other things, but I'm known only for that shower scene. Here's what happened: Letterman was doing his show in his office as an experiment. They wanted me to come early so David could show me around. He's got pencils stuck in his ceiling. He's got his own bathroom with a shower in it. When he showed me around, he asked, "Do you want to take a shower?" I said, "No, I don't want to take a shower." That night, we did the show in his office without an audience. It was like dead air. It was going out to millions of people and it was not entertaining. We started talking and trying to make a conversation. I'm thinking, Dead air. Big, big dead air. He asked me again if I wanted to take a shower. I said, "No, forget the shower." We all wore body microphones because there wasn't room for a boom mike. When the next guest appeared, the sound man said he wanted to take my body mike. I said, "No, because I might say something while I'm sitting here." He said, "We have only so many body mikes." During a commercial, David said, "Come on, take a shower. It would make the show more interesting. Just do it." I said, "No, forget it. I'm not taking a shower. It's stupid. Stop it." The sound man was bugging me about the body mike. Finally, I said, "OK, take the fucking mike. I won't say anything anymore." As soon as I handed him the mike, the sound man said, "She's gonna take the shower!" That was on the air. I decided, what the hell. I went into the bathroom. I thought, This is just a joke. It's just some kind of a titillating, sensuous idea, but all right, I'll take the shower. It was live TV and I went in there and started to take my clothes off and thought, What am I doing? Why? David's at the door, saying, "Turn on the water; we're running out of time." I turned on the shower, and I had my underpants on. I had to walk home with wet underpants. They didn't plan this. That was my foray into "living theater" and live show business with David Letterman browbeating me into doing it. People love to see people with a firmness crumble. It must have been some kind of a sexual conquering.

8

PLAYBOY: What have you learned from the Eighties?

GARR: Condoms.

9

PLAYBOY: Is fidelity part of your vocabulary?

GARR: Of course it is. That's the only thing that's fair. It's also completely human and natural to flirt with people and have sexual feelings, as Jimmy Carter said. You can't deny that that goes on. Fidelity is also sticking up for your friends and your ideals. It's the only kind of good thing about the Mafia.

10

PLAYBOY: Whose thighs would you die for?

GARR: Arnold Schwarzenegger's. They're very well developed; every muscle is defined. I don't want to say I'm envious of any other woman's body. It's a bad myth to perpetuate. Women have enough trouble liking themselves.

11

PLAYBOY: When do you know you're in love?

GARR: It can be an instant thing. It can be a guy at the cleaners who makes a joke and I can walk out of there and think, I love this guy. I've spent so many years being defensive and wisecracking that it's very hard to let myself know. I'm very defensive about it. It's because of men I trusted who left. I'm scared of it.

12

PLAYBOY: Describe your worst date.

GARR: One? I have 20 and they all make me shut the door just a little bit tighter each time. I was very naïve. I came to town by myself and dropped out of college and had my own apartment and was going to be an actress and was going to be a dancer and I had roommates. I was prey to all kinds of awful situations. Men are out to get you—I'm sorry—if you're out there and you're vulnerable and you're nice. I had to learn the hard way about how to protect myself. Once, years ago, I was on *The Dating Game* and I won a date with this guy and we had to go to Las Vegas. It was like prison. I didn't want to do it. This guy was in a singing group called the Fuzzy Lumps. It was pretty bad. I played the nickel slot machine all night and came home. Thanks, dream date. I wanted to be dead.

13

PLAYBOY: When was the last time you lied?

GARR: Just now. Sometimes, you tell people things to protect them. You know what's best, because you know better than anybody and that's why you lie. So, it's OK. I have a hard time with my family.

I keep certain things from my mother. I keep certain things from my brothers. I don't call it lying, but if I tell them everything about my life, then they worry. So it's not really like lying.

14

PLAYBOY: What is an irresistible combination of features in a man?

GARR: Sense of humor is on the top, which also connotes some kind of intelligence and wit. A man should be able to dance. When I was in high school, these were the two big things: Guys had to have a great car and they had to dance. Somehow, this stuff got lost through the years. But I'm bringing it back. Men who work on cars having always been very appealing to me. I like to say, "What have you got in there? Dual cams? You got two sixes? You got three fours? What have you got?" I like these guys.

15

PLAYBOY: What's it like being the other woman?

GARR: Being the other woman is something you unconsciously do on purpose, because you don't have any self-esteem or you don't want a relationship. You know he's not going to leave his wife, so you're putting yourself in this painful place. You're putting yourself as second fiddle and you accept it. You don't feel that you deserve or are entitled to be the number-one person. I once went out with a guy who was married—I didn't know he was married at the time—and when I found out, I went nuts. I said, "You can't do this. This is unfair." What about the wife? There's something about a man who wants to have all kinds of people he's committed to or faking it. What does that say about his ego? Being the other woman is torture. But at least it's something.

16

PLAYBOY: When you're dateless, what are some good things you can do only alone?

GARR: I like to get into my car and drive around. It's very meditative. I've always had a fantasy that I could get a pickup truck and drive around, bash it up, go way out, just drive. It's because I'm from Southern California. We learn to drive when we're young. When you're an adolescent and you're going through such insane angst, anyway, and the minute you're 15 and a half, you have this learner's permit, you start driving. I would drive everywhere—just get on the freeway and see what it's like. I'm like the woman in Joan Didion's *Play It as It Lays*. Driving is my acting research, because I can check out how different societies live and what their day is like.

17

PLAYBOY: How do you perceive yourself? Beautiful? Perky? Vague?

GARR: Perceptive. Energetic. Curious. Malevolent. Hostile. Empathetic. Compassionate. Precise. Occasionally, confused. There is one word—I'm not going to tell you what it is—that is used to describe me all the time. If I hear that word one more time, I'm going to eat my shoes. I guess it's my own fault for trying to be charming and please everyone. You finally get to the point where you go, "Fuck that shit. I'll just please myself."

18

PLAYBOY: What's the Teri Garr workout regimen?

GARR: This is pathetic. I used to be really good about the running. I did a lot of running. I do Jane Fonda's workout at least three times a week. That class is like the Marines. When I go to work, it's so hard to do any exercising that the best I can do is, like, ride a bike. I hate running any more. I hate fucking running. I won't do it. I'm going to start swimming. There is no regimen. I feel so embarrassed about this. It's catch-as-catch-can. I joined three gyms. I've been to two of them once. When I'm on location, I think, The best I can do is to walk around and shop today. I'll get some exercise. Tighten my butt as I walk down the street. I'm beginning to hate it all.

19

PLAYBOY: Who wears the pants in your life?

GARR: I do. I'm pretty much of a leader. My mother, sister-in-law and I are all from the same place, Island of the Bossy Women. You should see my brother get bossed around, and he's a surgeon, he's not a *schlep* guy. All women are like that on a certain level, because they're not allowed to do it anyplace else. So women develop this thing where their home becomes the Land of Bossiness.

20

PLAYBOY: Where were you when Elvis died?

GARR: I danced in a lot of Elvis' movies when I was starting out and studying acting. I was in Mobile, Alabama, doing *Close Encounters*. Elvis was doing a concert there. He was right upstairs in a suite and I thought, I should go up and say hi to him, because I know him. I didn't, and he died the next year and I felt like, You see, you should say hello to people you know. We're circus people. We take care of our own. I'm fascinated with Elvis, because he came from nothing and was given a lot, and how did he deal with that transition? Where's the party? There is no party. Where's the level of fun? There is no fun. It's just another level of your life, but you have more money. If he were alive, I bet he'd be a health nut, a nondrug person. But he just didn't make it around that corner. Too bad. Nice guy.

COMEDIANS

Robert Crane

The Man Show

Adam Carolla and Jimmy Kimmel want to establish themselves as the anti-Oprahs. Their show is funny, sophomoric, and offensive to women. What's not to love?

Originally, The Man Show was supposed to boost ABC's short list of bright, hip shows, joining Bill Maher's Politically Incorrect. Unfortunately, the executives at the Disney-owned network were appalled by the pilot—scantily clad women bouncing on trampolines, endless fart jokes—as well as by the gross and obscene language and visuals. ABC passed.

Comedy Central loved what it saw and promptly brought The Man Show to its Wednesday night lineup, following South Park. Jimmy Kimmel, already a Comedy Central veteran by way of Win Ben Stein's Money, hooked up with his longtime friend Adam Carolla, co-star of MTV's Loveline, to host this celebration of all things male.

Robert Crane talked with Kimmel and Carolla on the Ben Stein set in Los Angeles. Crane reports: "After Kimmel had taped three shows, he and Carolla settled into Kimmel's dressing room. The atmosphere was fraternity-like, interrupted occasionally by adults. Ben Stein popped in to announce that 'Jimmy Kimmel is the funniest white male alive,' and an assistant informed Carolla that he would have to move his illegally parked BMW."

PLAYBOY: Which groups would be unlikely to find any redeeming qualities in your show?

JIMMY: Women in suits of any kind.

ADAM: Groups that use acronyms. Female, male, all of those acronym groups are going to be pissed. We're not intentionally setting out to offend people, but I think we would both be disappointed if we didn't. We'd feel as if we weren't doing our jobs. We've been successful in offending pretty much everyone throughout both our careers. I don't see why this will be any different.

PLAYBOY: You claim that estrogen is one of the most poisonous substances known to man. Can you name others?

JIMMY: Mountain Dew.

ADAM: Anything by Bijan.

PLAYBOY: Can you think of any women who deserve to be on a pedestal?

JIMMY: Any woman you see in this magazine. The truth is, lots of women deserve to be put on a pedestal. The problem is, not every woman deserves to be put on a pedestal. We're not antiwoman, it's just that television promotes the idea that men are stupid and don't wear the pants. But men aren't stupid. For the most part, men run things. Men, for the most part, invent things. Men, for the most part, are the best cooks. It's phony to pretend that men are stupid, but TV shows kind of ram that down your throat. I don't know why it's been accepted for so long. Maybe it's because of all the Tim Allens of the world—he's a bumbling idiot and the wife is the one who runs the show.

ADAM: As males, we've been ashamed of our success for too long. The guys built the studio, they built the bleachers, they built the camera, they built the stage, they run the studio. They do everything involved with the TV show, and then the guy who plays the star on the sitcom is a buffoon. It's ridiculous, and we want to right that wrong.

JIMMY: If something like this were attributed to a race or religion—for example, if all Mexicans on TV were stupid—people would be outraged.

PLAYBOY: What should the male response be when a woman cries?

ADAM: Have they had sex yet? If they haven't, he should nurture her.

JIMMY: Otherwise, get the hell out of the house.

PLAYBOY: What are some fun things to say to women?

JIMMY: I can't really think of any fun things to say to a woman. You know, you start saying fun things and she starts saying stuff back, and then she wants to know what you're thinking and it really gets out of hand.

ADAM: I think what Jimmy's saying is, there's nothing wrong with a conversation on occasion, but once you set that precedent, then you're having them all the time. It's no longer just during long drives. You're watching TV *and* you're having a conversation.

JIMMY: Here are some fun things to say to women: "Let's turn on the TV." "Your ass is blocking the set." "I can't, I'm watching TV."

PLAYBOY: If you're in a relationship, what should you say to continue the relationship?

JIMMY: I don't know that women even want you to say anything; they just want to make sure that you're listening to what they have to say. I mean, every time I say something, she gets pissed off.

ADAM: That's true. My girlfriend says to me four days a week, "You're not listening. What did I just say?" I've never said to a woman, "Repeat what I just said." Never. I don't think guys ever say that.

JIMMY: Yeah, guys don't care that much, except if it's about the car or something. "Take it and get the oil changed." Then you want to make sure they understand. For me, a relationship is almost like a phone call that you're trying to end. You say, "Yeah, uh-huh, all right, all right, OK, I don't know, we'll see." Ultimately, men just want to be left alone. Of course, there's a honeymoon period, or maybe you're out dating and stuff, but ultimately we want to be left to ourselves. We want to go to the room where there's a television and no one talks to us at all.

ADAM: That's why the garage shouldn't be attached to the house. There's never a bathroom in the garage because then the guy would never come back.

PLAYBOY: Complete the sentence, "A woman's place is in the...."

JIMMY: Closet? I don't know where a woman's place is. I know where their places aren't, and their places aren't on the golf course, in the bowling alley, in the living room. My wife told me, "I'm thinking about taking golf lessons." I said, "Are you going lesbian?" She said, "No, it'll be nice. We can go play golf together." I was like, what the hell are you talking about? Play golf? I don't go to play golf. I go to walk around with some other guys for six hours—and get away from you.

ADAM: The idea is that you get to walk around with guys. Sometimes we just walk—we'll pass three or four holes without even playing. Women are constantly trying to think of hobbies that men and women can do together. They don't realize that guys have cooked up hobbies that they know women will hate, just so they can be left alone.

PLAYBOY: Construct a curriculum on how to be a man.

JIMMY: We think of this show as a graduate program on how to be a man, because, you know, there are so many aspects that a lot of guys really don't understand. Being a man is not about having a penis; being a man is an internal thing. Even some women are men. You know, the women who seem like one of the guys. They're kind of hard, and that's who the show is for. Being a man is more about the things you don't do than the things you do. There's a lot of room to be a man, but there are certain things you can't really be party to. I caught a 25-year-old guy who works here calling into a radio station to win Billy Joel tickets. I said, "What are you doing?" He really had no idea why it was wrong.

PLAYBOY: Your show is predicated on the fact that men don't have to say we're sorry—but surely men have to say sorry for a few things.

JIMMY: Only those that are to our advantage. Certainly, there are times you have to say you're sorry, but only to get sex, or to get them to leave you alone. It's purely to keep your life more pleasant. If you say you're sorry too much, when the chips are really down you have to start crying or something like that. That's why it's important to almost never say you're sorry, so when you pull it out, it's a big gun. Remember how Fonzie would never apologize for anything on *Happy Days*? But when on the rare occasion he choked up with Mr. C and said he was sorry, it was a big deal. He got a big round of applause.

PLAYBOY: Jimmy, do you have advice for men in your condition?

JIMMY: My condition—you mean being married? I would never say don't get married, because there are definitely good things about being married. I'd say don't give up your testicles. A lot of guys turn into a child and their wife becomes mommy. I never want my wife to be mommy. A lot of guys do. They give up their power or their edge. They give it up in exchange for being taken care of. I won't do it, and I hate to see guys who do. I see it happen to friends—they just wave the white flag. It's like they just get too tired.

ADAM: They're not even getting anything in return after a certain period. It's not like they get breakfast in bed every day. The wife becomes some sort of troll who's sleeping under the bed, and you got to tiptoe around the house because she'll come out in a bad mood. But it's not like the troll is cooking breakfast. Men just hit the point where they don't want to piss her off.

PLAYBOY: List some bulletproof arguments for the right to a boys' night out.

JIMMY: Any woman who keeps you from hanging out with your friends is a bad woman. It's natural for guys to hang out together. You have to do it, or else you become a woman.

ADAM: You have to get out of the habit of asking. I mean, you gotta tell 'em.

JIMMY: You never ask, you announce.

ADAM: Here's the deal. You can't be cruel or mean, but you have to be firm. Women like that, whether they want to admit it or not. They like the guy who stands by his convictions. You can't start arguing and sniveling, because they'll see that as a weakness and then pounce on you. You have to be fair and you have to be firm. You can't go out five nights in a row, but you have to say, "Look, it's been almost 18 hours since I was drunk, I haven't shot any snooker in four and a half hours and the chili I spilled on my shirt is starting to dry." You tell them. If you start asking them, then you're fucked. But you don't yell it at them, you just tell them: This is what I'm doing.

PLAYBOY: You guys talk big, but what's your secret fear of Oprah and Rosie?

JIMMY: Our fear is not a personal fear; it's fear for the nation. It's a fear that there's a focal point for women, and it's a powerful one. Oprah has a lot of power. If Oprah said, "Ladies, enough is enough. It's time to start chopping off testicles," I guarantee you'd be hearing them hit the floor like gumballs all over the country. I hope to God she stays slim, because when she flips out like all these fat celebrities seem to flip out after a while—name one sane fat celebrity—we're all going to be in a world of trouble. There are always a couple of picketers outside a nuclear plant. We're the picketers outside the Oprah and Rosie plants. We may seem nuts, but somebody has to focus on those two.

ADAM: We have to chain ourselves to something. Like Stedman's Mercedes.

PLAYBOY: We're not saying GQ is run by gay guys, but don't you think inordinate attention to style runs counter to basic self-esteem issues?

ADAM: All those male magazines, the Men's Fitnesses and the GQs and all the ones where guys are Rollerblading with the six-pack stomach in the cycling shorts—it's all gay porn. That's all that is. Regular guys aren't interested in 15-minute abs. That's ridiculous. Wouldn't it be great to live in a world where we can ask a young man, "Do you know where your abs are?" and he just points to his ass?

JIMMY: I don't buy clothing. I operate like a seven-year-old boy does with food. He doesn't go out to restaurants or the supermarket. I wear what is given to me. I wear what I get for Christmas and whatever free T-shirts I get along the way. Occasionally I get a couple pairs of jeans. The only item of clothing that's appropriate for a man to spend a great deal of time buying is sneakers. That's the only thing. I cannot go by a Foot Locker without stopping in.

PLAYBOY: What don't women understand about the subtle cunning of male interior decorating?

ADAM: You mean the cinder blocks with the pine boards?

JIMMY: What they don't understand is this: It doesn't matter how nice or how shitty anything is, you will eventually get used to it and not notice it at all. When I first came out to California, I thought, Wow, it's really beautiful here. It's so green. Now I walk outside and don't think twice about anything. We have five bedrooms in our house, and I live in one room. I share it with my cousin Sal. We got a computer in there. We got all our books and, you know, an eight-foot stand-up of Troy Aikman and some baseball cards scattered around. The room is filthy, but I don't notice it. You become acclimated. Women like to move furniture around. I could never imagine moving furniture except to make way for a bigger TV set.

PLAYBOY: What natural sounds and smells occur in the male environment and need no excuses?

JIMMY: I fart a lot, and my wife never, ever farts. It's a weird thing because, you know, we eat a lot of the same stuff. Maybe there is some difference physiologically between men and women. But she gets crazy. She gets so mad when I'm just lying in bed farting, which is every night. She threatens that we're gonna have different rooms and all this stuff, and I just laugh harder. It just makes me laugh so hard that sometimes I get stomach pains from laughing. I can see how it's disgusting, but on the other hand, I have no plans to slow down.

ADAM: It's an interesting point you bring up, because women physiologically don't operate that much differently from men. They drink a certain amount of fluids, they urinate a certain amount, they defecate a certain amount, blood pumps at a certain rate—everything's the same but the fart. I don't think farting gets cultivated in them at a young age. A tip to women as far as the farting goes: If you don't want your guy to fart, do not make the mistake of laughing or even coming close to accepting it, because that's a big green light. That's all he needs. If the very first time Jimmy farted in front of Gina, she said, "I can't believe you would show me that disregard. Don't ever do that again," and really spun out, it would have a set a different tempo. On the other hand, it's important for men to break wind early and often in a relationship and really let the women know where they stand.

PLAYBOY: How can we disable the inbred female imperative to make projects out of their boyfriends and husbands?

JIMMY: You can't disable it. The only thing you can do is fight it as much as possible. Occasionally they might have a good suggestion.

ADAM: Women's hobbies are guys. We got cars, we got model stuff, we got sports, we got hobbies; they don't have hobbies. Their hobby is you. You look like a big fucking Erector set to them. That's what they see: some kit that's not finished. Interestingly, lesbians have hobbies because they don't have guys to work on. In lieu of busting a guy's balls all day, they go play a round of golf.

PLAYBOY: Women on trampolines: they like it, we like it. Is it one of the intentions of your show to celebrate life's uncomplicated pleasures?

JIMMY: Our show is about what is true and what isn't. It's no bullshit. I mean, *Baywatch*, *VIP*, these shows are T and A shows, but they pretend to have a plot in all that stuff. We are not pretending; we have girls jumping on trampolines. That's as honest as it gets. We like to watch girls on trampolines. We're not going to make them carry machine guns and pretend to be busting up some kind of drug run. We just want to look at the nipples.

ADAM: "The Pope's in town, Pamela, he's going to need protection. It's gonna be hot out there. We better wear something loose fitting." Just put her on the fucking trampoline.

PLAYBOY: What are the only acceptable things to say when opening a gift from your girlfriend or wife?

JIMMY: I'm always very honest and it pisses my wife off, but when you're married it's like it's your money and she's wasting it. My wife will get me gifts sometimes, and I look at them and I can't imagine who her husband is. For Valentine's Day my wife bought me this art deco digital clock at a flea market. I wanted to just throw it right into the garbage, because it is exactly the opposite of anything I might possibly want. It was ugly. I had no idea why she bought it for me. I said, "I hope that wasn't expensive." "It was kind of." "Can't take it back, can you?" "Nope, flea market." "All right, well, I guess we ought to hold on to it 'cause it cost money." But I haven't seen it since that day and I will never see it again.

ADAM: It's ironic: When your wife buys you a gift, she buys it with your money. She could buy you a Rolle-Royce, but you'd be pissed off because it means you bought yourself a Rolls. It's sort of like when they give you something from your pet or from your five-year-old. The kid didn't go buy it and the cat didn't go buy it. You bought it and it got recycled through them. It's like money laundering.

PLAYBOY: Describe a perfect day off for a man.

JIMMY: I like being in the house alone because I can masturbate in rooms I'm not normally allowed in. It's really great when you live with people. I would not want to live alone; I'd get stir-crazy after a while. But when you live with a family and then have the whole house to yourself, it's like when the dog gets out. It's running and sniffing everything and leaving its scent.

ADAM: Yeah, you can pee in the sink, run around in your underpants. And when you cook, you take the time to fix something weird, like waffles, or something messy.

SCTV

Video's wild bunch waxes witty about sex, satire, networks and the things they can't do on television.

The seven people who make up the critically acclaimed "Second City TV" write, produce, direct, perform and edit their 90-minute show from an otherwise normal TV studio in Toronto. We sent Robert Crane into that center of creative chaos to talk with the talented group and to see if he could survive their pace for a week. He reports: "The energy from this cast could light up much of Canada. They tape here because they don't want to be part of the scene in New York or Los Angeles—the very places where the shows they satirize are made. Here are some brief impressions: John Candy is the lovable bear, a warm, funny man; Andrea Martin is the least inhibited and the most accommodating; Eugene Levy is careful and the most precise; Rick Moranis may be the best impressionist; Dave Thomas is the most opinionated and thought-provoking; Joe Flaherty is the most shy and introverted off-camera; Catherine O'Hara has the most changeable appearance and has the best bod in the group."

1

PLAYBOY: OK, who's the funniest performer in the group?

LEVY: I don't think there is one person who's the funniest.

MARTIN: I do. I think there're some weak people. If you want to be honest, I don't like—

FLAHERTY: Physically, John is the funniest. Rick is the quickest. Catherine makes me laugh. Gene makes me laugh, but he's not the funniest.

THOMAS: The way to find out would be to get all of us in front of 1000 people. I think I'm funnier than Rick.

2

PLAYBOY: Some people think your show is pretty outrageous. How do *you* think it stacks up against the rest of what's on the tube?

FLAHERTY: I can't believe *Three's Company's* is on television. But there are tons of bad shows. I find Norman Lear offensive under the guise of being a television messiah. Let's face it: A sitcom is a sitcom. He claims it's relevant or hard-hitting. He took himself so seriously. I remember that terrible thing he did, *All That Glitters*. It was like a real bad propaganda thing: "Look, I believe in the women's movement, I'm Norman Lear."

THOMAS: When I look at *The Dukes of Hazzard* and try to attack it from the standpoint of satire, I don't know what to do. What do we do, wreck cars? I don't understand the level at which it operates.

CANDY: I can't believe *The Richard Simmons Show*. And Richard Dawson—one of my all-time favorites. He's so obnoxious. He has everything going for him—the accent, the charm—and he blows it by being insulting. He isn't allowed in my house.

3

PLAYBOY: It's conceded that you folks are the best imitators on TV. But are there people or shows that are off-limits to satirization?

CANDY: It's hard to do close friends. You know, they're nice people. I'm very political that way. I kind of do them, but it won't be a full-out version.

MARTIN: I was thinking that Sissy Spacek would be a great person to imitate, and then I thought, No, she's too good and I like her too much.

O'HARA: I don't want to do some people, not because it would hurt them but because it would be too much of a compliment to them.

CANDY: On the other hand, we tried to do *Laverne & Shirley* one time. We shot a scene and it looked just like *Laverne & Shirley*. No matter how shticky we got with it, how bad we took it, it just looked like one of their regular shows. There are some shows you just *can't* do.

4

PLAYBOY: What's the best drug to take before watching your show?

MARTIN: A nice glass of warm milk.

LEVY: Johnny Carson is the best drug to take before viewing our show. But some of the shows are unconsciously better appreciated if you've had a couple of tokes.

O'HARA: All I can think of is my mom reading this.

LEVY: I think a lot of people interpret the show as stoned humor, but it's not. You won't find a straighter bunch of people than us doing a late-night show.

MARTIN: I picture our audience drinking a cold glass of white wine.

MORANIS: With some spinach salad and nice Venetian blinds behind them.

LEVY: Egg-salad sandwiches and a milk shake.

O'HARA: Rusty nails and cigarettes.

THOMAS: I think grass is the best, because it will keep you from being too fidgety. It will allow you to revel in the subtle nuances of what we do. I recommend sinsemilla above other types of grass, because that keeps you up a little longer.

5

PLAYBOY: What's the most fun you can have with your clothes on?

MORANIS: Eat at a five-star restaurant with Eugene.

LEVY: Yeah, having a lovely *paillard* of beef that is beautifully seasoned and a nice tall Coke.

O'HARA: Come on, bar hopping and parties are better.

MORANIS: Wait a minute. I've changed my mind. I think the most fun you can have with your clothes on is a dry fuck.

CANDY: Yeah, I've got to go along with Rick on the dry fuck. Time is short and you're just in a hurry, like we are on this show a lot. A lot of that happens—the zipperless fuck.

THOMAS: Nah, the most fun to me is picking my nose. No question about it. It relaxes me in a way that Rick has to take his clothes off and do things with someone.

6

PLAYBOY: Why isn't there more sex on the show?

FLAHERTY: Sex, like drugs, is a very easy laugh, so you tend not to use it. Catherine and Andrea won't dress up in panties and see-through bras just for a laugh. They're much better than that. I did do *Dr. Tongue's 3-D House of Stewardesses*, though. I thought it would be real risqué to have them strip to their bikinis. But it was silly, it wasn't sexual.

O'HARA: Also, we don't waste our time working on something that's going to get cut anyway. And everyone's married in the cast except Rick and me.

THOMAS: We have big-breasted girls who appear in the background of a lot of scenes, but basically, we don't think they're funny or, certainly, not funnier than we are. Andrea has a sketch about how to fake an orgasm and NBC at first bumped it from the show. The network relented because it felt that most of the people who are offended by sex go to bed early. That's good network thinking.

MORANIS: Also, we're Canadian and very provincial and we like to keep sex inside the bedroom.

7

PLAYBOY: Is it because you're Canadian that there are no blacks or Third World members of the group? Don't you think they're funny?

MARTIN: I'm Armenian.

MORANIS: We have an Italian, two Jews, an Armenian, an Irish person, a Scot. What's John?

O'HARA: Irish.

MORANIS: When you come from the Great White North, there aren't a lot of black people.

MARTIN: I'm about as black as you get.

THOMAS: This show started from a stage cast that was in Toronto, and there were no black comedians in the show at that time. It would be difficult for me to accept NBC's saying to us, "We want you to put one black and one Mexican and one more woman on your show. We want you to appeal to our demographics." Why force us to change what we do? Nobody appreciates that. Mexicans and blacks don't. A lot of what Garrett Morris did on *Saturday Night Live* looked as if it were just pandering to the blacks. Really tokenism. I was insulted by that: I'm sure he was. Intelligent and thinking blacks would be insulted by that, too.

8

PLAYBOY: Does it disgust you that unhygienic acts occur while your show is televised?

MORANIS: Well, it bothers me that herpes may be spreading during the show.

MARTIN: If I can help somebody's sexual act, I'm happy. I wish I could get aroused watching myself.

9

PLAYBOY: Are there any secrets you'd care to reveal about yourself or the other group members?

CANDY: Well, I'd like to tell the government that I *am* paying taxes and would appreciate a green card. I spend a lot of money and I would help the economy. My main secret is that I'm bald and really 100 pounds lighter than this. This is just a suit that I wear. I don't want that to get around, because it'll wreck my career. Another secret is that this show is being done out of South America with laundered *Nazi* money.

FLAHERTY: The truth about Catherine is that she's like a lot of Irish-Catholic girls—a nonswinger. She lives a dissipated lifestyle without being dissipated. She keeps bad hours, she eats the wrong food, but her vices are so innocuous. If you can pick vices, you should really have vices like humping away all night. Not Catherine. Her vices include French fries and staying up all night by herself in her hotel room watching TV. Rick and Dave are pretty straight. Andrea used to be wild in the milder sense. John has the most vices; he's a big guy and a big guy needs big vices. He has funny vices, such as he spends too much money. The group isn't excessive except for John; he would have to be our Belushi. But I don't see any dark streaks anywhere in the group.

MORANIS: Wait a minute. A good, little known fact is that Eugene sent back three bottles of Chateauneuf-du-Pape one night in a five-star restaurant. It was the highlight of my life.

MARTIN: The truth? Rick would like to sleep with every extra who comes onto this show.

10

PLAYBOY: OK, then. Graphically describe some of the sexual relationships that are occurring within the group.

MARTIN: It's certainly not a big party group, with the exception of Catherine, who would *kill* to party every night. Eugene and I used to go out with each other. Every time I mention that, he gets upset.

O'HARA: Hey, I went out with him once, too.

THOMAS: It's all part of being a family. And there's a point with any brother and sister at which they say, "You show me yours and I'll show you mine." Andrea is really refreshing, because she has no inhibitions at all. Catherine has loads of inhibitions, so they're a nice contrast to each other. You can drop your pants in front of Andrea and Andrea will go, "Good, dear. So that's what it's like, huh?" Catherine will be down the hall and out the door, will have ordered a cab and got *into* it before the belt hits the ground.

11

PLAYBOY: What are your feelings about censors—the standards-and-practices people?

MORANIS: They're just earning a living. The problem is, they're not reporting what is offending them so much as what they are told *might* be offending Middle America. They're bureaucrats and they should stay out of the creative process.

MARTIN: I'm a little bit more compassionate. Everybody tries to hold on to his job and he's scared. He doesn't really know what his job *is*.

THOMAS: Well, I know it's really hip to despise them. And there's no getting around the fact that you are, to some extent, what you do. Unfortunately, the real power always goes to the older guys. In entertainment, that's fucking deadly, because, ultimately, they will not have contact with their audience.

12

PLAYBOY: What's the most distasteful sketch you've written that never got approved?

THOMAS: I wrote a piece called "Pocket Pal." It was about an electronic detector that would warn you 15 seconds in advance of mid-air collisions in aircraft. Bernie Sahlins, our executive producer at the time, was horrified. I was mad, because I thought it was funny: "Shocked by the recent negligence of air-traffic controllers and the number of errors committed by overworked pilots? Well, you don't have to worry about mid-air collisions anymore, thanks to an amazing piece of hardware developed by the Ronco corporation called the Pocket Pal, which can predict mid-air collisions, sometimes as much as 15 seconds before impact." Well, Danny Aykroyd eventually did the piece on *Saturday Night Live*. Matter of fact, Aykroyd told me I was the only outside writer who ever got a piece on that show. Our producers called me when they saw the bit and asked me what the hell was going on—was I writing for *S.N.L.* or what?" They said, "Hey, you wrote that for our show." I said, "Yeah, and you rejected it. So piss up a rope, Jack." I didn't receive any money for it. I just wanted that idea to get on the air.

13

PLAYBOY: What are some of the other censorship battles you've won and lost?

MARTIN: Brenda Vaccaro for maxi pads. Giant pads, like diapers. "I'm Brenda Vaccaro and I like that." I walk off and I can't get through the door. They censored it.

LEVY: Rick's had a problem with a character, Guy Friday, a very funny gay character who was in the syndicated show, but we can't get him on network.

MORANIS: It's not a fight I'm interested in, because I know the gay groups I've talked to aren't offended by the character. It's the standards-and-practices people who are afraid, because they have had pressure from gay groups in the past and they think this will cause them problems. I don't want to lend credence to their position.

THOMAS: Sometimes, we'll take a shot at something to see if it can get through. We can say "The silly bastard" on TV, but we can't say "You ugly bitch"—which makes a lot of sense.

FLAHERTY: We've had a few pieces dropped, but I feel that the pressure is more a liberal pressure than a Moral Majority pressure. I don't think the Moral Majority is up at that hour, to begin with. Besides, we're not into trying to get "Fuck you" on the air.

14

PLAYBOY: This is an opportunity to say all the things you can't say on TV.

CANDY: I was taught that fuck was a scared word. If you use fuck properly, you'll always get a huge laugh. It's a good word that's wasted a lot.

THOMAS: What I think about the network is something I can't say on TV: It's a beast on its side heaving its last.

MARTIN: I got scared that I couldn't say breast feeding.

O'HARA: Turd. They won't let us say turd.

15

PLAYBOY: Which television shows did you watch while you were growing up and which ones do you watch now?

O'HARA: I watched *Combat, Captain Kangaroo* and *The Three Stooges* as a kid. Now I like *Lou Grant*.

LEVY: I don't know whether it was part of Grant Tinker's deal at NBC, but I'm glad *Hill Street Blues* got renewed.

MORANIS: When people mention Ed Sullivan, I still get a pang in my stomach, because it reminds me that I have to go to school the next day. I used to watch *I Love Lucy* and Dick Van Dyke. Nowadays, I watch *Nova* and Jonathan Miller's *Body in Question*.

MARTIN: I watched *American Bandstand* while I was growing up. Now I can't watch any television without thinking, Could I parody that?

THOMAS: I used to watch 50, 60 hours a week, easily. All the Westerns: *Rawhide, Lawman, Cheyenne, Sugarfoot, The Rebel*—I can still remember most of the theme songs.

CANDY: I loved watching Jack Benny, Jack Paar, *The Honeymooners*, Burns and Allen, George Gobel. *The Munsters, Rocky and His Friends, Howdy Doody, Rin Tin Tin, Lassie*. I wasn't influenced by any one show, I was influenced by the medium.

FLAHERTY: I tend to watch sports, movies and PBS.

16

PLAYBOY: *Saturday Night Live, Fridays* and *SCTV* are inevitably compared with one another. How would you characterize each show?

LEVY: *Saturday Night Live* was innovative and contemporary with what was going down. Outside of a bad skit about Claudine Longet, you could put up with most of the stuff. It broke ground for our show's getting into syndication. But I just have no respect for *Fridays*. It's a blatant rip-off of a successful show.

MARTIN: I've seen *Fridays* only twice. But when I think L.A.—where the show is made—I don't think comedy, I just think hype.

LEVY: *Saturday Night Live* and *Fridays* were the brain child of one person. For example, Lorne Michaels [producer of *Saturday Night Live*] was very successful and deserves a lot of the credit for casting the people he did. But we dictate what our show is. Nobody comes down and tells us what to do. We do it ourselves. I don't think we'll ever have this power again. You get an idea, you write it, you tape it, you edit it, you follow it through in post-production. This just won't happen again.

17

PLAYBOY: Who should immediately be put into the comedy retirement village?

FLAHERTY: I don't find John Ritter funny. Nor George Carlin. Obviously, I'm not even gonna mention people like Jack Carter or any of those old-line comics. They're almost funny again because they're just so unfunny. A lot of people doing TV comedy have no right to be there. The people on *Fridays*, for example. But they're actors; they don't create the show themselves.

CANDY: Don Rickles should definitely go away. Alan King. Jerry Lewis. The Rat Pack in its entirety. Marty Allen should just be there for a long time. And Tony Randall has lost that magic for me. I hate the Mighty Carson Art Players. I think Carson will agree with me sometimes. It makes you laugh because it bombs. He just stands there with egg on his face.

18

PLAYBOY: One of your show's most popular features is the Great White North segment with Moranis and Thomas. Matter of fact, it has led to a hit album and there's talk about a movie. How did that skit start?

MORANIS: Doug and Bob McKenzie were conceived because of content regulations that the Canadian government imposes on media. Three out of ten records a radio station plays have to be Canadian. When our show was bought by the Canadian Broadcasting Corporation, we gained two additional minutes because of fewer commercials. The producer said, "OK, for those two minutes, we need Canadian content." And we said, "OK, we'll fry up back bacon and drink beer for two minutes."

O'HARA: Americans love it because they think Canadians are just like that.

THOMAS: Entertainment is not an issue of nationalism. That's why I hate those Canadian-content regulations and why I reacted so hostilely in the creation of Bob and Doug McKenzie. But it's turned out to be a boon.

19

PLAYBOY: It's your business to pin down other people's personalities. Can you characterize yourselves in a sentence or a phrase?

THOMAS: I used to bill myself as, "the Beaver" because I'm a workaholic. I can tell you what I think of the rest of them: John is the big, lovable lump. I've never met anybody who hated him. Rick is really an imp. Gene is one of the slowest people I've ever met in my life. Nobody moves slower or more methodically than Gene. Catherine has the nickname "the Cheezer" because of her throaty, gravelly voice and her long chin. I can't look at Andrea without thinking of her as an Armenian. Joe is one of the most complicated, richly textured individuals I've ever run across: an amazing blend of Irish and Italian. It's a pretty unusual group. Did I leave anybody out?

LEVY: There's a citizenship award in grade two that reads: TO EUGENE, FOR BEING POLITE, FOR BEING KIND TO OTHERS, FOR BEING THE BEST BOY IN ROOM 15.

MORANIS: I received an award in Hebrew school for being runner-up in a Hebrew spelling contest and they spelled my name wrong.

MARTIN: Somebody described me as a hip Hobbit. I thought that wasn't funny, so please don't publish it. I think of myself as really being a conservative—

MORANIS: Whore.

MARTIN: I think we're all middle-of-the-road people.

O'HARA: I'm not middle-of-the-road. I'm just faking it because I'm with a bunch of older people.

20

PLAYBOY: Do you ever fake laughter just to be nice?

MARTIN: Oh, that's disgusting. Are you kidding?

O'HARA *(as Lola Heatherton)*: Haaaa ha ha ha. Our laughter is our sexual release, so, no, we try to do it sincere as often as we can.

MARTIN: I like a good cigarette after I laugh.

O'HARA: Yeah, let's all get naked and laugh together.

Roseanne

Barr-none, she is the season's hottest and funniest television star. But behind the laughter is a woman with a troubled past—and a present and future that is not all fun and games.

"If I had grown up content and sheltered, I wouldn't be making a lot of money and be very happy now," Roseanne Barr shouts above the din of the lunch crowd at one of Los Angeles' trendy restaurants. "Since I was three my dream was always to be a comic or a comedy writer. I grew up in Salt Lake City, Utah and I'm Jewish. So that's why I'm like this!"

The 37-year-old star of ABC's *Roseanne* was told, as a child, by her parents that she and her two sisters could say anything they wanted as long as it was funny. "My family was real poor and the only thing we had was watching comedians on Ed Sullivan on Sunday night. My father would shout 'Comedians!' and we'd all come in and watch," Roseanne remembers. Her father, Jerry, was a blanket salesman and a comedy "groupie." She attributes her dichotomous religious background to her mother, Helen. "When I was three, I fell against a table leg in the kitchen," Roseanne recalls. "Afterwards one side of my face was paralyzed. The first thing my mom did was call the rabbi. He came and said a prayer over me, and nothing happened. So the next day, Mom called the Mormon priests and they came and said prayers, and the paralysis went away. My mother took that as a sign from God and raised me a Mormon—although I still had to be Jewish on Friday nights when we went to my grandma's for kosher pot-roast dinner."

When Roseanne was 15, she thought she found in a medical book the explanation of what had happened to her face 12 years before. It was a condition called Bell's palsy, and it generally lasts for 48 hours. So much, she thought, for religious miracles. The next day she went out and drank, and smoked pot. "It was awful," she says.

But it signaled the onset of a period of rebelliousness so intense that Roseanne would sometimes walk across busy highways, forcing cars to swerve around her. Finally, a car hit her and knocked her unconscious, with a deep gash in her skull. After this, with her parents' consent, 17-year-old Roseanne checked into Utah State Hospital, where she remained for eight months.

Upon her release from the hospital, Roseanne went back to her senior year in high school, but unable to fight the boredom, she dropped out. She told her parents that she was going to visit a friend in Denver, but actually she was leaving home. In Georgetown, Colo., she met Bill Pentland, the night clerk at a motel. "He was really weird," she says. "I loved him right away." Soon Roseanne got a job as a dishwasher and moved in with Bill. They got married in 1973. "We really lucked into something," Roseanne says, breaking into her Cheshire cat smile. "Bill makes up for a lot that I had to live through."

While Bill worked as a garbage-truck driver and, later, as a mailman, Roseanne stayed home, raising their three kids who quickly came along—Jennifer, now 15; Jessica, 14; and Jake, 11. Roseanne also cooked, cleaned, wrote poetry—and got fat.

"Fat people are beautiful people," maintains Roseanne, who weighs nearly 200 pounds. "But nobody talks about us in a positive way."

When mounting credit-card debt forced Roseanne to get a job, she dieted down to 105 pounds and became a cocktail waitress at a Denver lounge. There she began to use her acerbic wit on her customers, playing against the role of the stereotypical waitress who will do anything for a tip. "The drinks are six bucks," she'd say, "and it'll cost you three dollars more for me to take them off the tray." She not only got tips, she got laughs.

In 1981, Roseanne visited a Denver comedy club where she was quickly outraged at the sexism of the male comics. She wrote a five-minute act which was, in effect, a rebuttal, and she persuaded the manager of the club to let her perform it. The laughs didn't come easy at first, but she persisted and she was soon performing a longer act at small clubs in and around Denver.

"I just try to say stuff that I think not everybody thinks about," she says. "I go back to the things that have stuck in my head from when I was growing up, and look at them honestly. Almost invariably, they are things that men have said, and then I turn them around to what I feel, and what I think a lot of other women feel."

With the encouragement of her younger sister, Geraldine, and her friend, comic Louie Anderson, Roseanne auditioned for Mitzi Shore, owner of Los Angeles' renowned Comedy Store. She was hired after a six-minute audition and moved to Los Angeles, temporarily leaving Bill and the three kids in Denver.

Initially, Roseanne was rejected by women who thought she was insulting their husbands. But now her audience of men *and* women understands that her routine is the language of her life. "I suddenly knew I could do what Richard Pryor did for himself—get inside the stereotype and make it three-dimensional from within. I am a housewife. And I could call myself a domestic goddess. I could say, 'Hey, fellas, you've had it wrong all these years. We women are not the jokes. You are the jokes!'"

Mass audiences soon took notice of this large, honest, working-class housewife who told it like it was and seemed completely at ease with her earthy body. Roseanne seemed like a real person, not a professional actress. "I perceive myself as a poet. I don't feel like I'm a comedienne. I feel like I'm funny, but I'm selling ideas."

Roseanne appeared on the Carson and Letterman shows, she did an HBO special and headlined at places like Carnegie Hall and Las Vegas. Then she achieved every comedian's goal: her own network situation comedy, with Roseanne as a working-class mother of three and John

Goodman as her husband. The show was an immediate smash hit. "I play a *real* mom on my show," Roseanne says. "She doesn't clean her house. She isn't sweet all the time. And she doesn't pay attention to her kids and husband."

Now living in a large home in Encino with her children and husband-writer-retired mailman Bill (who is writing for her show), Roseanne says she finally feels inner peace with herself. "I feel comfortable with people, and I never felt that before," she admits.

However, despite her seemingly upbeat persona, she is not encouraged by what she sees happening to women in daily life. "I don't think women have made any progress," she says, no longer smiling. "I think things are worse now than years ago. The more technology we get, the worse it will be for women."

"The thing women have got to learn is that nobody gives you power. You just take it. I raise my son to listen to women. I raise my daughters to go out and fight with the world. Boys need to be taught humility because the world gives them something else. I try to teach my kids things that the world isn't going to give them."

Still, her enormous success has brought many changes. "I get a lot of credibility that I never expected," she admits. "People are friendly and they're not freaked out the way they used to be."

As we finish lunch, I finally ask her if she has a workout routine. "I got myself a treadmill for exercise," she says, proudly. "I'm getting in shape. By next year, I'm going to be thin. I have a trainer and I've lost three ounces. It's great. I want to lose three ounces a year."

The waiter appears and asks whether we would like dessert. "Yes, I would like chocolate cake," says Roseanne. "The whole cake . . . "

Phil Hartman's Guide to the Holiday Office Party

How to Get Down with the Boss—and Other Essential Advice from the Departed Comic

THE ARRIVAL

Be fashionably late. Arrive half an hour to one hour after the designated start time. You don't want to appear to be one of those needy nerdlets who are too grateful for an invitation. Because the host is usually your boss, make a perfunctory greeting. This will be followed up later, when you're more inebriated, with fawning, butt-nuzzling comments. The main thing now is to name your poison. The party doesn't really start until everybody is in an altered state. Since this is the office equivalent of Mardi Gras, it's your one chance to really go wild. Don't hold back. You can always blame inappropriate behavior on the booze. Everybody understands that. Everybody will be out of control.

THE BARTENDER

Make friends with the bartender. You can do this quickly with a well-placed $20 bill. You want him to push on your enemies the more sickening drinks like manhattans or mai tais or other fruity, sugary concoctions. You might say to the bartender, "Jim loves kamikazes. Whatever he asks for, give him a kamikaze." Tequila drinks, especially those made with cheap tequila, can drive your foes mad.

CHOICE OF DRINK

I recommend scotch because of its extraordinary properties. It makes you loud and shockingly uninhibited, true, but don't forget that it also makes you more handsome, triples your wit and gives you the power to read minds. Go for the highest quality you can find—something aged at least 12 years. No generic brands. Any scotch made in Detroit, for example, is not a legitimate elixir for our purposes. You want to get a few under your belt right away, and then you can make small talk with your supervisors and lieutenants. Nothing substantial is going to occur until you get into your new mantle of superhuman scotchoid. You'll want to have some kind of snack so you don't peak too suddenly. You want the scotch to blend in. You don't have to worry about avoiding garlic or salsa or onion dip because another wonderful thing about scotch is that it's the ultimate disinfectant and mouthwash. It destroys anything that it comes across. Feel free to go for the most vile offerings on the buffet table—salami, beef jerky, whatever. They're no match for a great scotch.

I was a child of the Sixties—I've done it all—but I think scotch is the perfect nothing-makes-you-smarter drink. It's psychedelic, too. You really feel like you can see through walls, and you could have a flashback to the days of love-ins.

IMBIBING

Go two double scotches in the first ten minutes. That's straight up or on the rocks. I prefer rocks. No soda, no water. Then you can go one to two double scotches an hour. You wouldn't want to do more than 12 double scotches, probably. One of the great things about scotch is that it's the most controllable form of alcohol. It burns at an even rate. There are no sudden spikes of inebriation. Being a purist, I would never touch a punch bowl. You know damn well that the kid from the mail room has poured in some Grateful Dead substance. You don't want anything to put you off your game. I'm a strong believer in designated drivers. Take a cab. You don't want to risk everything for one mad moment behind the wheel.

ALLIES AND ENEMIES

Never take a date unless it's someone with whom you have an absolute understanding. One of the best things you can do is take someone from your office clique—someone who has her own agenda and will be running down the same moves. If it's an ally, you can work in concert. Never take a date you're going to have to pander and cater to throughout the party because, after all, it's part celebration, part commando raid. You're there trying to work magic. It's the one time of year when the rigid corporate structure is in disarray. You want to be able to float around like a ninja with all your senses finely tuned and enhanced by 12-year-old scotch.

The best way to snake someone's woman is to find that brief moment when you can sidle up to her. You don't have to speak to her directly—just get within her auditory range while he's distracted. For example, I like to back up to a woman, pretend I'm talking to somebody else and then say something that would be embarrassing to your rival, like, "Gee, Jerry's transplants look great. It's like a natural hairline," or "Jerry's calf implants are wonderful. If I had skinny calves, I'd do that," or "Sure, Jerry has a great smile. Dental plates are cheap." Or just impugn his ethics and morality—"Yeah, Jerry was with Joey Buttafuoco that night. How he got off I'll never know." Those kinds of comments work on a woman's mind in the most subtle ways.

Look for the married guy who takes off his wedding ring when he attends a party. I always keep a pocketful of wedding rings. When the married guy is hovering over some delectable creature, walk up with a wedding ring and say, "Jerry, I found this on the washbasin. Is it yours?"

THE BUFFET LINE

You don't go to a party to diet. If your eyes are crossing regularly, if you're seeing double or quadruple, get some fat into your system fast—a good sour cream-based clam dip or any kind of sausage in a blanket or ice cream will do. You need something to cut the absorption of alcohol. But if you're feeling OK, avoid the food. A real scotch drinker can control his intake so that when his eyes are just starting to cross, he can, through force of will, separate them and keep them on track.

You're going to want to make use of the cookies. Holiday cookies are mainly fun props—put them over your eyes and pretend you're a blind man or stick a chocolate chip cookie to your forehead and ask if anybody has any Clearasil.

POSITIONING ONESELF

Once you're in the zone, you have to stake out an area to perform in. You need a place to run your show. I like the Xerox room and its paper supply, because you can make paper airplanes—a true art. They're fun and they have that poke-somebody's-eye-out quality that can be so exciting.

In every office there's a prim and proper woman, most often the boss' secretary, who at the holiday party is the one who gets up on the coffee machine and dances topless. You want to draw her into your sphere as quickly as possible. She'll act as a magnet and draw others into your orbit. By the time you get to the Xerox-your-butt stage of the party, you are master of the entire situation. If one of your rivals is on some game that's drawing a bigger crowd, you have to work harder. You have to Xerox a butt without underpants. You have to entertain. It's like any other form of show business—it's competitive. You have to do your best. At this point, there's bound to be an office conga line. That's when you take the party from your power base and snake your way around the entire facility. That's when you express, in concrete terms, that you're a people person and that you have an elevated appreciation for humanity, though most people you despise on an individual basis. A conga line is a great common denominator. You just grab some hips and join in. There's no discrimination. It's where people from the loading dock can mingle with management and the FedEx delivery guys can grab on to the boss' secretary. It's just one big, happy, twisted DNA chain of humanity working its way around the office.

MANAGING THE BOSS

Sooner or later you're going to steal focus from whatever the boss is doing. You may notice that the boss is left in an impotent, innocuous position, sitting in his office with only the most sycophantic of his agents still hanging on while the party is like fireworks outside his door. That's when you move in. Have some sort of agenda to run down on him, and have it planned out ahead of time. You have to go through the back door with this kind of brownnosing. You can't be direct, like, "Have you lost weight?" or, "I didn't even know that was a rug." Find out his ethnic background and compliment him accordingly: "I've always felt the Lithuanians are such brilliant people." If you can, mention a famous Lithuanian: "If Vaclav Hershel hadn't invented the convex lens, all hyperopic people would be in a terrible jam right now. What would have happened to the world?" It's a way of stroking someone without being an obvious brownnoser.

I find I get very emotional when I drink scotch, so it's a chance to really share my feelings and get a little misty-eyed about last year's profit-sharing plan. It's the one time you can hug your boss or, if you're really successful, kiss him on the mouth. A kiss on the mouth has more power than is visible to the naked eye for two reasons: One, it may be the highlight of his night romantically, and two, it may be the most embarrassing moment of the year for him. In the latter case, you have something on him. He's going to be conscious of that for the rest of your tenure at the firm, however brief it may be. You can always say, "He initiated it."

ASSESSING THE PARTY GUESTS

You can tell how drunk a woman is by how high her knees lift when she's doing the watusi and how quickly her head snaps from side to side when she's doing the jerk. Just watch the dancers and you can quickly find an easy mark. Also, by the middle of the evening, figure out who at the party has remained the most sober and get him or her to promise to drive you home.

WORKING THE ROOM

Be a people person. Say hello to everyone. It's easy when you're loaded. Take extra effort to make eye contact with people you wouldn't usually give the time of day. Just bond. You never know when you're going to need a favor from somebody. Try to learn people's names, for goodness' sake. People are happy when others know they exist. It's good to have a party list. That's part of the homework—to know who's going to be there. Go through your photos from last year's party.

It's always great to carry a mistletoe harness. You can make one with a coat hanger. It goes around your neck and up the back and hangs over your head. When a worthy target presents itself, you can slip it on and say, "Oh, look where we are!"

Making out on the sofa where the coats and bags have been thrown is absolutely proper. It's easy to go through wallets—not with the intent of stealing anything but to learn which neighborhoods people live in and who might be worth getting to know. Look for country club membership cards, who has a gold card, who doesn't. Sometimes a frequent flier card means a cheap companion ticket.

If you can accidentally mistake someone else's Armani for your Mani, who's going to know? It's a difference of about $2000. There's always the chance that you won't get called on it.

THE DEPARTURE

I'm a big fan of the phantom exit. If you've done your work properly, you've sort of mind-fucked the boss. Wait for some of the key players to leave, and always leave after your office rival, because a few well-placed comments will plant the seeds for his undoing.

Wait for things to quiet down and when you know your boss is watching, do a little cleanup. Show that you're a team player. Help straighten up the buffet table and collect some empties. Show that you're Mr. Ecology and separate glass bottles by color. Make sure you're in your boss' sight line, but never establish eye contact.

Another way to endear yourself to your superior is to serve as a bodyguard. If your boss is making out with his secretary or a co-worker in the corner of his office, brace yourself in the door. Be a human rampart. He'll be grateful. Those little contributions help.

Whatever you do, don't crash at the party. If you do, you prove you're no samurai. You are of the lower caste. You're an untouchable. A true samurai never lets the flag touch the ground.

Joe Rogan

Is the new host of The Man Show just a sensitive guy underneath that macho exterior? Like hell

1

PLAYBOY: Now that you've assumed the recliner throne as host, how will *The Man Show* be different?

ROGAN: Obviously, Jimmy Kimmel and Adam Carolla were funny hosts and it was a funny show, but they had a lighthearted take. My take is more unapologetic. My co-host, Doug Stanhope, and I are going to do shit *we* think is funny. Here's what's ironic, though: The person at Comedy Central responsible for approving the bits in *The Man Show* is a woman. We're already running into censorship issues, and I don't know how much of our vision is going to get across. Rest assured, though, whatever does get across will be a lot darker and will make a lot of people angry. And that's fine with me.

2

PLAYBOY: Could you give an example of when you butted heads with the censor?

ROGAN: We came up with a bit called the Fuck Bed, about a bed built of steel girders, monster-truck shocks and gym mats. The sketch starts with a guy having sex with his girlfriend. She's about to have her first orgasm, but the bed falls apart. So we test this gigantic bed with a 370-pound bodybuilder having sex with a blowup doll. The censor said that was misogynistic. How could that be misogynistic? Is sex misogynistic?

3

PLAYBOY: What happens when you see a perfect pair of breasts?

ROGAN: I just go, "How great is it?" It just goes right to your DNA. Breasts to a guy are like a lightbulb to a moth. But if I had to choose between no tits and a nice ass, or big tits and a flat ass, I'd go with the nice ass every time.

4

PLAYBOY: Is there any subject that's just not funny?

ROGAN: There is no subject that isn't funny. Funny is funny, but you can't force it. A good comedian says things he thinks are funny. A bad comedian says things he thinks you're going to laugh at. There's funny in everything—executions, abortion, cancer. All of it can be funny if it is treated properly.

5

PLAYBOY: You started in stand-up. Which comics do you admire and which do you hate?

ROGAN: The comics I hate are thieves. Nothing's more disgusting than a guy who steals another person's ideas and tries to claim them as his own. Stand-up comedy is supposed to be "Here's the world through my eyes." It's supposed to be your observations, your thoughts and views on life. When you snatch little pieces of other people's lives and try to palm them off as your own, that's more disgusting than anything. Robin Williams is a known thief. Denis Leary is a huge thief. His whole stand-up career is based on Bill Hicks, a brilliant guy who died years ago.

6

PLAYBOY: You've mastered tae kwon do, kickboxing and Brazilian jujitsu. If an obnoxious bar patron picks a fight, how do you determine which martial art you should employ to whip his ass?

ROGAN: It depends on how obnoxious he is. Martial arts remove the need to prove yourself. If someone calls you a dildo, are you really a dildo? If I don't feel physically threatened, chances are I won't do anything. If you're on a quest to kick the shit out of all the douche bags, you'll never get anything done, because there are more douche bags than normal people.

7

PLAYBOY: Describe the erotic applications of martial arts.

ROGAN: Increased flexibility can lead to more interesting positions. Whether they admit it or not, women are attracted to men who know how to fight. Women are always turned on by the dominating male, because we're all 99 percent chimpanzee.

8

PLAYBOY: You hosted an all-Playmate episode of *Fear Factor*. Are Playmates uniquely equipped for reality TV?

ROGAN: Clearly their architecture is suited for television, because we're most likely to get good ratings by putting on people you would really like to have sex with. We had a girl on who works for IBM as an account manager, and she's beautiful. If she were a Playmate, people would be paying a lot more attention to her. It's a stamp of approval. It's validation that people want to fuck you.

9

PLAYBOY: How many times has something on *Fear Factor* made you throw up?

ROGAN: Only once, and I was at home. I was watching an episode with a contestant drinking cocktail glasses filled with earthworms, and she kept chucking them onto the table. She would get them in her mouth, and they would come flying out. The editing on *Fear Factor* is phenomenal. Those guys know how to add music and sound effects and the close-ups of sweat beading off her face. Dude, I ran into the kitchen and just puked right in the sink. Pathetic. I was so embarrassed. Then I started thinking about how many people across the country probably threw up at the same time. Look at my job and how strong my stomach is, and the fact that 20 million other people are watching that same thing. At least a million people had to puke. I would like to hear from those people.

10

PLAYBOY: How far are we from reality TV being like *The Running Man?*

ROGAN: We've got to get prisoners into the mix. As soon as we start offering prisoners parole if they can get past a certain number of challenges without dying. We need something to lower the value of human life, like a nuclear explosion in Cleveland. I'm trying to pitch a show called *Eat Shit*. You take 10 people and put them in front of 10 scales. In front of those 10 scales you put 20 pounds of dog shit, and whoever eats the most dog shit in one hour wins $20 million. Can you tell me people wouldn't do it? Twenty million dollars for one hour of misery and humiliation? I'm rich, and I would do it.

11

PLAYBOY: What are we three years away from in the field of adult entertainment?

ROGAN: Mainstream celebrities doing porn. I may do it someday if I want to get out of my *Fear Factor* contract. I may really consider doing porn, because I don't know if I'll be able to do an eighth season of *Fear Factor*. They'll have to pump me full of ephedrine and push me onto the set. How many fucking helicopter stunts can you do before it's enough already?

12

PLAYBOY: You've said that having a dick means you're untrustworthy. True?

ROGAN: There are two different men living inside one body. There's the guy who pays your rent, chooses your career and asks the girl out to dinner. That guy thinks he's running shit. Then there's the other dude who comes out when you get a hard-on. The guy who thinks he's in control is really just driving around the dick, putting it in a position where it's most likely to get some. When you get a hard-on, it feels like you're no longer driving your life but sitting in the back of a long bus watching some other dude drive it. You're trying to talk to him, but there's all this engine noise. "Do you even know where you're going?" He's yelling back, "You shut the fuck up. I'm in control here." When I'm fucking, that's when it's clear to me that I'm really just an animal. We're monkeys with Tivos, but we're just monkeys, man. I'm not buying all the spirituality. C'mon, religion is like a *Charlie's Angels* movie. If you pay any attention to the plot, you're going to lose interest.

13

PLAYBOY: Give us three cardinal rules of dating.

ROGAN: Rule number one: Don't believe the hype. Don't get sucked into some Sandra Bullock movie in your head. She's not Meg Ryan, you're not Tom Hanks. Rule number two: Be honest. You like watching porn? Don't hide that shit when she comes over. You think Christianity is for sheep, don't lie because she's wearing a cross and you're trying to get in her pants. Rule number three: If you find yourself in a situation in which you can't be honest because you don't have access to a lot of women, you need to change that situation.

14

PLAYBOY: You know you're in trouble with a woman when . . .

ROGAN: I'm on a date and a girl says, "I'm very spiritual, and I'm looking for a man who's very spiritual," because then I know she has a crazy checklist. When a girl's got checklists—"My last date didn't open the car door for me, which was rude and disrespectful. I like being treated like a lady"—any of that crazy shit, just run. And a girl who says she doesn't like sex? Run. She doesn't like giving head? Run, run, run. Don't try to talk her into it, just run like your ass is on fire and the nearest fire hydrant is a mile away.

15

PLAYBOY: Defend marriage.

ROGAN: People are still getting married? That boggles the mind. My friend got married last weekend. Okay, you're following an ancient tribal ritual that binds you to this person and makes a legal contract recognized by the state. If your best friend came up to you and said, "Listen, man, you know we're best friends, right? Let's sign a contract that says we're best friends for life, and then if we ever decide not to be best friends, we go to court and you give me half your shit." You'd be like, "That's retarded."

16

PLAYBOY: If women are so much trouble, why bother?

ROGAN: Here's an area that gets gray when you become a celebrity, because they're not that much trouble anymore. When you're a regular Joe Schmo working for UPS, if you find a gal, you better hold on to her. If she senses you're not into commitment, she'll find some other dude. But throw celebrity into the mix, and all of a sudden a guy like David Spade becomes attractive. Look, he's a cool dude and I'm not dissing him, but why are chicks attracted to him? They're attracted to him because he's rich and famous, and that's just how it goes. It's a distortion of their natural instincts.

17

PLAYBOY: Have women gotten funnier?

ROGAN: No. There's always been Lucille Ball, and today there's Sarah Silverman and Margaret Cho. The expectations for women are different. They don't get as much of a break. When a woman steps onstage at a comedy club, she doesn't get the same reception men do if she talks openly about sex or, especially, about politics. It's like running with weights on.

18

PLAYBOY: If you dated a comedienne, who would it be?

ROGAN: I wouldn't do it. I won't date actresses either. It's not worth it. The probability of their being normal is so small. A lot of celebrities date other celebrities because they figure they're the only people who understand them. Plus, it compounds your own celebrity. Melanie Griffith and Antonio Banderas haven't made a good movie between them in a long fucking time, but they're still celebrities because they're married. I'd much rather date an artist or a painter. Those are the kinds of girls I'm into now.

19

PLAYBOY: If you woke up in bed with Sarah Silverman, would you ask her to blow you just to get her to be quiet?

ROGAN: I think Sarah's funny, so no. And I wouldn't ask her to blow me, because I like her boyfriend, Jimmy Kimmel. He's a good guy. That would be kind of rude, and I hope he would extend the same courtesy if he woke up with my girlfriend. I would just say, "Oh, can I give you a ride somewhere?"

20

PLAYBOY: Are you the antidote to Dr. Phil?

ROGAN: I always tell ladies, "Don't take relationship advice from a guy you don't want to fuck, because he's never going to tell you the truth. He's going to tell you exactly what you want to hear because that might get you to fuck him." You ask George Clooney a question, you're going to get an honest answer, because that guy could fuck anyone. When you ask Dr. Phil, that fat prick has to tell you what you want to hear, like "Before getting a divorce, you should exhaust all possible avenues for working out the relationship." Bullshit. He says that only because he doesn't have any options, that goofy, Donkey Kong-looking motherfucker. The ultimate *Man Show* stunt would be the kidnapping of Dr. Phil. We'd pick him up in a limo filled with strippers, get him drunk and make him admit that it's all a scam.

Robert Crane

Hoseheads Go Hollywood for 'Strange Brew'

TORONTO – Evil comes in all shapes, and one most familiar is Max Von Sydow. He usually represents to the movie going world that grim side of the Human Condition. Here, at the eerily abandoned Lakeshore Psychiatric Hospital on nearby Lake Ontario, he is cast in another strange role in a strange movie called "Strange Brew."

And "strange" is selected with precision. Von Sydow and his partner in mayhem on this assignment, Paul Dooley, are decked out in earmuffs, toques, hiking boots and extra-large parkas. If one were not to look closely, they would strike one as unusual if not spitting images of Canada's two stooges, Bob and Doug McKenzie.

As part of a convoluted plot, the evil pair must eliminate with extreme prejudice the real Bob and Doug in order to take over the world. The beer-guzzling, doughnut-chomping McKenzie brothers who have raised the practice of clod to the level of art form?

Those Great White Northern hosers, Bob and Doug (as portrayed respectively by Rick Moranis and Dave Thomas), are the just-retired stars of the late-night silly series, "SCTV." Their first album, featuring the hit rock single, "Take Off," plus other songs and nonsense, has sold a million copies. But in the cold of winter here (before they wrapped the other day) they are actors, writers and directors of a $5-million film to be released by MGM in time for the summer vacation.

Moranis says, "It's kind of like 1980, G'day, welcome to our TV show; 1982, G'day, welcome to our album; and 1982, G'day, welcome to our movie."

While $5 million isn't much by the standards of movie making in this day, it might seem an enviable amount to contribute to young, untried TV comics. But it is merely the latest example of Hollywood trying to tap that wonderful, free-spending demographic that goes to the movies.

Could this be another "Animal House"? The plot involves Bob and Doug, beer, heroes and heroines, villains, beer, car chases, loads of special effects and beer. The producers hid scripts from the reporter, but the plot in this genre of the film art is normally of small importance.

Like sensible neophytes, Moranis, 29, and Thomas, 32, have surrounded themselves with veterans—executive producer Jack Grossberg, whose credits range from Woody Allen's first films to the American Film Theater; producer-manager Louis Silverstein, "I look after the business, they look after the creative"; deadpan character actor Dooley from New York theater and Robert Altman films; and Von Sydow, whose appearance in this type of film would require explanation.

Thus Silverstein notes, "Rick, Dave and I were sitting in Freddie Fields' (president of MGM) office in Los Angeles, and he asked who we wanted in the film. Max Von Sydow was at the top of our list. Freddie picked up a phone and said, 'Get me Max.' In a matter of moments, Fields had Von Sydow on the phone. 'Hello, Max, this is Freddie. Have you ever watched "SCTV"? Have you heard of Bob and Doug McKenzie? Hold on, here's Dave Thomas.' Dave got on the phone, explained the storyline and told Max he'd be reaching a new audience. Within three weeks, Max was signed. We got a touch of Hollywood."

Von Sydow, recently a villain in "Flash Gordon," plays Brewmeister Smith. Von Sydow says, "Smith is just a terrible person who is trying to manipulate mankind. It's nice to get a chance to do something which is not too serious just for once." Von Sydow laughs. Why did he get involved with a comedy? "My sons, who live in the States, are 'SCTV' fans and they persuaded me to appear in the film."

Although there are veterans on the set, it is strictly a Moranis-Thomas project. Director of photography Steven Poster says, "They're receiving input from everyone and loosely following a storyboard." He adds that they've done 80 camera setups in the last day and a half (giving Sidney Lumet a run for the money) and lately out of 5,000 feet of film exposed, 2,800 feet were printed.

Thomas, born in St. Catherine's, Ontario, spent three years with the Second City improv troupe in Toronto that featured the pre-famous Dan Aykroyd and Gilda Radner. He wrote and performed in the "SCTV" syndicated show before it went on to NBC. His specialty is his nose-on impressions: among the victims, Bob Hope and Walter Cronkite.

Moranis, a Toronto native, wrote and acted on Canadian radio and TV before joining "SCTV" in 1980. His arsenal of characters includes Woody Allen, Dick Cavett and Merv Griffin.

Film neophytes or not, Moranis and Thomas seem to know what they want, film-wise, and the fastest way to get it. How do two people direct and act simultaneously?

Moranis says, "One person takes the lead for the day. The storyboard has been 70% helpful to Dave and 30% helpful to me. So, make it 50% helpful." Thomas: "Rick directs me and also himself. He's being a nasty, fascist director. We sort of watch over each other. I've never really had a handle on the character of Doug."

Do they miss television, namely "SCTV"? Moranis: "I had more fun with 'SCTV,' but it was getting harder and harder to do. I miss it but, if I were still there doing it, I probably wouldn't be enjoying it. Dave likes this more. He likes the idea of 80 people following his instructions. He calls it the Snake."

Why are they doing it all in their first film? Moranis: "Initially, you ask yourself a lot of questions, trying to be pragmatic about your career. But the real motivation is, 'We've never done this before, so let's try it.'" Thomas: "We never had anything. You don't risk anything in this business because you never had it in the first place. Try to hold mercury in your hands. That's your career, so forget it."

Was Thomas on safer ground with "SCTV"? "We had parodied everybody and everything. I hear they're doing 'Towering Inferno.' Half the cast is dead. It's time to retire the show. The cast should try new things. That's why Catherine (O'Hara) left. She's parodied every actress. I don't think they're all going to be there too much longer whether the show goes on or not. It's strange. Now we're working with real actors and actresses. The same kind of people we've parodied."

The McKenzie style is affecting. Crew and actors alike are talking hoser language. One of two Panaflex cameras is identified as "camera EH," chairs for Moranis and Thomas are marked "Bob" and "Doug," and in the director slot on the camera slate reads "McKenzie Brothers." "Take off, hoser" is heard everywhere.

When the cameras stop rolling, Moranis and Thomas easily slide from the McKenzies into some of their impersonations for the benefit of a video crew that is taping a promotion special for "Strange Brew." Thomas, as Bob Hope, talks to the camera in a hushed voice until he comes upon the name "Joey Heatherton." A moment later, he's Richard Harris doing his high-pitched machine-gun laugh.

Moranis does Woody Allen, whom, incidentally, they asked to appear in a cameo role. Allen declined, as did Steven Spielberg, who said his first and last acting job was in "Blues Brothers."

In the production office located in a building dubbed the Little Thalberg Building, Silverstein was off the phone for a moment. "Frankly, we're holding off on supplying everyone's demands. We have another album coming out, a television special lined up and Rick and Dave are hosting 'Saturday Night Live' in a few weeks. There's no limit to what we could be doing. We have hats, buttons and T-shirts out. We've had offers for puzzles, beer holders, beer thermometers, a guide to hosers, and, of course, personal appearances. An appearance in Regina set off a reaction not unlike Beatlemania. A few years ago, it was toga parties. Nowadays, it's hoser parties."

If the somber setting created by the never-ending lawns and the dozen or so cracking and peeling brick buildings doesn't remind one of the "One Flew Over the Cuckoo's Nest" location, the scene currently being rehearsed inside one of the former hospital's corridors will. A group of patients line up for their medication. The film's Dudley Do-Right-type character, played by Angus McInnes, takes a sip of the mind-controlling drink and spits it out. Behind him in line is a dead ringer for Jack Nicholson, peaked eyebrows, demented smile, who sees this and provokes a confrontation with McInnes.

Dave Thomas, directing this sequence, yells, "Cut, stop! Stop acting!" and huddles with the Nicholson look-alike. An assistant director cracks, "It's nice of the Ontario government to supply us with all this equipment for therapy."

As final lighting and camera corrections are made, Thomas gets Moranis in a headlock right in front of the video camera's constantly probing lens. How are these Canadian knuckleheads, the McKenzies, able to capture such a large and enthusiastic following in Canada and the United States? "It was something that everyone could collectively look down on," Moranis says. "They seem to be sub-everyone's intelligence." Thomas adds, "They're recession characters. In a downward spiraling economy, people can look at Bob and Doug and say, 'I have more money than them. Look how sad and pathetic they are. Maybe things aren't so bad after all.'"

How do they react when called Canada's Cheech and Chong? Thomas smiles. "We should be so lucky as to do as well as they did at the box office. This isn't the kind of movie Cheech and Chong would do." Moranis says, "This story deliberately is a fantasy. This movie is not the comedy you'd expect from Second City or from Dave and I. It's a comedy from Bob and Doug."

The other comparison is to Dan Aykroyd and John Belushi. Brian McConnachie, who wrote for "Saturday Night Live" and "SCTV" and plays a mad scientist in "Strange Brew," offers, "Rick and Dave complement each other so well. They support each other. Aykroyd was in the shadow of Belushi. They weren't equals."

Moranis and Thomas, who have impersonated Francis Coppola and Steven Spielberg on "SCTV," are handling direction of major special effects quite easily. Thomas says, "I admire Spielberg and George Lucas. Spielberg knows how to direct people and machines, which I think makes him exceptional. I'm interested almost as much in machines as I am in people." Moranis adds, "I admire anyone who can complete a film and stay with it. I'm not being facetious." Thomas says, "It's an art of being able to handle compromise in a crafty and intelligent way. We have setbacks on this thing every day. We have compromised our fannies off, and there's no way around that."

The crew has made the proper adjustments for lighting and camera. They await Moranis and Thomas. How long will Bob and Doug go on? Moranis says, "If by some fluke this film becomes successful, I'm sure MGM will want a sequel. So we'll be together for another year." Thomas mocks, "After next year, that's it. I never want to see him again. I draw the line on two years." Moranis says over his shoulder, "It's already been three." Thomas wraps Moranis in a headlock, and they walk back to work.

Chevy Chase

He stumbled into America's heart by falling on his face, and it's been clumsy going ever since. A pullout from the show that made him famous. A jerky plunge into movies. And a head-on collision with the word "sellout." Life is lonely near the top.

Cornelius Crane Chase was hard to figure from the beginning. A funny writer who wasn't ugly as sin. An Eastern WASP crashing on the Lower East Side. A preppie who couldn't keep his finger out of his nose.

So, when he made the world's fastest leap into stardom, anchoring "Weekend Update" on Lorne Michaels' Saturday Night Live, he was as surprised as everybody else. And what followed was pure soap opera.

Successful comic faces tough career choices. Grabs megabucks. Leaves nest. Goes Hollywood. Makes nice. Loses wife and "perspective." Becomes superstar.

Sort of. Chase is too intelligent and self-conscious to lie down that comfortably in the mold. His movie experience consists of a starring role in the hit Foul Play but, as he says, "I want to do everything." He'll have his chance soon enough: Currently he's working with Michael O'Donoghue on a screenplay, Saturday Matinee, and will also write and star in more NBC specials.

OUI correspondent Robert Crane conducted the interview at Chase's Emmy-laden office in the MGM Studios. As you'll see, Chevy may have lost his perspective, but his madness is still intact.

OUI: You've become quite a celebrity since you came to Hollywood. How do you handle all the women who constantly seem to accost you in public?

CHASE: Between the two big toes. Normally, I would just say between the toes, but for the purposes of this interview I'll say the two big ones. I'm very flattered by it, actually. I love it. But there's a way you can be polite and say, "Excuse me, I really have to be going"; and there's a way to say, "Look, I *really* have to be going," and then push a little harder. Recently, one pack of girls actually wanted me to go watch them play volleyball. I really did have to be going, and as I walked away one of them yelled, "Faggot!" as loud as she could. So I figure the next time I'm accosted by a group of women, I'm going to make all of them pregnant.

OUI: What is it in a woman that turns you on?

CHASE: What magazine is this for?

OUI: OUI.

CHASE: That's funny. My publicist told me it was for *NON* magazine. *N-O-N.* Well, it figures that OUI would want to know what kind of woman I like. Actually, I like very, very overweight Japanese women—short, overweight Japanese women who cannot speak Japanese.

OUI: What about Goldie Hawn?

CHASE: She's not short enough. She's not Japanese enough. But, yeah, she's a very lovely woman. She's just what you see there on the screen—a little deeper, actually. She's bright and she's very clever. She was a delight to do that love scene with. We worked it out ourselves. We wrote it. [Chevy answers his buzzing telephone using a Japanese accent. It's Gilda Radner.] Gilda? You're calling me from New York? Yes, I have your laundry. I burned your shirts and we lost the rest of it. Should I send you the burned shirts? I'm having an interview even as you speak to me . . . Yes . . . you're very sweet to say that, Gilda . . . Yeah . . . you like that, huh? . . . I'm still here; I just think it's so sweet of you to call and tell me that billions of women all over the country love me. Actually I'm in the middle of an interview with OUI magazine . . . OK, you finish . . . [Chevy puts the receiver up to our microphone and continues to talk with Gilda.]

RADNER: . . . Stick it up your bum!

CHASE: I can't hear you.

RADNER: Don't let them hear me.

CHASE: What?

RADNER: Have you got me on a loudspeaker?

CHASE: No. Do you have a loudspeaker?

RADNER: No, but I mean, am I, like—can they hear me?

CHASE: Oh, no, they can't hear you.

RADNER: OK. Chev?

CHASE: Yeah.

RADNER: My favorite moment [referring to *Foul Play*], when you two were gonna kiss. That's what people really say. They say, "What'd you think of me the first time?" That was wonderful.

CHASE: We were just talking about that scene when you called.

RADNER: Oh, Chevy, it was wonderful.

CHASE: We wrote that scene.

RADNER: You did?

97

CHASE: Uh, Gil—uh, Goldie and I—I get you and Goldie mixed up.

RADNER: I get it all the time, yeah. Everyone calls me Goldie, and when I go up to Harlem they yell, "Oh, there's the girl on *Laugh-In*!"

CHASE: Oh, those silly black people. [He takes the receiver away from the microphone.] Yeah . . . no, I know; I really am in the middle of an interview. I love it that you're calling . . . When are you coming out? . . . Thank you . . . no . . . oh, Gilda . . . is it a simple D and C? No, nothing. I'm kidding. I'm coming to New York on Tuesday. Can I see you? . . . OK, so long as you have something . . . OK, I'll hang up on you now . . . I love you . . . I can't wait to see your little face . . . gesundheit. [Chevy hangs up.]

OUI: You were talking about that love scene with Goldie . . .

CHASE: Gilda was calling me about *that* love scene. Isn't that amazing? The first time Goldie and I met we read that scene. Finally I said, "Let's throw the script away and do it this way." It felt very natural. It's easy to play a love scene with her. There's no reason why you wouldn't want to kiss her. The only thing I didn't like was that little dog. The idea that I would have a little dog! I would have shot that dog if there were one more day of shooting.

OUI: In your own love life, what line have you found never seems to fail with a woman?

CHASE: "Use an ointment." Never fails. I don't have any lines; I'm married. I don't take the opportunity to ask everybody, "Will you marry me?" Generally speaking, I find that if a girl is susceptible to "lines" and clichéd come-ons, I probably wouldn't be interested in her to begin with. I think snappy patter and banter has its place up to a point, but the concept of "picking someone up" is an anachronism long since gone and I don't care for it.

OUI: So, you wouldn't make out too well at a singles bar?

CHASE: Well, I wouldn't go to one in the first place. I did go to a singles bar once, however. I was the only person in it.

OUI: What is it about you that women find so difficult to resist?

CHASE: I have very, very huge feet, as you can see. I wear a thirteen; I'm six-four. I suppose there's some—oh, golly—axiom or thing about big feet, big hands, big something. I don't know what they're all talking about but, apparently, they appear to find the knee area kind of irresistible. I don't understand it.

OUI: What about those comparisons of you to Warren Beatty?

CHASE: No one compares me with Warren. Warren's sperm count went down to four about three years ago. It was well publicized. Also, I understand Warren has a serious sexual problem with women.

OUI: And what's that?

CHASE: He doesn't like them. He and Buck [Henry] have a little thing going. I have some pictures that I will show you later. I can't, unfortunately, release them to the magazine, because I promised Buck that I'd return them. I don't compare myself to Warren; I compare myself to Buck. I find myself taller than Buck, better looking than Buck, just generally more successful than Buck, bit of a better writer than Buck, better actor. Warren? Why waste my time?

OUI: Is it true you never wore underwear on *Saturday Night?*

CHASE: No. I always wore underwear on *Saturday Night*; in fact, I only wore underwear. It's just that I had my underwear made to look like other clothing. My Yves St. Laurent suit was, in fact, underwear designed to look like a suit. It is true that Garrett [Morris] never wore underwear. Whenever Garrett took his pants off in the wardrobe room, there was a large thump that could be heard in Studio Six-A, two floors below. Finally, they put a sign up at Fifty-ninth and Fifth: "Garrett, please bring your Jockey shorts or a fuckin' roadbuilder, will ya?" Garrett wore underwear after that. *Anybody's* underwear. The problem was he never wore it in the right place. John [Belushi] wore underwear that, on occasion, made an attempt to walk away from him. I understand they recently scraped some of it off him and put it in the Smithsonian. I remember that Jane Curtin never wore underwear and that it was always a treat to hide under the "Update" desk. I would get these long letters from Danny Aykroyd about Jane not wearing any underpants. It's really none of my business and I'm sure it's none of the magazine's business.

OUI: What do you usually say during sex?

CHASE: During sex? Uh . . . "Have you got the correct time?" "While you're up, get me a Gauloises," "Can I have a warm washcloth?" "Is that yours?" "Not quite on it?" OK. Let's see.

OUI: Anything with batteries?

CHASE: No. I never say anything with batteries; I always just use my own voice. In all seriousness, I don't say much during sex that I would ever tell you. There is no such thing as "during sex." Life, to me, is continual sex. Even if I look like I'm writing, working, walking or driving, my mind says sex— always. That's also a lie, but I know your goddamned fuckin' editor wants some fuckin' goddamned raunchy fuckin' sex thing here. But I don't say anything I would say to you, certainly. Well . . . that's not true. If you and I were to, sort of, get it on, I might say, "Use an ointment."

OUI: Do you have any recurring fantasies?

CHASE: I do have one. I wake up in the morning and walk outside to run my twelve miles and swim and do my pushups. A helicopter appears overhead, and lowered from it on a dinky rope is the very beautiful and lovely body of Charo, being held by one ankle. Her body is slowly lowered in front of me while I run. While her one ankle is being held, the other leg is sort of spread away from it and dangling with her body spinning wildly, and she's going, "Cachelacabreca chalcabre," and singing songs. The helicopter keeps a nice pace in front of me for twelve miles; and just as I'm finishing, exhausted, I reach up and, lo and behold, they pull her up into the helicopter and it explodes. Every morning I have that fantasy. I'm so sick of that goddamned fantasy!

Robert Crane

OUI: Was your first sexual experience a traumatic one?

CHASE: Not particularly. For a number of years, I had no idea at all how to relate to girls because everybody around me—and this was in the Fifties and Sixties—all they did was brag about their sexual encounters. Of course, there's always the "make-out king," all of this thing *Grease* is about. I didn't go to that kind of school. I never saw a lot of gay greasers dancing and singing, pretending to like women. I was more like eighteen or nineteen when I really got started, and it was with a steady girlfriend, you know.

OUI: Are you as clumsy in bed as you are on camera?

CHASE: Much worse. For one thing, I'm wearing this stupid underwear that looks like a suit.

OUI: Have you ever been turned on while working with one of the prettier hosts of *Saturday Night*?

CHASE: Uh-huh. Rob Reiner. I remember when Rob first came out—it was the third show—he was wearing a wig because he was doing this piece. I don't know what happened to me. I got so goddamned hard and I must have been hard throughout the entire show. Now, this has never happened to me with any other high-caliber woman.

OUI: How do you feel about the increasing emphasis on sex in the new TV shows?

CHASE: I don't watch them much. I like *Charlie's Angels* because I've had a tremendous amount of sex with all three of them, and I like to watch them on TV and compare them. But I really don't care for Fred Silverman's principle of programming. I mean, it works from a business standpoint, but from a creative standpoint I couldn't care less about half-hour situation comedies or half-hour series.

OUI: But you have called Freddie Silverman a "brilliant genius," haven't you?

CHASE: He is not only a brilliant genius but a very *rich* brilliant genius who must find a good outlet for that money. I'm gonna have to talk to Fred about that.

OUI: If you were Silverman, how would you change television?

CHASE: That is a tough question. Freddie Silverman did not write *Laverne and Shirley*. He did not conceive *Happy Days* or *Charlie's Angels*. He's a businessman and a counterpuncher who discovered that half-hour sitcoms and pretty girls week after week are just about what the average agriculturalist would like to see after coming home and having his quart of beer. But the question is: Is he bringing in quality television? I'm with NBC, and I'm deeply in love with Freddie; I think he *is* brilliant. But there is a side of me that says, "That crap is crap wherever you put it"—and just because he can program doesn't mean it is good TV.

I think NBC has consistently been in the forefront of innovative comedy programs. Ernie Kovacs, Milton Berle, Sid Caesar, *Saturday Night, Laugh-In.* Tom Snyder. Of course, whether or not they get the ratings is the only issue, because television sells products. Yet, in spite of that, programmers appear to have some integrity, putting out stuff that is new and innovative. I hope that Silverman is able to understand that, as I think Herb Schlosser [president of NBC] did when he thought of *Saturday Night Live.*

The way I would change television would be to go to another country. The very nature of television is such that no one is going to take chances, because if one bottle of catsup isn't bought, that chance is too risky . . . and that is the essential flaw in television. It is its own—pardon the expression—house of Atreus. It is its own tragedy. It is there to sell products; yet, despite itself, it is also the most informative and the most powerful educational force in the world. There's nothing much Freddie can do about it except try to come up with *Chevy's Angels* and slot it against Charlie's. I wrote him a note to that effect, but I haven't heard anything from him yet.

OUI: You're a natural to guest-host the *Tonight Show,* but according to some reports you're on the Carson shit list.

CHASE: This is a fallacy; people write about it continually. The real fact is that I get calls from Johnny all the time; I had to change my number. He *wants me on that show;* he asks me week in and week out to come on. I don't know why. I guess he just needs some help. Seriously, I can understand Freddie de Cordova; he's right. There is a list of very bright, funny people ahead of me. They've got so many talents to get through first, you know. I think Leon Bibb will be doing it for a week. I understand they signed Karen Quinlan.

OUI: What do you watch on television?

CHASE: Game shows. I think that they tell us a lot about all we teach Americans to aspire toward. I like *60 Minutes.* I can't wait for the day Wallace comes to me and he hits me with, you know, "Mr. Chase, is this not in fact *your* driver's license?" I'm gonna say, "Mike, do you not in fact really *wipe* quite as much as you should? Are these not in fact *your* underpants, Mr. Wallace? Let's take a look." I'm ready for him.

OUI: A tight close-up.

CHASE: Yeah. He says, "Now, didn't you say, Mr. Chase, that you robbed a bank?" My answer might be, "Yes, I said that, but I believe I said that in a song written by somebody else." Of course, the edit would be, "Yes," and on to the next question. I do like that show; I think it's interesting, but I think they are getting more and more sensational. There's been a movement toward sensationalism in journalism lately. *People, Us*—these are magazines that have lots of photos, lots of gossip and lots of mistakes.

OUI: Is there anything you are particularly paranoid about?

CHASE: Afraid of or paranoid? One who is paranoid rarely knows what it is one's paranoid about; one who's afraid has a very good sense of it. I'm paranoid about people who keep writing that I'm paranoid. Actually, I'm afraid of it. I have moments of paranoia. Put a joint in my mouth at a point of insecurity, and about an hour later I might not be around. You know, I'll just be sitting alone somewhere. But that's probably about the same as anybody.

OUI: Does smoking grass have any effect on your comic abilities?

CHASE: Depends on the situation. I think that all drugs are the same—from smack to grass to coke to liquor—they all induce one form of psychosis or another; and you either interpret that as a happy occasion or you interpret it as a fearful and frightening one. Grass is a very hallucinogenic drug— more so than other, so-called heavier drugs. If you're with friends and you're relaxed and everybody's just getting wiped out, you may find yourself on a roll. You may even be able, under the influence of drugs, to write well with friends. Generally speaking, you can't do that alone. When you're straight and you look back at what you've written, it appears to be a little off. I remember when we were doing *Channel One* [the progenitor of *The Groove Tube*]. The assumption was that people who were going to see us were going to be stoned. So therefore, it seemed permissible. But if you're working on a national television show or making a movie, you can't assume that everybody's going to be in rhythm with you. Even doing *Lemmings,* you couldn't get stoned, because your timing would be thrown off and therefore you'd be out of sync with the others. If everybody's stoned, everybody's timing is off. So, for performing, it's real dumb to be stoned. And writing being part of performing, your best writing is probably straight, although there can be exceptions. There's no set rule here.

OUI: Were there ever any occasions on *Saturday Night* when somebody's "timing" was a little off?

CHASE: Well, I certainly wouldn't talk about whether they smoke *grass* up there or not. That's not my business, because if they do, I feel sorry for them—that kids that age have to lean on something like marijuana or co . . . what do they call it, cocaine? Jesus Christ, if those poor kids up there need drugs or are under the influence of them to create B-minus comedy, I feel very bad for them, very sorry; and I hope the heck they can pull themselves out by their own bootstraps and, goddamn, get out there and jog.

OUI: But Belushi seems to be—

CHASE: John, you misunderstand, *eats* drugs. That's his diet. When John wants to get high, he sucks on an apple.

OUI: Were you happy with *Foul Play*?

CHASE: It did very well. I am happy, and I'm happy people enjoyed it and that I apparently got away with it. You *can* fool all of the people all of the time, apparently. Well, not all of them. Mom didn't think it was that great. My family's seen it. They enjoyed it.

OUI: Were your parents critical of your aspirations to write and perform?

CHASE: No. They were always critical of my inability to come to grips with a specific aspiration or goal—which was the way to be back when I was in high school and college. I always believed they would find out that I could become very good at quite a few things and not just be a good doctor or something. I wasn't sure I'd become a performer, but I always liked music and I was always comfortable performing. I've never yet had an aspiration, to this day. I just know that I keep getting better and it's always been fun. And these magazine editors who want to write that I'm unhappy--let them eat, uh, very nice pork.

OUI: Has the media amplified or created problems in your personal life?

CHASE: Yeah, I don't think *amplify* is the correct word. The media exists by fabricating and then amplifying the fabrication. I realize that it's my "responsibility" to share a certain amount of myself with the public but, for the most part, I look on an interview like this as, number one, a propitious thing to do from a business standpoint in terms of promoting something. Number two, it may be fun—just as everything I do is fun. Interviews are part of that whole experience of being a star or being famous and, therefore, being interviewed is a learning experience of how to deal with the press and how they deal with you. I don't expect to get much back. I mean, I know what my life is like, and people real close to me know. Frankly, it has never been accurately represented in any article or any interview. It's always been the subjective view of the writer, and if the writer's good, then it's probably fun to read because it's good writing. If the editors have a different outlook or want "an angle" or some way to sell their magazine—and that's what this is all about—then it will take on another quality. I've been represented as defensive, paranoid, sexy, bright, stupid, dumb, an asshole, a very sexy and bright asshole, and a very, very, stupid, sexy asshole. I don't know. I've been represented as everything, and I prefer to think that I'm all those things, plus many more on any given occasion. I think my friends, with the exception of—who is it?--Golda, will bear that up.

OUI: You've been accused of having lost your perspective. Have you?

CHASE: Always. That's the one criticism I always get from everyone, and I have to agree with all of them. I always lose perspective, whenever I can.

OUI: Moving out to Hollywood, starring in pictures, creating your own films, sitting with Sly Stallone, as you like to refer to him, at the fights in Vegas, auctioning off Cher's mink at David Frost's ERA party. Are you ever scared of "going Hollywood"?

CHASE: I am Hollywood, and it is deeply frightening. But there is no way to stop going—and growing—from the ages of twenty-eight to thirty-one. "Going Hollywood" and "selling out" are semantical inventions that allow people to categorize others and keep the youth happy. Imagine anybody in the world in any other profession, given the opportunity to make much more money and to work at a higher level, not taking it because of some kind of crazy thing people would like to call integrity. I don't believe in that horseshit: "I will never lose my honor. I will stay in New York and do late-night television." What are we talking about here? I have always sought change and development, and I would like to continue to make changes at bigger levels, in prime-time markets or in films or in other areas.

I went to Hollywood, clearly. Yes, here I am in Hollywood, but Hollywood is really about the same as Times Square, you know; you don't say, did you go New York? He left Hollywood; he went "New York." Times Square and Hollywood are one and the same. They're little areas in a large town. It is more commercial here and it is harder to make decisions because there are so many more to make. When you are not making a lot of money in New York, and you are doing *Lampoon*

Robert Crane

or underground shows or off-Broadway stuff, you can make all the comments you want about Hollywood. It never occurs to you that maybe in ten years you will be a big success, and people who remember you from the other stuff will tell you that you are a sellout. You become more visible and, therefore, open to more criticism, just as you are open to more adulation.

I'd like to do everything. I'd like to experience as much of those things that people reading this article will never in their lives have a chance to experience, and I'm no different than they are. I got the chance to do it, and you bet your ass I'll do it all, even if it means doing a bad musical, or some pie-in-the-face stuff or simple clowning humor. It is all grist for the mill in my life; it is all fun and all new, and it's a very rich life within the confines of the entertainment world.

OUI: Are there any things you miss about doing *Saturday Night Live*?

CHASE: Well, it's been two years, so what I've missed has changed over time. I think that the high point for all of us was being accepted by the very establishment that we appeared to shun, when we received Emmies. What I miss is the initial impetus and the novelty of a show where, suddenly, people who were relatively unknown received tremendous recognition in the television world and from the public. What happened afterward was that there was a bit of an anticlimactic letdown. I miss the camaraderie, the late hours, the feeling that this is an important thing I'm doing. But in retrospect, I can see that there are other important things in the world and that one can get boxed in. *Saturday Night* was all-encompassing, and there was this feeling among us: "We're from New York; we know the answers. We're on late; we can say *fart* and you can't." Now I don't miss it much at all. I think everybody there is probably looking forward to moving on. You really can't go back.

OUI: What was it about you that clicked with the public and the critics and distinguished you from the rest of the cast?

CHASE: The cleft. That was a metaphor for everything that made that happen. Aside from the figurative, my name was mentioned every week. People today still say, "I love that Danny Agralucrasacra" [Aykroyd]. They can't pronounce it. It's spelled funny. Belushi is finally being pronounced correctly . . . by polar bears up in Alaska, who are all horny and want to meet him. To be really honest, I think that it's McLuhanesque. That's what advertising is all about, too. You see Bon Ami enough on TV, you probably find yourself buying it, as opposed to buying Foamo cleanser, because you hear it more.

What I gave *Saturday Night*, by hook or by crook, was somebody to bridge the gap between the reference points that the average American television viewer is used to seeing on television and those found in troupes like *Second City, National Lampoon* and *Groove Tube*. I look more average American, more preppie, more "he looks like a responsible fellow; I guess I'll watch this show." I was enough of a straight-looking guy to bridge the gap. I could charm my way through a filthy joke in the President's face. Also, quite frankly, I was good at playing the camera. I have a background that proved to be the best for that kind of a show, playing to videotape cameras for years with *Channel One* and *Groove Tube*.

104

OUI: What were the problems you had to deal with when it became apparent that you were the star of the show?

CHASE: Well, I must say that there were no problems between me and the rest of the cast at all. I loved it. I liked being famous. They liked me. We all worked well together. If there were jealousies, they may have come out much later.

OUI: There's never been a sense of love between you and Belushi.

CHASE: There has never been a harsh word between us since I've known him, with the exception of my trying to keep him alive on occasions. We don't spend a lot of time together because, you know, I stopped walking dogs back in '48. Actually, there's a very close relationship there. In fact, we used to instigate a rivalry for press and college audiences. Wherever he is and whatever he's doing at this moment, I'm sure he's doing a job on me, just as I do on him. You really can't believe what you read, you know. Hopefully, you'll believe some of this, assuming I can continue to lie this well.

OUI: As far as the rest of the cast goes, who is genuinely funny on-screen, off-screen, with or without written material?

CHASE: Aykroyd is hilarious. One of the funniest men I've ever met. When he gets on a roll, *wow*. Danny is also very private. He doesn't like to do interviews. I think he's anxious to get back to the tractor in the Hudson Bay area and scrape the ice for seal pelts. Gilda's funny but, again, as Gilda. Generally speaking, she's self-deprecating in a funny, kind of delightful way—not particularly sexually appealing, but I don't believe she wants to be. If she wanted to be, she would be. She can complain about it as long as she wants, but until she comes to grips with the fact that she enjoys complaining about not being appealing, she'll keep herself that way and that's her problem.

A very funny person off-camera is Michael O'Donoghue [writer of some of the more outrageous *Saturday Night* skits]. He's quick as a whiz. He's a great writer. He was the first editor of the *Lampoon* and gave it the flavor that it has which, basically, is skid marks. Anything that involves death or people being demeaned or injured, Michael jumps on like a vulture. The minute Larry Flynt was shot, Michael's tape recording on his phone answering system was announcing "Hustler's Gone Red." You know, I mean this man is ready.

OUI: Can you tell us about the film you're writing with Michael?

CHASE: There isn't much to tell you except I have two hundred forty pages of script and need only a hundred ten. Cutting it down is going to take more time than it took to write it, which has been a year already. It is hilarious and I love it, and it's going to finish me in the film world because . . . well, you know Michael O'Donoghue. It could be very heavy and abrasive if I didn't lend some, uh, temperance to it. It's called *Saturday Matinee,* and it's like going to a matinee but, of course, the difference is it's Michael O'Donoghue and Chevy Chase writing it. I had this idea years ago and, apparently, Michael did, too. I think he had another name for it. I sat with him in the offices of *Saturday Night* and said, "Mike, let's make a movie." He said, "OK." I told him what my idea was and he said, "Well, I've had the same idea for a long time." I sued him. We settled out of court and there it was—that's how it started. And now, of course, I'm in *Who's Who* and he isn't. Michael gets migraine headaches on occasion; gray matter actually spurts out of his ears when he can't come up with a punchline.

OUI: Speaking of O'Donoghue, at what point does comedic satire stop being funny? Where do you draw the line?

CHASE: There are two limits: One is when you die; there's nothing really funny anymore. The other limit is when you stop laughing. That's about it. It seems to me that the second you laugh, any learned preconceptions, any superego difficulties go right out the window. Now, that begs the question: Is laughter necessarily connected with funny? Most of us connect it with funny. And is it connected with happiness or hurt? That's an ambiguous question. I draw the line at gratuitously hurting somebody, knowing it's a cheap and easy shot. An example of that was a very funny line written by Alan Zweibel for "Update." It was during the Patty Hearst trial. The joke was: "Patty Hearst denies that she had sexual relationships with any members of the SLA . . . she said she was saving herself for the right army." Now, that's a good Zweibel joke, but I wouldn't do it, based on the fact that I thought she'd had enough, you know. It's not as if Patty Hearst went out and maliciously killed people. I find it hard to believe she fell in love with anybody, being closed up in a closet like Steve McQueen in *The Great Esc*ape. She really went through hell there. So, these are places there where I had to draw the line, where I thought people were being hurt.

OUI: Was there ever a period of your life when you didn't feel funny?

CHASE: Sure, there have been many periods in my life of low self-esteem or vulnerability which, depending on the nature of my emotional life at that time, could last over a period of time. You've got to have the balls, the confidence, to do something that's funny. And if you don't feel you have balls on a certain day, you don't have them. During those periods I play a lot of music. I'm a good musician—I always have something I'm doing.

OUI: Why does it seem like most comedians have musical backgrounds?

CHASE: Well, thinking back on it, I feel that my favorite comedians, people I thought were the funniest, in fact, do have musical backgrounds. This goes hand in hand with rhythm and also goes hand in hand with athletic ability. Most, in fact, are short—lower to the ground—like Chaplin; they have a better sense of balance. They are probably better athletically; they are more streetwise because they are smaller. If people really get laughs, it is because they have good, surprising physical moves, even if it's just the rhythm—the way a line is said. It's basically, ultimately, an athletic musical thing. I'm trying to think of comics who aren't musical, and the ones I think of aren't funny, either; so I tell you, it was a good question.

OUI: As far as long-range film goals go—if you can project yourself into the future for a second—would you rather be Cary Grant or Woody Allen?

CHASE: Neither. Is this the lady or the tiger? I got no choice? If that's the case, I prefer to be Woody Allen, because I do the same thing he does. Nobody will ever be another Cary Grant, but I don't believe Grant ever cared whether he had control, or that he aspired to get his perspective out there. That's Woody Allen's life. Then again, I would prefer to look more like Cary than Woody, just so I could get into a restaurant. I don't want to be used to scour pans.

OUI: Do you think there will be room for, as far as the public is concerned, a serious Chevy Chase?

CHASE: No, I'm an entertainer; don't expect me to get up there and start telling you where I'm coming from seriously and how it all came about and all that horseshit. No one wants to hear that. At least, I don't want to hear it. I'm there to make you laugh. The idea is to surprise. In an interview of this nature there are no surprises; it's right there on paper and inflections are lost and physical movements are lost, but my work, as far as the public is concerned, is to be funny. In my own life, I am very serious about things. I think a lot. I care about people, and that element I don't think I would care to share with forty million people. I would share it with people I am close to, really. I think America is going to be ready for a funny President in twenty years. If I can hide my high school transcripts, they may just be ready. Sooner or later they're gonna say, "I'm so sick of these solid and upstanding nice guys. At least they could have been funnier." I think it is time the country had a President who's a good put-on artist, who can pick up the red phone at any point and say, "Brezhnev, I've lost my mind, I don't know what has come over me. Goodbye." Hang up and give them like five seconds to try to get the forces going, pick up the phone again and say, "Just kidding." Just keep people on their toes.

OUI: Does show business ever seem meaningless to you?

CHASE: Do I ever feel sometimes, "Why am I doing this?" Is that what you mean? That show business is such a shallow area? I feel that almost everything is show business now in this country, and every area in life has its elements of it. Show business, as we put it, has elements that are gratuitous and meaningless and silly and exist for the buck. It's the same with journalism, which I find is concerned with selling a paper or a magazine, and doesn't really give a shit about who the person is they are talking to. By the time the editor gets it, it has to fill this space or that space. I think that politics is show business. I think that journalism is show business. I think that the entertainment industry is only one part of show business. We are in an age of show business, and it's been thrust upon us by our own ingenuity in developing systems of communications that inform us continually of what the guy next door, four thousand miles away, is doing. So it's a nonstop act, this world. We can make better use of it. I think everything has its meaningless moments; I'm for anarchy whenever possible in any one of them, so that you can sit back a little bit and throw away the papers and start again.

OUI: How would you like to be remembered after you're gone?

CHASE: Ah, on my tombstone? That's nice. Well, I think I'd like my epitaph to say, quite frankly, "Jamie Farr." You know, just to be serious for a moment.

107

Joan Rivers

The bashful comedienne defends her role as sex symbol and social commentator and explains why she isn't Liz Taylor's best friend.

Joan Rivers enjoys one of the most active schedules in show business. In addition to seemingly nonstop appearances in Las Vegas, Lake Tahoe and Atlantic City, she is preparing two film projects. Robert Crane caught up with her at her palatial Los Angeles estate. He tells us: "Television doesn't show how really lovely she is. She's even funnier in person. And don't believe her when she says she has Jewish thighs."

1

PLAYBOY: You're the sexiest comedienne working today. Despite the fact that you're married, do you get hit on a lot?

RIVERS: Yes, I do. A lot more than my husband realizes. I was asked to pose nude, but then I really took a look at my Jewish thighs. No, I do get hit on and it's funny, because the ones who hit on me are very interesting. It's always out-of-town businessmen or real Hollywood dumb machos. The kind who haven't read a book since *Dick and Jane* and are really impressed when I tell them how it ended.

2

PLAYBOY: Who turns you on?

RIVERS: My husband. My manager. Cary Grant, a little younger, though. Roy Scheider, Kris Kristofferson. I have a great fantasy life. I can look at an old Laurence Olivier movie and just have the best time for the next week and a half. Who else turns me on? Dark-haired Italian men that I could tame. Oh, and, well, situations—if I were stuck for days after an earthquake with a really handsome Italian guy and we both were just there together with champagne and a fire going. What could I do? I thought the world was over.

3

PLAYBOY: Why is it still difficult for audiences to accept funny women?

RIVERS: I don't like funny women. I come out of that generation where the woman should be beautiful and sexy and a wonderful flower attached to a man, even though my whole life has been the antithesis of this. To this day, you don't expect a woman to be funny. That's why someone like Dolly Parton is so wonderful, because she's pretty and yet out of her mouth comes funny. That's like an extra bonus. Or a Loni Anderson. Or Lily Tomlin, who is really very pretty. Nobody likes funny women. We're a threat. *I* don't like funny women. I don't think I'm funny. I think I'm witty. Also, who I am onstage is not who I am in private life. Tremendous difference. Onstage, I complain for every woman in America. In private life, I'm just a shallow, calculating bitch looking for a rich Arab to take me away. I could clean him up. We could be very happy.

4

PLAYBOY: Being funny is still considered a male thing, especially telling dirty jokes.

RIVERS: I don't like to see a woman telling dirty jokes. People say I'm dirty and I always stare at them. My areas are just very "women's" kind of areas. I have a routine now, which my husband hates, that for Christmas he gave me a box of Rely tampons. That's not dirty. I think that's very funny. It's such a woman's joke and it shows what your husband thinks of you. To me, a dirty joke is two nuns and a rabbi were screwing four Chinamen—

5

PLAYBOY: Who makes you laugh?

RIVERS: Lenny Bruce, still. I'll still listen to his records. My daughter. Albert Brooks. Jackie Gayle, who is brilliant in a club. Shecky Greene. Johnny Carson. David Brenner makes me laugh. And Rodney Dangerfield, even though a lot of us are very angry at Rodney because he runs around screaming at everybody, "You stole my material." It's a joke now among comedians—"Rodney says I stole this one from him." We laugh because he's so paranoid. But, anyhow, I think Rodney's very funny.

As for women, Lucille Ball is the best of the comedy line. Bea Arthur as Maude, if you're going into character comedy. Carol Burnett is the best sketch performer—ever. Lily Tomlin: You just want to put your arms around her and laugh and protect her at the same time. However, there are a lot of ladies doing comedy these days who should *not* be doing comedy. I love to see a serious actress who tries to get funny, or a serious actor. You want to go, "Oh, God, go back to drama. It's easier."

6

PLAYBOY: How do you handle hecklers?

RIVERS: Badly. I cry. Or I shoot them. Usually, I can handle them. Cher once did something that I'll love her for the rest of my life. She had an Arab who walked onstage *during* her act to get to his seat. Total arrogance. He walked past Cher, who was singing, and sat in front with his girlfriend with no regrets, no excuse-mes. She stopped the show and had him tossed out. I loved her for that. They threw him out and the girlfriend and the camel.

7

PLAYBOY: What were your first sexual experiences like?

RIVERS: Positive. My first encounter, as they say, was with a man I had been in love with since I was a child. So it was a very meaningful, if short, moment. I went out and bought a special dress for the occasion. It took longer to pick the dress than the whole sexual act. I guess our theme song was [sung to *I Feel Pretty*] "I feel nothing." But we were very much in love and that was very important. I waited through college. I'm glad I started that way. I've had very few sons of bitches. I've been very lucky. I was careful who I fell in love with. I came from a generation where you knew nothing;

you learned by doing. My old joke was: "I thought you took turns moving." Whoever had the good position moved. You had to learn. Where nowadays they know everything.

8

PLAYBOY: Is your husband romantic?

RIVERS: No, I wish he were. He is very unromantic and it is upsetting. It's horrendous sometimes, because you just would love someone to say, "Don't you look fabulous" or that roses would come to the house. When we first got married, when we would have fights—I love gardenias—dozens of gardenias would come and I'd go crazy for that. Or I'm always looking to open a rose and find a diamond ring in it. Well, after you've pulled apart 2000 roses, you just go out and buy your own ring. The nicest thing my husband can say to me is, "You don't look bad." It's very English. When you float down the stairs, you want something. The thing that I don't like is when my friends' husbands lean over and tell me how great I look. I hate when a friend's husband puts the hit on you.

9

PLAYBOY: Does that happen a lot?

RIVERS: Enough. Sometimes I feel everybody is looking. I don't like that. Let a stranger tell you, that's OK. The romance is out of my marriage, which is horrendous. But what can you do? My husband is a terrific man, so I just buy myself the diamonds.

10

PLAYBOY: When you and Edgar were married, did he realize that one day he would be a part of your act?

RIVERS: I don't think he realized it. He married me when I was already successful. But I was always autobiographical in my humor and it just evolved. He became a part of my act the same way my daughter became part of it, because I talk about my current experiences. My act now is more leaning over the back fence and saying, "Can you believe Nancy Kissinger? Isn't she a horse? When I met her, she was wearing a saddle from Gucci and the queen of England! If I've told her once, I've told her 1000 times, 'Shave your toes'" and like that. So there's less of the husband in the act.

11

PLAYBOY: What do you think of Elizabeth Taylor's comeback?

RIVERS: I hear she looks terrific. In real life, she's a dear friend of a dear friend of mine. She said to him, "I've dieted all my life. I want to get fat now. I'm happy. Let me go." That's her right.

But it's also my right to say what America's thinking. I think a comedian can never be an insider. I could never be a friend of "the greats." Every friend of mine who is a comedian and has become a friend of the greats is no longer funny. I won't go into names. You can't dine with the biggies and then walk on a stage and still be a common person. So, when Elizabeth Taylor got fat, that was great, because I could walk on a stage and say, "Wow, her thighs are going condo." Thank God she's fat. She lost weight for a while and I went into shock. I was so upset. I mean, I have a mortgage.

They say black makes you look thinner. So she should hang out with the Supremes. One of the reasons I enjoy making jokes about her is men still *adore* her. When I say she's fat, men get upset in the audience, and then you can scream at them—"OK, so she's not fat. I took her to Jack In The Box and she ate Jack." Then it's fun. But the men still find her very sexy and beautiful. God, her eyes. Especially that right one.

12

PLAYBOY: How do you feel about Hollywood people entering politics?

RIVERS: I think it's a great idea, because I'm planning to do it eventually. I think I'd be dynamite. I'm gonna tell Nancy Reagan to get out early so I can redecorate. Is she or is she not a Stepford wife? She's so perfect.

13

PLAYBOY: The sense of fun has gone out of a lot of areas of life. Sports, for instance. Everything is salary. Has that gotten out of control?

RIVERS: I don't care, because I hate sports. When I was single, I had to participate. I mean, picture this Jew in tennis shoes. I used to go sailing. You understand, I was going out with a guy from Harvard. I used to get hit in the head with the boom. I had concussions every spring. Try to sail and hide your thighs at the same time. Try to sail in high heels. It isn't easy to run on the deck with Spring-O-Lators.

But somebody was saying to me how disgusting it is with the salaries in Las Vegas. If you can bring them in, and they want to give you that, you're a fool not to take it. I'm all for big salaries. I'm also for big payoffs under the table. I'm looking to become a tool of the Mob. I'm looking for some big *mafioso* to say, "Get your hands off her. She's Sinatra's woman." I'm waiting for that. That has never happened. Those are my fantasies—"Leave her alone. She's Bob Mitchum's gal." I met Robert Mitchum at a party. I just stood and laughed into his stomach—he's so big.

14

PLAYBOY: Having lived on both coasts, what are the differences between New York women and Los Angeles women?

RIVERS: New York women are, by far, brighter, snappier, better dressers and doing more with their lives and are unafraid. California women are much more beautiful, nobody is over 11 and they're all frightened to get old. I have friends who exercise under their desks. In California, there's always the successful guy with the great-looking blonde on his arm and she lives only to stay "the great-looking blonde." In New York, you may have a great-looking woman, but she's also an art historian working for the Metropolitan Museum. In California, the women are much more "men's women," much more athletic, and they all look like Rod Stewart with hair bows. They're all thinner out here, too. Very depressing. Except it's cheaper when you give a dinner party in California.

15

PLAYBOY: Why is that?

RIVERS: In California, you don't have to serve anything. Just six Quaaludes and everybody's happy. In New York, they're looking for fine French food.

16

PLAYBOY: How do the Eastern rich differ from the Western rich?

RIVERS: The Eastern rich know how to spend it. The Eastern rich are not frightened to have French furniture or own an old master. They're not frightened to go to Europe. I mean, that's what the fun of money is: to go and buy clothes over there *at* the showings. Eastern lifestyle is much more formal. The only time you see anybody in California in a tuxedo is when they're burying him. Here, the rich don't spend their money the way I like to spend it. Let me put it this way: If I see one more piece of country French furniture or Lucite, I shall throw up. I have a very formal living room because it's nice to have a formal living room as we sit in our warm, comfortable den. It's nice to have a formal side to your life, too. These people out here are a little frightened of that. I bring finger bowls out at parties, and people out here get very nervous when they see that. They think entertaining means a bathing suit and a bowl of chili.

17

PLAYBOY: How do you keep creatively sharp living in Los Angeles?

RIVERS: We read everything in sight. The only extravagance we have, besides putting a bid in for Buckingham Palace, is we go into a bookstore and buy anything we want. That really keeps you very up to date. You have to be up to date; otherwise, you're dead in my business.

I also read the *National Enquirer,* because when I go onstage, that's what they want to know about: that Princess Caroline is a tramp. And poor Grace Kelly, no wonder they say she boozes—her daughter is sleeping around Monaco—and Caroline Kennedy is a bore. Second-generation kids are *pugh.* A lot of it has to do with the parents' not being there when they should have been. I mean the mothers more than the fathers.

18

PLAYBOY: Besides being a comedienne, you've also directed a movie. What did you learn from your experience with *Rabbit Test?*

RIVERS: It got lousy reviews on the whole. PLAYBOY loved it, Denver loved it, Chicago loved it. I can tell you who loved it: Gene Shalit should only die. His mustache should pull him down into the pool. I remember Gene Shalit when he was a flack, hanging out at the Upstairs at the Downstairs, saying, "Think I'm funny?" He was a big, fat boy. He knew I'd mortgaged my home to finance *Rabbit Test* and he said on television *twice,* "I hope she loses the house over this." I know he's a really funny guy and can be a lot funnier than me, but *his* special came in last place. That's the way it goes. I hope he reads his reviews.

Think I get a little defensive? It doesn't sound like much now, but we put up $492,000. When we paid off the note, the bank did a photo reduction of the signed document and pasted it on a bottle of wine and gave it to us, which was very sweet.

19

PLAYBOY: Now that we're out of the "me" decade, what is going to happen to the gay culture that was flourishing at the end of the Seventies?

RIVERS: First of all, I am so pro-gay. I owe my career to the gays. They found me first. But the Seventies got too liberal at the end. On the other hand, the born-again religious fanatics are very terrifying. It's scary, you know, when God only listens to certain people.

The women made their point in the Seventies. Let's all relax. Unfortunately, it's gone so far. I don't want to watch *The Phil Donahue Show* and see elderly gays telling me there's an alternative lifestyle for my child. This is not an alternative lifestyle. This is a lifestyle that will happen because of something the child has no control over. But it is not a choice. I think of myself as a fat Queen Victoria now, and yet I was the first straight person to put my name in the ad against Anita Bryant.

Don't you love how she swung around, that bitch, when she suddenly found a rich guy who doesn't feel the way she does? A lot of conviction there. But she lost the commercials. Weren't they smart, how they did that? Just very quietly, they eased her out.

Enjoy yourself. You go through life once, do anything you want—but quietly. I'm so bored with guilt. If you really see an animal you like, why not? But don't tell me about it and don't ask me to double-date with you and your chimp and *don't* say to my daughter, "Have you tried a great Dane?" Keep it to yourself and don't try to convert anybody.

20

PLAYBOY: What comes between you and your Calvins?

RIVERS: Longies and body wrapping. If my Calvins could talk, they would yawn.

Andy Richter

Conan's Former Couch Potato on Pornography, Overeating and his Plan to Rebuild Iraq

It wasn't that Andy Richter had a problem with being second banana to Conan O'Brien for seven years. The problem was, Richter, 36, star of Fox' Andy Richter Controls the Universe, had the acting bug and couldn't shake it. The Michigan native attended the University of Illinois, studying film and video. He then worked with several Chicago-area improve pros, including the late Second City veteran Del Close.

Before joining Conan, Richter appeared in Chris Elliott's notorious bomb, Cabin Boy. *Toward the end of his* Late Night *run, Richter upped the ante with appearances in Robert Altman's* Dr. T and the Women *and, in 2002, Barry Sonnenfeld's* Big Trouble.

*The Emmy nominee for Best Comedy Writing (*Late Night *and* Universe*) continues his big-screen career with roles in* The Guest *and* Frank McKlusky, CI.

Robert Crane caught up with the posse-free Richter at La Luna in Hollywood.

1

PLAYBOY: What does your Richter scale measure?

RICHTER: Just my passing judgment on everything and everyone at all times. It's my dark secret how truly judgmental I am. I try to be nice about it. I used to get criticized a lot for being cynical or too critical, so I had to surround myself with like-minded, professional bitches. And now I'm one of the more sunny people from my circle.

2

PLAYBOY: How did you remain interested in the process during all those years of sitting there listening to celebrities babble?

RICHTER: This is nothing against Conan, but frequently the interviews are pretty much the same. So, as a diversion, you look for the plastic surgery scars. I had a good angle, because I was looking right at the backs of their ears, which is where all the flesh gets gathered and is snipped off. Then you begin to notice the liposuction scar in the middle of the chin, the face-lift scar that's in the hair. Also, you notice the beard growing behind the ears, because all of that skin has now moved north a few degrees. You can see that some men have to shave behind their ears after a while. The things I love, and that I feel are intimate little secrets, are the spider veins on a supermodel's leg. Or the pit stains of famous actresses are exciting—I felt lucky to see them. One supermodel was wearing clear plastic pumps and her feet were getting hot, so the shoes were fogging up with her foot sweat, and I just thought that was one of the best things I'd ever seen.

3

PLAYBOY: Any tips on how to behave on a couch for hours on end?

RICHTER: Well, if you want to look good, don't sit on the couch, because it makes you slouch. That was always the secret on the talk shows. And you'll notice the host gets to hide behind a desk, because everyone looks good from the sternum up.

4

PLAYBOY: Define second-banananess.

RICHTER: In the *Ziegfeld Follies,* there was a number where all the dancers came together dressed in banana costumes and formed a bunch of bananas. The star of the show was at the top and the second star was the second banana. It's a good thing to be a supporting player. It makes you less vulnerable, that's for sure.

5

PLAYBOY: List styles of obsequiousness that approached the line but didn't cross over.

RICHTER: I didn't have to worry about it that much, because in instances where I've had to actually conduct interviews when I've guest-hosted, or when I'm interviewing someone whose work I'm not particularly fond of, I don't think I'm ever obsequious. I'm a little susceptible to people laughing at my every word. When my wife asks me what my opinion of somebody is I say, "He laughs at everything I say. I think he's fantastic." That's a hard one to beat, unless you're not trying to be funny.

6

PLAYBOY: You are the third-highest scorer in *Celebrity Jeopardy* history. Was there a question that was particularly hard?

RICHTER: One thing you have to understand about *Celebrity Jeopardy* is that it's really not in the show's best interest to make celebrities look stupid, so the questions are pretty simple. Because it was taped in New York, there was a category about naming stores in New York. Like, "It starts with a Z and has lots of food." "What is Zabar's?" *Jeopardy* is also a unique athletic competition, because it is a battle of thumbs. You have to get the rhythm of when to push the button, because if you push it before the question is over you're locked out for two seconds. There are lights on the side of the board that the audience doesn't see—the countdown is three, two, one and then you're free to answer. A friend of mine, who was head writer on the *Conan* show for a couple of years, was a legitimate *Jeopardy* champion—he took home 60 grand. When I was done he said, "You didn't try to ring in on the questions you didn't know the answers to. That's an interesting strategy." And, I thought, No, it isn't. I would look like an ass if I rang in and didn't know. But I guess other *Jeopardy* people figure that they'll take a chance, no matter what the question.

7

PLAYBOY: Give us your blueprint for rebuilding Iraq.

RICHTER: Satellite dishes for everybody wouldn't hurt. I'm not a real political guy. I get confused and have a hard time seeing only one side of an issue. That's why much of my comedy is apolitical. There's something political about saying, "Everyone should be nice to each other." That's a political statement, but in terms of any particular issue or taking a particular stand, aside from murder being bad I'm not sure.

8

PLAYBOY: Any plans to visit Baghdad like Sean Penn did?

RICHTER: No, no, no. It would be embarrassing, because nobody would know who the hell I was. Did they know who Sean Penn was?

9

PLAYBOY: Any plans for all those palaces?

RICHTER: Starwood Resorts. I'm in their points program, so I might get something out of that.

10

PLAYBOY: Does the word Scud actually describe the aerodynamics of that particular missile?

RICHTER: I'm not sure. Maybe that word sounds better when it's said in Arabic. Maybe it means something really good.

11

PLAYBOY: Share some of the sartorial tips you've gleaned from the great one, Jackie Gleason.

RICHTER: Don't be afraid of color. A purple suit looks good on anybody. As Anjelica Huston says in *Prizzi's Honor,* "Shapes come and go, but colors are eternal."

12

PLAYBOY: We've heard you're an office hooligan. What are some fun things we can do without getting caught?

RICHTER: If you find a camera at someone's desk—not a Polaroid but a regular-film camera, disposable or not--it's always fun to go into the bathroom and take a picture of your genitals and then replace it without being discovered. It's always a nice surprise, and, depending on how well known you are, you're probably not going to be identified. At Conan's show, NBC had firewalls against accessing porn. Some of it was silly, like if you wanted to look up information on breast cancer, they would keep you from doing it. So I started to find different code words that the NBC firewall people didn't know, one of which was bear—which is slang for big hairy gay men. So, you could look up bears and find lots of interesting stuff. I got the knack of sidestepping the industry firewalls and accessing terrible pictures and leaving them as somebody's wallpaper on their computer. And I could do it quickly. It got to where I could find some really unnerving pornography in less than a minute—in the time it would take someone to go to the bathroom.

13

PLAYBOY: What was the worst image you left on someone's computer?

RICHTER: I've done it only once on my show this year, to one of the writers. I put a picture of a dolphin vagina on his computer, and that was pretty disturbing. I *assume* it was a vagina.

14

PLAYBOY: Are the days of bare butts on Xerox copiers over?

RICHTER: Well, I know somebody who broke the copier glass with his ass. People are aware of the dangers now.

15

PLAYBOY: Janeane Garofalo has said that you're the sexiest person on TV. How does that make you feel?

RICHTER: Pretty good. She's a friend of mine, so I don't know. She's ironic—she might have meant something else. She could have just been in a publicity mode. It's nice. Who doesn't want to hear that about themselves? Even clerics like to know they're sexy.

16

PLAYBOY: What pranks and dumb things from our childhood should we resurrect for our adult lives?

RICHTER: I think the wedgie has a lovely equalizing feature. The world would be a better place if people were giving those out more freely.

17

PLAYBOY: What are your favorite subdivisions of porn?

RICHTER: I'm really not a big pornography consumer, because I mostly get distracted by wondering, "Whose house is that? Look at the weird socks that guy is wearing. Yeah, I think they rented that bedspread." Also, when I find myself wanting porn, I need it for only three or four minutes. How can you be a connoisseur? After that, it's goodbye Spectravision, hello Discovery Channel.

18

PLAYBOY: If you had to guess, were you not replaced on *Conan* because you're irreplaceable, or was it an occasion for the network to economize?

RICHTER: I don't think the network is allowed to economize. They hired a couple of writers—that money was spent somewhere. The budget doesn't go backward, it only goes forward. I don't know if I was so much irreplaceable as Conan probably didn't want to break anybody else in. You know, you've got a roommate you're pretty comfortable with and he moves out and you can afford the rent yourself. Why the hell would you want to get another roommate?

19

PLAYBOY: Describe the Andy Richter diet.

RICHTER: I try moderation. My family lives in the Midwest, and the way people eat there just blows my fucking mind. I mean, I'm a carnivore, I enjoy meat and I like cheese, but there has to be some moderation. I don't have a steak at every meal. You go back to Illinois and everything is a Fred Flintstone meal with cheese sauce on it.

20

PLAYBOY: Describe the Andy Richter workout regimen.

RICHTER: When I started working out, for the longest time I had an adversarial relationship with my body, and I still somewhat do. Janeane Garofalo talks about how she and her vagina are like roommates—"We just happen to share the same space; we're not pals or anything." That was the way I was with my body. My wife talked me into going to yoga once, and I am the only person who doesn't want to go back because yoga made me so angry. It's supposed to make you feel good, but it was all about getting into these contorted positions. "Now you should be feeling this on the right side of your lower back." "I don't feel it there, fuck this!" If I'm not able to do something well, I usually don't do it. And it took a long time to get over that and learn how to lift the weights right and to isolate the thing you're supposed to be isolating. I need to start up again with a trainer, because that's the only way. I'm not getting out of bed to lift weights unless I'm paying somebody who's waiting for me. It's a combination of the money and the fact that there's another human being I've committed to. I'll back out on my own commitment. A commitment I make to myself? That's easy. Fuck that guy.

Sweetmeat

He is the humerus maximus of late-night TV, the Falstaffian funnybone of Second City's version of Friday Night Frenzy. Finally given a network shot last year, mirthful, girthful John Candy is the logical successor to the comedic crown that once belonged to John Belushi.

When people think of John Candy, they think of John Belushi. Both funny men. Both stars of new wave comedy. But John Candy doesn't like to be reminded of the other John. Belushi was a good friend, he admired him, but he's gone. John Candy is the personification of life. He looks forward, not back.

The main attraction of SCTV, the syndicated late-night comedy show that picked fans from its former lead-in, Saturday Night Live, *John Candy is fast becoming as popular as his late friend. Even though his humor is highly satirical and often political, thousands of teenagers tune him in every week. Comedy has its own fashion, and what tickled our grandparents is not necessarily funny today. Like the Not-Ready-for-Prime-Time Players, Candy and his company of comics have a direct line to the humor consciousness of the younger generation.*

Candy started out with the Toronto and Chicago units of the Second City *stage show—the same company that spawned John Belushi, Dan Aykroyd, Gilda Radner, and Bill Murray. When* Second City *decided to try its own television show, Candy joined as a performer-writer. After three seasons, he left to front his own show,* Big City Comedy. *Although the show lasted only one season, it made a star of Candy—in Canada. Then came featured roles in 1941, The Blues Brothers, and* Stripes *(in which he mud-wrestled two voluptuous women). Just before* Stripes *was released, SCTV became part of NBC's late-night Friday line-up, and Candy rejoined his original group to air on network TV.*

Candy is an imposing figure. He stands six-feet-three and easily weights over 250 pounds. This man doesn't get lost in the crowd, and when he pulls one of his famous practical jokes—he once tucked Chevy Chase into a wrestling headlock at a party, dragging him around for several hours—he's not easily forgotten.

Neither are his SCTV characters Candy is a connoisseur of sleaze, a man with a fine appreciation of cheap pomades and jailhouse tattoos. Only Candy could have invented the unctuous Johnny LaRue or Harry ("the guy with the snake on his face"), owner of a chain of sex-supply houses. That selfsame love of society's slimy underbelly (or so he claims) made big John eager to talk to OUI contributor Bob Crane and to associate himself with what he affectionately terms "one of the sleaziest porn magazines I've ever had the pleasure of reading."

We're dubious, but feet up and Molson in hand, we plunge bravely into Candyland.

OUI: How did John Belushi's death alter your life?

Candy: When you lose anyone you know, it causes you to reflect on your own life, to look inside. John's death is very tragic and very untimely. I think all death is untimely. I'm not a big fan of it. It made me look around a little more—how I was living, what can happen to you, how things like that can happen. It's easy to do. He was the Bear. He was indestructible, and it didn't turn out that way for him. He wasn't the Bear. This is a very hard subject for me. John meant a lot to a lot of people. He was a very giving man. I just hope people remember the good things about him and what he brought, instead of the bad, what people assume is bad.

OUI: Did you see that terrible report on him by *20/20*?

Candy: No, I refused to watch that. I can tell what kind of lady that was, you know. I heard stories. I just didn't watch it. It was too close, too rough for me. My love goes out to Judy (Belushi). She's tough, but it doesn't matter how tough you are when you lose someone you love.

OUI: Why are so many young comedians burning out and dying or almost dying—Prinze, Pryor, and now Belushi?

Candy: Well, I guess it's the nature of the beast. I didn't know Freddie Prinze and I don't know Richard Pryor. John lived real fast. We all have a tendency—we being the group of friends that I have—to live pretty fast because you work real hard and you play real hard. After a while, it takes something like this to jolt you and say it's not worth it. Nothing's worth that. Freddie Prinze, I guess, was very young. His success came when he was around 17 or 18. It's a lot of pressure, and it must have been too hard for him. Richard Pryor—I don't know. That was very unfortunate. A lesson to be learned with matches there, I think. I don't drink rum and Coca-Cola much, you know. I did learn that because of that incident. I don't drink a lot of that anymore, and I did before. So, I did learn from that one.

OUI: The former stars of *Saturday Night Live* and the stars of *SCTV* have followings now like the old rock 'n' roll stars.

Candy: Comedy groups are becoming like rock 'n' roll bands. I hope, like a lot of groups, we don't break up. We're a new type of hero, I guess. *Saturday Night Live* really did that. They came on real strong, and people could relate to them like they could to the music in the sixties. I don't think it was as strong a wave as the Beatles or the Rolling Stones—those groups influenced a lot more people. This influenced the North American market at a time when music was sorely sagging. There wasn't really a trend outside of disco. There was a lot of musical undercurrent—no wave and new wave and punk—starting in the early seventies, but it really wasn't getting much attention. People were just waiting for something, and *Saturday Night Live* was that answer. They could relate to the cast, and they had rock bands on; so, there was a marriage there.

OUI: Do you lead a life of excess?

Candy: At times, yeah, I do—to a point. I do split myself up. I'm Jekyll and Hyde at times. I think I'm greatly affected by the moon. I have a tendency during a full moon to go crazy. No one comes near me. As soon as the new moon starts, I'm fine, I'm my old self. I honestly live a quiet life in the country with my wife and my daughter, and I find that my favorite time. When I'm living the other side, more like Johnny LaRue's taste, there is a tendency to go overboard. I try to keep a close rein on that.

OUI: Can you recall some incidents that you wish hadn't have happened?

Candy: There are so many. Where do you begin? Many parties where I went a little too nuts. I carried Chevy Chase in a headlock for a long time. I dragged him around a party. We had a big party in Los Angeles in 1976 or '77, and about 350 people showed up. Steven Spielberg was there and all our friends were there, a lot of good people, and Chevy came, and for some reason, I started playing wrestler with him and carried him under my arm in a headlock for a while. Or so I'm told. That was one.

Another time, we were at the New York, New York disco when it was just opening, and they wouldn't let us in; so, I started barking out front, like a live sex show. That wasn't taken too kindly. I was hustled off for that one. There are a number of times when I've had a little fun. There are some that are just too embarrassing to bring up.

OUI: During one of your forays into too much drink or what-have-you, were you ever in a situation where you woke up and didn't know where you were?

Candy: I've done that in my own house. Walked straight into the wall. I thought I was in another hotel, but I was actually in my own bedroom. I've walked into the closet in places and just stood there for a while, and then I realize I'm in a closet. I get a little foggy in the morning. I'm not exactly the swiftest man in the world.

OUI: Most comedians seem to have had an unhappy childhood. Was yours?

Candy: Mine wasn't unhappy. I was unhappy in the sense that I lost my father at a young age. That certainly had an effect on me psychologically, I'm sure. But I had a good upbringing; my mother, my brother, and I lived with my grandparents and my aunt. It was a normal upbringing. I watched *Leave It to Beaver* and *Ozzie and Harriet.* I was an avid Mouseketeer fan. I played soldiers and cowboys and played with my little cars. I have no complaints about my upbringing.

OUI: Why are most comedians also musicians?

Candy: There's a frustration there. There are a lot of rock stars who want to be actors and a lot of actors who want to be rock stars. I guess the grass is always greener. I try to just master one thing, and that's hard enough.

OUI: *SCTV* has always been a better show than *Saturday Night Live* was or is, but it's still not as well known. Why?

Candy: We're riding the crest of the wave they started. They came at a right time—all the right people were in the right place at the right time, and it just hit. It was good, it was funny, it was timely. It was unfortunate, but they lost a lot of their cast at once. It's like any team: When you lose your best players, that's what the fans remember. So, anybody who comes in there—no matter how good they are—they're always going to be compared to the originals. That's not fair to any cast.

Our success is just really starting now, since we've been with NBC, and I think that is one of the major reasons—the fact that we are with NBC now. We're in more markets, and we're on kind of a regular schedule. They're still bumping us around in this graveyard slot on Fridays. This is an expensive show to do, and there's not much money generated at that time—12:30 at night until 2 in the morning. It's hard for them to justify our being there. What gets them is we keep getting such good press. They can't just drop us.

OUI: Do you think you would be as funny if you were thin?

121

Candy: I would like to think so. I mean, my brain isn't that fat. Maybe it is. I don't know. Maybe people do just think of me as being that fat actor who's funny. I'm six-three and I stand out in a crowd. In terms of my abilities, I'd like to think that I could do anything. I'd probably be able to do more if I were thinner. You do get restricted with weight. I've always had a running battle with it. I've got to lose 40 pounds in two months for this new picture, *Drums Over Malta.*

OUI: Besides the Bob and Doug phenomenon, why do you think you've been singled out as the star of *SCTV?*

Candy: Probably because I'm fat. It usually works. I try to use it to my advantage as much as possible. I don't know if I'm considered the star of the show. I don't think I am. My God, looking at everyone's talent in this group, it's hard to pick *anyone* over anyone else. There are seven equally talented people.

OUI: I think you've been singled out like Chevy Chase was singled out on *Saturday Night Live* the first season.

Candy: Maybe it's because I've done some outside work, some films—*Stripes, Blues Brothers,* and *1941,* though I wasn't in that a lot. I've worked at it a long time, and I think that has something to do with it. It's the number of months spent on a movie, I think, that makes you a star. I wouldn't say I'm the star of the show. I would say all seven are equal.

OUI: Why do you produce the show in Toronto and not in New York or Los Angeles?

Candy: It all started in Toronto. The show was conceived in Toronto. We all worked together on the *Second City* stage show. It just all happened there, and we found Global Network. Bernie Sahlins, Sheldon Patinkin, Del Close, Andrew Alexander, Harold Ramis, Joe Flaherty, Dave Thomas, Gene Levy, Andrea Martin, Catherine O'Hara, and myself all came up with it. Bernie and Andrew approached us to do a TV show because they saw they had the talent here, and *Saturday Night Live* was just really starting to kick in. They had facilities here cheap, and I think part of the move was not to lose us. My feeling initially was that it was a make-work project. It was, like, to keep us going, because we had done other shows and pilots that were just fiascos. This one just seemed to work. As soon as the idea was brought out—a fictitious television station—it worked. Material was endless for that. It evolved very nicely.

Everybody happened to be here, even though the cast is from different cities. Joe is from Pittsburgh. Gene is from Hamilton, Ontario. Andrea lived here, although she's from Portland, Maine. Catherine lives in Toronto. Harold was living in Los Angeles. It just evolved in Toronto.

Then we went to Edmonton because the finances went bad, and we shot the show there. I left that year for a number of reasons, moral reasons. I didn't like the way the show was going. It was time for me to leave at that time.

I came back in when NBC stepped in. There was a little more credibility there for the financing. The producers dug in and kept the show on the air. Their reward will be down the line. They're putting all their money in now. It's a very expensive show to do. We outgrew the facilities in Edmonton, and Toronto was really our home and it was hard for us being on the road; so, we came back.

OUI: Is it possible for women to be both funny and sexy? There is still a stigma about comediennes.

Candy: I don't know if that's true. I think you should have the ability to play both. A woman shouldn't be afraid of playing sexy. If you're an actor, you should be able to do all parts. You can put that question to a guy as well. Tell a male stand-up comedian to be real macho out there. If it doesn't work for him and his act is playing the wimp, then that's what works. You play with what works. If a woman is doing a stand-up act and it works for her to be sexy, then that's what she should go for. If it works playing the Joan Rivers-type character, you know, or the Phyllis Diller-type character, then go for it.

OUI: Why is it harder for women to succeed in the comedy field?

Candy: It's a male-dominated business to begin with. It's an uphill battle for a woman. The good ones just rise, you know. It's a numbers game. There seem to be more men in comedy than there are women. Scripts usually call for more men than they do women. It's always been real hard for women to find great parts. Bette Davis and Katharine Hepburn always had to fight for those roles. They're great actresses, and they had to really struggle. It seems a lot easier in this business if you're a man.

OUI: Who are some of your favorite actresses?

Candy: Judy Holliday was one of my favorites. I loved her. She made me laugh. Marilyn Monroe was real funny. She and Jayne Mansfield could play that dumb blonde so well. Marilyn Monroe was incredible, very talented. Lily Tomlin—excellent, excellent comedienne. Valerie Bromfield, who's on *Best of the West*—excellent. Mary Tyler Moore does a great job. There are so many who do it well. Rose Marie was real funny on *The Dick Van Dyke Show*. She had great timing, and working with those guys, you've got to be good. I really think that Catherine and Andrea are two of the finest comediennes on television or anywhere in North America. I haven't been around the world, so I don't know—there may be some in France.

OUI: You have an up-and-coming film career in motion. Which actresses can you envision starring with?

Candy: Starring with? Where do you begin? Actually, I'd love to work with Katharine Hepburn or Bette Davis. We're trying to get Bette Davis for *SCTV*. My dream girl for a leading lady? I'd better say Catherine and Andrea to play it safe. Carrie Fisher is very good. I worked with her before. Pia Zadora—you just wonder about that one. Morgan Fairchild is doing a fine job. Christie Brinkley. I'm talking heavy comedy here. Slapstick, broad comedy, pie-in-the-face, the whole bit. Bo Derek. She's kind of going down, isn't she? She's getting old. I like to keep them around 15, you know. I didn't mean that. A young Brigitte Bardot. A young Sophia Loren.

OUI: Why is Johnny LaRue the favorite character of most *SCTV* viewers?

Candy: People can identify with him. They all know some loud-mouthed jerk like him, some pompous ass. There's a little bit of that in everybody. Kids love LaRue—the heavy smoking, the drinking, he gets very indignant, always hung-over, always loaded, carousing at all hours. There's something nice about him, a nice quality.

OUI: Who is your favorite character?

Candy: I like LaRue. He's fun to do. Dr. Tongue is a lot of fun now with Woody Tobias, Jr., a.k.a. Bruno. Gil Fisher's a lot of fun now. I like Harry, "the guy with the snake on my face." He's opening up more Harry's Sex Shops. All the employees will have snakes on their faces.

OUI: The characters you've mentioned are all slightly bent. How do you come up with these people?

Candy: I always look for the sleaze in somebody. If they're sleazy, I can believe them. That's just the way I see people.

OUI: Like the character Harry, are you also an aficionado of porn and sleaze?

Candy: Oh, yes. That's why I'm doing this interview for this magazine. This is one of the sleaziest porn magazines I've ever had the pleasure of reading. I enjoy flipping through the pages of OUI Magazine. I have since its creation.

OUI: What kinds of filth turn you on?

Candy: This magazine. Any sex. *Any* sex. I've been working so hard these days, anything will do. These days, I get excited watching an elevator going up and down. A subway going in a tunnel. A woman smoking a cigar gets me going. A big Panatela. Just everyday things. It's lonely here.

OUI: Are you a fan of porno films, like Johnny Wadd films?

Candy: Johnny Wadd? Yeah, good guy. Hell of a nice guy. He killed how many? I'm not saying there's a tie-in with violence and porno. I'm not saying that at all. He got caught. Okay. It could have been anybody. But Johnny Wadd got caught.

OUI: Johnny Wadd also claims to have made it with 14,000 women.

Candy: That lousy...they're gonna love him in prison. Just that thought of him walking in. He's had more than his share. This is kind of like penance. Think of the wonderful stories he'll be telling the prisoners. He'll keep them captivated for hours.

I met Harry Reems. Nice guy. I'm kind of embarrassed around that. These are big stars—Jamie Gillis, big star. They intimidate me. I just can't live up to those guys.

OUI: There have actually been a few well-produced films starring these guys.

Candy: I saw *It Happened in Hollywood*. I loved that one. Very funny. There was the flying fuck, I think it was. A guy was on a unicycle on a high-wire, and the girl was sitting down below, and he took the brakes off and went all the way down. That was funny. They should do more comedy pornos. If you do porn, it should be funny. We were talking about doing a porn, one day, in make-up. Catherine would do Elizabeth Taylor or something. I could do Orson Welles. We'd do a cheap porn, make a fast buck, and go.

OUI: Do you ever hear from the people you impersonate, like William B. Williams?

Candy: Never. I don't look anything like William B. Williams. It's Joe Flaherty's fault. I look nothing like him. He's graying, he's thin. I'm expecting something from him. I do it jokingly, I swear, William.

OUI: Have you heard from Divine or Shelly Winters?

Candy: I haven't heard from any of them. I'd love to know what Luciano thought of my Pavarotti. I'm trying to get a tape to him. Jimmy Coco was fun to do. I did Ed Asner—it wasn't that bad. Dave Thomas met Bob Hope, whom he does. I don't think Joe heard from Jack Klugman. He does a great Quincy. Phil Silvers saw Rick Moranis do him on one of our shows—he loved it. Herb Ross wanted a copy of our Christmas show. Neil Simon got a copy, but I don't think he was too pleased.

OUI: The English love drag humor. Why do you think so?

Candy: I guess it goes back to Shakespeare, when the men played women's roles. Milton Berle made a whole career out of that. *Some Like It Hot* was a huge success—two guys in drag. It just looks funny. It's when you take it very seriously—that's when it's a problem. When you like dressing like that and wander around the house—that's when I'd start worrying about myself. I hope that I could catch it at that time.

OUI: What are your predictions regarding the cast after *SCTV* ends one day?

Candy: I see everyone doing extremely well. Everyone is so talented. Everyone will go off and do well, unless everyone just turns into a wino. Everyone is very clever, and they have good business minds and creative minds. It would really take an act of God really zapping somebody for them not to make it.

I would like to see this group stay together for a while. We're in our sixth year now, and now we're starting to reap a little profit on this. I wouldn't mind paying off my farm first, then we'll talk about leaving. I think we all feel that if we're going to leave, we should all leave together.

OUI: The cast doesn't appear to be another group of drug-crazed comedians.

Candy: Very clean cast. I'm the only real heavy drinker, and I'm not that bad. Don't get me wrong—I can drink real good. It's nothing I'm proud of. Canada's more of a drinking country. They like their booze up here; they like their beer. I guess it's the isolation of being north. Long winters.

OUI: You know and have worked with most of the *Saturday Night Live* original cast. Any comments on their post-SNL careers?

Candy: Bill's done real well. *Stripes* did real well. John and Dan did great with *Blues Brothers*. *1941* was so-so. Gilda's movie did all right.

OUI: Are they better-suited for television?

Candy: You're in the public eye more on television. They see you week after week. In movies, the audience tends to forget you unless you're working constantly. Chevy works all the time. He must do three or four movies a year. As a result, people keep up with him more. It's a hard decision. They were right on top. To go back to television, I don't know if their thinking is, Gee, will people think less of me because I didn't make it as a film star? I hope that they don't think that. Careers are lifetime. We're all still very young.

I think everybody's just exploring different things, learning their craft. It's nice, sometimes, to get away from it all for a while, just to recharge the batteries so you can offer more later on as an actor. If you don't experience a lot of things, you've got nothing to say or to relate to. If you don't see anything fresh coming in, because you're working all the time, there comes a point when your performance starts getting stale. That's when you've got to pull back out of it a little bit.

OUI: What is left to explore comedically on television?

Candy: A better way of doing an old joke. *SCTV* is fairly innovative, but it was an obvious innovation. It's usually the obvious ones that work. I'm sure there's a show like this buried in someone's desk.

A lot of the cable programming right now, the big attraction to it is that it's uncensored. There's good and bad there. What you couldn't say on prime-time television, you can now watch in detail—over and over and over and over. After the shock wears off, is it any good? Is the quality good? I'm not saying that the quality on the networks is great. PBS. What happened to PBS? They're taking their funds away. That's unfortunate. There's some good quality programming there. I think the networks and cable should take a lesson from PBS. Good programming.

There's room for everybody out there, for every type of show imaginable. They have to build the TVs bigger now—more channels, and they're going to fill them all. It's the kid in the candy shop. Can you eat everything? Your eyes are bigger than your stomach. It's gonna be weird.

I was sitting at home, and I looked at my big 28-inch Sony and my ¾-inch machine and my Betamax. I remembered when my dad got a gel to put on top of our black-and-white set for color. What's my daughter gonna have in 25 years?

OUI: What are your limits for bad taste?

Candy: I thought cancer was sacred, you know, until I went to this bar the other night and heard a guy use cancer in a song. It was an up song about Terry Fox, the kid who ran across Canada. "Terry, you're a rarie" was one of the lines, and then "He died of cancer." I can't remember the exact lyric, but my mouth dropped. I couldn't believe that you could ever use cancer in an up song, but this guy did. That, to me, was fairly tasteless.

It depends on the house, who you're playing to. We did a stage show for a group of people who booked the theater, and they made condoms. These were the guys who worked on the line. That was a good show, a very strange evening. I think some of those guys had ties on for the very first time. Any reference to sex, they stood on the table. They're around it all day, so I thought they'd be bored with it, but it had the opposite effect on them.

You can get real tasteless. It doesn't bother me. Lenny Bruce did it with an edge to it. If it's done properly, you can go real tasteless. Michael O'Donoghue threw cats in a swimming pool. That bothered me. I'm sure the joke was just that—to get to somebody. He has cats. I don't think he maliciously wants to throw them in. It got me pissed off.

OUI: When has *SCTV* gone over the limit?

Candy: We're good censors. I don't think we've really gone over the edge. Even with Mother Theresa, we treat her with respect. We just put her in a situation with jerks around her. That's the way we see it. I always envisioned her coming to Hollywood because they want to do a life story on her or something. She's just this saintly woman besieged by these sleazy agents. That's how we surround her doing the *Lola Heatherton Show.* Mommy Theresa—that wasn't tasteless to me. I think if we would have made her strip and had her wear garter belts, that would have been tasteless. You don't do that. *I* don't do that—although I'm sure there are people who would. There's a movie out where Vikings rape nuns. That is tasteless. Oh, God, give me a break.

OUI: Are Los Angeles and New York dangerous to one's ego, creative life-span, or sense of humor?

Candy: It depends on how you deal with yourself as a person and how you deal with your success. If you've got your life under control, your family life and yourself and your business, you've got it—you know how to deal with it. If you're bad on one, you'll go into a tail-spin. I've seen it happen to people. You've got to keep your eyes open. You've got to be aware. It's very easy when life looks great and everyone is telling you you're good. After a while, you lose objectivity, you lose sight of what got you to that point. If you start believing all those things all the time, pretty soon you're going to fall. It's inevitable. No one is that great.

OUI: Do you think you'll ever experience as much freedom creatively as *SCTV* allows you?

Candy: No, I think this is a rare instance where we have control. I feel like I'm in college sometimes or in high school. We're just doing our show, and we get it done our way. Budget has some restrictions on us. I know it's going to change. It's happened to me already. When I did *Big City Comedy*, I thought I had creative control and I didn't have it at all. As a result, the show didn't do that well. I'm not saying that I could have saved it, but I would have liked to have been given a shot at it.

OUI: What happens to old comedians?

Candy: They end up on *SCTV* in some form. It's sad. Look what happened to the Three Stooges. They were good comedians. Once you get set into a routine and your routine is the same and your act hasn't changed and you're still using hippie references in 1982, that's when you should really start thinking about taking a little time off. Take a look around you. Stop and smell the roses for a while. See, the thing is, there's always a crowd. Once you make it as a big star, you can ride on that afterglow for years. There's always going to be some lounge that you'll play where they love you. "I remember you. You're great. You're wonderful." It pays the rent.

Styles have changed so much, it must be hard on these old stand-up comics. If it wasn't for Atlantic City and Las Vegas, it would be the Holiday Inn circuit, the Ramada Inn circuit. There are not that many great lounges to play anymore. A lot of comedy clubs are closed down. Television's your big break, or Atlantic City or Las Vegas or feature films. A lot of these guys are just not going to cut it in any of those places. A hard, cruel business. They eat their young here.

OUI: What does one do when it's all over?

Candy: I don't even want to think of that. You've just got to keep working. You've got to keep it fresh. Look at Bob Hope. The man's all over the world. He keeps it fresh. He keeps a whole pool of writers around him. George Burns—he's got the energy going for him. You make it work for you. You keep it fresh. You keep it going.

There are times when I would like to just make enough money, pay off my house, and just quit. Pick a project every now and then, and just enjoy my family. The urge is getting stronger and stronger. I think maybe I just need a rest. I haven't had a vacation in 10 years. Once you start the ball rolling, your career starts going, you're always afraid to take some time off because, if you do, people will think the worst of you and they'll forget about you real fast and you'll be gone.

Things are going real nice for me now. I don't intend to blow it by burning myself out. It ain't worth it. Nothing's worth that—no career, all the notoriety, it means nothing. It's wonderful and it's hard to give up, but I think I could. Busting your tail, no matter how much you love the business and you love what you're doing, you ain't gonna love it if you're in a box under the ground or if you're in some hospital, shaking in the corner and doing Big Bird imitations.

OUI: Each of the last few decades has featured a different kind of humor. What kind of humor will be featured during the eighties?

Candy: Times are so hard now, it should be a comic's field day. It's getting harder and harder to make people laugh. Times are real bad. What's popular about our show is it's television. People are now laughing at television. It's an inside laugh now, it seems. It's real hard to say what's going to happen. We just happen to be here, and it's '82. I don't think we're going to change the course of comedy for the eighties.

OUI: Do you think Steve Martin, for example, starting out today would make it?

Candy: That act when he first came out—put an arrow on your head and blow balloons up—I think it would still work. It's funny. People just laughed at the guy. You knew guys like that at parties. There was a certain overkill to it, but he's a very talented man. He'll get by. The New Christy Minstrels—I don't know if they would now. The Kingston Trio might not make it now. Steve Martin would.

OUI: So many comedians have come and gone, and so many comedy series have come and gone, but Johnny Carson has endured for almost 20 years. Why?

Candy: He's good at what he does. He's a great host. All the intimate experiences late night, he's been part of it. He can maintain night after night. That's a long grind. You feel comfortable watching him. You laugh when he bombs. When he's on a roll and he's got somebody on like Rodney Dangerfield or Dom De Luise he goes crazy sometimes. You can tell when he doesn't like somebody—that pencil starts tapping and the next thing you know you're on a commercial and they're not there anymore. That man has control. Hats off.

OUI: Do you see any differences between East Coast and West Coast comedians and comedy?

Candy: Just the jokes vary. In New York, they say, "You know I just got in from L.A. and the funny thing about L.A. police..." and when they go to Los Angeles they say, "You know I can't get used to the traffic here. What about those New York cops?" That's the only difference—in the police jokes back and forth. "You know, L.A. police are so laid-back. In New York, they're so heavy, man."

OUI: What do you do for fun when you're in New York or Los Angeles?

Candy: In New York, there's just so much to do. It's wonderful there. There's just so much of anything you want. John Belushi once told me, "This is Rome. It has everything here." I said, "I prefer the suburbs, John. I'm sorry." But he was right. It has everything. It's a wonderful place.

In L.A., there's so much to do there, but it's so spread out. It's got the weather, but it's got the smog, too. That drives me crazy. Driving wears me down there. You really have to plan your day—starting in one section, you just kind of work your way over the hill, down the other side of the hill, go to your meetings, back up the hill, and go to the other side. Everyone goes to restaurants there. Nobody ever stays home. I like staying home.

OUI: Does it bother you that many *SCTV* viewers are stoned during the program?

Candy: No. Do whatever makes you feel comfortable. It's nice to watch it without anything, too, sometimes. That's a different view of it. Then, ratings might drop again, I don't know. A lot of people just get real drunk and watch our show and pass out.

OUI: Can you do drugs and comedy at the same time?

Candy: No. Your timing's way off. You smoke a joint and forget it. You can't. I know people who do. It's a giveaway. Their eyes are just like mirrors.

OUI: Do sex and comedy mix?

Candy: Uh, yes, they mix. Of course, they mix. Of course. How foolish of you. I think sex and watching the show is wonderful, a wonderful experience. Two big jokes going on—in my case, anyway. Sex and comedy. Would you like some examples? Good shows can ruin good relationships, I guess.

OUI: Are there *SCTV* groupies?

Candy: I haven't seen any yet. See, that's where rock stars have got it made. I guess ours are called jokies. All male kids with braces who want to be comedy writers.

OUI: Ever get accosted on the street by 15-year-old ladies?

Candy: No, and I try. Damn, I try, but it doesn't work. I wear my costumes. I wear LaRue's outfit, and Joe and I will go down the street—he's Caballero in a wheelchair. We try anything. Joe and I went to a strip show one time in a bar. There was an act going on. The place you don't want to get recognized, that's where we get recognized. The stripper recognized us. I was walking past her, and she was grinding it out on stage, and at a crucial moment, without skipping a beat, she said, "John Candy. *SCTV*. Love the show," and went back to what she was doing.

I think because of the disguises we wear on the show, people don't really know what we look like. We're trying, but nothing. Just the young kids who are writers, male kids in high school: "We'd love to write on your show. Do you take material?" No, we don't. Do you have a sister?

129

Robert Crane

MUSICIANS

Robert Crane

Nelly

The Multiplatinum Mayor of Nellyville Holds Forth on Halle, Hummers and—Whoa, It's Getting Hot in Here

1

PLAYBOY: It's common among guys who suddenly reach your level of success to get a Ferrari, a huge house and an entourage. You now head a corporation. Give us a sense of your payroll and health plan.

NELLY: Yeah, I'm a businessman now—Dirty Entertainment. The payroll is about $30,000 a month. That's if nothing's going on, if we don't do a show. My mom is probably the only one who gets paid who's not traveling with me now. But the payroll can range anywhere from 30 to 150 grand. It depends. We all just took physicals for our insurance plan. We got our cards. My movie production company is under Dirty Entertainment, as is Vokal, my clothing line. It's in stores now.

2

PLAYBOY: Before you made it big, you worked at McDonald's. What would revitalize the Golden Arches?

NELLY: Broadening the menu a little. I think people are getting tired of the McDonald's regular menu, especially with so many other franchises opening up. People's tastes are changing. But there will always be kids who can't wait to get a Happy Meal.

3

PLAYBOY: If you can't have it your way, which way would you have it?

NELLY: Probably Halle Berry's way.

4

PLAYBOY: How does one dress for hip-hop success?

NELLY: That's the thing: Hip-hop allows you to do it any way you see fit. Hip-hop doesn't limit you to the Wall Street type of success. It allows you to be a businessman and an artist. I like to chill out in athletic clothes, but I want to put on a suit every now and then, clean it up a little bit. As long as you have clothes, you can handle your business. Hell, you can be dressed in your underwear and still make a lot of bills.

5

PLAYBOY: When you're selling apparel, is it a good idea to have a song urging women to take off all their clothes?

NELLY: Unfortunately, when I sang that song, we didn't have a women's line out yet. Apple

133

Bottoms—that's the name of my ladies' line. So look for the Vokal *Hot in Herre* remix. I'll be singing about putting 'em on.

6

PLAYBOY: Are you concerned with how the clothes will look on the floor?

NELLY: Maybe lingerie. You're on your way to the bathroom, then you see this nice thong that used to be on her. It gets you back in the mood real fast.

7

PLAYBOY: What makes for better mood music—Nelly or Barry White?

NELLY: It depends. Barry White puts it out there for you. He sets the mood—probably not for my generation, but for my father's. When I was little, if you walked in the house and Barry was on, you'd go to your room and shut the door, you know what I'm saying? Because there was something going down you didn't need to be a part of.

8

PLAYBOY: Is bling-bling a competitive sport?

NELLY: If you have jewelry, you notice jewelry. It could be earrings, watches. You'll notice a bang-ass ring—you may not stare at it, but you notice it. The first guy who really excited me about jewelry was Jermaine Dupri. He had that big "72" necklace and it was all diamonds. I had seen it before I had a deal, and I was like, "Oh! I've got to get one of them!" It was extra inspiration for me. So when I got my first deal, I bought a big "Nelly" in diamonds on a chain. All of us take notice of what other guys have around their necks.

9

PLAYBOY: But Jermaine Dupri is having money problems now. Aren't you supposed to put the money in the bank and not around your neck?

NELLY: As long as you have more in the bank than you do around your neck, you'll be cool. The problem gets mixed up when it's the other way around. But luckily we don't have that problem.

10

PLAYBOY: Ice-T, Ice Cube, LL Cool J, DMX, Puffy—whose career would you like to emulate?

NELLY: What I'm going to do is try to take pieces. I would try to get the longevity of LL. Everybody would like Puffy's status, because even if he's not doing as well as he would like with his records, he still maintains his fame. I'd like to extend my acting career like DMX has. So for me and my generation of hip-hop, we're looking at those guys and trying to branch out.

11

PLAYBOY: Do you drive a Hummer?

NELLY: Yeah. I had the big steel one but recently got rid of it. I've got the H2 now. I liked the big one, but driving it was a workout. There's no power steering. You can't just drive that up and down the block every day, park it, take it back out. The H2 is more streetwise, but it still gives you a little Hummer feel if you're ready to go all-terrain.

12

PLAYBOY: Can you do drive-through with that?

NELLY: Yeah, with the new one. It's just a hassle trying to turn tight corners and stuff. A lot of times I just go over shit. It's like, "The hell with it." One time I ran over this guy's hedges and he came out—he wasn't really tripping off it, because he saw it was me. I said I was sorry, and then I gave him 100 bucks and told him, "Here, buy yourself some new bushes, man." He was cool with it.

13

PLAYBOY: What's your favorite drink?

NELLY: We drink a lot of pimp juice—Malibu rum with peach schnapps and pineapple juice. They call it pimp juice because it's real sweet and ladies like to drink it. It's easy for them. But after you've had about six and you go to stand up, you're like, "Whoa!" Between the rum and the schnapps, it kind of sneaks up on you. It's real good.

14

PLAYBOY: Xzibit, Outkast, Ludacris, Fabolous. Ever thought about giving these guys a dictionary?

NELLY: It's all about being original. It's about putting your mark on it and making it something of your own. When we spelled Vokal, of course we took it off the word vocal, but we thought, Vo-kal—just let the clothes speak for themselves.

15

PLAYBOY: East Coast versus West Coast. If you had to shoot somebody, who'd it be?

NELLY: Right now probably Rams coach Mike Martz for putting Kurt Warner back in the game. Me and a host of others in St. Louis would line up.

16

PLAYBOY: Has anyone ever said, "Whoa, Nelly" and meant it?

NELLY: Yeah, I've had quite a few people say, "Whoa, Nelly." Usually girls.

17

PLAYBOY: You've said you like it doggy style. Whose head would you most like to see the back of?

NELLY: Halle's. Who else? Although J. Lo is engaged, the back of her head would look very nice. Actually, I doubt I would see the back of her head, because I'd be looking down too much.

18

PLAYBOY: Women say they like lovers, not fighters. What do you think?

NELLY: I think they really like a combination. I don't think women like a man who's unmanly, so to speak. I consider myself both, so I guess if they're messing with me, they get a lover and a fighter.

19

PLAYBOY: How can you tell when a guy is lying about his sex life?

NELLY: Nine times out of 10, the guy who raves on a lot isn't doing it like he says. Because if he is, he doesn't have time to talk about it too much.

20

PLAYBOY: Why will a guy hook up with a random skank even if he has something nice at home?

NELLY: I watch a lot of the Discovery Channel—animals in the jungle, stuff like that. The lion spreads his seed endlessly in different territories. Man is the only species that really narrows it down and says, "You must be with one." Why would we have millions of sperm for just one partner? It's a willingness to be devoted. When we do that, we're showing our commitment to the female. It's more mental than physical. Otherwise, I think a man would just run wild in a world without diseases. A world without diseases would be heaven for men. They just get that urge. They don't mean anything by it. It's just that they get on, they let it roll. It's a hard life.

Peter, Paul and Mary: Just Plain Folk

You'd think that after twenty-eight years, eight gold and five platinum record albums and thousands of sold-out concert appearances around the world, audiences would be able to tell one member of the legendary folk singing trio Peter, Paul and Mary from another.

"We sometimes confuse ourselves," admits Peter Yarrow, who is fifty years old and the shortest of the threesome. "Paul goes by 'Noel' offstage. Poor fellow, he's lost his hair. Obviously, I have a full head of hair. Actually, he's more easygoing and soft-spoken and funnier than I am."

Paul—er, *Noel*—Stookey, now in his late forties, a Michigan State alumnus and a former stand-up comedian, continues: "Peter is the one with the glasses. Of course, added to the confusion now is, who's Noel? I sometimes deal with calls in my office where I answer the phone 'Noel,' and the caller says, 'I'm a personal friend of your brother's.'"

There's no mistaking Mary Travers—except for the fact that she recently shed thirty pounds and looks more like she did in her Greenwich Village days than she does on the *Peter, Paul and Mary Holiday Concert,* which premieres on public television this month but was taped in New York last February. The mother of two daughters in their twenties, Travers recently became a grandmother— an astonishing realization to those who still picture her as a hip young folk singer. "Life is very full these days," she says, "full and terribly sweet. I don't think I've ever been happier."

After exploding on the scene in 1962 with their debut album, *Peter, Paul and Mary*, which spent three-and-a-half years on the *Billboard* charts, the trio embarked on a rigorous recording and concert touring schedule that lasted through 1970, introducing such classics as "If I Had a Hammer," "Blowin' in the Wind," "Puff, the Magic Dragon," and "Leaving on a Jet Plane" to millions of fans.

"We became a family at the age of twenty-one," recall Stookey. "We have stepped on each other's toes, taken each other for granted, ignored each other and, in the early years, were competing with each other for our individuality."

Despite their phenomenal recording and performing success and a shared commitment to human rights that included marching on Washington and Selma with Dr. Martin Luther King, the trio amicably disbanded in 1970. Stookey moved his family to Maine, Travers and her daughters settled in Connecticut and Yarrow maintained his household in New York City. During the seven years that followed, each of the three made solo albums and concert appearances, producing a body of interesting if not wholly memorable work.

While organizing a major antiwar rally at the Hollywood Bowl in 1978, Peter asked Noel (Paul) and Mary to join him on stage. "We hadn't sung together in six years," says Travers. "We realized that we missed each other personally and musically. We decided to try a limited reunion tour. We wanted to work enough together to have it be a meaningful part of our lives, but not so much that it wouldn't be fun." They signed with Gold Castle Records and decided to limit their yearly schedule together to one album and sixty concerts.

With the recent resurgence of interest in folk music—fueled by such young artists as Suzanne Vega and Tracy Chapman—veteran folkies like Joan Baez, Judy Collins and Peter, Paul and Mary are now reaching yet another generation of music lovers. Though the trio resists the narcissism of trying to understand their continuing popularity, Yarrow nevertheless attempts an explanation. "Every so often the pendulum swings" he says, "and right now we're watching it swing very powerfully in the direction of the kind of music we've been singing for a long time. This kind of music is being taken to heart by people; it's moving and affecting them."

Stookey agrees, and feels that public television has contributed to the group's longevity. "It is through community broadcasting that I think folk music will have its opportunity," he says, "because of all the words that one could pick to describe why folk music is popular and still alive, it would be the word 'community.'"

A few years ago, Peter, Paul and Mary celebrated their twenty-fifth anniversary by taping a concert special that became public television's all-time greatest pledge drive program. That milestone behind them, the trio now dares to look forward to the fiftieth. "I think the temptation is going to be to dress in tuxedos," Stookey jokes, "and be a little overweight and probably be acknowledged by some institution. If we have our smarts about us, I think we'll wear blue jeans and play at a small coffee house in Greenwich Village."

With their upcoming special, the re-release of their first Warner Brothers album on compact disc, and a continuing tour schedule that allows them to balance life as a trio with their individual lives, Peter, Paul and Mary have plenty of blessings to count this holiday season, and they hope their followers will join with them in the counting. "It's a time for stopping the world," says Yarrow, "and taking a look at things that are meaningful. It's a time of giving thanks. The holidays give us a break from the travail of our times. Whatever is troubling us, it is very helpful to recall that we are, indeed, fortunate. It's something we need to do at least on a yearly basis."

Openers' First Annual Rock-'n'-Roll Celebrity Bubble Gum Blowing Competition

JOAN JETT (*The Runaways*): "My favorite bubble gum is Carefree Sugarless. We buy it by the boxes and take it on tour with us. It's good for your teeth and you can blow good bubbles and I like the color."

LITA FORD (*The Runaways*): "I like the Carefree shit, too. Bubble gum makes me horny because of the way it wraps around your tongue and the way it sticks on your face. The secret to blowing [big bubbles] is to wrap your tongue around it and blow. I chew gum 'cause it's better than smoking. It's fun, too. It makes you feel like you're from New York."

ALICE COOPER: "I know the real story behind bubble gum. Bubble gum was originated as the very first contraceptive. What they would do in the old days was, the woman would chew it up and, depending on how big the man was, would blow a great big bubble, and then the guy would stick his boy's thing in, and the bubble would break around the head of his cock and that would stop the sperm. The only problem was that there were so many people getting stuck together once it was on the end, and bigger men were pulling the insides of the woman out accidentally because the bubble gum was sticking to the insides of her girl's thing. So they stopped that idea because it was sticky business.

"My favorite kind of bubble gum is the kind that comes with baseball cards. There's nothing nutritious about it. We're a sugar generation. It's a real upper. I wonder if Hitler chewed a lot of it."

DEBORAH HARRY (*Blondie*): "I blow-o-o-o-o, shoobie-doobie-doo. My favorite is SuperBubble, the big new sugary kind. I've been blowing bubbles since 1802, when I was a child."

The Art of Bad Rock:
Making 'Spinal Tap'

Michael McKean as David St. Hubbins—Lead Singer: *McKean does an about-face from his most famous role, greased-up goof Lenny on 'Laverne & Shirley.' He starred in the film 'Young Doctors in Love.'*

Christopher Guest as Nigel Tufnel—Lead Guitarist: *Comedy writer Guest is best known for 'National Lampoon' work. He's also an accomplished musician, has written songs with McKean for 15 years.*

Harry Shearer as Derek Smalls--Bassist: *Shearer is a founder of L.A.'s popular satirical group, the Credibility Gap, and formerly of 'Saturday Night Live.' Film debut: 'Abbott and Costello Go to Mars.'*

LOS ANGELES—The word is out: *This Is Spinal Tap* is one of the most hilariously original movies in years.

What started as a skit on a TV special six years ago has rolled into a rock phenomenon. A mock documentary about a rapidly tarnishing British heavy-metal band's last gasp, the film is attracting record crowds in New York, Los Angeles, Boston and Chicago, and is to open nationally Friday.

The spoof has been so successful, people are walking into record stores and requesting such nonexistent Spinal Tap albums as *Smell the Glove* and *Intravenous de Milo* (a soundtrack album is available on PolyGram, however).

There's no way just one twisted mind could be responsible for inventing a band that sings lyrics such as these: "Just crank that volume to the point of pain / Why waste good music on a brain."

In fact, there are four twisted minds, and they also star in the film. Director Rob Reiner, best known as Archie Bunker's son-in-law Mike Stivic on *All in the Family,* is filmmaker Marty DiBergi, the man who turned down *The Attack of the Full Figured Gals* to immortalize Spinal Tap on celluloid. His co-creators, comic veterans Christopher Guest, Michael McKean and Harry Shearer, play musicians Nigel Tufnel, David St. Hubbins and Derek Smalls, respectively.

Shot with handheld cameras in 16mm and blown up to 35mm to achieve the proper docu-graininess, the film is spookily authentic—mainly because of its totally improvised script.

"We shot the film in five weeks and Rob cut it from 50 hours down to 82 minutes," McKean says. "We never rehearsed a scene with maybe two exceptions for logistics and move."

While there was no screenplay, there was an elaborate band history—listing scores of personnel changes (Spinal Tap's drummers have an unfortunate habit of exploding onstage), name changes and record titles spanning 17 years.

As a result, *Spinal Tap* gleefully wallows in almost every rock-documentary cliché, from the use of TV-show footage in The Who's *The Kids Are Alright* to the classic clash of personalities in the Beatles' *Let It Be.*

But most critics are comparing *Spinal Tap* to Martin Scorsese's loving look at The Band's final concert, *The Last Waltz.*

"If we took anything from *The Last Waltz,*" Shearer says, "it was that kind of self-consciousness verging on pretentiousness."

Unlike other media-made groups such as the Partridge Family, the Archies and the Monkees, the *Spinal Tap* actors played, sang and wrote all the songs.

"We've all watched these movies where any time a rock 'n' roller started to play it was like, 'Don't watch my fingers,'" Shearer says. "We thought it would be nice if someone did a film where you actually believed that these people were onstage playing this music. We seemed like the best-qualified people to do the job."

Adds McKean, "Actually, we were the low bid."

As for the songs themselves—such ear-splitting crunchers as *Big Bottom* and *Sex Farm*—Shearer says, "The music is parody music—it's a lot shorter than real songs would be. It gives you the feeling that you've been listening to this horrible music for a long time and it's only two-and-a-half minutes."

To warm up for the filming, Guest, McKean and Shearer, along with keyboardist David Kaff and drummer R.J. Parnell, played their repertoire of 11 parody rock songs at clubs around Los Angeles. "We were way out of tune and we couldn't hear each other and the wigs weren't right, but it was OK," McKean says.

The trio is now dealing with real-life record executives as the film's soundtrack album, MTV video and single, *Hell Hole,* get air play.

Is this the beginning or the end of Spinal Tap?

"There's a very old saying in the comedy business," Shearer says, "Leave them wanting more."

141

Robert Crane

Give Us a Little Respect

Temptations Otis Williams and Melvin Franklin, otherwise known as the Tempests in the Motown Teapot, talk (finally) about their celebrated split with soul-music Godfather Berry Gordy

The Temptations, after a 17-year association with Berry Gordy and Motown Records, which included 17 gold albums and a platinum album, have left the "family" in search of what any superstar group deserves . . . respect.

It was on their recent world tour that we caught up with them in Phoenix and talked to original Temptations Otis Williams and Melvin Franklin about their split with Motown.

OUI: What were your problems with the Berry Gordy organization?

OTIS WILLIAMS: Well, in the event that anybody from Motown should read this, I'm saying this in the hope that it will make them change. The problem was respect. We are human beings before we are Temptations, Supremes, Marvin Gayes or anything else. That was one of our main problems, aside from the contractual agreements and the finances. Anytime you have somebody telling you— here we are thirty-four and thirty-five years old at the time—"You guys get rid of your lawyer and things will be much better for you around here," you know things aren't right.

MELVIN FRANKLIN: It was difficult to leave. We were established there. They helped us maintain over the years but we didn't like their attitude towards us. Being in the business for sixteen, seventeen years, you learn a lot. You have to learn in order to make it and not wind up a "Joe Louis-type story" in show business. You've got to make money not only on your tours—you've got to make mechanical monies. You've got to get set up so you get money from publishing. There have to be incentives for an artist to do the right thing, to become a stable entity. There's a lot of money made in the record industry, and naturally the companies feel important, and they are. But the artists are important as well. They never gave us the opportunity to work toward some sort of financial security. We couldn't follow that path. We had to leave. We liken our feelings about the split to the sadness of a divorce. You may start off in love with a woman and then, after seventeen years, a whole lot of little things build up.

OTIS WILLIAMS: When you look back and think about the tired little contract we had while we were selling millions and millions of records, and then you think about the contract we have now, you realize how much they capitalized on the fact that we were so young and naïve. Detroit's not known for entertainment lawyers and accountants; so when we took our contracts to attorneys, they said, "Yeah, that's fine. Go ahead and sign it." We weren't conscious of what we were doing.

OUI: The Temptations, up until recently, were guided or managed by Berry Gordy. How can you get a good deal when your manager is also the president of your record label?

MELVIN FRANKLIN: You can't.

142

OTIS WILLIAMS: That's been one of the great drawbacks of the Temptations and, I guess, a lot of the other acts that were managed by Motown. Gordy and the company are naturally going to think of themselves first. How could they be objective? Melvin and I have always been the kind of guys who would go outside and talk to other people to evaluate what Motown had told us. That's why we've learned a lot, and that's one thing they didn't want us to do. What they thought of us was kind of summed up a few years ago when they wanted us to go to the Orient right when the United States and Korea were about to get into a conflict over the Pueblo incident. We said, "Hey, brother, we're not going over there if that's going on," and they said, "Oh, come on, you guys go over there and you'll have plenty of broads to screw." Well, we don't have to go all the way to the other side of the world for that when we get enough here. But that's how they thought of us—that all we wanted to do was get girls to screw and carry on, that that was all we knew.

MELVIN FRANKLIN: I remember once we were in a very serious meeting about management. We were trying to find a good structure for the Temptations to work independently of Motown. We needed management with objectivity. I told them being a record company and a manager was a conflict of interest, and they said, "That's a lawyer's term; you can't use that." In other words, we weren't supposed to have the intelligence to know that.

OUI: Did you ever discover any out-and-out questionable business practices on the part of Motown?

MELVIN FRANKLIN: Oh, yeah. We were the first artists who had enough nerve to audit Motown. People used to say, "If it's so bad, why have you stayed so long?" But it's tough when you're part of something from the first brick and you know the people personally. I mean, we sang at the funeral for Berry Gordy's mother. We felt part of the whole overall thing. But Motown execs should have found enough time to take a microscopic view of the entire Temptations situation. They kept looking out for themselves. Now it's time for us to look out for ourselves.

OTIS WILLIAMS: We questioned a lot of things Motown did. Back in 1975, when we had a big seller with the album *A Song for You*, they turned around after all that hard work and released an album with a lot of mediocre material by this producer and that producer. We told them that album wasn't going to do anything and, sure enough, it didn't.

MELVIN FRANKLIN: The people expected quality material from the Temptations. I'm gonna say this right out: They did it with Thelma Houston, too. She had a big record and they came right behind it with a low-keyed-type thing. It wasn't consistent. How can an artist ever get any good traction? They had the whole ball of wax. You should have read the contract.

OTIS WILLIAMS: That's another thing that made us mad. Motown was taking all the bows and I guess that's automatic, but it's not always the truth. Very seldom did they say, "Yeah, the Tempts were responsible for that."

MELVIN FRANKLIN: Like when our producer, Norman Whitfield, and Motown took the bows for our Grammy for *Cloud Nine*. We were known as the Norman Whitfield Singers back then. Boy, did that stab home. They just wanted us to sing. They didn't want us to write or try to produce. We were damn near producing the sessions a whole lot of the time anyway. They never even gave us a credit for helping with the production of the album, to let people know the Temptations had those abilities. That's why people like the Jacksons left Motown. Their father wanted them to produce, to grow, to have publishing. These are the mechanics that make you money ten years from now, your catalog becoming worth something. There's a person at Motown whom we mentioned publishing to once and he foamed at the mouth.

OUI: Do you think somebody runs Berry Gordy? The Mafia, perhaps?

OTIS WILLIAMS: You never know. I don't believe so. Personally, from dealing with Berry on a pretty close basis, I know that just about every time something goes down they go to him for the decision, and he throws out the yesses and nos and maybe-sos. It looks like he's the main man behind it. I guess those rumors started because Motown started out all black, and then after a while there were personnel changes. I think a lot of it was the way Motown ran the overall machinery, which tended to inspire those kinds of ideas. I do know they always check with him. I don't know if he has to check with somebody else.

MELVIN FRANKLIN: I don't know. I don't feel it, though. There was a time back in the Sixties that I thought maybe some takeovers were coming around. But in retrospect, I don't think the Mob is in there.

OUI: Then why are people afraid to talk about Motown?

MELVIN FRANKLIN: More than a fear, I think it's pride or shame.

OTIS WILLIAMS: People may be scared of a lawsuit.

MELVIN FRANKLIN: Berry delegated the responsibility of various acts to different people at different times. As the company grew, they got executives from other fields; like one time they got a guy who had worked for Coca-Cola. He had no knowledge of the record business but he was an executive type. They hired another guy who had been in politics. Berry Gordy was like the admiral. Otis and I could speak directly to Gordy, but there were usually other people to go through. We would save going to Berry Gordy as a last resort. We would try to work it out within the corporate structure. If Motown continues to grow and strive for success, they really should consider getting competent people, not just people who are there because they stroked Berry Gordy.

OTIS WILLIAMS: They killed my incentive for wanting to be an executive at Motown. I don't think you should have to fear somebody you work for. You can respect someone without having to be afraid to say something for fear he'll start cussing you out or whatever. Gordy's nothing but a man—he's no god. He doesn't warrant that kind of fear. Since we signed with Atlantic, we can see how differently they run their corporation. It's the way we always imagined it. You can see it. First of all, they treat you as people.

OUI: Since the Temptations have been around a long time, do you feel Gordy was tired of the whole group, the sound, the style?

MELVIN FRANKLIN: In the beginning, he had definite interest in us. He loved our good ol' harmonies, the fact that all of us could sing lead. He was a crux of a whole lot of the creative force going all the way through Motown, especially in its inception.

OTIS WILLIAMS: I think as time went on and as Motown became more and more successful, he wanted to get into movies and stretch out into other areas, and his interest in us and other groups wasn't as intense.

OUI: Did the corporate move from Detroit to Los Angeles have any effect on Gordy?

OTIS WILLIAMS: I wouldn't doubt it. After he left Detroit, where he was used to having everything pretty locked up, he encountered L.A., where the competition was pretty stiff. He was dealing with RCA across the street, Columbia, Warner Brothers, Atlantic, a lot of the other majors. These companies had a different philosophy. Motown's concept was they wanted it all—all the publishing, all the production. They stifled us from being creative people in areas other than singing.

MELVIN FRANKLIN: Motown had to become a more sophisticated organization when it moved to L.A., in order to compete with the real record companies.

OTIS WILLIAMS: When Gordy moved to Los Angeles, a lot of his acts started leaving. The Tempts wanted to leave as far back as 1968.

MELVIN FRANKLIN: It's been an eight-to-nine-year battle.

OUI: How long can the Tempts go on?

OTIS WILLIAMS: As long as the public wants the Tempts and we have our health and strength and voices. We plan on being around as long as God and the public permit.

Aimee Mann

The indie rocker hits some high notes on record labels, hackneyed lyrics and Britney Spears

Aimee Mann fears nothing. Not even a clichéd comparison to David and Goliath. The embattled singer, 39, has taken on corporate entertainment giants Seagram and Universal, labels Epic, Geffen and Interscope, and Svengali music executives Jimmy Iovine and Ted Fields. Despite her waifish appearance, Mann is a survivor in a landscape littered with show business casualties.

After dropping out of the Berklee School of Music in the early Eighties, Mann formed a seminal New Wave band, Til Tuesday, which became an MTV favorite. Voices Carry (written by Mann) made the Billboard Top Ten and the album sold more than a million copies. The band recorded three albums for Epic before leaving the label over creative differences—that is, Epic wanted more top 40 dance-pop. It took Mann three years to get out of her contract; in the meantime she was unable to record or release new material elsewhere. Finally, starting over, Mann went solo, recording the critically acclaimed Whatever, for the ill-fated Imago label. Her second solo album, I'm With Stupid, was eventually sold to Geffen Records, which released it to even more acclaim in 1996.

In 1999, eight of Mann's songs were featured in Paul Thomas Anderson's Magnolia, with one, Save Me, earning her an Academy Award nomination (she lost to Phil Collins) and a Golden Globe nomination. Mann's third solo album, Bachelor No. 2, went into limbo when Geffen became a casualty of the merger of Universal and Polygram. Mann and her manager, Michael Hausman, finally bought back the collection of songs and released it on her own label, SuperEgo Records, available through aimeemann.com.

Robert Crane caught up with the attractively lanky singer at the Coffee House in West Hollywood. Crane reports: "Mann is a fierce defender of artistic independence. Her husband of three years, singer-songwriter Michael Penn, has been through similar battles. They tour together, armed with a wicked sense of humor. Mann is dedicated and opinionated. She takes no prisoners. But she loves to laugh, and when she smiles, the whole room lights up."

1

PLAYBOY: What's Thanksgiving like at the Penn household, and who is the alpha brother?

MANN: I think Michael is, but my guess is each one of them would dispute that. Usually we go to Michael's mother's house—or we have in the past. And there's always some brother arguing with another. That's sort of notable.

2

PLAYBOY: If you ran a record label, how would you tell an artist you didn't like his or her album?

MANN: That was never my problem with record labels. They liked my record or didn't like my record. My problem was when they didn't like my record, wouldn't put it out and then wouldn't let me leave the label—you're stuck on a label that doesn't want you. If somebody thinks there's no way they can sell a record, that's an intelligent thought based on practical matters. But nobody has those conversations with you. They just say, "We're not going to put it out." They don't say, "Here's why. Here's our difficulty." It's like, "Well, it's not commercial enough. We don't think we can sell 3 million records. It's not worth our time." So there you go. As an artist, I never found any room for a creative alternative plan. "Well, how about we market it in this way? How about if we go for a different audience on a smaller level, in this direction, by these means?" Nobody wanted to hear that. If I were running a label, I would sit everybody down and brainstorm and see if we could come up with a way to work it.

3

PLAYBOY: We suspect that your fans are also your husband's fans. Whose fans are more ardent?

MANN: It's kind of the same ballpark. I think that at this juncture I probably have more volume because of the *Magnolia* soundtrack, but other than that, I can't really say.

4

PLAYBOY: When one of you writes a really good song, is the other jealous, or supportive?

MANN: Totally supportive. Jealousy never enters into it. For instance, he plays something for me and I go, "What a great line. That's a great phrase. I love this melody." You just point out the stuff you really like.

5

PLAYBOY: Ever rip each other off?

MANN: No, but sometimes we tread on the same territory and don't really realize it. More often it happens in phrasing or using the same type of metaphor, but I think that's inevitable.

6

PLAYBOY: Do you have pens and pads of paper on your nightstands?

MANN: No. You really have to be in the habit of writing stuff down, and I'm out of the habit because I'm in the touring-and-supporting-the-record mode, which is kind of a bad environment for songwriting. He's much better at it than I am. He has a much larger storehouse of ideas. I have virtually nothing on the back burner. There's no bank of ideas or pages. There's just pretty much nothing. It would have to be from scratch at this point.

7

PLAYBOY: Lilith Fair—care to spill the beans on the offstage antics?

MANN: I did only four shows. It seems that everybody is disgustingly supportive and extremely nice, offering to sing background vocals on other people's songs. There are no jealousies or power struggles of any kind, from what I could observe. It was not only devoid of that, but shockingly the other way. Sarah McLachlan said, "Oh, I love your stuff. I love this song. I'd love to sing it. Come up and play with us." It's one big happy family. And also it's summer, it's outdoors. It feels more like summer camp than being on tour.

8

PLAYBOY: We hear you hung out with Tom Cruise during the making of *Magnolia.* Was he an inspiration to you and the film?

MANN: He's just an amazing guy. Looking at movie stars, you always have to wonder. But he's definitely able to focus on you—whoever you are—when he's talking to you, which is kind of amazing, given that 8 million people are always trying to talk to him at once. But he never blinks, and I find that suspicious. He seems genuinely nice and a kindhearted guy. Pretty rare.

9

PLAYBOY: It seems like some young film stars would much rather be musicians. What don't they understand? Can you offer any advice?

MANN: Like Keanu Reeves? Don't they understand it's a fucking grind? It's a tough job and people have to get over this fucking narcissistic idea that how it looks is more important than how it is. Yes, I'm sorry, it looks really glamorous, but it's not. It's work, like any other job. And being on location for two months shooting a movie, at least you're in the same place every day. It's nothing like being in a different place every night and having to forage for food sometimes. That's my existence, anyway. I'm sure Sheryl Crow gets regular meals. You have to be in it for making records and writing songs, which is very rewarding. The other stuff is trying to sell it and that's never the fun part, unless you have a talent for it. If you're a good performer and have a desperate need to be loved by millions, a certain kind of dysfunction can help you along.

10

PLAYBOY: Is music still fun when you're mature enough to forgo indulgences that come with the musical life?

MANN: Music is more fun when you're old enough to really know what you're doing and insist on doing what you really want to do, as opposed to getting pushed around in a hundred directions, none of which you feel comfortable with but you feel you can't refuse, like when you're told, "You ought to learn some dance steps." And when you're young, you're trying to please people who shouldn't necessarily be pleased. They say, "You know, you guys should get a smoke machine." You're like, "Well, I always hated that kind of stuff, but maybe. OK, whatever." Michael and I do what we want with our live show. This is a true "we do not give a shit" rock show. One of the big things I used to hear from managers way, way back when I was in Til Tuesday was, "You have to talk more onstage. You have to talk more to the audience." They actually gave me a piece of paper, like, "Here are some things you should say: How are you feeling tonight? Are you ready to rock?" No kidding. So I've always felt this pressure to talk onstage. When Michael and I started playing Largo in Los Angeles, both of us felt awkward about bantering between songs, so we said, "Fuck it. Let's get one of our comedian friends to do it." So we have a comedian on the road who does our banter for us. It's an insane idea that is so great, and it's entertaining for us. We get a whole comedy show between songs while we're onstage. Couldn't be better.

11

PLAYBOY: Has the need for a single ruined music?

MANN: What's ruining music is record executives who think they know what a single is, without benefit of being a musician, knowing anything about music or fucking listening to music—like, not even being a music fan. If you're a music fan and you listen to 50 songs, there's one song that you keep singing at the end of the day. All right, that's the single. But record executives don't do that. They think there's a formula, and the formula is, "Make it like a song that's already been a hit." That is what has ruined music—executives at record companies who think they are better at making records than musicians and producers—the people who make records.

12

PLAYBOY: Describe examples of hackneyed lyric writing.

MANN: The first one is when you hear the first line and then you can pretty much telegraph what the rhyme is going to be. Like "sitting by the phone, here I am all alone"—that kind of thing. When somebody does a setup that's normal, and then comes in with something you didn't expect, that's pretty satisfying to me. I would also include gambling imagery, though I've done it, too. But cards and dice, those are always good. The elements—wind, fire, earth, nature—are usually bad. Weather in general. Oh my God! Rain—stay away from rain altogether. Rain and sun. The sun should never come out. No rain should come down ever again.

13

PLAYBOY: Can one sing about love too much?

MANN: You've got to change your angle. I mean, love—"Boy/Girl, I love you more than you love me"—yeah, you could definitely sing about that too much. The dynamic that I'm more interested in now is, "You love me and I'm totally incapable of having any kind of human relationship."

14

PLAYBOY: Jewel is now the world's highest-paid poet, reportedly earning $2 million for her book of poetry. Would you care to comment?

MANN: You're just looking for a catfight! Listen, how old was Jewel when she wrote that stuff? Read my lyrics when I was 23 and you'll find I didn't write lyrics any better than she writes poetry. But people are buying it, so somebody likes it. Obviously, nobody gives you $2 million for doing something they don't think is going to sell, so it's to somebody else's benefit to make that deal. And however naïve—or whatever assessment you want to make of Jewel and her poetry—she's the one with the $2 million. I don't think Jewel is naïve or simpleminded in any way. I think she's clever and canny, and she's doing what she wants. When does great art ever get its monetary due? It never happens. Whatever. I can't get that worked up about it. She's fine. She's great. She's beautiful. She has a great voice. She's perfect. She's exactly what everyone wants.

15

PLAYBOY: Any advice for the current crop of nymphet singers?

MANN: Where would you even start? I think these stars are primarily singers and performers. I thought of myself primarily as a songwriter and not a very good performer, so I come from a whole different mind-set. Also, they are moneymakers who won't encounter the kind of problems that I do. I don't think they're going to come out with albums that make anybody doubt their ability to sell them, but if they want to, they should stick to their guns. They'll get a bunch of shit for it, and

I'll quote somebody—I'm not sure, but I think it's Cyril Connolly: "It's better to write for yourself and have no public than to write for the public and have no self." My friend Andy Kindler is one of the comics we have on the road. One of his jokes is his advice to aspiring performers: "Take the high road—less traffic."

16

PLAYBOY: What two things does Britney Spears have going for her?

MANN: That's a pitiful question [*laughs*]. She's lovely and she can sing and dance. She's a great performer. She doesn't write, does she? I don't even know. Did she write that song? You never know, because these kids are so young. It's fun to dress up and dance and sing, but at the end of the day when they're done with that, maybe they'll go, "What I really feel best about is serious songwriting." But then it will be difficult because executives will always look at them with dollar signs in their eyes and know that they can market the hell out of them the same way they had before.

17

PLAYBOY: Do you think of your music as elitist?

MANN: Well, it's very niche-oriented. Yes, you might have to read a book. That is one of the basic requirements. It might help if you're familiar with the English language. I can't call that elitist. You don't need a glossary to fucking understand my language. I think my lyrics are conversational. They're the kinds of conversations I have. Everyone's invited. If you have a hard time keeping up, we'll give you some books to read first. I mean, c'mon. I'm not overly intellectual. I don't think I'm intellectual at all. But compared with people who toss lyrics on top of a little tune and don't care if it makes any linear sense at all, the contrast is fairly literate, I guess, but it's not arcane in any way.

18

PLAYBOY: The Penn boys are enormously talented. What are their hidden talents?

MANN: The other two, Sean and Christopher—first of all, I don't know that much about them. But nobody juggles at Thanksgiving, for instance. I think they're actors through and through. Michael is an extraordinary human being. He's extremely smart. It's not hidden talents so much; it's his hidden interests that are kind of surprising. He knows an enormous amount about theology, the history of the Catholic Church and the occult roots of Nazism. He's a fascinating guy.

19

PLAYBOY: You've complained that too much emphasis has been put on attractiveness. While it's a problem, you certainly qualify. Is it so wrong to get the message from a messenger who is physically appealing?

MANN: Lucky for me, because if I weren't, I'd be fucked. I don't think it's wrong, but I think we've been trained to dismiss music from people who aren't attractive. Janis Joplin could never get a record deal today. Carole King? C'mon. *Tapestry* was a big hit because it was a great record, and I think she's attractive. But she's not a goddamn model, and she would never get a record deal today. Never. Forget it. And that's why you have Jewel instead of Carole King, and if the music suffers a little bit, so be it. But we already have models. We can look at beautiful women until the cows come home. There are good-looking girls who are young and are great performers and that's always fine, but it's definitely at the expense of more-talented people who could really bring depth to one's musical world. But people aren't looking for that. They're overentertained. They're accustomed to constant entertainment, which has to be lighter, because you can't work with that volume of entertainment if any of it's meaningful.

20

PLAYBOY: Men have muses. What do women have?

MANN: Problems. Actually, I don't think men have muses. Michael doesn't. A woman dreamed up that one. "I'm going to be his muse. That's how I'm going to contribute to great art. I'm going to sit there and look hot." If you want to be his muse, give him a hard time. Then he'll really have something to write about.

Robert Crane

Ruben Blades:

Serious Salsa

With Central America's political corruption and bloodshed headlining the daily news, it was only a matter of time until a nonviolent, clear and honest Latino voice emerged for North America to embrace. Panamanian singer-songwriter Rubén Blades and his group Seis del Solar have impressed concert audiences and critics around the world with a blend of love songs, political ruminations, character sketches and everyday experiences, all of them set to the sizzling beat of the spicy music known as salsa.

"I am, in essence, a salsa or Afro-Cuban artist," says the subject of "The Return of Rubén Blades," an hour-long documentary that airs July 2 as part of the *Summer Night Music* series. "But the music has done itself a disservice by its lack of interchange with other musics." After years of recording big-band albums in Spanish on the Latin American Fania label, Blades finally signed with the American Elektra label in 1984. The result was a trio of ground-breaking Latin albums, all of them still sung by him in Spanish: *Buscando America* ("Searching for America"), *Escenas* ("Scenes") and *Agua de Luna* ("Moon Water").

Blades recently broadened his audience further by releasing his first-ever English-language album, entitled, with his usual sense of candor, *Nothing but the Truth.* This literate and visionary work utilizes rock, pop and ballad styles, along with Blades' trademark salsa, as it takes the listener on a journey through an agenda of pressing contemporary issues—among them the exploitation of Latin America, United States foreign policy, bigotry, AIDS. Song titles like "The Miranda Syndrome" (a look at the stereotyping of Latins, using Carmen Miranda as an example), "Letters to the Vatican," "In Salvador" and "Ollie's Doo-wop" (ironically commenting on the jingoistic philosophy of Oliver North) attest to Blades' disparate political concerns. And he has enlisted the help of some of popular music's most famous and politically aware players—Sting, Elvis Costello and Lou Reed. Although cultural chauvinists will disapprove of Blades' entry into American musical styles, his Latin American identity is still vividly present in every cut on the album, from the role politics plays in everyday life to the rhythms, arrangements and signature salsa sensibility.

"I'm always fighting stereotype—the rose in your teeth, ruffles, saying 'Olé,' small waistline, dancing tango," says Blades, who, before he became a full-time singer, earned a master's degree from Harvard Law School and worked as an attorney. "I've been writing political songs since 1969—social portraits of Latin America, not just songs that said, 'Come on, baby, let's dance.'" Unlike some popular artists who only play to the converted, Blades' point of view is so individualistic that he won't make the music or the lyrics easy, refusing to massage anyone's ears. "I wasn't about to become an adventurer in search of money," he asserts, unlike many of the current pop stars who simply seem out for a quick buck. "Nor was I interested in a popularity that is obtained by compromising one's position as an artist or a person. So it took me a while to realize that I was ready to perform in English."

Although the fact has not been widely publicized, Blades, in a change of pace, wrote the Spanish translation of Michael Jackson's recent hit "I Just Can't Stop Loving You" ("Todo Mi Amor Eres Tu"). And he coached the superstar singer through the recording session of the Spanish lyric. "I

152

was with him for hours in the studio," Blades recalls. "Michael turned out to be one of the most professional people I know," he says with evident admiration.

In addition to his albums and concert appearances, Blades has recently been answering Hollywood's call—a natural follow-up to his success a few years back in a salsa-inspired film called *Crossover Dreams*. In the past year, he has appeared with Whoopi Goldberg in *Fatal Beauty* and he won favorable reviews for his role as a New Mexican deputy sheriff in Robert Redford's *The Milagro Beanfield War*. Blades also has a cameo role in the upcoming Mickey Rourke film, *Homeboy*. And, as if that weren't enough, he is also mulling over more movie offers, is simultaneously writing his own film script and a short novel, and has just recorded a new Spanish-language album, *Antecedentes* ("Antecedents").

But it is the music that most inspires and drives Rubén Blades. "Today reality is stranger than fiction," he explains. "We are suppressing our love through violence. Hearts don't need visas. When you cry, you don't need subtitles. I'm coming from an emotional position." One of his goals is to prove that artists from different backgrounds, races, cultures and musical styles can collaborate as equals. He believes America is the logical place for this collaboration to happen.

In his song "Calm Before the Storm," Blades sings, "There was a time when ignorance made our innocence strong. There was a time when we all thought we could do no wrong." Instead of trying to recapture those times, Blades is moving forward, celebrating the opportunity to shape something new. He thinks of it as positive opportunism. After a glance at the daily news, any movement in that direction can't hurt.

Chris Isaak

The cable balladeer explains his broken heart, his broken nose and why he likes older women

Some performers collect armloads of awards every year. But Chris Isaak, a 46-year-old Stockton, California native, just hunkers down and does the work. To his amusement, the star of Showtime's Chris Isaak Show is finally receiving big-time kudos. He had a brief career as a boxer in Japan (where his nose was broken), forays into acting with small roles in Married to the Mob (playing a homicidal clown) and Silence of the Lambs (appearing as a SWAT commander) and years of fine-tuning his musical skills in clubs around the country. Then Isaak's profile took off with a monster hit, Wicked Game, which featured a sexy video co-starring supermodel Helena Christensen. He followed with several albums and videos, including a moderate success, Somebody's Crying, that caught critical attention but not the mass appeal of his initial hit. Isaak's good looks earned him a place on People's list of the 50 most beautiful people. He was a natural on the big screen in David Lynch's Twin Peaks: Fire Walk With Me (portraying an FBI agent), Little Buddha opposite Bridget Fonda, Grace of My Heart, and That Thing You do, directed by Tom Hanks. He appeared on television as himself on It's Garry Shandling's Show and The Larry Sanders Show and guest-starred on Friends, Melrose Place and the HBO miniseries From the Earth to the Moon.

Stanley Kubrick chose Isaak's song Baby Did a Bad Thing as the focal point of the soundtrack for his last film, Eyes Wide Shut. CBS commissioned him to compose the theme for its Late Late Show With Craig Kilborn. Then Viacom approached Isaak with an idea to star him and his real band, Silvertone, in a quirky cable series, the Chris Isaak Show. The Showtime series, now in its second season, has caught the attention of critics and guest stars, including Bridget Fonda, Jay Leno, Stevie Nicks, Green Day, Third Eye Blind and Everclear. Isaak recently released his ninth album, Always Got Tonight, and visited U.S. troops in Afghanistan with Dwight Yoakam, among others.

Robert Crane caught up with the reluctant star at Sutton Place Hotel in Vancouver, where the series is filmed. Crane reports: "Besides being handsome and talented, Isaak attracts women by being so damned low-key. They seem to want to take care of him. Among his female handlers are an assistant, a manager, publicists and record company staff. Nice gig. Isaak is also an accomplished artist. He drew 12 sketches during our interview, illustrating what he was talking about. His manager wouldn't let us publish them."

1

PLAYBOY: Have you kept any sand in a jar from the *Wicked* video with Helena Christensen?

ISAAK: I didn't keep the sand. I kept the memories. At the time, Helena wasn't a big star. They put her up in a really seedy, mildew-smelling motel. It was in Hawaii, on the big island. I had stayed in that motel before. That's the kind of place I stayed at. They put me up in this really fancy-pants place. Your monogram's on everything. I said, "I really feel it's a waste to put me in this room because it's not what I'm accustomed to. Why don't you put her in my room and I'll go stay at the cheap motel? It's not going to bother me. She'll feel good. She's a girl. She'll have nice fresh sheets." They said, "OK, if you want to." So we switched. At about two in the morning, my

154

girlfriend called and got Helena Christensen on the phone, and I never heard the end of that. To this day, I'm sure she believes there was some kind of hanky-panky. I wasn't even at the hotel, but she wouldn't take no for an answer. She said, "I know! I know what was going on. You can't pull the wool over my eyes." Often accused, often guilty, yet only convicted for crimes I didn't commit.

2

PLAYBOY: Your nose was broken when you boxed in Japan in your early 20s. When it was reset, did you ask for the upturn, like "Give me the Bob Hope?"

ISAAK: No, it was probably an uppercut that did it. I got what nature gave me. Somebody took a swing and that's what's left. The interesting thing is, when I quit boxing in Japan and was back in the States, some girl I knew was going to get her nose done. She wanted to go to the doctor. She was scared. She said, "Come with me and listen to what he tells me because I'll forget. I'm going to get nervous." So I went into the room. The doctor walked in. He looked at me and said, "Oh, we can definitely do something with it. Yes, this is definitely worth doing." I said, "No, I'm not the patient. She is." And he said, "Well, you know, we can take cartilage from your ear and then reconstruct your nose." And I said, "No! I'm fine. I can breathe through it if it's raining." I can't imagine going through surgery and taking cartilage out of my ear. My ear and my nose would look screwed up. I said, "I'll just wait a few more years. I'm a guy." I don't have to worry about that stuff. Ten years from now, who cares? I'll just be another gray-haired guy on a beach.

3

PLAYBOY: Who sings better love songs? You or Dwight Yoakam?

ISAAK: Dwight's a pretty good singer. He's a hell of a writer. It's always hard to judge your own work, but I would put Dwight at the top of his class. When you listen to the quality of his songwriting, there are real stories there, and you can take them into your own life. He's a smart guy. Don't let the cowboy hat fool you. I spent 23 hours with him on an Air Force cargo plane going to Afghanistan. We entertained the troops together. It was a lot of fun. Bridget Fonda was on my TV show playing my girlfriend, and that's his girlfriend in real life. So, for 23 hours, I kept saying, "Yeah, you know, Bridget is a hell of a kisser, Dwight. She's really got it going on. It must be a lot of fun, huh?" He's a funny guy. He's a pilot. He was in the front of the plane almost all the way. He was hoping they might let him fly the plane a little bit. I said, "No, I hope to God they don't let you fly the plane. It would be a desperate Air Force." He also gets extremely worked up if you mention the Taliban. He's ready to put on fatigues.

4

PLAYBOY: Whose idea was it to have a nude woman on the rotating turntable?

ISAAK: It's based on Bimbo's nightclub in San Francisco. We played Bimbo's because I wanted to have a home base besides my house. A place where you could say, "Where's the band? Where do they work out, play, hang out?" Bimbo's has a great restaurant, it's a nightclub big enough to have fun, but small enough to be intimate. And below the club there was a labyrinth of mirrors, with a woman rotating on a table and her image reflecting up through the mirrors into an aquarium behind the bar. This has been there since 1930. It's like some magical trick. So we thought this would be impressive for the TV show. Actually, it's better than a video game. If you have a few beers, it really looks like she's swimming in the fish tank. I went down there a couple of times. When you have time between sets, you don't want to go out into the club; it's noisy. So you go talk to the woman on the table. She likes the attention. She's just killing time down there.

5

PLAYBOY: Do you ever lose your lines?

ISAAK: Oh, because of that? No. A lot of people joke with me. "You must hate that, working with that beautiful nude woman." Bobby Jo Moore, who plays Mona, is the sweetest girl and as much like a sister as you could have. Every time I see her, it's "Hi, Chris." "What're you doing, Bobby?" "I'm making cookies for my nieces." "Hi, Chris. I'm decorating Christmas cards for everybody." I was on the *Rosie O'Donnell Show* and they asked me about her. I said, "She's this sweet girl who's always doing things for her nieces and nephews." Rosie said she should have her on her show. Bobby was staying at my manager's house. Rosie called her up, and Bobby said, "Are you kidding me?" Then she named all of Rosie's kids. I asked her, "How do you know all the names?" "Because Rosie works with children, and I want to work with children someday, too. And I'm really proud of her." And I was thinking, "Nice people. I forgot they existed." On the show she's naked, but there's no sexuality between us—she is totally a mentor. She has reached nirvana and she's helping me get there. I never hit on her and she never comes on to me. Sex is the last thing going through your head. What's really going through your head is, I have 10 seconds to deliver this line, because you have to hit the mark as she turns around. Those scenes are very exacting.

6

PLAYBOY: You find your own clothes, right?

ISAAK: I try to find my own clothes. They got me some stuff for the show because TV just eats up clothes. You go through clothes because you're shooting 20 different scenes every week and each scene calls for a different set of clothes. I try to go to the junk store with the wardrobe people once in a while and find secondhand stuff that's cheap. We get a few new things to sprinkle in with the old stuff. And to come up with something flattering.

7

PLAYBOY: Don't you have some of your outfits made?

ISAAK: The stage suits I have are things I get interested in. I'll actually sketch designs and talk to the people making the stage clothes. I meet rock stars who are on the show and they look at the clothes I'm wearing and ask, "Is that Versace? Armani?" I don't know. Usually it came from Goodwill [*showing label of sweater he's wearing*]. I think this is some Catholic school sweater. It is. School Apparel. I think that's an offshoot of Armani. It's nice to have designer things once in a while, but a lot of the stuff I have is junk. The only people who notice the good stuff are the people who can afford it. That leaves all my friends out. It's always hysterical to me when people look at a black T-shirt and say, "Is that by such-and-such?" "Yeah, if it was it would be 500 bucks. And it'll still be a black T-shirt." Prada. I think they must have a guy there who sews really slow. Nice stuff, but he just takes his time. I've always liked stage clothes that looked like you dressed up for the show. My band wears suits. None of us look like fashion models. We're not the guys you can put in Levi's and T-shirts and the women would scream. So I've always thought, Let's dress up and look nice. Let people walking in think they came to a nice show. "Look, honey. I spent 25, 50 bucks. I drove downtown, had to park the car. And these guys went to the trouble to get dressed up." It would bug me if somebody has gone to the trouble to come to the club, and you wander onstage half an hour late, in a dirty T-shirt, smoking a cigarette, in your Levi's. I've seen that. For some people, that's a good act. But for me—we're tipping our hat right from the beginning. Here we are. We're here to entertain you. Even if you don't like the music, we hope you go home and say, "You wouldn't believe what the hell he was wearing!"

8

PLAYBOY: You seem to have loads of monogrammed shirts and jackets. Do you have any monogrammed nonapparel items?

ISAAK: Well, "monogrammed" makes it sound like I'm classy. It sounds like David Niven. David Niven would have DN on all his shirts, demurely set in a corner of a sleeve. Think more like Jethro Bodine. Mine is in glittery, big letters and it's on my guitar in stick-on mailbox letters, like Stevie Ray Vaughan. It's on my guitar strap because I saw B.B. King had his there. It's on my belt because I saw James Dean did it on his belt. It's on my boots because I've seen other people monogram their boots. I put monograms all over things, partially because I always figured people won't know who I am when they're watching TV. And partially because some of the guys I work with aren't really trustworthy. It's like summer camp. My surfboard has my name on it in big letters. I figured if it gets lost at sea, they'll be able to bring it home.

9

PLAYBOY: Define what sort of music you do.

ISAAK: Seventeen years ago I had a three-piece rockabilly band. Seventeen years ago Sting was trying to be pop and now he's avant-garde. I think I am more vocal than pop. Roy Orbison was gleeful one time and said, "People ask me what kind of music I do. I tell them I'm the romantic balladeer." I thought that was a good description for what I try to do—romantic balladeer, and put some rock and roll into it.

10

PLAYBOY: What's the best way to take a vacation?

ISAAK: It's all about weather and food. I'm a basic animal. If I go to Greece and the food is cheap and plentiful, I'm happy. If the food is bad and the weather's cold, get me out of there. I don't care how much wonderful art they have. When I go on a road trip, I love to go to the old side of town. Usually there's a nice side of town, where there's a fancy mall and they have artistic things to do. I go to the old side of town, where there are pawnshops, places that sell hair products and a 5-and-10. Those are the places I love to haunt. They have interesting, weird junk. I never buy expensive antiques on the road. Cary Grant did stuff like that. I don't. Find a local to tell you where the places are to haunt. I went to Thailand. People asked me, "Did you hook up with a girl in Thailand?" That's the last thing in the world you need to do on the road—try to hook up on your day off. You don't need to chase women in some strange country. Just do the tourist things. It's hilarious. Most people won't do it because they feel they are too hip. When I was in Thailand, I went to the capitol building and the museums. All my friends went to bars and they all asked, "Well, what did you think?" I said, "I had a great time." They think I caught something!

11

PLAYBOY: What is the most wicked game you've ever played?

ISAAK: It's usually being played on me. As soon as I completely commit to someone, that's when something lands on my head. The gods are just waiting. For instance, I pulled into my girlfriend's driveway after I'd picked up some food for her because she said she wasn't feeling well. Did her a favor. Let her just lie there and rest. I rang the bell and there was no answer. Poor thing, she's probably so sick she can't get the door. Then I looked and noticed there was another car in the driveway. Well, at least I had my shopping done.

12

PLAYBOY: What's the difference between rock-and-roll fame and television fame?

ISAAK: Rock and roll is a small, specific group that likes your music. Television is a whole bunch of people who didn't particularly want to see you but did. They may like you, or not, but they know who you are because they were too lazy to get up and change the channel. It's like the difference between having a subscription to a magazine or a throwaway newspaper that comes to your house every day. TV is right there—accessible to a lot of people. Because I'm on TV, I'm recognized by people all the time. I was in New York and I walked into the Carnegie Deli. "Hey, Mr. Isaak, come on in. Right here, man. Here's your table." He acted like he knew me. I guess he feels that way because he saw me on TV. I'm glad when somebody knows me. I'm just happy to be treated well. Any kind of smile I get, I'll take. It's all wonderful and good.

13

PLAYBOY: Is fame addictive?

ISAAK: To tell the truth, fame doesn't really do much for me. I want the stuff that goes with it—that green stuff. You get the money and you get control over your art. Every time you're famous, or the band becomes famous, it means we have a few more years on our career—at least playing state fairs. I love playing music. It sounds like a joke, but I would be happy playing bars or state fairs. I would rather do that than sit at home. As far as the fame? My scenario is: Let's imagine Bill Gates calls me. He's watching TV. It's late at night. He and his wife are laying there in their big connubial bed and he looks at the screen and says, "Who's this creep Chris Isaak?" She says, "Honey, he's got a TV show." He says, "I hate him. He's creepy. I can't stand his singing, and I hate his show." "Well, what're you going to do, honey? What can we do about that?" He says, "You know something. I'm a billionaire. I'm the richest man in the world. Have somebody pay him off not to sing." "Really?" "Yeah." So if Bill Gates called and offered me $250 million to never appear on TV again, I'd say, is that cash or a check? Cancel my show. I'll stay home! I'll do all my singing on the beach.

14

PLAYBOY: The rock-and-roll groupie is dead—say it ain't so.

ISAAK: Damn, she was getting old. It's too bad, because I was hoping to get a turn at her, but I guess she's gone now. Well, God bless her. It was probably wearing her out, all these different bands. The word groupie is offensive to me because I think it's demeaning to the women. If you travel all the time, who are you going to meet on the road? You're going to meet everybody on the road. They're the only friends you have. I've always been a singer. Being a singer you end up going back to your room. If you go back with a girl and talk and go to bed and stay up until three in the morning, you won't hit the high notes the next day. I'm conscientious. My relationship with my throat is like a baseball pitcher with his arm. You're not going to blow it out before the game. The other thing is, there's a loneliness that comes with doing that. It sounds fun. People like to fantasize about it, but I think it's really lonely. I'm not blaming anybody. Take some sandwiches back to your room and watch CNN by yourself. I do that a lot. I read something Jewel said in an interview. She said after a gig she was back in her hotel room and all these people wanted her attention. Of course they want her. She's sexy. She said she felt alone. She's in her room saying, "What's wrong with me? Here I am alone. All these people apparently want me." The attention you get is not really about you. It's about the stage and the lights and your glittering suit. But when you go back to your hotel room, you're on your own.

15

PLAYBOY: When is a woman being predatory and when is she being brainy?

ISAAK: You look in people's eyes and the conversation you have with them, you get a pretty good idea of what people want. Some people are pretty bold and up front, and say, "I want you, baby. My girlfriend will wait in the hall." People can be really forward, which is always scary to me. In some ways it's exciting. But it's also terrifying, because you think, Where have you been? If these are your standards, if you'll go with me, my God, you'll go with anyone. I've been lucky to find people in my life who are smart. They're dangerous and I like the danger. In the long run, it's smart women who reinvent themselves, and are a challenge and a stimulus. They bring something to the table everyday. Somebody else who's just looking for breast size and a day care center—if they want to do that, that's OK. Infantilism is a laudable pursuit for somebody. I just don't know that I want to do it full-time. It takes all kinds. Everybody gets a chance to try different things. The best thing is to get somebody that you're physically attracted to and they have something else going on. Charles Bukowski said: Take any beautiful woman that you see. Look at her and realize that somewhere there's a guy who's sick of her. What I take from that is if it's just physical, you're going to get over that. Then you're just changing partners. For me, I'm shooting for the moon. I met somebody who's a complete knucklehead and very cute and sweet. Apparently, her extradition is not going well, so she's going to be here for a while. They're unable to match her fingerprints with the other bodies. So everything's looking good.

16

PLAYBOY: If you could have been in any band, which would it have been?

ISAAK: When I was starting off in the music business, I used to dream about being in the early Sun sessions. I would have loved to have been Scotty Moore, playing guitar in a three-piece, but I wouldn't have been as good. Or I would have loved to have been in the Beatles. What the hell would I have done? I'd have screwed things up. I wish I could have seen those bands. We've played venues where someone has given me a list of who has played there before, like 1960-something or 1955. One bill was Elvis Presley, Johnny Cash, the Everly Brothers, a juggler and some kind of 4H project. Admission was $1.50. I wish I could go back in time and see that. I would love to have seen Elvis playing the Airport Lounge. I read about this. He played at an airport when he was starting out. Somebody said, "What would you pay?" I'd give you $50,000 to see that. I'd give you $100,000 to see that. I would love to have seen the Beatles playing in Hamburg when they were doing three shows a night. I'd give you $100,000 to see that. That's how much of a rock-and-roll freak I am. Those guys are just so impressive and I want to see them when they were rough and raw, and just starting off. I heard the tapes of those early sessions. It's amazing. You always wonder, What did Sam Phillips hear? Sam Phillips is a genius—the guy who produced Elvis—a genius. You listen to the first Elvis tapes and they're rough and raw. But my God, the guy could sing. To digress for a second—I am sitting in my house in Vancouver, working on the TV show like crazy and reading some magazine. It's a Sam Phillips article. I love Sam Phillips as a producer. He started rock and roll. Genius guy and a crazy man. He just did it his own way. At the end of the article, it asked, "Who among modern artists do you like?" And he said Chris Isaak. And I cried! I don't know if he knows that that nice thing he said travels out there and goes to me. I always think that's so cool. I haven't talked with Sam Phillips, and I would love to. I'm such a complete fan of his work. Everybody in rock and roll owes him a debt. He really took chances. Today, there are certain people pretending to be dangerous. But there was a time when rock and roll really was dangerous. That was a time when they were saying, "Hey, this is something that unites black and white, young and old, and brings all these things together." I love that music can break down barriers. That's very cool.

17

PLAYBOY: Could you name some aesthetic offenses of the Seventies?

ISAAK: I can't think of the offenses so much as things I liked. You take any woman and dress her in Seventies fabric, and she looks a little tawdry—but hot. I like that. I'm also the guy who likes all the women on Mexican television because they dress like glamorous hookers. We know it's bad taste. We know it's not fashionable. But we go, "Look at those glittery clothes and makeup." Is there anything that white go-go boots can't help?

18

PLAYBOY: Who do you want on your show?

ISAAK: Mariah Carey. It seems like the press is having a field day saying she's having a hard time. But she wrote all those songs and she produced them. She isn't a piece of fluff. It would be funny for her to come on the show and make fun of the fact that somebody was knuckleheaded enough to pay her millions to be let go. She's going to turn around and have another huge hit. I think she'd be fun. James Coburn. I'd like to have him play my father on the show. A real bad-ass. He looks like my dad, so that would be good. One cool thing about doing this show is people think everybody in Hollywood knows everybody. One minute Shelby Lynn is on and the next minute it's the Goo-Goo Dolls. And Green Day, Third Eye Blind and Art Alexakis from Everclear. Every week is a music education. It's been raining gold, so I haven't been wishing for much.

19

PLAYBOY: Who would be a present to yourself?

ISAAK: She has to be sweet and kind—through the eyes of a child—yet a total freak. You know who I like? That actress who was in the movie *Hud*. She was also in *A Face in the Crowd*. Patricia Neal. That's my type of woman. I always go for the type who was a little older, smarter, been around, seen things. I like the soul. Patricia Neal always did it for me. I always thought Barbara Stanwyck was really hot. Older, but she was still hot. She just looked like somebody who'd give you hell. I need a woman who's smart enough to give me hell. I already have somebody who's giving me hell. It's funny what women think men want, and then there's the reality. You get a bunch of guys in a room and a girl who's drop-dead gorgeous. And there's another girl who's not gorgeous, but every guy in the room is looking at her and going, "Oh my God." It's the way somebody moves, the way they talk, the way they look at you. We were talking to this woman, and she must have been 60-something. I said, "God, she's hot! How is this possible?" My friend said life, it's just boiling out of some people. Other people can be beautiful, but it's like looking at a piece of cardboard.

20

PLAYBOY: Baby can do a bad thing. When is it real bad and when is it unforgivable?

ISAAK: I'm trying to think what I would not forgive if I'm in love. That's the sick thing about the way you love somebody sometimes. "Honey, I know you didn't mean to cut off my legs, right?" "I did! I did mean to cut them off." "Well, I forgive you." There's a song that goes, "I'm here at the barroom thinking of what you have done. I'm just sitting here with this bottle, trying to forgive you." It paints a picture of somebody who's saying, "You did something to hurt me so bad, yet I love you so much I want to forgive you and I can't find a way. Maybe if I get drunk, I can find a way to forgive you." If you really love somebody, you can always come around. When you get a little more experienced, it's harder to judge people. You go, "Yeah, she stole my money. Yeah, she shot my dog. Yeah, she wrecked my car. But you know something? I see why she did it." People don't do something out of downright crazy meanness. I've met a few people who were crazy mean. Usually, people are afraid you're going to hurt them first, so they hurt you. When you see that, it makes you feel sorry for them. Sometimes life does that—throws stuff right in your face and you're confronted with the limitations of your love. I don't feel like I hate the other person. I just feel bad.

Dionne Warwick:

The Hits Keep Coming

Superstar singer Dionne Warwick, together with the songwriting team of Burt Bacharach and Hal David, is responsible for an unprecedented string of hits that, during the sixties and early seventies, crossed the categorical borders between pop, rhythm and blues, gospel, blues and jazz. Reading the list of her song titles is like scanning a history of contemporary popular music: "Don't Make Me Over," "Walk on By," "You'll Never Get to Heaven," "A House Is Not a Home," "Message to Michael," "Trains and Boats and Planes," "Alfie," "Do You Know the Way to San Jose?"

Though tremendous credit is due to Bacharach and David, it is Warwick's powerful and elegant performances that linger in the memories of nightclub and concert audiences and radio listeners alike. Reviewing her distinctive singing style, a critic for the *New York Post* wrote, "Her technique is so remarkable that it almost defies description. With enormous range and dexterity, Warwick's voice is pulsing, veering, zigzagging current, but always sure, on the button, now light, now dark, now bloodied, now whole."

That remarkable voice had its roots in gospel. Dionne grew up in a gospel family and gained her first musical experience as an organist and occasional vocalist with the Drinkard Singers, a church choir group. Later, while studying at the Hartt College of Music, Dionne and her sister and cousin formed a trio, the Gospelaires. When the group sang backup during a 1960 recording session for the Drifters, Warwick's voice caught the ear of then-fledgling composer Bacharach. She started cutting demos of the songs that Bacharach and David were writing, and the threesome wound up with a recording contract from Scepter Records.

In 1962, "Don't Make Me Over," the first release from the Warwick-Bacharach-David team, became a top-ten smash. The string of emotionally and technically demanding ballads that followed would set a new standard as the most sterling recorded performances of the era.

"I would like to think that the public is as conscious of quality as I have been over the years," says Warwick, summing up a quarter-century of hitmaking. "The public expects it from the very first record on. Hopefully, I've given it to them. Working with two of the finest songwriters that ever existed, it was hard not to come up to that mark."

Her own favorite among all those hits is the poignant ballad "The Windows of the World." Explains Warwick, "It addresses a lot of things that unfortunately are still happening in the world today. The song is a way of saying, 'Let's do something about all the craziness in the world.'"

When the Warwick-Bacharach-David team broke up in the early seventies, Dionne experienced a dry creative period until Clive Davis and Arista Records signed her up. Now working with such diverse songwriter-producers as Isaac Hayes and Barry Gibb, Warwick picked up where she left off with hit records like "Déjà Vu," "Heartbreaker" and "I'll Never Love This Way Again." She still pins her success on her never-ending pursuit of quality. "As long as the song is good and the recording has the quality people are accustomed to," says Warwick, "the chances of it becoming a hit record are as good today as they were ages ago." And Warwick refuses to rest on her well-earned laurels. "I can't afford to be complacent," she says. "All these nice, wonderfully talented young people coming along"—including Warwick's niece, Whitney Houston—"have kept all of us vets on our toes."

Warwick's love of live performance has never wavered, and it's manifest in her July 30 PBS performance with the Boston Pops Orchestra on *Evening at Pops.* She enjoys seeing a gradual change in the people who come to hear her. "My audience is growing up with me," Warwick says with a smile. "What's even nicer is to see that they're bringing their families with them."

Secure in a musical role that now spans generations, Warwick has set her sights on a whole new set of goals. Her quartet with Elton John, Gladys Knight and Stevie Wonder, "That's What Friends Are For" (written by Burt Bacharach and Carole Bayer Sager), raised over a million dollars for AIDS research and was widely honored with awards and praise for the good work it accomplished. In a different vein, in 1986 she launched her own line of perfume, Dionne, which is selling well. There's also the occasional flirtation with acting, including an appearance in last year's movie *Rent-a-Cop,* which starred Burt Reynolds and Liza Minnelli. "I've always said that there were a lot of things I was capable of doing," Warwick explains, "and it's nice to be given the opportunity to show that I can."

Such successful stretches aside, it's still the remarkable voice, the glamorous yet understated sense of style and the matchless string of golden hits that define Dionne Warwick for millions of people and that will endure. And her love affair with her work and her life continues to be what matters most. "I enjoy what I do so much that that's ninety percent of the battle," says Warwick. "Everything else other than that is like having whipped cream and cherries on top."

Best of The Beatles: A Bittersweet Look Back

"Of all sad words of tongue or pen the saddest are these: It might have been." Pete Best missed out on more, by less, than most of us can fathom. Twenty years later, he's finally coming to grips with the phenomenon he wasn't part of.

Drummer Pete Best was considered the most popular Beatle by some when the young rockers, then known as the Silver Beatles, worked the raunchy Liverpool pop scene in 1962. Best toiled with John Lennon, Paul McCartney, and George Harrison in the early dues-paying days of the mop-top quartet, but he was replaced by the impish Ringo Starr shortly after their breakthrough Hamburg tour.

Why was Best abruptly dismissed just as the Fab Four were at the brink of superstardom? According to Best, jealousy, intergroup rivalry, and managerial deception all played a part in his ouster. Others insist Best was thrown out of the band because his playing was not up to par and Ringo Starr just happened to be a better drummer.

Following his split from the Beatles, Best worked with several local bands until he retired from show business in 1968. He finally took a mundane government job to support his family while he recovered from the shock of what might have been. But can there be life after the Beatles? How did he feel after investing so much time and energy into the band, watching it soar off without him to become one of the greatest musical groups of all time?

Best has now resurfaced, breaking a self-imposed, 20-year silence to promote a previously unreleased collection of the early Silver Beatles sessions. OUI magazine is happy to present this candid, revealing interview with drummer Pete Best, "The Lost Beatle."

OUI: You barely missed out on one of the all-time great show-business phenomenons. How does it feel?

BEST: Initially, a lot of heartache. The two years I'd been with them, we'd been through thick and thin, bad times, good times, and just on the virtual eve of the phenomenon, I was out. Consequently, it caused me a lot of grief, a sort of heartache inside because of the fact that I should have been part of the Beatles. It goes without saying, financially . . . well, that speaks for itself. Even my home life, my personal life was affected by it. But you've got to persevere. What I've strived to do is make the best of what's available around me and lead my life in an enjoyable way. That's the way I play it at the present moment.

OUI: What have the last 20 years been like for you?

BEST: There have been a few peaks. For the next six years, I stayed in show business. It sort of went up and down, but that's show business. You expect that.

When I finally decided to quit show business in 1968, my life took a dive. It went down to virtually zero. I decided I had a family to bring up, I wanted to get a routine job, become a normal person, get security for the family, and I thought it would be easy to walk into a job. That wasn't the case.

I went round to employers and filled in the employment sheet. "What have you been doing since leaving school?" Show business. They went, "Oh, oh. Hang on a minute. This guy's a fly-by-night. He's gonna ghost in for a couple of weeks, and the first time he gets the show-biz bug, he's gonna be back on the road again."

I persevered until the offer came to be a bake-house laborer, which wasn't paying a lot of money. It meant I had to work shifts, work weekends, overtime, work all the hours that God created to get a livable wage. During that time, my lifestyle had gone down to rock bottom, and apart from friends who stuck round me, I was an outcast. The show-business circle had closed. My own personal friends were there, shoulders to lean on, so to speak. They weren't the hangers-on or associates who disappear overnight once your credibility goes.

For 12 months, I pulled through until the offer came to join the government service which, again, is a secure job. Since then, the lifestyle has taken a turn for the better. I know that I can face people. I've got a lifestyle I adhere to which is happy for myself, keeps the family content, allows me to mix with the true friends. I know I can still pay the bills and spend a little at the end of the week.

OUI: How long have you been married?

BEST: This year will make 20 years. I've got two girls, 18 and 14. I'm still living in Liverpool.

OUI: How did you originally hook up with John, Paul, and George?

BEST: They initially opened my mother's club, the Casbah. It was a coffee club. They were known then as the Quarrymen. They were just a guitar lineup, no drummer or anything like that. They had another guy with them called Ken Brown, who left them over a disagreement about some cash. They used to play the club on a Saturday night, but they'd come by during the week, and we buddied up.

They finished playing at the Casbah and went to have an audition with Larry Parnes. During that time, they changed their name to the Silver Beatles. They toured Scotland with Johnny Gentle, and by this time, Stu Sutcliffe had joined them and played bass. They had a drummer who stood in called Tommy Moore. At the end of the tour, Tommy Moore said that he'd had enough, he was packing up.

I had a group, and we were playing the Casbah, but I knew that my group wasn't going to stay together much longer because some of the guys were going on to the university. Paul and the rest had seen me playing drums at the club with my group, the Blackjacks. I got a phone call from Paul, and he said, "Hey, Pete, we got an offer to go to Germany. We need a drummer. Are you interested in joining?" So, I said, "Yes, it sounds good." A chance to go to Germany. I auditioned the next day. I played about six numbers with them. They said, "Great. You're in." Two days after that, I was a Beatle.

OUI: Do you remember the six songs you played with them?

BEST: John started with an old instrumental called "Ramrod." It was a 12-bar blastaway thing to ease me in. Then George sang "Shakin' All Over." John did "Memphis" and "My Sweet Little Sixteen." Paul did "Over the Rainbow" to see if we could handle a slow number and then an out-and-out rocker which was "Long Tall Sally" or "Tutti Frutti." So, we bashed through it with no finesse, but they said it sounded good and I was in and that was it.

OUI: Here are some of the factors which seem to have contributed to your dismissal as a Beatle: George wanted Ringo; Paul was jealous of you because you were the most popular; Brian Epstein wanted you out because you had handled the business previously; and [Producer] George Martin didn't like your drumming. What do you think it was?

BEST: In a nutshell, jealousy. There are a lot of quotes that have been put into a lot of magazines and books, and I've just been a throwaway because someone simply said, "He wasn't a Beatle." They don't give any reason why or why not.

I'll go over the one with Brian first, get him out of the way. I tackled Brian about it. I said, "Is there any complication over the fact that I had handled the business side?" My reason for asking was that when we agreed for Brian to take over, it was a group decision. The way Brian had sold it to us was: "I think I can help you. I haven't managed before, but I've got a good business mind. I'm involved in records, etcetera, etcetera, etcetera." We said, "Okay, well, this guy's got a bit of cash and a bit of credibility, and he knows the people in the business. He's got a good reputation." So, we said "Yeah, we'll sign you up." He turned around and said that initially he'd use me because of the contacts I had, the business orientation. He wasn't afraid of that fact. A couple of times he called me into the office and said, "Look, Pete, we've got this deal. What do you think about it? Should we go back and work for this promoter?" And I'd say, "No, he's a bit of a shark. You don't get your money off him." He took my word on it. There was nothing to be scared of. When he took over as manager, I said, "You are the manager now. I am the group. Call on me if you need my experience." That was only going to be a matter of time, because a couple of months into the business, he'd have dealings with all the contacts I had anyway. He got the feel for it. He had his own ideas about what he wanted to do. I wasn't the father figure standing there sort of saying, "Hey, Brian, you can't do that, pal. I won't let you do that." He had nothing to be scared about.

When the ax fell, Brian turned around and said, "The others feel you're not a good enough drummer. They want Ringo in. They want you out." My first reaction to it was, "Why?" Later he opened up and said, "Well, George Martin mentioned the fact that you weren't a good enough drummer." Later on, when I sort of got my brains together and I was trying to get reasons for my dismissal, I contacted George Martin and he explained it to my mother: "Mrs. Best, it wasn't the fact that I wanted Pete out. What I meant by 'Pete's not a good enough drummer' was as far as recording actual record. The idea was to use a session drummer in the studio till Pete finds the line and adjusts it to the type of material they want to play. What happens behind closed doors in a recording studio, the public doesn't know about, but the physical appeal, the fact that he is part of the group, there's no need to change the lineup. I've been misquoted about that. I mentioned that Pete's not a good enough drummer, but there was no need for Pete to be axed out."

OUI: Would you have been happy with that arrangement, using a session drummer?

BEST: We went down and we sort of laid down the tracks. On that particular occasion, we only spent an afternoon there. George Martin never had the time to say, "Okay, we do it this way." He said we were talented musicians but not the professional musicians that they later became. At a later stage, when we would go back into the studios quite regularly, we could have sat down and discussed what it is that I'm going wrong on, what they wanted from me. I could have overcome that obstacle. You can overcome any obstacle by practice if you know what you're practicing for. But it happened and I was out. The funny thing was, Martin was unaware of the fact I was out because he had Andy White, who was a session drummer, standing by, fully expecting me to be on the session, to come back and do "Love Me Do." When Ringo walked in, White turned around and said, "Where's Pete?" and they said, "Pete left the group." As it happened, Andy White stood in and played a couple of takes on "Love Me Do," and Ringo stood in and did a couple of takes on "Love Me Do." George Martin, to this day, doesn't know which take it was that was released. Martin was expecting me back again as part of the group, and he didn't know anything at all about the fact that I'd been kicked out. It was a complete surprise to him.

If I was more popular than the rest of the Beatles, I wasn't aware of it. I know now from talking to people that it was starting to become Pete Best and the Beatles or Pete's Beatles. Whether they felt that there was too much attention being paid to me, hence the jealousy, who knows? People came around afterwards and said, "It was easy for us in the audience to see that there was jealousy there. They were aware that you were getting more attention than them," but I wasn't aware of it. If I got a couple of more screams than Paul or John, it didn't make any difference to me. As long as the group was getting the acclaim, it didn't mean a damn who was getting the screams. If they got screams and I didn't get any, what the hell? The group was popular, and that's all I was concerned about. They never mentioned anything about it. They never said, "Hey, play it down a little. You're getting too popular." Whether that contempt was laid and they discussed it afterwards and said, "Look out for this guy. If we go big, he's gonna be the one who gets all the attention, and we're gonna be shoved on the sidelines," I don't know . . . and I guess I never will.

OUI: How were you told you were terminated as a Beatle?

BEST: We played the Cavern on a Tuesday night. At the end of the session, I was loading the van up with Neil Aspinall. We were due to play Chester Ballroom the following Wednesday night, and I shouted out to John, "Do you want picking up? Do you want Neil to pick you up?" John said, "No, I'll make my own way over there." It was strange, because we'd always got lifts together, but I didn't think anything at all about it. Just as we were driving off, Brian came up and said, "Pete, I'd like to see you in the office in the morning about ten o'clock." I didn't think any more about it because I'd been called into the office quite a few times before to discuss certain things—five or ten minutes later, out again. I thought, Maybe he's got something he wants to discuss with me, new contract or something like that.

I went in there the following morning, and I got a funny feeling when I went into the office. Brian wasn't himself. He seemed agitated, apprehensive, nervous, sort of talking around the subject. After being in there three or four minutes, he turned around and very quietly said, "Pete, I've got bad news to tell you." I said, "What is it?" He said, "The boys want you out, and they want Ringo Starr in." Well, you can imagine my feelings because there had been no mention of it at all before. I was completely shell-shocked. My brain was going, Why, why? Brian said, "They feel Ringo is a better drummer." That didn't hold water, because, even to this day, I'm adamant that I was equal to if not better than Ringo. He apologized. I asked him, "Why aren't the boys here?" He said, "They left it up to me as manager." As I was being told by Brian, there was a phone call which I later found out was from Paul. Paul had said over the phone, "Have you told Pete?" Brian said, "No, I'm just telling him" and put the phone down. I asked when Ringo was due to join. Brian said, "He's going to join on Saturday."

So, it had been all arranged: Ringo was due to join on Saturday, I was out, and that was it. If they had mentioned anything to me beforehand, sort of said, "Hey, Pete, tighten up on your drumming a bit. We need to go places a little faster," I'd have worked on it, but there was no mention of it. We played. We got the great response from the kids. Yet, I didn't have anything to say about it before the ax came down. It was left up to Brian, and they didn't have the decency to be in the office and say, "Okay, give Pete time to defend himself. Let's see what his arguments are or at least give him time to get his thoughts together."

OUI: Why didn't Brian fix you up with another group?

BEST: For two or three weeks after that, my brain had gone. I was in the house, and I had friends coming up to the house saying, "Pete, what was the reason for it?" *Mersey Beat*, which was the local music paper at that time, had put out a story saying: "Pete has left the Beatles amicably." The fans were knocked out by the whole episode. I had offers to join other groups at that time, but I needed time to weigh the pros and cons and make a decision. In the meantime, I got a phone call from Brian, and he said, "Pete, I know you probably don't feel like talking to me after what's happened, but I would like to see you to discuss something with you." So, we arranged to meet. Brian said, "Pete, as far as the Beatles are concerned, it's over, but I do not want to lose you out of the stable." Brian was just starting to become the impresario, taking on other groups as part of his NEMS empire. There was another group called Mersey Beats, a very popular, up-and-coming group who styled themselves after the Beatles. Brian said, "I want you to join the Mersey Beats and build them up with your enthusiasm, experience, and drumming ability. I'd like to make them second string to the Beatles." I said, "Brian, look, I've been the number-one jockey on the number-one horse in the number-one stable for two years. Now you're asking me to drop to number two. You've got a lot of respect for me. You want me to build a group up. It's nice to know that you still want to manage me, but you still manage the Beatles and I'm still gonna come under that stigma—I should have been part of the Beatles. The Mersey Beats might get big, but I'm still gonna be second jockey. I'm always gonna be looking over there, seeing where they're going." He said, "To be quite honest, Pete, I thought you might feel like that. I'd have felt like that if it had happened to me. It was the answer I had expected, but I had to put the proposition to you just in case there was any way around it." So, I thanked him for the proposition and wished him well—it was all very polite and courteous—and a couple of weeks after that, I joined Lee Curtis and the All-Stars.

OUI: During your time with the Beatles, were you able to project who would be the major talent in the group?

BEST: As far as talent was concerned, we felt that as a unit. We knew that, by hook or by crook, somewhere along the line, we were gonna be rock stars. That was the driving factor. We knew that we had that something and that when the breaks came, we'd be there. If we'd have just gone into the English charts, that would have done us. I don't think anyone thought at that moment in time they were going to become the next phenomenon. We felt that the talent was there as a foursome. As the Beatles, we were inseparable, we could take on anyone.

Looking at it from a drummer's point of view, they were all talented performers, each in his own right. John, with his resilience, throw-away lines, charisma on stage. Paul, because he was press-relations orientated; he wanted to be the spokesman of the group. And Paul was a dynamic performer on stage because of his repertoire and vocal range—even then. He'd sing a ballad; then the next song he'd be belting out Little Richard. George, singing-wise, I wouldn't put him down as being as dynamic as the other two, more of a middle-of-the-road voice. Still, he got his numbers over well and contributed a great deal to the act but more in his music than his performing.

OUI: Who were you closest to and why?

BEST: Without doubt, John—simply because we spent a lot of time together in Germany. I liked him as a character. I had a lot of respect for him. We may have been out of the same blood-group, so to speak. I think I could get away with a lot more with John than other people could. If you rubbed John up the wrong side, you could expect a verbal whiplash from him. I've seen him give people terrible verbal lashings and walk away and think nothing at all about it, like a volcano calms down again and goes back to normal. When we came back from Germany, he spent a lot of time at my mother's house after we came back from the different venues we'd been playing. John would spend the night, and we'd sit around and play records, raid the ice-box. He was part of the family. He had a lot of talents going for him. Okay, Paul has a lot of talents going for him, but those are in songwriting, record A&R-ing, performance, composing, arrangements. Talented—you can't take it away from him. You go back to John—ready wit, his doodles and sketches which came to recognition afterwards as the phenomenon grew, crazy things he'd do on stage, he didn't give a damn. He had a resilience and latent talents he himself didn't know. He was a multitalented guy, but he thought nothing at all about it. He'd pen something and throw it in the corner. He had an oddball talent for literary composing. All of these things sort of rolled into one, and that made him the guy for me.

OUI: John had a tragic personal life—his father left early on, and his mother was killed when he was young. Was this dark side of his life evident?

BEST: It's something that he suppressed actually. He'd never talk about his mother. If anyone talked about it or mentioned anything about it, he'd cut off completely. Whether it was a grief he carried within him, I don't know, but it was something which he wouldn't open up to anyone about. It may have been a driving force within him, the fact that his mother, whom he idolized and held so much in respect, was knocked down and killed in a nonsensical road crash. She started him off, teaching him banjo chords and this and that, and then, all of a sudden, she wasn't there anymore.

OUI: Did John use and abuse women at that time, as he has hinted in several interviews?

BEST: He had a good sexual appetite, a randy sort. When it's thrown on a plate, you've got to take it. It was there. He took it whenever he got it.

OUI: During the Liverpool and Hamburg days and nights, who was the sexual star of the Beatles?

BEST: (pointing to himself) Let's be honest about it. We were young, healthy men, and we were sort of in the vice city. It was there on a plate. We could have it from normal female fans who were in love with the group all the way to a top-corps girl who wanted you for the night because she loved the way you smiled at her and she wanted to bestow her presence on you because she could turn around and say, "I was with him last night." So, the opportunities were there, and I think everyone claimed it. It's just that some of us got a little more than others.

OUI: Tell us about the Beatles orgies during your days with them.

BEST: I'll try and be explicit about it. We didn't have gross orgies—"Wheel the next 50 in, and we'll take our pick." We had numerous birds on occasion, gang bangs. It was readily available for us, and we accepted it. We had healthy appetites. It was more than readily available for them when they became a phenomenon, queueing up to do whatever they wanted to do. Whether in fact it was 50 or 60, I do not know. They've got to be going some for that. Even in the German days and times in

Liverpool, the appetites were healthy. If their prowess as sexual athletes increased, then there may well have been orgies. But I wasn't part of that, unfortunately. I can't complain, though.

OUI: You were described at that time as being the James Dean-type of the group.

BEST: This was an image which was sort of pre-cast for me. It wasn't something that I was going out to do, to be mean and moody, if you can understand what I'm trying to get at. The fact that I may have turned fans on may have happened, but I wasn't playing a role just to get them to do that. That was me. They either liked it or they didn't.

OUI: Describe a typical day and night on the road with the Beatles in Hamburg.

BEST: Performing on stage can be seven hours a night; on the weekends it can be eight or nine hours. So, on a weeknight, that takes you up to two in the morning. By the time you're finished playing, you get a bite to eat, you have a few beers, and you wind down, you're talking five or six o'clock in the morning. You go and meet the girls you have to meet, either shacking up for the night or going to a hotel. We'd be heading back to our digs as people were going to work, the people who'd been sitting in the audience the night before. We would sleep through seven or eight hours until half past two or three o'clock in the afternoon. You wash and shave, go out and get a bit to eat, wander into town to buy clothes or watch a picture show, and it was time to go back on stage again. Seven days a week.

OUI: Any memorable incidents or stories from the Hamburg days?

BEST: The funniest thing which always sticks in my mind again is with John. There were so many pranks that he played. We got aled up on stage one night—we used to get tanked, because the more ale we got down inside of us, the better the performance. It was a big thing for the German audiences to send drinks up. More ale and schnapps would land up on stage, and we'd drink it and toast everyone. This night, we really filled up before we went on stage. George put on a beret and a swimming costume, Paul put on an old dress or something like that, and John wore a toilet seat and stripped down to his underpants. We had to walk through the crowd, you see, to get to the stage. The crowd sees us coming out and goes wild. By the time we get on stage, the crowd is erupting. We're playing this rock number, "Sweet Little Sixteen," and when George takes the solo, John turns around and pulls his underpants down, and there's this big, bare bottom looking at the fans. The solo finishes, and John casually pulls his underpants up again. There's silence, and then the crowd erupts again. That one sticks out in my mind.

OUI: Were drugs a major part of the Beatles at that time?

BEST: I wasn't into that side of it; we should get that clear. I was a beer man. The pills they were into were more like diet pills which were available in Germany, and if you took them, they'd pump you up and keep you awake for a short while. They used these because of the long hours. It wasn't something that started the first six months we were there. It was more when we went back the second time at the Top Ten Club. That's when they started to use them, because they were free and easy to get ahold of. The effects made you feel good, and it kept them bouncing. There was no coke-sniffing or LSD or any of that. Compared with what they most probably took later on in their careers, which they admitted, it was kid stuff.

OUI: What were the goals of the Beatles at that time: to be famous, to get rich, to play America, to get laid?

BEST: All of that. If we'd have gotten to number one in England at that time, we'd have felt that we'd done good. We were a Liverpool band, and at that time, it was very hard to break into the London scene. It sounds funny when you think about it now. Liverpool and London are only 200 miles apart. London was the capital of the recording business at that time; so, for a Liverpool group to get to number one on the charts would have been one up for the Liverpool lads. That was the driving force. I don't think anyone, at that time, ever realized that they'd become the phenomenon they were. I don't think their aspirations ever reached that height.

OUI: 1964 was the height of Beatlemania: *The Ed Sullivan Show, Hard Day's Night, Meet the Beatles,* and their American tours. What was your reaction? Where were you, and what were you doing?

BEST: I never made a point of following the Beatles' career directly, like picking up a paper and seeing what they're doing today. I had my own group, and I was trying to get as far into the pop business as I could with that, but you couldn't get away from it. You put the radio on—Beatles music, number one. You put the television on—they've conquered the States, Ed Sullivan, the fans are going wild. You pick up the press—it's there. You couldn't switch off from it no matter where you went. You saw their style of clothing in the shops. You saw the kids walking around with the Beatle hairstyles. So, even though I never followed their career directly, I was always aware of what was happening with them simply because it was all around you.

OUI: Did you ever see them in concert?

BEST: No. Funnily enough, there were only the two occasions when the All-Stars played second bill for them very shortly after I was kicked out. But, in concert, I never saw them. The only time I ever made a point of watching them on the television was when they did the variety show in front of the Queen. John did his famous "Those in the front, rattle your jewelry." It was a milestone in their life, playing before royalty, and I wanted to see what the reaction was. I wanted to see whether they'd changed their style of playing to accommodate the fact that they were playing in front of a different audience. They were in front of the elite of the elite. They didn't change.

OUI: Did you see any of their movies?

BEST: I was playing with my group in Canada, and *Help!* was premiering at one of the cinemas there, and we were invited down to watch it. But I never made a point of seeing their films. I never saw *Hard Day's Night.*

OUI: When was the last time you spoke with John, Paul, or George?

BEST: The last time I saw them was at the Majestic Ballroom in Bergenhead. They'd just won the *Mersey Beat* popularity award, and Lee Curtis had come second to them, which was a good thing for us. The last time I actually spoke to them was the Tuesday night before I was kicked out, when we were performing on stage at the Cavern. Two occasions after that, we saw one another and no word was spoken.

OUI: Did you ever consider dropping in or calling up one of them?

BEST: No. There were several times when they landed up at my mother's house for one thing or another, but I wasn't there. I was out on the road somewhere, touring around Britain. The feeling wasn't there, simply because of the way it happened and the heartache—and I was deeply involved in my own career at the time. I didn't have time to step out. I wasn't concerned about it. I tried to wipe it out of my mind completely and pursue my own avenues.

Robert Crane

OUI: Aside from your participation with them, did you have a favorite period of the Beatles?

BEST: The first 12 months afterwards—mid '62 to '63, possibly early '64. The material they were putting out then—"Please Please Me," "Love Me Do"—was the Beatles I knew. It was good material. I could see they were progressing musically, but it still had that Beatle charisma about it. I could see that they were changing simply because they wanted to change. They didn't want to be branded as just coming out with the same old stuff. They were the leaders in the field. Even though their later music was good, it wasn't quite my style.

OUI: When John started writing songs like "Tomorrow Never Knows," "Strawberry Fields Forever," and "I Am the Walrus," were you able to hang in there with him?

BEST: It was a general trend; it wasn't just them. People were aware that they were on acid trips and writing about stuff which was hallucinatory. It was happening everywhere.

OUI: In 1969, the Beatles broke apart. Why do you think it happened when it happened?

BEST: I don't know the inner complexities of what happened with Apple—and the fact that Brian had died, and he had held them together, and they got into bad business ventures, and the fact that they had been at the top for so long, money didn't mean anything to them. But I think they were looking for contentment, to leave the rat race behind. Whether it was anguish within the group, rivalries between the members, forces pulling at one another, people who wanted to go out and do their own thing and not be branded as a Beatle but have their own identity, who can say? All you can do is make assumptions from the sidelines.

OUI: Who do you think succeeded artistically, post-Beatles?

BEST: It's got to go to Paul. He's still belting it out and getting number-one albums; he's got the Midas touch. George, looking at it realistically, is most probably semi-retired. He's backing Monty Python and other things, and he's probably not too bothered about the fact that he's no longer known as George Harrison, Beatle. He sits in with people, writes songs, and gets royalties from them. He's happy. Ringo does his own thing. He's not over-serious about what he does. He does things because the opportunity is there. Paul's way in the lead, but John isn't alive to contend. It would have been very interesting to see if John had stayed on his comeback kick, whether he could have gotten up with Paul.

OUI: How did you feel when you heard John had been murdered?

BEST: I was sick. People said, "You haven't seen him in 20 years. What difference does it make?" But when I remember John, I remember the person who used to stay at my house. It took me a long time to accept the fact that he had died. I was upstairs getting a shave when it happened. It was about six o'clock in the morning. My wife, Kathy, shouted upstairs, "Pete, John's dead." I thought, Which John's she talking about? She said, "It's on the radio." So, I came down. She said, "John Lennon." I said, "Come on, you've got to be joking. It's a sick joke." After hearing more reports coming in, it suddenly dawned on me. This isn't a prank. This guy who I knew for four or five years is no longer here through no fault of his own. It was such a nonsensical, bloody thing to happen. There was no reason for it, no logic behind it. I had to say to myself, Forget about it, Pete. He's gone. All I've got is memories, and they can't take them away from me.

My family has a belief that what will be, will be. If it's fate for you to have been part of the particular package, then you would have been. People ask me, "Are you content?" Yeah, I'm content. It would have been nice to have been part of it, to reap the benefits and the glamour and the acclaim which came from it, simply because I put so much of my life into it. But if it was fate that it wasn't meant for me, then okay.

OUI: Is there any evidence to the rumor that John Lennon and Brian Epstein were having an affair?

BEST: It's hard to say. John said that once he was at the top he would do anything to hold that particular status. Brian may have had a very close relationship with him, but who knows? I wouldn't like to be the one to say, "Yeah, it did happen," because I just do not know. I wasn't there. It's a rumor.

OUI: What was your reaction to Paul working with Linda and John working with Yoko?

BEST: I don't think it was needed. I don't think Linda has contributed a lot to Paul's group.

OUI: I always wondered if the keyboards she was playing were plugged in or not.

BEST: Whether it was a way for Paul to have her on stage, to get encouragement from it, who knows? Again, whether Yoko influenced John's life so much, controlled it, was a dominant factor in it, whether he couldn't do anything without her, and she was his support, who knows? They could have done it without them, but knowing the two guys, there's most probably some particular reason it evolved that way. It wouldn't have happened just because the women said, "Come on, I want to play in the band." There's some hidden factor there.

OUI: How did you get the rights to the Silver Beatles tapes?

BEST: This is something that's been handled by Backstage Records, the label it's out on. They've cleared all the legal problems. They're credible, the way they've handled the quality of the merchandise. The actual, inner legalities—I haven't gotten involved with that.

OUI: Why is the album coming out now, almost 20 years after the recordings were made?

BEST: If I hadn't been approached to be part of this, I wouldn't have been involved. I keep stressing the quality of the package, which is something that's taken a great deal of thought. It wasn't something that I automatically got with. I gave it thought. It sounded like a nice package to be part of; it wasn't a flyer, a ghoster. It's been handled well.

OUI: Have you speculated what Paul, George, and Ringo will think about your involvement with this package?

BEST: If it worries them, I don't know. If I was in the same position, I'd say, "What the hell." They've made the money. I had a similar type of thing when I was approached to be advisor on [the TV movie] The Birth of the Beatles. Paul said, "It'll be interesting to see what materializes." I don't think that they've got anything to worry about.

OUI: Why did the Beatles become a phenomenon and not someone or something else?'

BEST: You had a group with a lot of latent talents—singer-songwriters—and their presentation was different. There was a charisma about them. The talent there was unexplored. It needed to be groomed, channeled, and released on the public. Brian Epstein had a lot to do with this. There are so many talented people around who are unexploited—they haven't got the publicity machine behind them. When you take talent and publicity and you release that and it's an unknown commodity, you've got a winner if it's handled correctly. That's the underlying factor: if it's handled correctly. If it's not, then you can get a mini-explosion, a couple of months, a year, then it takes a dive. The Beatles were not content to remain the same. They wanted to lead the field. They were adventurous. Because of that and their publicity, people were aware of what the Beatles' next record was going to be. They always managed to do something slightly different—change the gear, different package, different artwork. People were ready to buy anything which was released by the Beatles before they even heard it, because the expectancy was there.

OUI: How have the public John, Paul, and George changed since your days with them?

BEST: I think you could see that the grooming was taking place. They were rough diamonds. You can polish a diamond, but there's still got to be that quality in it. They were becoming more at ease with certain pressures. Every now and then, the rough diamond would show through. So, it wasn't all polished and finessed. I looked for the unexpected from them because I knew that they couldn't keep that up all the time.

OUI: Who is a better drummer, really—you or Ringo?

BEST: Me. I've always been adamant about that. I believe in my own ability, and other people have believed in it as well. I can play drums.

OUI: Were you impressed with any of Ringo's drumming?

BEST: Yeah, there were a couple of things. Let's not knock the guy completely. He's a drummer. He's improved. He's picked up a lot of things by sitting in with other people. He's tightened up a lot. What improves with age are wine and cheese and drummers.

GORILLA, PORNO STAR, CHEF, MODEL, BARTENDERS & BODYBUILDER

Robert Crane

KOKO

Our favorite animal to go ape over sign language tells us what it's like to have hands on her feet and why her friend Michael is the gorilla of her dreams

Koko is the most celebrated gorilla in the world, and for good reason. She is the first gorilla that can use a human language. Dr. Penny Patterson has been her teacher since Koko's birth and is the director of The Gorilla Foundation in Woodside, California, where Koko now lives.

Robert Crane interviewed Koko, with Dr. Patterson acting as interpreter. He reports, "Koko, 15 years old and 230 pounds, sat poised and ready in her open-air living area. She looked me in the eye and, using American Sign Language, commanded, 'Show me your teeth,' which I respectfully did. She was delighted by the enormous amount of gold and silver in my mouth. Her mate, Michael, 13 and 350 pounds, who shares quarters with her, never looked me in the eye—something to do with the fact that I was a stranger and a male.

"Koko and Michael, who have an occasional spat, are, for the most part, nonaggressive. They are the subjects of an ongoing study by the foundation's research team. [Donations are welcome. Write to The Gorilla Foundation, P.O. Box 620-530, Woodside, California 94062.] Both gorillas seem happy and, in Koko's case, willing to deal with media attention."

1

PLAYBOY: Who are smarter, gorillas or humans?

KOKO: Koko Devil. Gorilla Koko love good.

2

PLAYBOY: What is the most fun to do?

KOKO: Please eat. Please eat.

3

PLAYBOY: What makes you happy?

KOKO: [*Slaps her chest*] Gorilla Koko love good. Koko love good fake tooth. [*Fake tooth is Koko's sign for a gold dental cap or crown.*] Feel Devil know. Gorilla polite happy Koko.

4

PLAYBOY: Do you think Michael is cute?

KOKO: Cute [*signed with two hands for emphasis equaling very cute*] sweet good.

5

PLAYBOY: What's better than bananas?

KOKO: Corn.

6

PLAYBOY: What's the difference between boys and girls?

KOKO: Corn there [*points toward floor*] good. [*Koko gets corn, because her floor is clean. Michael doesn't, because his is dirty. The morning before the interview took place, Michael hadn't received a corn treat, because he had urinated on the floor. The gorillas are toilet trained.*] Girl people. [*Koko thinks of herself as a person and of Michael as an animal.*]

7

PLAYBOY: Which sex smells better?

KOKO: Girl girl.

8

PLAYBOY: What do you want to be when you grow up?

KOKO: Polite want good. Gorilla good.

9

PLAYBOY: What don't people understand?

KOKO: Sorry good. [*When I say I'm sorry and I'll be good*] Frown look lip [her sign for female] pimple [people] fake tooth. [*They frown when I want to look at women's fake teeth.*] Gorilla don't know Koko love good. [*Gorillas and people don't know that Koko loves to be good.*]

10

PLAYBOY: What do you think of our language?

KOKO: Fake lie good.

11

PLAYBOY: What's your most troublesome thought?

KOKO: That. [*Points toward gold-foil pattern on one of her scraps of fabric. Koko wants a gold tooth so badly that the night before, she had put a piece of gold braid into her mouth and swallowed it. Koko puts the gold foil against her first right upper molar, as if trying to make her tooth a gold one.*]

12

PLAYBOY: When is the kitten more trouble than it's worth?

KOKO: Cat bad good. Frown eat there. [*Points to her cereal—referring to the fact that her cat has, on occasion, eaten it*]

13

PLAYBOY: What's it like having hands on your feet?

KOKO: Good there [*floor*] there [*mesh fence*]. [*They're good for use on the floor and on the fence.*]

14

PLAYBOY: What does it mean when you slap your chest?

KOKO: Gorilla good. Drink hurry good drink me. [*Koko beats her chest to intimidate Penny, to get her to give her drinks, which have been restricted for a medical test.*]

15

PLAYBOY: What do you want for your birthday?

KOKO: Earrings. Cookie.

16

PLAYBOY: What do you say when you really want to insult people?

KOKO: Dirty. Devil head.

17

PLAYBOY: How do you feel when you've eaten too much cake?

KOKO: Sad bad stomach.

18

PLAYBOY: What would you eat for the sheer pleasure of it?

KOKO: Champagne.

19

PLAYBOY: Is there anything else you want people to know about you?

KOKO: Me gorilla gorilla me Koko good... finished.

20

PLAYBOY: What do you say when you're tired of being asked questions?

KOKO: Gorilla teeth. Finished.

Traci Lords

The resilient actress on past lives, the current state of the porn business and how to handle an alien

Actress Traci Lords has enjoyed an eclectic career. The Ohio native has worked in many areas of the entertainment industry: sitcoms, miniseries, John Waters movies, big-budget films and now an action series. Lords, 32, is the heroine doing battle with aliens on the Sci-Fi Channel's First Wave. But things were not always this legitimate.

The former Nora Kuzma grew up in an unhappy family, living in West Virginia, the Midwest and, ultimately, southern California. At 14, looking to escape a dismal, fatherless home life, Lords accepted an opportunity to appear in an adult film. Taking the first name Traci from her best friend and Lords from the star of her favorite show, Hawaii Five-O, she quickly became a household name, appearing in more than 75 films until, when she was 18, her agent and two producers were indicted under child pornography laws for using a minor in their films. Video store shelves were cleared of Traci Lords products—except for those films made after her 18th birthday. Lords was losing her battle with a cocaine addiction. Still a teenager, she had hit rock bottom.

Lords tapped into her survival instincts and successfully dealt with her drug problem on her own. She studied acting at the famed Strasberg Institute. She was soon cast in her first feature film, a remake of Roger Corman's science fiction cult hit Not of This Earth. Then a call from eccentric filmmaker John Waters changed Lords' life. She appeared opposite Johnny Depp in Cry-Baby. Roles followed in Waters' Serial Mom (starring Kathleen Turner), Virtuosity (with Denzel Washington) and Blade (opposite Wesley Snipes). Lords has guest-starred on Nash Bridges, Tales From the Crypt and Married With Children, had recurring roles on Melrose Place and Roseanne and starred for two seasons on Profiler. She has appeared in Stephen King's The Tommyknockers mini-series and Intent to Kill. Lords showed her versatility with her singing and songwriting debut, Control, a dance club hit that rose to number two on the Billboard charts.

Robert Crane caught up with Lords in Los Angeles. He reports: "Traci could definitely kick ass on the Survivor island. She maintains a splendid sense of humor, a tempered perspective and a take-no-prisoners philosophy. She also has a great pair of legs. She was in the middle of a whirlwind tour. Lords was ready."

1

PLAYBOY: Who is easier to please in bed, a man or a woman?

LORDS: I would have to say men. I've been with women, and I'm much more comfortable with men. Women are lovely and they're lovely to kiss and I certainly have no problem with the female form, but you always want the pesky penis at the end, and plastic just doesn't do it. I'm completely comfortable with my sexuality and that I've been both places and explored, but that's something you do when you're 16. To do it now would be almost ridiculous. Not because I'm in any way, shape or form offended by women. I think they're great. I just know what I like, and it usually has a penis attached.

2

PLAYBOY: What always seems to work with a man?

LORDS: Every guy is different. It depends on how somebody makes you feel. I know what I don't do with someone I'm with, and that's to be fake. I hate the whole thing about women faking orgasms—women giving somebody credit for something he didn't do. It's really teaching him kind of poorly. 'Oh baby, baby, that feels so good' when it doesn't. Well, then, why are you there? Sex is a great thing. I love sex. It's really important and I don't like to waste my time with it. I choose men very carefully. I have to make sure they qualify. There's a test when you first meet them—see if they wear boxers or briefs, see if they like beer or wine. If I like someone, I'll watch him. His mannerisms, the way he walks, the way he holds himself. You can tell a lot about somebody by the way he moves. If somebody is overly into himself, physically, he's usually really lousy in bed, because he's worried about how he's going to look when he's moving a certain way. If somebody's not in his skin, if he doesn't own it, he's usually a lousy lover. There's that whole thing that women say, about a guy with big feet: Big feet, big shoes. I have to admit I tend to peer at feet, even though I don't believe that. I just can't help but go, Hmmm. And I love Gucci on men. Gucci shoes do it for me every time. Say, a size 14.

3

PLAYBOY: A person stays over for the first time. Why doe he leave stuff or pick up stuff?

LORDS: Oh, it's total marking. If I'm with a guy and I spend the night with him and leave something, it means I want to see him again. If I make sure that everything, every strand of hair, is attached to me when I leave, chances are I crept out in the middle of the night very slowly, so as not to disturb him. I've never actually taken something from somebody's place. I think you can be arrested for that, can't you? I've taken T-shirts from boyfriends. It's just the smell thing. I love a good semi-crusty T-shirt, with a one-day slight stench to it—I love it, if I'm really into the guy. Oh, yeah. There's something so primal and sexy about sweat. I love sweat.

4

PLAYBOY: A guy is going out with Traci Lords for the first time. What could he possibly do to impress her?

LORDS: It's really simple. A gentleman impresses me. I like men who open doors. I like men who are on time. I like men who bring flowers. I like men who call the next day. I like men who are confident. I like no-nonsense men. I don't like prissy boys. I don't like people who are afraid to say what they think. I like straight shooters. That turns me on.

5

PLAYBOY: Who benefits from lowering their standards, men or women?

LORDS: I don't think anyone benefits from lowering their standards. I think it's the greatest lie you can tell yourself. It's always lurking there no matter how you try to disguise it, how you try to color it. You know what the deal is. So when you lower your standards and think, Well, he doesn't really turn me on in bed, but he's really nice—we all know that's crap. It's the lethal package that I'm interested in. I want the guy who is physically appealing—pleasing to me. He doesn't have to be a drop-dead-gorgeous babe but somebody who I think is sexy, smart, funny, who knows what he wants. I don't want some beautiful dummy and I don't want some ugly genius. I want an average Joe. Isn't that frightening? Do you know how few of those there are? And if you find any, will you send them to me?

6

PLAYBOY: You've worked hard to see that children don't have to go through what you went through. What are the hard truths and realizations you acquired as a child?

LORDS: Not having my dad around really formed my life. I felt like I looked for my father for a long, long time, which led to bad relationships. When I was in my 20s that's all I did. I was lucky that I met an amazing man and married him. That was wonderful, but after we split I went through every bad boy because it was safe and comfortable and reminded me of Daddy, and that was a nightmare.

7

PLAYBOY: How long were you married?

LORDS: I was married for six years. He's an amazing man—my oldest friend and my oldest lover. I'm going to see him tomorrow, actually. I might get laid, as a matter of fact. The last time I saw him was three years ago. I knocked on his door and he opened it and took one look at me and we ended up in bed for three days. I saw him three weeks ago and it was the same thing. It was great. it's always great. He's the love of my life. I was just too young. We were so young and he's on one coast and I'm on the other. So we'll see. It's kind of funny to have an affair with your ex-husband every so often. It's pretty cool. He knows which buttons to push. It's like he has some sort of map of my body or something. He's the only guy I've ever met who actually screams louder than I do. I like that fearlessness in a man. God, what have I been doing? Why am I even fucking around like this? I have to go see him.

8

PLAYBOY: Do you think the adult film industry should be shut down or more strictly governed?

LORDS: I don't have a problem with pornography as long as it's consenting adults who are doing it for their pleasure. I have a real sore spot—no pun intended—about child pornography, because it's something I've had to deal with half my life and it's been very difficult for me. I don't think 18 is old enough. How come you can't buy a drink until you're 21? Because you're not mature enough to make that decision. But you can go out and have sex and have it recorded. That seems ridiculous to me. I don't think 18 is old enough to make a decision that's going to affect the rest of your life. It affected mine—changed my entire life. I was so young—14, 15, 16, 17. I did the best I could at the time. I thought that was cool then. I didn't really understand what it was going to mean later. I didn't think, What's going to happen when I'm 25? I thought, God, I'll never live to be 21. I was one of those kids.

9

PLAYBOY: What has changed the most about the porn industry since you left it?

LORDS: When I was in porn, it was still kind of underground. There were people who rented movies, but it was not like it is now. Porn is everywhere. The most conservative people I know like to watch movies. The Internet is a big factor, and there are women who really promote themselves as porn stars. That wasn't happening when I was around. I did what I did and hoped that nobody found out about it. Now people are like, "Yeah, I'm in a porno movie." It's pretty bizarre.

10

PLAYBOY: Should politicians be in the position to legislate moral issues?

LORDS: Well, they are in that position and they're not exactly the best role models. The bottom line is, there are good politicians and there are bad politicians. There's decadence and then there are people who are on the proper moral path—whatever that may be. I just don't believe it's cool to impose your views on other people and say, "No, you can't look at this, you can't do that," except with kids. It's not OK to exploit kids. They're our future. They should be protected, and more should be done to protect them. I mean that in every way—regarding safety and guns and violence and pornography. America is so obsessed with sex and with keeping it in the closet. I would much rather see people having sex than killing each other. You would think we would have learned that by now. I feel stupid even talking about it, it's so ridiculous.

11

PLAYBOY: We never ran into a 16-year-old like you. Were we in the wrong place at the wrong time?

LORDS: Well, that depends on how you look at it, doesn't it? I know people have the fantasy, the schoolgirl thing, the young innocent girl, the Britney Speaks phenomenon. But come on, guys, it's not right. It really isn't. You shouldn't be screwing the babysitter. It's really not cool. And as far as I'm concerned, I don't know if you would have wanted to run into me at 16. I was a nightmare at 16. I was definitely a wild child and sometimes to be around me was fun because I was just so over-the-top and outrageous. You never knew what I was going to do. Other times I was just so wounded and angry and pissed at the world that I don't know how much fun I was. I think it was that combination of rage and teenage sexuality. If I'm going to hit my sexual peak now, I'm going to lock myself in a room somewhere. I'm scared. What would that mean? Can you imagine? Frightened, I'm frightened. No, no more.

12

PLAYBOY: If a fan meets you on the street, should he keep his enthusiasm to a minimum?

LORDS: It used to really upset me when somebody would make a comment like, "Oh yeah, I've seen your early films," but now it completely depends on how it's done. If somebody's really vulgar about it, it depends on what mood I'm in. if I'm feeling sensitive it will be a different reaction every time, but basically I don't begrudge people whatever they say. If a guy has one of my old films and he has jerked off to it, I'm glad somebody got some pleasure. It's already done. I can't take it back. You can't save me from that part of my life. I sometimes find those films embarrassing, sometimes it pisses me off and sometimes it just makes me laugh and I go, "Yeah, well, I give good head." What am I going to say? That's probably the only thing porn taught me—how to give a blow job without messing up my lipstick. Which comes in handy from time to time.

13

PLAYBOY: You worked with Patty Hearst. Ever discuss victimhood?

LORDS: No. Patty and I never really spoke about anything serious. She played my mom in *Cry-Baby*. I didn't know her very well and I didn't want to offend her or put her off. It was her first acting job, and I guess I was coming from a place of "I get sick of hearing it" so she was probably really sick of hearing it. I wasn't going to go there, and I didn't. We talked about baking and cakes and recipes, mother-daughter stuff. She never said porn, I never said robbery, it was beautiful. Mutual respect.

14

PLAYBOY: Anything you miss from your former life?

LORDS: No. I'll say that it was much easier when I was marching to the tune of, "Oh it doesn't matter what I'm doing, because I won't live to be 21." Having zero responsibility, being fearless, because I didn't care if I lived or died. That's sort of a tragic statement. If I miss anything, that's it. It's a lot harder being conscious. It's a lot harder being grown-up and thinking about what you're doing and how it will affect people around you. It's a lot harder giving a shit.

15

PLAYBOY: What's different about craft service on adult films and legit films?

LORDS: Craft service on adult films has condoms and douches, and craft service on regular films certainly doesn't. There are no lubricants involved. On First Wave we have the best. Everything from pizzas to grapes to coffee and a big basket of vitamins because we're all sick and malnourished, working too many hours. There's lots of aspirin and gum because there's a lot of stinky breaths from working 16-hour days and drinking coffee. It's Vancouver, so there's mounds and mounds of sushi. Salmon, unbelievable. It beats porn craft service and vodka at six A.M.

16

PLAYBOY: What should you do if you're confronted by an alien?

LORDS: You should definitely haul ass. I don't think you should say anything. Not, "Hi, how are you? Nice to meet you." Just go. If you watch First Wave you'll notice that whenever there are aliens around nothing good comes of it. It's just bad, bad, bad.

17

PLAYBOY: So is the only good alien a dead alien?

LORDS: Yes. Absolutely. The aliens on our show are not like E.T. They are more like the ones Sigourney Weaver fought—the big, horrible ones. They do nasty things. Currently, I'm having something nasty done to me by one of them. They've done all kinds of things to me. They've strapped me to devices and changed my consciousness and tortured me. I've actually gone to hell and met Satan.

18

PLAYBOY: Are your aliens the gooey or the metallic type?

LORDS: They grow bodies that are called husks. The Gua are the aliens on our show, and they are always exquisitely beautiful because aliens are not stupid and they realize that in our society it's beneficial to come into a beautiful husk. So our aliens are always stunning. They put their consciousness in these husks, and then when they die they basically disintegrate.

19

PLAYBOY: What kinds of movies make you squirm?

LORDS: Horror movies, Stephen King movies. I find the books more frightening than the films, because when you're reading, it's all up here [*pointing to head*]. I like sci-fi a lot. I think that's probably why I've done so much sci-fi in my career. I saw *The Cell* recently and thought some of the effects were really disturbing. *Silence of the Lambs*—type movies just freak me out.

20

PLAYBOY: Your soft side: Who gets to see it?

LORDS: I guess whoever's looking. I don't consider myself a terribly hard person. I have been, but I don't think that's where I'm at now. I feel like I'm pretty open, but I can be shut down really, really fast. If I feel like I'm in danger, I can be very firm, but I don't really hide behind that badass persona anymore. I did for a long time. Now I'm kind of like, "Hey, I'm human. I'm not getting laid, just like you." I wanted to be perfect for so long and I think I felt I had so much to prove: "Hi, I'm really smart." "Hi, I'm really talented." "Hi, I'm really a serious actress." I was so busy trying to prove to everybody that I was all of those things that one day I said, "Oh my God, I am these things. Why am I so insecure about it?" No one's arguing with the fact. It's me. It was my head trip the whole time. That was the biggest joke of all. I was the only one who didn't believe it. It's like, "Oh shit, you idiot."

Holiday Dish

The Food Network's Sara Moulton sounds off on her fellow chefs, the current state of American cuisine and disasters in the kitchen.

SARA MOULTON IS THE ULTIMATE unsnob foodie in the middle of the Food Network's ruling boys' club that lists Legasse, Flay, Batali, Tsai and Puck among its members. A mini-conglomerate on the heels of Martha Stewart (without the impending insider trading rap), Moulton is hostess of Sara's Secrets *on the Food Network, executive chef at* Gourmet *magazine, food editor of* Good Morning America *and kitchen shrink at her web site:* saramoulton.com. *She is also the author of* Sara Moulton Cooks at Home *(Broadway Books, $29.95) and is married and the mother of two children.*

She's a graduate of the Culinary Institute of America, founder of the New York Women's Culinary Alliance and proudly claims Julia Child as her mentor and one of her closest friends. Although Moulton's nonstop schedule doesn't permit much time for sunbathing, she cites Palm Springs as her favorite vacation destination.

Robert Crane met with the diminutive Moulton at Gourmet *magazine's offices in the Conde Nast building off Times Square in New York City. After a tour of the Frank Gehry-designed cafeteria (spectacular), and Moulton's office (tiny) and the test kitchen (a dream), Crane and Moulton settled down in the executive dining room.*

111: You host a live cooking show—what was your biggest disaster?

Moulton: What is my biggest 100, you mean. It happens almost nightly. I don't consider it a disaster because I think it's my job to make mistakes. I'm trying to empower people to get into the kitchen, and if I'm perfect, why should they bother? It's unattainable. But I think, honestly, the worst is Wednesday nights; we do a cook-along and we make the meal in real time. So there's no cheating, there are no swaps, there's no nothing. What you see is what you get.

111: Any examples?

Moulton: I ended one Wednesday cook-along with raw veal chops on the counter, never even got them into the pan. So I would say that's probably the worst but we've had burned pancakes—I seem to have a problem with pancakes.

We forget to oil the griddle. I seem to burn the croutons every single time. It's mainly burning, although I will tell you also we've had three fires in one week on-air. So that was interesting, although one of them I wasn't there for but that's my favorite story.

The guest host was David Rosengarten. For awhile I was doing two shows and I must have had a full-moon week because that's when all that stuff happened. Anyway, you know when you have a cutting board down, you have a towel underneath it to keep it from sliding. And we had a bunch of guests sitting there, including Andrea Immer who's a wine lady, very elegant. And David had done his show, my 7 p.m. show and now my 10 p.m. show. He's wasted. He's a wreck. So, the burner's right here and the towel catches fire and *this is on the air!*

David jumps back and says, "Oh, there's a fire." Now, meanwhile sitting next to him is a chef and Andrea Immer, I forgot who exactly. And he just stands there. He does nothing. He's exhausted, right? So Andrea Immer gets up... the woman saves the day. Grabs the towel, throws it in the sink and she's the wine lady, right, puts it out with a beautiful bottle of red wine. Very depressing.

111: The Food Network features Emeril Legasse, Mario Batali, Martha Stewart, Wolfgang Puck, Too Hot Tamales. OK, dish.

Moulton: Too Hot Tamales are no longer there. They're very talented, nice people, but they're no longer there. Wolfgang just got started. We all really get along, quite frankly. We really do. We just had to do this Christmas special. They made us do one last year and that one was much phonier. The idea for the show was for us to think of our favorite Christmas memory and get up and tell somebody else. And everybody was acting, oh, it was just awful. The next year, though, they put us into a room and let us do what we wanted. Emeril is one of the nicest guys who ever walked the earth. He does have an entourage and he's very hard to get next to and he always has a lot of women surrounding him. Although now that's he's remarried, I think that has slowed down a bit.

Two years ago there was an awful article written about him in *The New York Times* that really was mean, mean, mean and said that his show wasn't serious, that he wasn't a good chef and that his recipes didn't work and that he was a horrible teacher. It really hit below the belt and I know Emeril from way back. He cooked in my dining room years ago. And I had a lot of fun with him. I loved him, I know just how talented he is. I wanted to tell him that he didn't have to worry about this *Times* article. I just wanted to say something positive, because I knew he was feeling bad. But in order to find him, to get through to him, because I couldn't get through to him straight, it didn't matter if I said, "Hi, this is Sara Moulton from The Food Network." I had to talk to my producer at *Good Morning America*, who is also his producer, find out under what alias he was staying, at what hotel, call him there, leave a message and then he called me back and then I was able to tell him.

He's a lot of fun, though. His dressing room is next to mine so we bump into each other every so often. I'm there every night. He's only there when he comes and shoots. So he's a really nice guy.

Bobby Flay comes off as a real bad boy and he certainly is a ladies' man. When he did an event out on Long Island in a tent, it was a Food Network "live" thing. And I remember at the end of the evening he was doing shots and he had like 12 beautiful ladies around him. They were all doing shots or something. He just attracts them. On the other hand, he's really good to women. Both he and Emeril just love women—in a good sense. And Bobby apparently has a lot of women who have worked for him. I just recently meet the chef of Bolo, who's a woman and I had no idea. She said he's great, she's worked with him for two or three years and I've heard that from other women, too. He's always been so respectful of me. Like when I first started my show, he actually sent me a tape of something he was doing to have me critique it to see how I thought he was doing. And he used to call me and nudge me about things on the show live.

Like we had this big argument going about whether there is any such thing as a male and female eggplant. There isn't. They go both ways. They may switch-hit, these eggplant. But he and I had a fight about it. He doesn't come off warm and fuzzy but he's very respectful and I think his food is excellent.

Mario Batali is a wild and crazy guy. He's larger than life. I don't know how old he is, but he's pushing the limits. However, I know he is a family man also. He's got two adorable babies—well, they're bigger now. And he's married to the daughter of the people who own Coachfarm Goat Cheese. And his wife is a smart, cool lady. But he's just a big character. I think he is one of the finest chefs in the country. I think his food is just superb. Have you ever eaten at Babbo? He's just so good. And he's nice. I have to tell you overall when I'm with all of these men, I feel slightly more like the mascot or the housewife.

It's probably partially my fault. I remember one time we were in an airport, me and Mario. And this lady comes up and all she sees is Mario. He's very distinctive looking. And she's like, "Oh, can I take your picture?" And so I said to her, "Well, why don't I take your picture with him?" And she looks at me and she's like, "Oh, it's *you!*" I'm in the shadow of these guys but they're all very sweet with me. They're very nice.

111: Who else? OK, here's a trick question. What's the deal with Martha Stewart?

Moulton: We've tried to get her on my show and she says yes but she never shows up. We all love to dis her. She's an easy target. But, frankly, finally one day my husband called me on it. He said, "Why are you so negative about her?" And I said it's because she's so obsessed, she's so anal. He said, "Well, what do you think about her work?" I said, "I think it's incredible." And since then I've stopped being mean. Julia [Child] thinks the same way, which is so funny because Julia never sees the bad side of anybody, of course. Julia just thinks Martha is misunderstood, so she's going out of her way to be nice to her.

One night I remember I was decorating something with flowers and I made a reference to having a "Martha moment," and one of these days I know that's going to come back to haunt me. But anyway, we all poke a little fun at her. We can't help it; she's too perfect. On the other hand, I'm the anti-Martha, so un-perfect, so there you go.

111: There's the Naked Chef. Have you ever cooked in the nude?

Moulton: No, it's dangerous! Damn! I wear sneakers in the kitchen. I wear high-tops. I have 12 different pairs. That's my little fashion statement—besides the fact that I don't wear white jackets, which horrifies the old school.

But other than that, I wear the long-sleeved jacket and I make sure I have the apron, I make sure my hair is up. There are reasons why you wear these outfits and at home I can't cook without an apron. It's like the hands don't work if the hair is down and the apron's off. It doesn't happen. They don't function. So it's like a professional thing, but I wouldn't want to cook naked. I'd feel naked and naked is not for cooking.

The late James Beard used to. And he was sort of a flamboyant guy, he was an actor before he became a famous chef. He had this townhouse on 12th Street and apparently he had an outside shower, or at least a shower that was visible from the backyard. And he would get in that shower and shower all the time. The neighbors could just look out and see this big old guy having a little shower. So he apparently had no problem with it. I don't know actually if he ever cooked naked but he had no problem walking around naked.

111: Please rate popular cookbooks.

Moulton: I love Alfred Portale's books. He's done two for the home cook and we made some of the recipes in the dining room and they're really just excellent and they really, really work. I mean a whole bunch of chefs came out with cookbooks and Charlie Palmer has a nice book. Oddly enough, I bring up the chef's books on the show. I don't know why. There's a *Retro Desserts* by Wayne Harley Brackman. I like that a lot. I love any book by my buddy up in Chicago at Frontiers Grill. I love (Rick)

Bayless' books and he's got one out right now called *Mexico: One Plate at a Time*. It goes with the TV series.

111: What's the one cookbook every chef should own?

Moulton: I have one that I like a lot, just because I would hand it to the newlywed couple, because it's got everything in there you might possibly need and that's the *Doubleday Cookbook*. It's co-authored by a friend of mine, Jean Anderson. So if I'm making pancakes, I know there's a good recipe in there. If I want to make a standing rib roast, I know I'm given parameters and three different ways to cook it. If I want to make chicken pot pie, it's even got all the downhome recipes. There's more elegant stuff there, too, so you can stretch in either direction. It's the tome, it's about that big. So it's a good cookbook. Why did my cake rise so high? Why did it fall in the middle? Why is my meat tough? She's got all of the answers so it's a good empowerment cookbook.

111: It seems that a lot of chefs and restaurants, in fact, a lot of food is overrated. Name some of them for our readers.

Moulton: You think I'm going to do that? I'm not going to give you names of overrated restaurants. Okay, there's one thing that absolutely drives me crazy and this is not a type of food, this is a trend—chefs adding sugar into every place possible. I don't mean straight sugar necessarily, although sometimes it is straight sugar. It might be in the form of some fruit juice or some mango puree or something. But suddenly, I don't know what's my dessert and what's my entrée and it really pisses me off. Sugar, like salt and acid, really balances, has a place in many savory dishes. But it's gotten to the point of being ridiculous, it's so overdone... so that drives me crazy.

Also, as much as I love Alfred Portale, he created this sort of vertical cuisine and some followers of his take it way too far to the point where you're looking at your meal and you don't even know how to attack it. It's like this construction project. I don't like overly crossed-over food, although he does it beautifully. It's just his imitators who don't do it as well.

111: OK, how about the chefs you consider to be underrated...

Moulton: I can tell you who I think are some of the really talented chefs in this country. They're mostly pretty well-known. I think Jean George Vongerichten is great, because he's gotten completely out of the box. The trouble with French training (which is what I had) is that it took awhile for people to branch away from it, to stop using the cream and the butter and the meat-based stocks, and he just goes out there. He just does wild and crazy things and different sauces and much lighter food and much sharper flavor. I think he's brilliant.

Robert McGrath, who's a chef in the Southwest, I think he's also brilliant. He does southwestern food, but it's not heavy. It's just beautifully balanced.

Wolfgang Puck, I think now his restaurants are as good as he is. I went to the original Spago years ago and I didn't think it was that great. I was at the new one recently, Spago Beverly Hills, and I thought it was fabulous. But I knew how well he could cook because I did prep for all the chefs at *Good Morning America* all those years and he was one of the regulars. And his food is extraordinary.

I think Lydia Shire in Boston is very, very talented. I think Mario Batali, wow! I think his food is just extraordinary. All those unsung heroes—partly because they stay in their restaurant. There's one here in New York. He's a sweet guy; he's cute but he doesn't have that big personality. I'm referring to Bill Telepan at JUdson (sic) Grill. I think he's completely underrated and I think his food is fresh and wonderful and exciting, but not being overly so.

I'll tell you what I've seen too much of and that is French food. I think it's because I'm getting pretty old, so I've tasted too much food and I'm now looking for something new. Now, I love French food—my parents took us all to Paris in April, including the kids and us and we had so much fun. We ate out lunch and dinner for 10 days mostly at little bistros, so you could walk. You walk into any restaurant and it's just about as excellent.

But I'm tired of the French stronghold on this country. I think it's slowly letting go but classical French food, I'm tired of it.

111: Guide us through a romantic, seductive dinner. What are essentials?

Moulton: Champagne's an absolute must. Women are suckers for flowers and candles. This is a whole different issue but I talk to all these young people and even old people who are trying to get dates these days, there's always "How much does he want and is he just doing this so he can get me into bed?"

It has to be quite clear that that's not the only reason you're cooking, although you may end up in bed anyway, but you don't want to feel used. So women, this is good. If he puts a lot of attention to the table setting, they'll think, How sweet. He's thinking about how nice he's making it for me.

So put the candles all over the place and some beautiful dark roses. Go to a really tasteful florist, no carnations, dear, please! And then the Champagne is de rigeur and with all the foods that say "romance." There are obvious ones like caviar and foie gras, maybe some beautiful chilled shrimp or some raw oysters. Of course, then you have to slurp them. You've also got to make sure ahead of time that she likes oysters!

Get the best caviar. I recommend Osetra. Beluga's the big name and that's the perceived expensive one but real foodies like Osetra which is the middle-sized, the intermediate-sized caviar. It's got the most flavor.

Last Valentine's Day we took two guys who had never cooked before and got them to cook a romantic meal. Rack of lamb, it's such an elegant dish. Essentially, it's a rack of lamb and you put on a little mustard, mayonnaise, you sear it, then you make rosemary scallion crumbs with hot pepper flakes and you put them on top and finish in the oven. And you take it to just medium-rare and let it rest. But when you carve it, it looks like two hearts.

111: What's the greatest restaurant city in the world?

Moulton: Well, I think it's New York. West Coast people don't agree. Los Angeles is a contender. San Francisco would consider itself a contender. Chicago is becoming a contender but almost every city is really happening now. Miami's very exciting; Boston's really happening, but no, I'd still say New York.

I still think Paris is extraordinary but I'm very embarrassed to say I have not been to London since I was 13 and I hear that the food's exciting there. I was in Madrid; we had some wonderful meals but I've never been to Barcelona. I hear that's incredible.

111: What's your favorite fast food?

Moulton: Anything fried, but that's not necessarily what you get in a fast-food restaurant. Oh gee, I don't know because I don't go to McDonald's. In terms of unhealthy habits, I have plenty, though.

My favorite thing is roast duck, foie gras, deep fried, mayonnaise, those are my favorite, lamb shanks, all that really fattening, horrible stuff. I love it.

111: You live and work in New York; where do you eat?

Moulton: It changes all the time. I love Babbo. I haven't been to Gramercy Tavern in a while but I'd like to go back. I think I'm going back to Union Square Café, these are all tried-and-true places. I love Tabla. These are oldies.

Interesting enough, these are all Danny Meyer restaurants. I told you about JUdson Grill. I like Picholine. March is another one I like. I need to get out more. My husband and I have a date on Friday nights, so we're eating at a new restaurant. It's just easier to go to the same old places because I don't get around to making plans until late and can't get a reservation on Thursday night for a Friday.

As a matter of fact, you can't even get it for the next Friday or the Friday after that, so I have to do the really obnoxious thing if I know the chef. I call up straight and say, "I'd like a table for two." She'll say, "Oh, no we don't have anything at all." So then I'll say, "Well, supposing I know the chef. I'm a friend of the chef's." And then you go through the whole thing about, "You know, I had the chef on my TV show," and then you pull the strings to get in.

111: Tell us about the drink that will get you into trouble every time.

Moulton: Tequila. Mostly, I don't do it. I'm a wino, I love red wine, but it doesn't get me into trouble because I have wine with dinner.

Another one I love is aged port. That can get me into serious trouble. I can choke down a cognac but doing tequila shots—I used to work in a bar, we used to do that and that can get you into real trouble. But no, I guess aged port would be the one.

111: When you worked as a food stylist, what was the most unattractive food you ever styled?

Moulton: Just about any stew is awful. It's just lumpy, brown food. You always reach for the green herbs to fix it up. Winter food is very hard. Summer food is very beautiful.

111: Please evaluate the current crop of wines.

Moulton: The trouble for me is drinking with dinner. It's not a trouble but it's expensive. So I'm looking for value wines so those are the wines that I am mainly focusing on.

So Spanish wines, I know there are some good Chilean wines, although I haven't come across one that I like as much as the Australian or the Spanish. I think California's still happening. I think it's still exciting out there. And the rest of the United States is catching up, too, all the different wine areas. The wine guy here at the network is always teasing me. He says I like the ones I can chew on, and the Australian cabernets are pretty big. I mean, I love Italian wine.

111: You worked with Julia Child. Is she your culinary god?

Moulton: Yeah, she really is. She's a great example for women also – even though she will not call herself a chef, she calls herself a home cook. She feels she never was a chef in the sense of running a kitchen. She's gotten everything she wanted. She just kept going against incredible odds and she's never stopped learning. She's insatiable. She also happens to be really funny and really well-rounded. She's a riot.

She's just constantly learning. If she came in here right now, she'd want to know all about you. You could barely get anything out of her about herself. She wants to know all about everybody.

And she taught herself so much about food. She's learned so much and she thinks about every different angle of how you roast a duck, how you cook a goose. She's just right there, like the kid who first got out of cooking school—she's got as much excitement as she did 30 years ago.

111: What are the most important lessons you've learned from Julia?

Moulton: The biggest lesson that I've learned that's obviously stood me in terrific stead on this show for TV purposes is: Make a mistake and then fix it. Julia sometimes goes out of her way to make a mistake. It makes the person at home less nervous, and then she can show you how to fix it. It achieves my goal, which I think is her goal: to get people cooking. The other thing is to be a team player. You don't get anywhere by yourself. That would be an important lesson. Also, just work hard.

111: You're so damn cute. Does it ever get in the way of your credibility?

Moulton: Almost every minute of the day. I graduated from CIA (Culinary Institute of America) in 1977 and I've done just about everything you can do in the food industry – I've done a lot of heavy-duty things. But after all these years, I'm still just a woman. And it's maddening and it's just about daily. I don't think it helps that I'm short either and that I look a little younger than I am, which is actually very nice, but sometimes, people don't take me seriously. I gave a graduation speech recently at CIA. I made a point of spending a few minutes talking to the women and essentially saying, "Don't let any man out there tell you there's something you can't do in the kitchen." In some ways I think women are better suited. We're much cooler under pressure. (It's the man who throws the temper tantrum when a rack of lamb is sent back.) So I make a point of talking to the women. It's a very big part of my crusade – besides getting people to cook and to sit down to dinner.

Carol Alt

NYC's model citizen on slashing, bad boyfriends and how Amazon differs from Gilligan's Island

Being called the most beautiful woman in the world by hundreds of magazines could alter a person's perspective. Model and actress Carol Alt credits it all to plain luck. She's never bothered making plans. Alt, 40, a native Long Islander, was discovered by a photographer while waiting tables at a steak house during her freshman year at Hofstra University. Her father, a fire chief, and her mother, a former model, tried unsuccessfully to talk Alt out of moving to Manhattan to pursue modeling full time. She bolted and soon commanded $2,000 a day posing for Valentino and Sassoon jeans. The Sports Illustrated 1982 swimsuit issue featured her on the cover. More than 700 magazine covers followed, including Life magazine, which called Alt "the next million-dollar face." She entered the rarefied world of the supermodel.

Juggling a career of endorsement contracts and posters, calendars and exercise videos, Alt eventually realized something was missing—she wanted to become an actress. She began studying and made her stage debut in Bob Fosse's Sweet Charity as Ursula, a Swedish blonde bombshell. Putting her successful modeling career on hold, Alt moved to Europe, where she got lead roles in multinational films such as Via Montenapoleone, My First 40 Years (opposite Elliott Gould) and Love for Life, for which she was named actress of the year by Moda magazine.

Alt returned to the States, where she continued modeling. She also appeared in such domestic productions as the television miniseries Anna Karenina, Under the African Sun (a series of two-hour films) and a syndicated series (Peter Benchley's Amazon). Alt also acted in Private Parts opposite Howard Stern and Revelation with Jeff Fahey.

Robert Crane caught up with the itinerant Alt on a recent stopover in Los Angeles. He reports: "Alt never stops. Next, she was off to Russia to visit her boyfriend, hockey star Alexei Yashin. She was previously married to former New York Rangers defenseman Ron Greschner. She swears she's not a hockey hag. She just happens to like athletes who skate fast. Alt settled her six-foot-plus (with heels) frame into a big chair and sat sideways, her open blouse occasionally revealing her left breast. She refers to herself as a tomboy."

1

PLAYBOY: Describe the supermodels' retirement village. Who's the gossip? Who has the drinking problem? Who's the slut?

ALT: I don't want to point the finger at anybody. I work with a lot of these girls. It's not like I get into their personal lives. Most of that stuff is all gossip anyway, so you never know who's sleeping with whom until you're in the bedroom with them. It's better not to repeat unwarranted gossip. I could describe what the village would look like, of course. There would be a gym, a nutritionist, a beauty salon, a health food store and the bedroom. Most likely it'd be by the ocean. Most of us like the ocean. It's probably someplace in the Caribbean where it's quiet. But it has its moments of being hot, because everybody comes in the wintertime. I think most of us like our quiet time, but at the same time we have split personalities, because we live for those moments of being in the public eye. We're all going to live there one day. We'd all have our own little problems.

2

PLAYBOY: Would there be a ban on the young models who are coming up, like the Brazilians?

ALT: Like I said, they're all going to be in the village one day or another. They wouldn't be young kids when they got there. Let me tell you how sexy those Brazilian babes really are. Oh, baby. They are sexy, sexy people. I shot a movie there and it's really beautiful to watch people totally comfortable with their bodies. And there's no menace about it. Men don't leer. They're so used to it.

3

PLAYBOY: Which photographers put you through the most pretzel-like poses?

ALT: There isn't a photographer who doesn't put you through a pretzel-like pose. But the worst was Irving Penn. And there was someone – I can't remember his name—who worked for *Vogue* in the early Eighties. I literally sat for five or six hours in one position for both of those guys. With Penn I sat straight up on a stool for five hours, my head turned to the side. For the next day it was as if I had been in a car accident. With the other guy I sat with my feet over one arm of the chair with my head leaning back. I sat like that for six and a half hours for *Vogue*. I was so happy to be working for him he could have sat me there for 20 hours and I would have done it. I loved the pictures in both cases.

4

PLAYBOY: Any long-term chiropractic problems?

ALT: I find that I go for chiropractic just for maintenance, and because I have a cute chiropractor. I have a very cute doctor. So, maybe I have a little incentive to go. I can look at him and feel happy.

5

PLAYBOY: What was the most ridiculous shoot that helped end your modeling career?

ALT: Every shoot. There isn't a shoot where I don't think that. It's a ridiculous business. I got hypothermia shooting skiwear. I was absolutely freezing. It was 36 below on top of a mountain at four in the morning and I was wearing a shirt that didn't even have filler over a little turtleneck with a pair of pants and ski boots. No hat, no scarf, no gloves, no coat. I talked myself out of being cold to the point where it almost killed me.

6

PLAYBOY: What do you look like first thing in the morning?

ALT: Pretty much like I look right now, except no lipstick. Do you want me to take my lipstick off so you can see? I sleep with my mascara on. I hate taking mascara off because you have to rub your eyes to do it. I'm not wearing any makeup right now. I came out of the car and it was raining on me while I was in the car. This is not a science fiction movie—it was raining in the car.

7

PLAYBOY: Are hockey players the most aggressive athletes on and off the ice?

ALT: Off the ice, definitely no. They are Jekyll and Hyde. What I like so much about hockey players Is that they aren't brought up in a system where they're stars or where they're adored and admired and given scholarships and all the stuff we do with football and baseball players. Hockey players fight every step of the way. You end up with people who are thankful and appreciative of what they get. Hockey is in a strange position now. They have players who are thankful for working, for sure. But they're worth money and yet they're not paid like baseball and football players. One of the things about my boyfriend, Alexei Yashin, is that he's not a fighter. He's talented in terms of strategy and scoring. I've seen him do things in practice I've never seen any other player do, and I've watched hockey for 20 years. He's not a fast skater, but he's a strategic player. He's not a fighter because he has what they call hands. Why break those hands if that's what you need to play?

8

PLAYBOY: Do hockey players have adequate dental coverage?

ALT: My ex-husband was hit in the mouth and lost all his teeth in the last game of his career. Everything was covered. They are prepared for problems like that.

9

PLAYBOY: How do you imagine it feels getting slammed against the boards?

ALT: I have asked my boyfriend that. In fact, I don't think it's as bad as it looks. I've seen his elbow padding. I've walked into one of the rooms in the apartment and he had everything out to dry because he was packing for the World Championship. He has shin pads, knee pads, hip pads, protection in the front, shoulder pads, stomach pads, elbow pads, wrist pads, gloves and a neck thing. They're unbelievably padded. So when they smash all these pads into all those pads, and it's a clean hit. I don't think it bothers them at all.

10

PLAYBOY: After watching hockey, is it possible for you to appreciate men's figure skating?

ALT: I love figure skating, I love watching it, and Alexei and I watch it together. My ex-husband and I were at Billy Joel's house one night, and Billy was playing music. He just sat there, jealous, looking at Billy playing music. As we got into the elevator he leaned over and said, "You know, I always wanted to play the piano." And Billy looked at Ronnie and said, "You know, I always wanted to be a hockey player." Then they started comparing hands.

In this industry we're all fans of one another, because we realize what it takes to get to a certain level. You can appreciate the talents of people who reach that level. Alexei watches the figure skaters not just because they're fellow Russians, but because he can appreciate the talent and the time it took to get to the championships.

11

PLAYBOY: How is *Amazon* different from *Gilligan's Island*?

ALT: *Gilligan's Island* was, obviously, a spoof. We are trying to do reality-based TV. Peter Benchley came up with the idea. What if a plane goes down, and nothing goes right for the survivors? The rescuers don't find them. They wake up two days later. The plane is gone. All the dead bodies are gone, and there's stuff there, cell phones, which everybody thinks work everywhere. Hey, they don't even work in Laurel Canyon, for heaven's sake. So what happens to these people?

12

PLAYBOY: Were you the Ginger or the Mary Ann?

ALT: I was Mary Ann. And the truth is that I probably wanted to go that way more. I didn't want to be too sexy because that's obvious. I wanted to go a little more risky, and risky for me was no makeup, baggy clothes.

13

PLAYBOY: If you could do anything to Howard Stern, what would it be?

ALT: I would probably want to hold him close. He's the only person who hugged me and would turn off the cameras and say, "Carol, how are you?" And I would want to pay him back when he needs it. I absolutely adore Howard. I think he's a genius.

14

PLAYBOY: Is it important for a model making her first movie to not have a Baldwin brother as a co-star?

ALT: I don't think it was a Baldwin problem to begin with. Any model who is going to do a movie, especially if she has an amazing opportunity in front of her, has a responsibility to take classes. It's as simple as that.

I have two amazing acting coaches. I worked in Europe for many years because I didn't feel ready to come here. I didn't want to be one of those models stepping out and getting slashed because I didn't know my craft. For me, craft is the most important thing, not coming to America and getting a role I couldn't handle. I wanted to have a technique and know my craft and I didn't care where I had to go to do it. I studied for a long time, even before I got my first role. I started studying acting when I was a kid. I did dance, theatre, I did everything. I took ballet when I was three. When I was studying to be a doctor, my mother looked at me and said, "You should be a lawyer or an actress because you are so dramatic." So I took her advice.

15

PLAYBOY: How do you get a cab in New York City?

ALT: "Hey, yo, buddy. That's my cab. Get out of there!" Actually, I just pull up my skirt and stick out my leg. It always works. I usually get 10 or 12.

16

PLAYBOY: Hooking. Slashing. High-sticking. Which is which?

ALT: Hooking is kind of nice, especially when it's somebody you like. You take your stick and hook it around another player's arm, neck, leg or foot to prevent him from receiving a pass from another player. High-sticking can be kind of nice, too, actually, but it's usually after you shoot the puck. You bring your stick up a little too high, up into someone's face. It's considered dangerous, which is why a lot of people wear visors these days. Sometimes you can high-stick on purpose because you know a guy is coming at you and you can hit him in the face. But a lot of times it's just the heat of the moment. Slashing seems intentional. That's nothing but hitting somebody with your stick. There's no reason for it.

17

PLAYBOY: Have you ever had air rage?

ALT: I have had ticket rage. I have had airline rage. Air rage? No. I enjoy flying. I probably should have been a flight attendant because I love to fly. I'm a lazy flier. I like to get on the plane and fall asleep. It's the only time the phone doesn't ring and no faxes come in. I get good sleep on an airplane.

18

PLAYBOY: Why do supermodels pick inappropriate boyfriends?

ALT: I think it's availability. We have such horrible schedules and most of us are businesswomen, so we don't want to adjust our schedules. Modeling is also a business of opportunity. You can't always adjust your schedule because you might miss a really big opportunity or a big job. So we're at the mercy of the jobs that come in. Most inappropriate men are opportunists. They see this void. These men see very busy, very lonely women who are on the road working all the time. You rarely find a successful businesswoman who can work out a relationship with a successful businessman. Ronnie Greschner and I were both successful in what we were doing. That was ultimately the demise of our relationship, because we just didn't spend enough time with each other. When you're successful, you're successful because your other partner in marriage is your work. It takes one person in your relationship to give up something to be with the other person. But we didn't realize that until it was too late. I think a lot of these girls find a guy who fits in, who'll go anywhere. A guy who will show up at any time and do anything they need. That is great, because every woman likes to feel taken care of. But if someone is that willing, that's a sign there's a need beyond just wanting to be there.

19

PLAYBOY: Married to a hockey player. Now going out with a hockey player. What's this hockey deal all about?

ALT: It just happened. It's not that I particularly go for hockey players. I do like sportsmen, and of all the sports—no offense to the NFL or the AL or the NL—I just like the temperament of hockey players better. I've never heard of a hockey player doing drugs, beating his wife, attacking anybody or fighting anybody in bars. Again, I could be naïve, but they seem to be much more humble people off the ice. I guess I like that temperament better.

20

PLAYBOY: Give us a list of scary things completely out of character for you and a schedule of when you'll do them.

ALT: Being nude. That's completely out of the park for me. The funny thing is I have no problems with PLAYBOY and nude pictures. I love seeing nude bodies. I appreciate going to museums and I see statues and my favorite ones are the nude ones. I'm just shy—I can't imagine walking around the set naked. I have a hard time in the gym. It's totally scary for me to wear a bathing suit on the beach. I don't like it, yet I can do it. There's that little switch that goes, I can do it for a camera, but that's my job. And there's something that separates me from my job. It's not an ego thing: I want to be so sexy and show off my body, because I won't do it on a beach. I give my bathing suits away. I go to Vegas and do the Sky Screamer. I love that. I don't have problems with that. I try to do my own stunts. If you're talking about physical danger—I love danger. Danger's my middle name. Actually trouble's my middle name, but that's another story.

Rich Man, Pour Man

Meet 5 Ventura Boulevard bartenders... and why you should grab a barstool and have a drink with them.

JACKSON, OAKFIRE PIZZA

Popular Oakfire Pizza features one of the longer bar-tops along the Boulevard, and bartender Jackson Kuehn works it like Mick Jagger works a stage—tirelessly and pleasingly. "I always smile while I pay attention to my customers' needs and wants," says Kuehn, 34, looking more like actor Matthew Perry than he needs to. "I feel good when the patron feels good. We're like rock stars. Everybody loves a bartender."

The son of a government official (read C.I.A.), Kuehn was born in Austin, Texas and grew up in cities around the world. He observes that there's a common denominator among the earth's human inhabitants. "People love to talk incessantly about their current state of affairs," acknowledges Kuehn. "I'm similar to a psychiatrist in that I listen, but I'll occasionally offer advice like, 'Don't ask me to make some drink you ordered in Las Vegas at four in the morning.'"

He shamelessly plugs Oakfire's pizzas as the best in L.A. and has been known to direct some of his female fans toward the Rocky Road dessert. "They leave with their eyes gleaming with pure happiness," he quips.

Kuehn's 10 years of nights as a bartender (he's also presided over Beauty Bar in Hollywood) have supported his days as an actor. While his theme song is "Don't Stop Believing" by Journey, his refined accuracy and supersonic approach are what makes him a leading mixologist on the Boulevard. Still, his ultimate goal is to someday open "a sophisticated, aesthetically pleasing coffeehouse, unlike the one in *Friends*."

SIGNATURE DRINK: ICE CUBES, HEAVY POUR OF VANILLA-FLAVORED VODKA, DASH OF CHAMBORD AND PINEAPPLE JUICE. SHAKE VIGOROUSLY, GARNISH WITH FRESHLY-CUT LINE.

SERVE HIM: OLD FASHIONED OR BELGIAN ALE

JUAN, DAILY GRILL

The unofficial Bar Code of Ethics casually states that a tender of bar needn't engage his or her client in trivial banter. To the consumer who frequents the hardtop at Daily Grill (Studio City), under the tutelage of Juan Rosas, the conversation is anything but mundane. In fact, much laughter can be heard over the big-screen news and sports programming. The comfort factor rates highly. And Rosas doesn't make a bad drink either.

Despite 20 years of experience, Rosas, 43, of Mexican origin, acknowledges, "I'm still learning from my guests. Every day, regulars and new patrons walk in with their own stories. But at the end of the last pour, we're all good people." With Studio City housing many thespians, don't be

199

surprised if you're sharing bar space with actors like Robert Forster, Cuba Gooding, Jr., Johnny Knoxville, Cote de Pablo, and William Devane.

Rosas likes to think of himself as the coach—behind the line but in control at busy stretches. His personal theme song—"We Are the Champions" by Queen—reflects his style. He says a visit to his bar on the busiest day, Valentine's Day, is mandatory. Rosas grins, "If you tell your sweetheart how important your relationship is with a delicious meal and fantastic drinks provided by me, it will make my day. I'll be happy—mission accomplished."

Apparently one of the few bartenders without a second career, Rosas quickly amends that. "I'm a father. It's more difficult than tending bar because there is no handbook for raising children," he says. "But I married my sweetheart, a wonderful woman who has nurtured our kids into becoming decent, respectful young people who will find their own careers."

SIGNATURE DRINK: TEQUILA, FRESH LIME, LEMON JUICE, FRESH MINT, SHAKE WELL.

SERVE HIM: CLUB SODA WITH CRANBERRY JUICE

MEREDITH, SPARK WOODFIRE GRILL

If every bar has an employee who radiates like a welcoming committee, then Spark's spark is Meredith Eckles. Born to a U.S. military family serving in Wiesbaden, Germany, Eckles credits her father, who tended bar in college, with showing her the ropes of her decade-long trade. "I prefer creating drinks to being a waitress, because I have control of the outcome," says Eckles, 32, her smile displaying confidence.

Oklahoma was a destination for her peripatetic tribe when she was a youngster. The importance of where she grew up is not lost on her. "I'm the tailback at Spark," she confirms. "If we're running the ball, then we're playing well. If I fumble, the entire team suffers."

Eckles' idea of a piece of music that perfectly captures her cozy bar is "Here Comes A Regular" by the Replacements. Her regulars include noted somebodies like William Shatner, Billy Corgan, Paula Abdul and Alex Trebek. But she claims the one-time sightings are more exciting. "Barbra Streisand, Slash, Robert Downey, Jr., Kiefer Sutherland and Larry David top my list."

Her enthusiasm never curbed, Eckles thinks Valentine's Day at Spark is the perfect place to snuggle. "There are only half a dozen seats at the bar, so you'll be able to hear your date talk better than at another bar," advises Eckles. "Plus you can act like you planned to sit there when you actually forgot to make a reservation."

Spark may have to punt soon. A seamless transition to a career in massage therapy is in progress for Eckles. She acknowledges that she's ready to "hang up my martini shaker," knowing that she could be "contributing more to the world than the perfect lemon drop."

SIGNATURE DRINK: MEREDITH'S FAMOUS SPICITINI: ABSOLUT PEPPAR VODKA, SPICY BLOODY MARY MIX, TABASCO, WORCESTERSHIRE, LEMON, LIME, OLIVE JUICE. SHAKEN AND SERVED IN A LARGE MARTINI GLASS WITH A SALTED RIM AND FRESH GROUND PEPPER ON TOP.

SERVE HER: CHIMAY BLUE LABEL BEER, A NAPA CABERNET, AN OAKY, BUTTERY CHARDONNAY OR A GLENLIVET

STEVE & KIRK, STANLEY'S

If you've never seen Butch Cassidy and the Sundance Kid, it's playing four nights a week at the perennially well-attended, long-time watering hole Stanley's. Steve DeWinter and Kirk Driscoll, like a cool, modern version of Butch and Sundance—still always having each other's back—preside over a square, marbled bar with numerous satisfied customers returning for the well-crafted drinks as well as the comradery. DeWinter's and Driscoll's track record of 21 working years together makes imbibers feel at ease. "We have many regulars, because Stanley's is a comfortable, neighborhood bar where we have fun," explains DeWinter, 48. "The main reason clients return, though, is that I have the booze!"

Besides working 40 hours a week, the San Fernando Valley natives find time to follow their creative muses. For Driscoll, that includes being a highly commissioned photographer of the female form and landscapes. His work was displayed at Orlando Gallery in Tarzana. DeWinter enjoys a rock-and-roll life with his band, Daddy and The Innocents, performing club gigs throughout Southern California. One wild night at Stanley's, he played a CD of '40s cartoon music composer Raymond Scott over the house system. DeWinter smiles guiltily, "It added a zany, wacky quality to the bar."

The saloon hosts enjoy a certain autonomy found in photography, music and bartending. "Just as Annie Leibovitz controls her shoot, bartenders are given the run of the bar," says Driscoll, 58. "We're rewarded—and not only in tips." The bounty includes a celluloid chat with Tarantino, a beer with Gretzky and singing a song with Dolly Parton in the bathroom for Driscoll; and hanging with the late Lakers announcer Chick Hearn, talking shop with songwriter Jimmy Webb and carding singer Pink for DeWinter.

Their bar adventures have resulted in another creative niche: book writing, *Burn the Ice* (Amazon Kindle, and in an effort to fully disclose, co-authored by yours truly) details "all the unexpected episodes at Stanley's that landed in our pile of ice behind the bar, so to speak."

STEVE DEWINTER'S SIGNATURE DRINK: CLASSIC MANHATTAN: BOURBON WHISKEY (MAKER'S MARK), SWEET VERMOUTH AND A DASH OF BITTERS.

SERVE HIM: MILLER LITE

KIRK DRISCOLL'S SIGNATURE DRINK: KIRK'S COFFEE: ESPRESSO COFFEE, GRAND MARNIER, BAILEY'S, DARK CREAM COCOA, STEAMED MILK.

SERVE HIM: WATER

A Star is Formed

Rachel McLish, 30, the most celebrated female bodybuilder in the world, likes the smell of sweat. "Sweat is a cleansing mechanism," she says. "If you have a clean body, sweat has a clean smell. If your body is full of junk and smoke and you have bad habits, such as not bathing, you'd better leave." And if McLish tells you to leave, you may want to listen—she's the holder of two Ms. Olympia titles, the author of two best-selling books (*Flex Appeal* and *Perfect Parts*) and has been known to start her day with a five-mile run and an hour of weight training. She's now channeling her discipline into her embryonic movie career, which already includes *The Man Who Loved Women*. "The roles offered to me are *Conan*like, where I decapitate people," she complains, insisting that when she does make a movie, it will be on her own terms. Who's going to argue?

ACTORS

Robert Crane

Nicolas Cage

The intense actor on Lisa Marie, his uncle's wine and how he cured his hunka hunka burning love

1

PLAYBOY: After playing twins in *Adaptation,* were you disappointed to play only one con artist in your new Ridley Scott film, *Matchstick Men*?

CAGE: Absolutely not. *Adaptation* was the most difficult film I've done in terms of special effects. We'd decide which twin to shoot depending on which side of the bed I got up on that day.

2

PLAYBOY: Neither you nor Scott is known for comedies. Did *Matchstick Men* feel like new territory?

CAGE: Gee, when I consider all those heavy dramas I've been in, like *Raising Arizona, Moonstruck, Adaptation* and *Honeymoon in Vegas,* I kind of understand how you can ask that question.

3

PLAYBOY: Oh yeah, thanks for the reminder. Do you seek out films that have a Vegas theme?

CAGE: It's totally a fluke that I've made three or so movies that take place in Las Vegas. I don't know how that happened. Also, for a while, it seemed as if I was making movies that had the word moon in them—*Racing with the Moon, Moonstruck.* It's just one of those strange things. I'm sure there's another moon movie in my future, because things tend to happen in threes.

4

PLAYBOY: You changed your famous last name when you started acting. What can a Cage do that a Coppola can't?

CAGE: Be a movie star.

5

PLAYBOY: Do you get your uncle Francis Coppola's wines at a discount?

CAGE: For the holidays, Francis will send me a case of wine. That usually lasts awhile. It's a nice gift. My new favorite is my cousin Roman's wine called RC Reserve. It's a quality syrah and a good value. We went to Venice together and had the first tasting of his wine in Europe. It was great.

6

PLAYBOY: Would you like to do a movie in which you don't have to torture yourself for the role?

CAGE: Those roles are just the ones that stand out. I think of *Family Man* as being about a guy who isn't really on the edge, or my character in *Guarding Tess*. It seems I gravitate toward characters who do have some sort of dark edge to them. I don't know why that is. Maybe I'm just a dark-edged kind of guy.

7

PLAYBOY: Is it best to work out troubling things in movies, or would it save time to go to a psychiatrist?

CAGE: The best way to work out anything is through expression and—in my case—through movies, whether it's acting, directing or producing. Take negatives and turn them into positives through creativity.

8

PLAYBOY: In *Leaving Las Vegas*, your character suffers the erectile problems characteristic of a heavy drinker. If there were a cure, would its name be Elisabeth Shue?

CAGE: The only time my character ever gets hard is at the very end of the movie, with Elisabeth's character. For the majority of the film, he is unable to do anything because of the massive amounts of alcohol he's drinking. But on the other hand, I think he breaks free just before his death.

9

PLAYBOY: Is there a time during the making of a movie when you think it isn't going to work out at all?

CAGE: There's always a moment in every movie when I become possessed by self-doubt, because I never want to get comfortable in anything that I'm doing. That's part of the reason I haven't taken a straight line in my career trajectories, because I wasn't comfortable making some of the choices that I made. I thought perhaps by doing that I could learn something or grow in some way as an actor. I'm always trying to stay on the high wire.

10

PLAYBOY: Divorce for actors is especially hard because it's so public. One school of thought has it that to make it easier, give her everything she wants. Having been down that road twice, do you have any advice?

CAGE: My general rule is to try my best not to explore my family dynamics publicly. But I will say that I always think it's best to be generous.

11

PLAYBOY: What are some things you really like, and what do you just not give a shit about?

CAGE: I really like Venetian glass. I like nature. I like biology. I like Gaudi architecture. I like inspiring acting. I don't give much of a shit about watching a ball game.

12

PLAYBOY: You auctioned off your comic book collection. Did you hold back anything from the hammer?

CAGE: I've parted with most of my collection. I kept the old horror comics. I like those—some of the *Tales of Suspense* comics. By and large I was going through a streamlining process where I made a decision that everything you own owns you. I got too caught up in the collecting. Now I'm trying to find other ways to stimulate myself besides collecting other people's stuff.

13

PLAYBOY: Was there any role in which you were completely comfortable or found a familiar emotional center?

CAGE: I generally don't ever get totally comfortable. I'm always trying to find myself still in a state of tension. A long time ago I was making a movie called *Amos and Andrew*. It wasn't a very successful film. But I remember at one point I sat down on the couch in that movie and started talking about Sea-Monkeys. The character was talking about his mother buying him an aquarium with Sea-Monkeys in it. In that monolog I felt very centered and comfortable. But the character was smoking a lot of weed.

14

PLAYBOY: Were there any roles you were not offered in which you thought you would have done a better job?

CAGE: I can't ever say that I would have done a better job than anybody, because a movie finds the right cast for one reason or another. I do think that if I had played the Joker in *Batman* I would have made him madly in love with Batman. But I think Jack Nicholson was great.

15

PLAYBOY: What are the best thing and the worst thing a director ever told you?

CAGE: The best thing a director ever told me was on *Wild at Heart*. David Lynch had a very exuberant way of saying, "Nixer! Solid gold, buddy!" That was probably the best thing. The worst thing was on *Moonstruck* when Norman Jewison said to me on Christmas Eve, "The dailies aren't working."

16

PLAYBOY: Some of the actresses you've worked with include Sarah Jessica Parker, Elisabeth Shue, Bridget Fonda, Cher, Penelope Cruz, Meg Ryan and Kathleen Turner. Considering the quality of the company, were there movies you would have liked to go on a little longer?

CAGE: It's funny, when I make a movie I really want to get it over with. I see the light at the end of the tunnel, and when I see the palm trees swaying at the end of that tunnel, I know I'm almost done. For me, acting and being in a movie is like being on a hot grill. I just want to get off that grill.

17

PLAYBOY: In romantic situations, is it easier to try something for the first time when you're acting or when you're not acting?

CAGE: Probably when you're not acting. There are so many different places you can go to find an attraction. It can be a memory. It can be a picture that you saw. Or it can be the person standing right in front of you. For me, the set is never a very romantic place to meet somebody. There are all these people around, cameras and people observing you. it's not a comfortable zone for romance. For such a thing to happen, it would have to be off the set.

18

PLAYBOY: Have you listened to the album by your ex-wife Lisa Marie Presley?

CAGE: Well, yeah. I heard her record before it came out. I think it's excellent.

19

PLAYBOY: Have you ever experienced a hunka hunka burning love?

CAGE: I have, but I've been taking antibiotics and it has cleared up.

20

PLAYBOY: Which son-in-law would Elvis have preferred—you or Michael Jackson?

CAGE: I can't speak for him. I just hope he would know that Lisa Marie and I tried.

Jamie Foxx

The funnyman on fly girls, the trouble with rap and that hot Condoleezza Rice

Actor-comedian Jamie Foxx, 34, was born Eric Bishop in Terrell, Texas, where, he says, "Everyone who is African American is either a yardman or a maid." Foxx' parents were divorced when he was six years old, and his mother's adoptive parents adopted him as well and raised him as their son. So, legally, Foxx' biological mother is his sister, and his grandmother is his mother—and chief source of comedic inspiration.

Foxx' family encouraged him to take piano lessons, and when he was 13 he was playing Sunday services at his church. Upon graduating from high school, Foxx won a music scholarship to the United States International University in San Diego, but he soon realized classical piano wasn't going to be his life's work. He enjoyed making people laugh too much. After Foxx moved to Los Angeles, where he did stand-up at local comedy clubs, he changed his name to the androgynous Jamie Foxx when he noticed most club owners booked women sight unseen. Foxx' act at the time consisted mainly of impersonations—Mike Tyson, Louis Farrakhan and O.J. Simpson, among others, and his alter ego, Ugly Wanda. It was Wanda who caught the attention of the producers of Fox Network's hit series In Living Color. Foxx appeared on the show for three years, co-starring with Jim Carrey and Damon Wayans. At the same time, he played Crazy George on the critically acclaimed Fox show Roc.

Foxx moved to the big screen in 1996 opposite Janeane Garofalo and Uma Thurman in The Truth About Cats and Dogs and in The Great White Hype, co-starring Samuel L. Jackson and Jeff Goldblum. The WB Network then offered him his own series. The Jamie Foxx Show, which he co-created and executive-produced, enjoyed a successful five-year run. Foxx headlined such films as Booty Call, with Vivica A. Fox, and Antoine Fuqua's action comedy Bait. His 1999 performance in Oliver Stone's Any Given Sunday garnered a Best Supporting Actor nomination from the New York Film Critics Awards. Foxx currently portrays Drew "Bundini" Brown, Muhammad Ali's cornerman and inspiration in Ali, starring Will Smith and directed by Michael Mann. He recently completed his Cold Comedy stand-up tour, and he's kept his musical roots, releasing a top 20 R&B album, Peep This, in addition to contributing songs to the soundtracks for Any Given Sunday and Bait.

Robert Crane caught up with the comedian at his production office in Los Angeles. Crane reports: "Foxx appeared without his entourage, half an hour late. He constantly adjusted his do-rag, picked at his lunch and looked me in the eye. He seems incapable of not having a good time. A former high school football player, Foxx looks more like a wide receiver or defensive back than someone in show business. He'd be ideal for Deion Sanders' biopic."

1

PLAYBOY: Should the U.S. government hire Suge Knight to fight the war on terrorism?

FOXX: Suge would probably scare everybody. He'd just do a huge drive-by—Afghanistan, Pakistan. It would just be one red Mercedes and all of our problems would be over.

2

PLAYBOY: You cut your teeth on *In Living Color* with all those Wayans kids. Didn't Mr. Wayans Sr. have a hobby? What was he thinking?

FOXX: I think he really loved his wife and she was understanding to have that many kids. And Keenan is following that path. There's the Wayans, and then there's Wayans Light. They're all hilarious. I would love to sit down with Keenan's father to find out where they got all the comic genius.

3

PLAYBOY: Do you keep in touch with the Fly Girls?

FOXX: No, but I have some new fly girls I keep in touch with, and they don't dance. They just do their thing. J. Lo was a Fly Girl. She's moved on now, huh? She's still fly, though. I knew all of them very personally. I knew them all, and they knew me, and they remember that whenever they see me.

4

PLAYBOY: You starred in *Booty Call*—what were you thinking?

FOXX: I needed a job, and I needed to do something fast in order to take a step in my career. Maybe not an Academy Award performance, but definitely a peek-a-boo performance on Sunset Boulevard.

5

PLAYBOY: You threatened to spank Prince at the MTV Awards if he wore those butt-revealing pants. Are you sorry you didn't?

FOXX: A little. If nobody would find out about it, I'd spank him publicly—if I had on a veil. I don't know how he'd take that, but he'd have to take it, because I'd spank him with my index finger up.

6

PLAYBOY: Name one black star who couldn't take Prince.

FOXX: Who couldn't beat him up? Gary Coleman couldn't take Prince—actually it would be a draw, because they're about the same size.

7

PLAYBOY: Help us understand the conflicts brewing in the hip-hop community. We hope it's not about money but rather about art.

FOXX: Come on, man. You think it's about artists? Of course it's about money. If you can't get any height—because, really, rap stars are just poets who have fallen into this society of bad boys—you've got to be the guy who goes to jail. That sells records, so that's what they do. It's not really about the art, because the art died a long time ago. There aren't too many guys out there who are actual artists with the words and stuff. Now it's about how big my record company is, how many jewels are on my necklace.

8

PLAYBOY: What's your party mix?

FOXX: It's just enough ghetto to remind me I haven't left the hood, with some high-end people from the Hollywood crowd and a couple of white girls who dig me. My food is gourmet wieners and hamburgers—not quite doing it like Hef does. I'm like the black version of Hugh Hefner without the budget. I'm Jerome Hefner. I'm putting it down like that. Finger foods in more ways than one.

9

PLAYBOY: How do you tell a girl, "It's check-out time." Or do you have people who do that?

FOXX: I just say, "Bounce! You know what it was all about. You didn't care about me when I was just walking down the street. Get out of here. It's over." I've been thrown out, too, so it's pretty equal.

10

PLAYBOY: We know what your character learned from Al Pacino in *Any Given Sunday*. What did you learn?

FOXX: I learned how to be modest. Al Pacino is nothing like the characters he's played. He is a professional in that he doesn't use his status to beat you over the head like some actors do. He doesn't do that at all. That's what I learned—to be modest no matter what the accomplishment. To see him be just a normal cat made me go, "Oh, it's cool to be normal. You don't have to do all the antics." That's the true talent.

11

PLAYBOY: Do you think Condoleezza Rice is hot? She could make your ass disappear in a second.

FOXX: Sounds good. Can I get some of that Condoleezza on my rice? My brown rice, as a matter of fact. Can I perform Condoleezza on you, Ms. Rice? I want her to do that to me, because once I'm done, she's going to have to make me disappear, because I'm filming it.

12

PLAYBOY: Whose picture should be on the wall of the young African American?

FOXX: I would have to say Muhammad Jordan-Smith, Muhammad Ali mixed with Michael Jordan and Will Smith.

13

PLAYBOY: Would there be a place for your photo?

FOXX: Not unless they just want to have a good time. I'm the party cat.

14

PLAYBOY: Women—leave them laughing, or wanting more?

FOXX: Leave them laughing, because once they start laughing, they will want more. That's what I've learned. I don't care how beautiful a girl is. If you can make a woman laugh, that's it. They'll always want to be around you. You don't necessarily have to have all of them, or sleep with all of them. Just the fact that all of them want to hang around you makes people say, "Is he fucking them? What is he doing? They're always around him." I don't like young girls. I usually stay with girls close to my age. I'm 34, so I stay with 29, 30 and up. At least we can reminisce on some things.

15

PLAYBOY: What was the deal backstage at the MTV Awards?

FOXX: Michael Jackson's ass. Jesus Christ. He has 60 bodyguards. I started screaming at the top of my lungs, "Fuck Michael Jackson. Who does he think is going to jump on him, Britney Spears? Should we shoot him? Can we break his leg? What should we do?" But that's because I feel in this business there's a huge gap between what you have as an entertainer and what you have in your personal life. Nobody puts his arms around Michael Jackson and says, "Dude, regardless if you sell one fucking record, I'm not going to let you do this to yourself." Nobody takes the time to say, "Hey, we're going to love you anyway. Maybe you can't sell 20 million records, but at least you can live your life pretty much sanely, as opposed to being the butt of everybody's joke. You've kind of lost touch as far as being a human is concerned." Sad thing.

16

PLAYBOY: What material always works?

FOXX: What I call "human material"—things that happen to you every day. Relationships—do you love them or do you hate them? I talk about jealousy, which happens to everybody who falls in love. I say, "Have you ever been jealous of a person who isn't even with you?" You see somebody you think you might like, and you think, Look at this good motherfucker. "What's up, Jamie?" "Fuck you." "What's wrong with you?" "You're looking at my girl." "You don't have your girl with you." "Well, she's with me in spirit." So I deal with things that I call the human things.

17

PLAYBOY: What material has bombed?

FOXX: It doesn't bomb, but it makes the crowd real quiet when I talk about going to the health clinic. But it's simply this—it's about communication. I say, "Have you ever gotten VD from a girl, but the girl is so pretty you don't want to blame it on her, because you might fuck up the relationship?" I was going out with this girl—this is a personal story. This girl was so pretty, but I couldn't tell her that I thought she gave me something, because I didn't want to fuck it up.

18

PLAYBOY: What's funny now?

FOXX: You talk about your fears. When you're on a plane now and see somebody Islamic, you automatically feel a different way. It's good for me as a black person living in the San Fernando Valley. I can drive up and down the streets at 100 miles an hour and look at a policeman and say, "Hey! America, man!" It's good to have the heat off me now. You know what I'm saying? Now they're charging up to the 7-Eleven. You make light of it, but you don't walk light. Don't be afraid to make jokes about it. It is a sensitive situation, but at the same time, life has to go on.

19

PLAYBOY: Is it true you got your role in *Any Given Sunday* because P. Diddy throws like a girl?

FOXX: That's what they say. I've never seen Puff actually throw, but I don't give a damn how I got the role. He is making millions. He can buy a fucking mechanical arm, or somebody who looks exactly like him. I didn't know that Puffy was up for the part when I went in. So maybe he threw like a girl, or whatever, but I got the part. Shit, he's got enough money to pay for whatever he needs to get it done.

20

PLAYBOY: How will your film *Ali* improve upon Ali's film *The Greatest*?

FOXX: For one, Muhammad Ali is not as good an actor as Will Smith. There are things in this movie that are going to enhance Muhammad Ali. And because you have Michael Mann at the helm, who pays such close attention to detail, it's going to be the last time they ever do the Muhammad Ali story.

Matthew Perry

The ex-Friend is going The Whole Ten Yards to make sure you'll see him somewhere besides reruns

1

PLAYBOY: Now that *Friends* is over, what would you have had Chandler do differently?

PERRY: I would have had him rethink the sweater-vests.

2

PLAYBOY: Listen closely and you can actually hear the ulcers perforating at NBC over the prospect of a *Friends*-free Thursday night. Can you name all the failed must-see wannabes?

PERRY: I'll do my best. There have been about 20 of them. *Coupling*, of course. *Boston Common*. And *Pig Sty* on UPN, which I auditioned for and did not get. Nobody can find the "new *Friends*" because, for lack of a better word, magic occurred in 1994 when these producers and this cast were put together. It's luck—and timing. *Friends* was my sixth television show, and I think it was Jennifer Aniston's seventh. Two weeks before I shot *Friends* I had no money, and I did a pilot called *LAX 2194*. It was about baggage handlers in the year 2194, and my job on the show was sorting aliens' luggage. Two weeks later I was playing Chandler.

3

PLAYBOY: You were raised in Canada. What are trips home like for you now? Has anything been named after you?

PERRY: Yes, the Toronto Blue Jays are now called the Toronto Perrys. For the most part trips back have an initial kind of strangeness with my buddies, and then 10 minutes later we're right back where we were. My pals don't care that I'm in people's living rooms on TV. I can just hang—and that's nice.

4

PLAYBOY: So who are funnier, Americans or Canadians?

PERRY: I think ordinary, everyday people in Canada are funnier than people in the U.S. Canadians have a certain dry humor. Maybe it's so cold up there that we have to be funny, but everyone, even the bank teller, can make you laugh. That's why we have the Jim Carreys and Mike Myerses and Michael J. Foxes. I think their success has a lot to do with the fact that they're Canadian.

5

PLAYBOY: You attended a private boys' school in Ottawa. What did you learn there that you wouldn't have learned in public school?

PERRY: The desire to have women around, always.

6

PLAYBOY: Did you get hazed much?

PERRY: I was a pretty popular kid, but when I needed a defense mechanism, I had one: If anybody got really mad at me in school, I would just try to make them laugh. I had a little trick—if somebody was coming at me on the sidewalk, I would trip over the curb and the guy would just laugh and walk away. It's a defense mechanism that I'm trying to get away from now, by the way.

7

PLAYBOY: The show has made you insanely rich. You were in the *Forbes* top 100 celebrities last year.

PERRY: I believe I was actually number 25. I was surprised to see Bruce Springsteen at 26. That was a very surreal moment for me. Britney Spears was number one the year before and then wasn't on the list. That was odd. It suggests how strange the list is.

8

PLAYBOY: Who can you now get on the phone that you couldn't if you hadn't been on *Friends* for the past 10 years?

PERRY: Short of the president of the United States, just about anyone. If I placed a call to Tom Hanks, it would probably get returned eventually. That's very interesting. I placed a call to Steve Martin a few weeks ago, and he called me back after about 20 minutes. That's not normal. There's a lot of giggling under my blanket about what I'm able to do now, and I have taken advantage of those things. I can say to a group of people, "I want to see the French Open. Let's go to Paris tomorrow." And that's amazing. But in order to stay sane, I have to *realize* that it's amazing. I realize I won the lottery.

9

PLAYBOY: You were a top-ranked junior tennis player. Who was your favorite pro?

PERRY: Jimmy Connors, my favorite athlete of all time. I love McEnroe, but I was always a Connors guy. I had the same temperament as Connors when I was a kid—and the same bad haircut.

10

PLAYBOY: Which female tennis players do you like to watch?

PERRY: I have to say Jen Capriati, of course, because I'm friends with her, and that changes everything. I mean, there are pictures of me having mental breakdowns while cheering her matches. I was with her seconds after her big semifinals loss at the U.S. Open. I said, "The only way you can handle this is to go into the press conference and make a joke." So when the reporter asked, "How do you feel?" she said, "What do you mean? I won, didn't I?" It's also fun to watch the players who are just beautiful athletes. Jelena Dokic, of course, is great-looking. And it's awfully nice that they wear those outfits for me.

11

PLAYBOY: What is must-see TV for Matthew Perry?

PERRY: *SportsCenter. Inside the Actors Studio*, because of what I can learn from it. And any of your porn stations. I really don't watch much. I stopped watching *Friends* a long time ago, just because I was there and I knew what was going on. Sometimes when I see it in syndication it's a nice look back and I remember my Charlotte Rampling hairstyle.

12

PLAYBOY: What is television doing too much of?

PERRY: I think television is getting lazy. Sometimes reality TV is fun to watch—I admit I watched the first *Joe Millionaire* every week. I had people over to the house. But producers are getting lazy and cheap, and if it continues that way there won't be another *Friends* or *MASH*. It's so much more inexpensive to use real people—you whisper to them what to say and then they say it, which is what I believe happens on reality television shows, frankly. I don't buy the "I love you" and "Let's get married" and all this fake craziness.

13

PLAYBOY: What's the weirdest story line discussed but never used on *Friends*?

PERRY: There was a discussion about Chandler going to a male strip joint every day just because he loved the sandwiches. It's very funny, but that's the one story line I nixed.

14

PLAYBOY: Besides the added yard, how is the sequel *The Whole Ten Yards* different from *The Whole Nine Yards*?

PERRY: It has a different style. It's more of a *Midnight Run*-style movie than the first one. We tried to tap more into the chemistry between Bruce Willis and me. Who knew that this man who saves the world in other movies would be able to ping-pong funny stuff with me? The first one was mostly me. I was the pitcher to whoever came up to bat, and this sequel has a lot more of Amanda Peet, Bruce and me. This time we have Kevin Pollak playing an 85-year-old who steals every scene he's in. He made me laugh so many times that we had to cut the camera because I was making involuntary sounds—not all of them oral.

15

PLAYBOY: Does Amanda reprise her memorable topless scene from the original?

PERRY: First, I wasn't allowed on the set that day, which was a terrible experience for me. She didn't want to do the scene in the first place, and I said, "You've got a great role in this despite that scene. And you're going to get a lot of attention, not just from that scene but from the work you do in the movie. Do it." Amanda is one of my favorite people in the world. She is dorky and beautiful and wonderful and talented, with this innate sense of timing that I really respect. So without taking her clothes off this time, she is probably sexier than she was in the first. Amanda, I hope you read this.

16

PLAYBOY: You're one of the few celebrities we see regularly wearing glasses. Why don't you just get that operation?

PERRY: I'm a little wary of laser surgery because of the earthquake that could potentially occur right when it's happening. I'm nearsighted. As I'm sitting here with you I can see you completely clearly. But if you were 20 feet away, you'd look like a black woman.

17

PLAYBOY: Who will be the first *Friends* cast member to guest-star on Matt LeBlanc's spin-off?

PERRY: I guess the correct answer is whoever is asked first. Oh, probably me. Matty and I are very close, and I support him in all his endeavors.

18

PLAYBOY: How will Matt let you know that it's *his* damn show now?

PERRY: He won't.

19

PLAYBOY: What's your post-*Friends* career nightmare, the one that wakes you in a cold sweat?

PERRY: That I won't be able to continue the creative growth that I have experienced as an actor in the past 10 years. I was so inspired watching Bill Murray in *Lost in Translation*. If that went away all of a sudden and I went, "What a minute—carpentry!" that would be a nightmare. To be honest, I don't want to star in any more what I call *Love Boat* movies—boy meets girl, they have some kind of problem, maybe on the fiesta deck, and then they make up and kiss and the camera pans out to the entire city. I think I've been in three or four of those. On the fourth I was like, "Really? We're going to end this way—again?"

20

PLAYBOY: It seems every hit TV series is remade as a movie these days. Can you cast the *Friends* movie for us?

PERRY: I think the idea of recasting *Friends* is absolutely insane. That said, I think Matthew Broderick would be fine as Chandler.

Jack Nicholson

The varied and highly successful film career of Jack Nicholson began in 1958 with *The Cry Baby Killer*. Before that, the native of Neptune, New Jersey, bounced around studios, doing odd jobs and such occasional television shows as *Divorce Court* and *Matinee Theatre*. After *The Cry Baby Killer*, Nicholson was featured in psycho-exploitation films like *Little Shop of Horrors, Too Soon To Love, The Terror, and The Wild Ride*. In 1964 he made two films in the Philippines with Monte Hellman. This was followed in 1965 with two low-budget westerns, *The Shooting* and *Ride In The Whirlwind*, in which Nicholson co-starred. He had also written the screenplay for the latter.

Although these films didn't catapult Nicholson into the limelight, they supplied him with important filmmaking knowledge.

In 1967, he teamed up with director Richard Rush and cinematographer Laszlo Kovacs, to do an A.I.P. classic, *Hell's Angels on Wheels*. Nicholson played a disillusioned gas station attendant, who tries to find Nirvana atop a Harley-Davidson 1000. In this film, we get our first look at the Nicholson anti-heroic, soul-searching, loner, in quest for the real America. It is Nicholson's schizophrenic ability to be aloof and concerned at the same time that gives his character an unapproachable level of brilliance.

The team that worked so successfully in *Easy Rider* came together for the first time in *The Trip*. Scripted by Nicholson, it starred Peter Fonda and Dennis Hopper. But it was *Easy Rider,* another low-budget film which gained Nicholson national attention and his superb characterization resulted in an Academy Award nomination. This was followed by another great performance in *Five Easy Pieces*, and a second Academy Award nomination.

Nicholson debuted as a director with *Drive, He Said*, a film about alienation which he also co-produced and co-scripted.

This controversial work was followed by performances in *Carnal Knowledge, A Safe Place, The King of Marvin Gardens,* and *The Last Detail*. His brawling, cursing, hard-nose portrayal of Billy "Bad Ass" Buddusky brought him his third Academy Award nomination. He also received the Best Actor Award at the 1974 Cannes Film Festival.

Rounding out his 1974 schedule were leads in *Chinatown* (hailed by many critics as the best American film of 1974), in *The Mousebed Fortune* and in *One Flew Over The Cuckoo's Nest*.

The Genesis interview, conducted by Robert Crane and Christopher Fryer, took place at Nicholson's hilltop house off Mulholland Drive, in a living room that overlooks his redwood-decked pool and Coldwater Canyon. The walls were decorated with memorabilia from his movies, a poster in Japanese advertising *The Terror*, and a large photograph of an oil field, reminiscent of the locale of *Five Easy Pieces*.

After clearing the room of friends and people who were constantly dropping in, we settled into a brown suede sofa for our conversation.

Genesis: Having been connected with films from all angles, which aspect of filmmaking do you like best?

Nicholson: Well, because I've done all these things I can't come to any real conclusions about that. I first produced about nine or ten years ago, when I was twenty-seven, and the problems for a twenty-seven year old producer in Hollywood are enormous. I mean a producer in Hollywood doesn't go out and rent trucks at U-Haul, and go down and pick the wardrobe at Western Costume. I was originally drawn to films by a creative drive, so I really almost did any film. I'm not much involved in what the credits are. When I'm *involved* in a film I'll do whatever I can. Because acting is where I started, I feel most comfortable in that role. I've only been a failure as a director, so I'd like to get back into that and make use of the experience that I've had. It's also the most expressive part of filmmaking. I don't like the fact that if you're going to author, write and oversee a film, that it takes a minimum of a year. That's a lot of time to give to a film, especially for something like *Drive, He Said*, which didn't find a wide audience.

Genesis: Why do you think *Drive, He Said* failed at the box office?

Nicholson: Everyone analyzes these things. I don't know. What I do, just to keep myself creatively sharp, is to say, "Well, it was a perfectly satisfactory film to me." I mean I honestly feel, based on the way I do things, that I did the best that I could do with it, which is all you can ask of yourself.

Genesis: Did working with Mike Nichols on *Carnal Knowledge* give you any insights into your own work as a director?

Nicholson: Yes. He's a very precise director. The environment he creates on the set, the pace he shoots at, where he places his concerns, the kind of dialog he gives to his characters, and his own temperament relate to the moment to moment experience of directing. He's very specific about it. There are a lot of things that he does that are worthwhile for anyone to adapt. It won't ultimately affect the contour of your product, but it'll affect the efficiency you get it together with.

Genesis: Do you have a favorite film of yours, so far?

Nicholson: No. When I first got started in movies, most of my thinking about it was very theoretical. That was so, because of where I was functioning—in low budget films and horror movies that everyone else hated, including my best friends. I had a conversation with a guy I lived with for a while, another actor, and he frankly admitted, even though he was in classes with me, that he never thought I'd be a good actor because of all those horror pictures. Because of that, sort of protectively, I started thinking of my own work as a body of work.

There are a lot of projects where I think I might just pluck characters out of the situations that I left them in in several movies, and as a writing exercise take them and let them see how they feel about one another. It's an inwardly energizing thing for me that gets my particular insight and feelings about a character going.

Genesis: How close to you are the characters that you portray? Are they an extension of yourself?

Nicholson: Well, I work very personally. Their life and their behavior are extensions of my behavior. There are always differences between the characters and myself. I always try to translate them into characters with a positive philosophy. In other words, I try to feel that what they're doing is what they think is the right thing, and what is motivating their life force, and so on. In that way, it's an extension of my thinking but it's separate.

An interesting phenomenon is that sometimes—and this has only happened in the last three films, and never in any of my other work—you play a character that creates such a large impression that you're suddenly dealing with the feedback from the character you played, and it will change your life after it's done. I suppose I'm a symbol for male chauvinism at this time because of *Carnal Knowledge*. Actually, that's not an area that I've ever been particularly into. I've always had very good relationships with women, but because the new women I meet have this super image of me, I'm in the dialog whether I want to be or not.

Genesis: So in that respect, has being a movie star affected your relationships with people you're close to?

Nicholson: Absolutely. It's impossible to be a movie star and not have all of your relationships affected. All of them.

Genesis: Do you think it has affected your acting?

Nicholson: It has affected the rhythm in my acting. I don't do as much as I used to.

Genesis: How careful were you in choosing scripts after *Easy Rider*?

Nicholson: I've only accepted one job since *Easy Rider* that I hadn't already been committed to do. Considering all the offers that you get after becoming a known actor, that's pretty selective. It's based on being able to do only so much work; and, I've really done as much or more work than anybody around. Before, I've never been able to afford to be selective. Now I am, and I'm affected by it.

Genesis: Was your script for *The Trip* based mostly on your own experiences with LSD?

Nicholson: Mostly, and also on what was going on in my life at the time. I felt that it would be good. I always shoot for well-rounded, unbiased views of a subject. Although I never felt that the film was going to be 100 percent brilliant, or really cover it or anything like that, I felt that my being in it with Roger (Corman) meant that between the two of us we would make it a more well-rounded film than if he had made it alone or with someone who didn't have as much experience with the drug as I did.

Genesis: Have you acted while under the influence of drugs?

Nicholson: Yeah, I've acted stoned.

Genesis: Does it help or hinder your performance?

Nicholson: For the most part, it's not a help. For one thing, being stoned takes a lot of your energy away, and that's difficult. The only thing that being stoned has helped me with creatively is writing. It relaxes you, and makes you a little more content to be in a room all by yourself. It's easier to entertain yourself mentally. It produces a lot of shit, too.

Genesis: How much of a script makes it to the screen?

Nicholson: Well, with *The Trip* it was a particularly small part that made it. I knew they wanted to show the interior mind of fantasy, which is wrong for the movies. It's exactly the thing you don't want to do when you put a novel on the screen, unless the fantasy has a scenario of its own. The images are much too specific to go as fantasy images, so I did that part with subliminal cuts, or very fast cuts, and not a lot of them at once, so that you almost couldn't see them. That was the technique that I thought would be wise to use, even though I went to the trouble of specifying the content of each image.

The idea of the script was seeing the objective camera-eye experience of the guy actually on the trip when he's got the orange. He can't believe it. Or seeing an actor when he's regressed to where he's three years old, and talking that way or not, but seeing the objective experiences by juxtaposing the little flashes as a key to what might be going on. That was really the balance of my script. They blew up all of the fantasy images and minimized the juxtapositions greatly by doing so. In that case, while all the words were said, maybe sixty percent of the images made it to the screen.

Genesis: Why did you do *On A Clear Day You Can See Forever*?

Nicholson: Primarily, for the bread at that time. I needed it.

Genesis: Do you feel you've reached a plateau?

Nicholson: I've reached a plateau, but I've never been that much in love with my own work. I still have a certain desperation of wanting to get beyond it, and into where I'm doing it the way I think I can. I don't have very strong limitations because of the kind of worker that I am.

Genesis: But you sound as though you want the "bubble" to burst. Do you want to get back to the basics?

Nicholson: No. Hmmm, the basics. I don't want to get back to anything. I want to go on. I want to open it up.

Genesis: Do you feel you've reached a plateau with the "Jack Nicholson, anti-hero" role?

Nicholson: I think it's easy to group things as an anti-hero. But you could put all American films under that. I think that the films that I've done show a lot of diversity, and more than most actors ever get to show. Most of the characters are very, very different. When you really look at it, they're tremendously different. You can group the overall themes of the pictures as anti-heroism, but you can say that about every other picture made in those years, or in the last ten years since *Angry Young Men*. I don't vibrate too strongly to that kind of character.

I think the most impressive thing about me, unbeknownst to most people, is that I've done twenty to twenty-five films, and none of the characters are alike. That's a lot of characters to have played. Even the two westerns I did, which were filmed back to back, had characters that were totally different. You could easily categorize them if you want, but in reality they're totally different. I feel I function well and properly in that area. That's not an area I'm concerned about. It's other things, you know, like styles rather than thematic content of the characters that I'd like to open up.

Genesis: Do you think that your characters from *Carnal Knowledge, Five Easy Pieces,* and *Easy Rider* represent the 1970's hero?

Nicholson: Well, I think that's where it's been. None of these characters covers a lot of people. They're specific characters, but many people identify with them totally. Some would only identify with one out of the three, and others all three. I think heroes are bailing out the boat today, trying to get it so that it'll go. I think it's a very difficult, transitional period. People are overloaded now, not only with information, but with philosophical interpretations. Coupled with that is the fact that most human beings are in a striving situation where their mind is not really quiet. I think that people are suspended. They don't really know, nor maybe should they know. I think the person who could be considered heroic is someone who's trying to keep his own humanity vital, and trying to bail out the boat and keep the thing ready to go if it's called upon.

Genesis: Who were your heroes?

Nicholson: Early on, I would say Brando was a big hero of mine. Castro was a hero. I like Galbraith. Dylan. Actually, I haven't had lots of heroes. Joe DiMaggio was one when I was a kid. Some friends of mine have always seemed heroic to me. Women that I've lived with have given me a lot in that area—things they go through.

Genesis: Would you like to win an Oscar?

Nicholson: I wish I had already won one. The only thing that's tough about it, is going up to accept it. In other words, everything else is just like a real nice party. It's nice if your peer group singles you out.

Genesis: Do you see a lot of films?

Nicholson: Yes. I see as many as I can. It's almost my entire social life. But, I like to do other stuff. This year I've been skiing in Switzerland and visiting friends in the Bahamas in the sun.

Genesis: How much has the L.A. culture affected your life?

Nicholson: I've been living here over half my life, and I'm very into it. I like it here. I see L.A. win people over who totally hate it when they first come here. There's no other city that you can compare it to and that's one of its charms.

Genesis: Do you ever find yourself mentally and emotionally through with a part before you start shooting?

Nicholson: No, I almost always grow with it during the filming. One of the things that was wrong with my work in low budget filmmaking was that the films were shot in two weeks. I'm really not into the character for the first week and a half. I've got it, and in my mind I know where I want it to go and I've got all the impulses, but specifically I don't have this diamond-hard gem carved out. You tend to over-characterize when you first step into a part, and you tend to show it. But when you've done it for a while, and you're thinking about it all day long, you get with it much more. In a two week picture all you've done is that early stage of overshowing a character.

Genesis: Do you consider the audience when you write or act in a film?

Nicholson: Yes. I take a relatively classical position. The fact that in ten years from now *Drive, He Said* will be shown around, and that people will say, "Hey, why didn't I see that before?" doesn't mean a lot to me. That's because I classically work for the moment. It's not fair to make a movie for ten years from now.

I'm very eclectic in style. I don't say, "You must shoot at eye level; no dollies; you must always move when you're moving." When I think about a movie, I think about styles, that is, which ones to use or not to use, whether or not to try new ones, or where to try and force it open.

Genesis: Do you feel that people approach you as Jack Nicholson, movie star, rather than Jack Nicholson, person?

Nicholson: Everyone approaches everyone else with an erroneous image of who and what it is they're approaching. People have as complicated a way of approaching A as they do B, so it really doesn't make that much difference. A lot of people make a great effort to show you that they're not going to relate to you.

Genesis: Do you always tell the truth?

Nicholson: No, but I always try to.

Genesis: When do you find that you can't?

Nicholson: When it involves the confidence of another person. Actually, that's a problem I haven't had for some time. But, in a relationship when you're with a chick, and you ball somebody else, it's hard to tell the truth in that situation. I've tried it. I find that's the general area of most people's dishonesty. Some people can't even be honest about what they think at a given moment, because they think it will down them socially. But I always tell the truth in that situation. I sort of relish it. I've cleared a few rooms in my day. I can be rude, and I don't admire that quality at all. And then, I have this horrible tendency, after I've been rude, to say, "What did I do?"

Genesis: What qualities don't you like in people?

Nicholson: I don't like the head ushers of the world. Officious people. People whose office in life keeps them out of touch with reality.

Genesis: Perhaps a touchy question, but what caused your divorce?

Nicholson: My divorce was good like the marriage was. It was a clear, non-violent, non-tumultuous decision. My wife Sandra (Knight) and I had just come to a very real separating of the ways. It was obviously the only thing to do, and we did it very simply. The probable cause was that she became stimulated in a mystical area, and I couldn't get with that. I didn't want to get caught in a situation where I was in competition with God, or something like that, and I felt I would be and that I would do it myself, because I felt the strength of this new flow into my ex-wife's life.

Genesis: Would you ever get married again?

Nicholson: I don't really know about that. I don't have anything specific against it. I don't envision myself being stimulated to stand up and take a major oath before God, or something like that, because I don't imagine myself ever creating that kind of a God image. I don't feel the ritualistic need to announce my social position before a community, because I am before the community a lot anyway. Since my divorce, I've probably offered to marry someone a couple of times in some half-assed way. No one took me up on it. I don't know whether that's fortunate or not.

Genesis: Why is it that you refuse to appear on talk shows?

Nicholson: For a lot of different reasons. I have done radio interviews and stuff like that. And an interview like this is also different. Even though you transcribe the words I say and someone reads it, the process is removed enough so that I don't feel like the person has this total, definitive, picture of me. They have some idea of my thoughts, and they can agree or disagree with them, but on a television show you're sort of captured in there. I don't really understand the format, emotionally. Why am I having this conversation with a stranger in front of the nation? That's one reason, for not doing a talk show.

Then, there's the feeling that I wouldn't be particular interesting on a talk show, because in that kind of situation I tend to get very laid back. I've always hated acting interviews, like every actor does, so I've completely broken down my anecdotal style.

Also, I felt it wouldn't be good for my work. I feel it would be good for my career. In terms of movies, I probably am in a weird position, in that I'm a fairly popular film actor, but I'm not as widely known as anyone else who's ever held that position simply because I don't do television, and they don't know me.

A lot of people never go to the movies, it's as simple as that. I'm trying also to maintain a certain level of anonymity regarding my work. It's that, and also I don't like television. It's at the throat of my livelihood.

Genesis: So you can't ever see yourself doing a television series?

Nicholson: I'm sure I'll have to wind up making my living in that way. All old actors do. I mean, you have to go on making a living. Do you know any completely retired film stars? Cary Grant's maybe the only one. He doesn't have to do a television series. John Wayne probably never will, either. These are all people that have had twenty-five year film careers, which is not too usual, and most of them have been broke at some time during it. I mean I will do everything I can to avoid doing a television series, you can bet on that.

Genesis: What is the hardest thing you've had to adjust to with your success?

Nicholson: Entering and exiting rooms. There's a lot of people to say hello and good-bye to.

Genesis: Getting back to films. Where do you think they're going?

Nicholson: Into a more figurative, less prosaic, direction.

Genesis: Such as?

Nicholson: Anything in Cocteau's area, or *King of Hearts,* if you saw that French film or Godard. These kinds of films are what I'm talking about.

Genesis: How about Dennis Hopper's *The Last Movie?*

Nicholson: I thought more of it than most people who saw it. I thought it was a very fair expression of Dennis, the filmmaker's, work. Like anyone involved in the editing process, or seeing the film in other stages. I thought some good things were lost in the editing, but essentially I think the editing followed what Dennis wanted to say at the time. I personally enjoyed seeing the movie. Saw it a couple of times, in fact.

Dennis always tries to make a classic. He said what he wanted to say. If there's anything really wrong with the film, it's that he said it too many times within the context of the film. It was a difficult film, a difficult filmmaking experience, and a difficult time for Dennis. I think it's a very pure kind of confessional movie of some kind of depth. What the film essentially says is that the industry of movies was created in America, and the magic of movies was released through America. The germ of movies was picked up most strongly in the American psyche at the time when America was at the perimeter of civilization. The motivation for films and what they're about is superficial related to what they are in actuality, and what they do create. Not only the action of making them, but the action of having viewed them; the fantasy and values created by them. This is sort of what he's saying, and what I feel he says very well in the film, and for me, very movingly.

Genesis: How important were your early films to the advancement of your career?

Nicholson: Very important. Any work that you do as an actor is important. This is how you develop. You have to work. Very few actors have been any good in movies before they've done a few. What's happened in the commercial marketplace is that only the young people are pulling the people into the theatres right now. John Wayne, or any of these guys, aren't really pulling. This has caused the young actor to be more prominent than he would be normally. I always felt that I was lucky to be doing all those movies, even though I felt that at least half of them were really stinky. A lot of actors have to learn. I was having a conversation with Warren Beatty, and it's hard for someone like Warren to have to learn the acting while doing it at a very important commercial level. It's a painful and difficult experience, one that I'm glad I didn't really have to go through. Warren did it very well, I think. He did mostly good, interesting films.

Genesis: How much of your life is a put-on?

Nicholson: Very little. I'm not attracted to that style. Sometimes, conversationally I don't like to be serious every single minute, but I prefer non put-on situations really. I suppose there are mild forms of put-ons that everyone indulges in, that's just a part of them. But, basically, I'm not attracted to that.

Genesis: Is there anything that particularly impresses you about females?

Nicholson: First of all, that they are females particularly impresses me. I'm very democratic. I've got about the same number of female friends as I do male friends. They'll change any group of men that they walk into. There is an amazing change in the atmosphere, and that impresses me. Actually, I'm totally intrigued by females. And now that there's a feminist movement, I'm even more intrigued. I feel that the dialog that's coming from that area is very interesting.

Genesis: Is there something in particular that you want to say?

Nicholson: Well, for acting purposes and performing purposes very often it's important that you reduce the concept down to a very small, skeletal, germinal idea that's really an over-simplification, and then the process opens it up. At this level, and we're discussing "What is it that you would like to say," and so on and so forth. If I just wanted to say something, I wouldn't make a film. I'd just go around and say it. I'd say, "Be nice to black people," you know, or "Try and share the bounty of the world with one another." The movies that I make I hope would say a lot of things. I think in my movies all the characters have something to say, and that's how you give a larger picture. I believe in the positive philosophy of all my characters. If my work is non-total, it's because my work doesn't include a character who's totally negative or totally negatively motivated. Like this killer in *Flight To Fury*, who's totally positively motivated, and he's ready to discuss it with anybody. His rationale is "There will be murders." It's as simple as that. Everyone will agree with that at this point in society. There will be arranged murders. Everyone will agree with that. His point of view is that that's not his problem. He's just filling a job category, because he happens, through no fault of his own, through accidents of birth to be attracted to that kind of work, and to do it well. He does it better than other people, and it's a function that will be done, so it should be done well.

I think, for instance, right now, the most positive function in film is literally for people to have something to do outside their homes that they can relate to. It's nothing more complicated than that. Forget about the inner content of ideas, or what is effective.

Genesis: Can you characterize Jack Nicholson in one sentence?

Nicholson: He just wanted to make it nice.

The Jedi Directs

Mark Hamill's mockumentary, *Comic Book: The Movie,* is on DVD this month. Did he use the Force?

PLAYBOY: What inspired this movie?

HAMILL: The first fake documentary I ever saw, *Take the Money and Run. The Rutles* inspired me. *Spinal Tap.* Not to run afoul of the lawyers, I had to come up with my own versions of Superman, Captain Marvel, Batman. Kevin Smith talks about writing a Commander Courage movie, but he's really talking about writing the Superman film. We satirize Hollywood from the standpoint of a layperson, not an insider.

PLAYBOY: Why set it at a real comic-book convention?

HAMILL: The convention in San Diego is a half-billion-dollar set with real, authentic people. The movie would have worked as a straight documentary, but we use the convention as a backdrop to our story line. It's a genuine examination of why I'm enamored of something I should have outgrown when I was 12.

PLAYBOY: Hef has a cameo. Should he keep his day job?

HAMILL: It's always a pleasure to meet icons and get to know a dimension of them that you never knew. To be able to finally do something with him is a thrill. He plays himself, so we didn't need an audition.

Ben Stiller

A young prince of Hollywood sounds off on self-hatred, self-esteem and the downside of the onscreen boner

Growing up on the road with his actor-comedian parents Jerry Stiller and Anne Meara, Ben Stiller often watched six hours of television a day. He felt at home with "Bewitched" and "I Dream of Jeannie." He could recite every word of every episode of "SCTV." He was more familiar with Will Shatner than with Will Shakespeare. Eventually, Stiller learned to read, write and direct. Predisposed to a career in show business, he studied theatre at UCLA for a year before opting out of college and heading home to New York, where he made his professional acting debut on Broadway in "The House of Blue Leaves." Stiller persuaded some cast members (including Swoosie Kurtz and Stockard Channing) to appear in a short comedy film he directed, "The Hustler of Money," a spoof of Martin Scorsese's "The Color of Money." The film aired on "Saturday Night Live," and Stiller was soon hired as a featured player and apprentice writer. After an unhappy five-week stint, Stiller left the show and created "The Ben Stiller Show" for MTV. That show moved to Fox, where it won an Emmy for comedy writing but flopped in the ratings. It was during the series' run that Stiller established his on-going comedic collaboration with Janeane Garofalo. They shared the big screen with Winona Ryder in Stiller's feature-length motion picture directorial debut, "Reality Bites." Stiller followed with a leading role in the hit "Flirting With Disaster," then turned director again for the controversial $40 million Jim Carrey film "The Cable Guy." Now Stiller is back to acting, with starring roles in "Zero Effect" opposite Bill Pullman and "Permanent Midnight," based on Jerry Stahl's dark Hollywood memoir. Stiller is working on an adaption of Budd Schulberg's unrepentant Hollywood novel "What Makes Sammy Run?" which he hopes to direct and star in.

Robert Crane caught up with Stiller at the King's Road Café in West Hollywood. He reports: "For me, Ben—handsome, unshaven, wearing a white T-shirt and black pants—could have been the guy behind the counter, the owner or the poetry reader on Friday nights. He definitely does not have an entourage."

1

PLAYBOY: The real scourge of today's youth—drugs or TV?

STILLER: It's probably a combination of the two. I've had more experience with television. It's detrimental to your thinking process. Once in a while I run into somebody who doesn't watch television at all, and it's astonishing the way he or she talks about ideas and books. When you stop watching TV, it's like coming off a drug. I'm not into prime-time television. I watch the late-night stuff or the fringe cable channels. Television has become an atmospheric presence in my house, which is probably even scarier.

2

PLAYBOY: You're one of the chief theoreticians of and apologists for the post-Generation X mind-set: Ironic disposition, deadpan demeanor, dark clothes. Are we missing something?

227

STILLER: I like dark clothes. When *Reality Bites* came out, there was so much Generation X bullshit about it, I wanted to jump off the Eiffel Tower. It got ridiculous. I never viewed myself in any way except by what I was doing. *Reality Bites* was written by Helen Childress. If anybody deserves credit for a generational voice, it's her.

3

PLAYBOY: There's isn't a lot of nudity in Gen X movies. Why all the modesty?

STILLER: *Reality Bites* isn't really about sex. It focuses on two people who have been in love with each other for a long time. It's not supposed to be a *Red Shoe Diaries* episode. I like sex in movies as much as the next guy. I'm considering doing a movie about the porn industry. If the sex scenes were relevant to what the movie's about, I'd show as much sex as the next guy. I'm constantly asked to do sex scenes. I'm sick of people seeing me as just a piece of ass. I'm self-conscious about my body. I had a scene in *Flirting With Disaster* in which I had a boner. I had to deal with the fall-out from that. It seems to be people's favorite: "Oh, man, the scene where you had the boner—that was the best. How'd you do that?" It was fake, but I had to walk around all day with it on. Somehow, it wasn't embarrassing for me to do that scene. I felt silly and funny. The sex in that movie was dealt with in a very real way as opposed to being romanticized; it wasn't meant to be hot or erotic. People in this society are so repressed about sex. That's why *Playboy* is successful. I started reading *Playboy* when I was ten.

4

PLAYBOY: Describe the lifestyle of the posthip.

STILLER: My dad had a hip replacement and he's doing fine. He has much more mobility.

5

PLAYBOY: Janeane Garofalo says she's self-hating but has high self-esteem. Is that common among the posthip?

STILLER: I think most actors have incredibly big egos, but they're also incredibly insecure. That's a bad combination. I include myself in this group. For whatever psychological reasons, we want and need approval from everybody in the universe, though we also think we're totally unworthy of it. We need to validate ourselves through our work.

6

PLAYBOY: Why is the literacy rate in the U.S. among the lowest in the developed world?

STILLER: The U.S. is geographically isolated from other countries. We don't come into contact with other populations. I just got back from Europe, where everybody is at least bilingual, usually trilingual, because the countries are so close to one another and people are in contact with different nationalities and cultures. American culture is sedentary. There's something very wrong with the educational system in this country. I went to a private school on the Upper West Side of Manhattan. I was able to skate along and not work very hard because I knew my parents had money and would be able to send me to college.

7

PLAYBOY: Say you're doing a remake of *War and Peace*. Would you get the book or the Cliffs Notes or rent the original from the video store?

STILLER: I would probably use the notes as a guide as I watched the video. I'm a multimedia sort of person. I used to read and have the TV on and listen to a CD all at once. I've been trying to focus on one thing at a time. So I'd start reading the book, and as time progressed, I'd realize I wouldn't ever get through it. Then I'd switch over to the notes and watch the end of the movie to figure out what happened. That would take two hours. I usually flip through a script to the end to see if my character is still there. Now I'm trying to enjoy the experience of just reading.

8

PLAYBOY: People call you the nicest guy in Hollywood. What would they be shocked to know about you?

STILLER: I'm repressed. Every once in a while my dark side comes out—in a way that has never hurt anyone. I don't really do drugs. I have never done heroin. I have experimented with the minor drugs. I've never done cocaine either. I'm taking this opportunity to tell you which drugs I've never done. Once in a while I have weird little adventures. All those things we repress in American culture are present in me. I'm working hard with my therapist to bring them all to the surface in a way that will be safe for everybody to deal with.

9

PLAYBOY: We understand you dislike jokes. Which joke forced you into a joke-free environment?

STILLER: Right now I don't think I could recall one joke, except maybe a riddle from when I was ten years old. My parents never really told jokes in their act. They did sketches and characters. Humor catches you off guard. So when somebody says, "Here's a joke," the laugh is never going to be genuine. I was watching *Harold and Maude* recently by myself, and a couple of times I laughed out loud. Also, I love Hal Ashby movies.

10

PLAYBOY: Of the jobs you've had, which should have been fun that weren't?

STILLER: For a summer I was a busboy and waiter at a place in New York called Café Central, which was a hip, trendy restaurant in 1985. First I bused tables and was really bad at it. I'm clumsy at carrying plates and glasses. You had to have a swiftness and facility for carrying stacked objects. That wasn't me. I was interested in who was coming in, because it was an actor hangout. I would want to see who was talking to whom and what they were saying—basically, stuff you shouldn't do as a person of service. Dudley Moore came into the restaurant and I was really interested in what he was saying. I kept going over to make sure that he and his companion had enough coffee and that their plates were cleared. I think I really annoyed him. I kept changing the ashtrays with that move where you put the clean ashtray over the full ashtray and remove both and put back the clean ashtray. I think I did that one time too many. Then I became a waiter there, and dealing with orders and the kitchen was worse. It prompted me to get acting work.

11

PLAYBOY: We hear you dislike auditions. What happens when you're directing a film and a friend does a bad audition for you? Can you say, for instance, "Janeane, you blew that one"?

STILLER: First of all, I don't think I could get Janeane in to audition. She's too difficult to get on the phone now. She's doing films with Sylvester Stallone. Second only to auditioning on my own, in terms of torture, would be to watch a friend audition. It's hard to maintain a sense of dignity in an audition. I have done so many auditions where I've put it out there and have been met with that kind of blank stare—"Great! Thanks! OK! Great work! Thanks for coming in!" At the door I'm thinking, What the hell am I doing with my life? If I want to work with friends, I just offer them the parts.

12

PLAYBOY: What about the appropriation of contemporary movie titles by the X-rated industry? For example, *The Cable Guy* could become *The Able Guy*. Is there a pornoproof movie title?

STILLER: I haven't seen one for *Get Shorty*. That's not going to bring a lot of people to a movie theatre. I enjoy seeing what they do with the porno movie titles. I never fail to chuckle when I see a clever one.

13

PLAYBOY: Is irony the only form of rebellion left when you admire your parents and their work?

STILLER: My early rebellion was that I wasn't going to be funny. That's what I thought when I was in high school. I was going to be a serious actor and make serious movies. I tried to do that for a while, but unfortunately you can't help what's in your system. As much as I tried to get away from it, I kept coming back to things that made me laugh—*SCTV* and things like that. You have to rebel against your parents when you're that age, so what happened was that my humor took on the second-generation cynical edge that I saw in all the show-business parodies they did on *SCTV*. That show was made for me. Nobody else got it as much as my sister and I. We would watch it when we were both 14 and see things like "The Sammy Maudlin Show" and think, Oh my God, we've actually lived this. We've seen this happen.

14

PLAYBOY: What was the most unreasonable position that your parents took with you?

STILLER: The time my mother forced me to go to camp comes to mind. She insisted I go and I hated it. I couldn't understand why it was so important. Now I see she was helping me grow up. My parents put me on an airplane and I freaked out and made the pilot turn the plane around. I went home that day, but the next day they made me go back. At the time I thought my mother was Hitler. I wanted to stay home: "I love you. I want to be with you and Daddy." Now I realize they were doing the right thing. They were great parents. I love them.

15

PLAYBOY: What would life be like if you were going through it as Ben Meara?

STILLER: I'll always be associated with both of my parents in some way. You have to embrace that. I've been lucky enough to carve out my own career. It's hard for the kids who have to live in the shadows of these huge celebrities. A friend saw my dad and me at a Knicks game. He saw a father and son watching us. The father said, "Look, there's Jerry Stiller." The son said, "There's Ben Stiller." Neither knew who the other guy was. It's different audiences.

16

PLAYBOY: Is David Letterman the spiritual leader of Generation X?

STILLER: I think David Letterman is the comedic persona of the Eighties and Nineties. Letterman's attitude has been copied by so many shows. He has influenced a generation of television personalities. Letterman is the guy Generation X grew up with. It's been interesting to watch him mature and become like the establishment. Now there's a counterculture to him, but he'll always be the king to Generation X. He is funny five nights a week. I did *The Ben Stiller Show* for 13 episodes. I was almost relieved when we got cancelled. It's hard to keep up the quality.

17

PLAYBOY: Describe your perfect world since *Reality Bites*.

STILLER: A world with no indecision. I'm really indecisive. I wish I didn't have to make choices all the time because they drive me crazy and I always second-guess myself. A perfect world would be to know what's right and what's wrong and act on it and not worry about hurting people's feelings. I have a lot more to learn about life. I need to experience the world more. I like to explore, but I also like to go home to my comfortable bed.

18

PLAYBOY: Given that Gen Xers don't exercise, tell us about your workout regimen.

STILLER: I'm working on my abs a lot, and my glutes. I have a treadmill in my house and I like to run at this lake in Hollywood. I just try to run a lot. I like to swim when I have access to a pool. Once in a while I lift weights, but I start to look like Stretch Armstrong. I need to do more of the aerobics stuff. I can get neurotic about that. There is a real advantage to working out. When you're not feeling well or you're depressed and you go out and do something physical, it can change your attitude.

19

PLAYBOY: Discuss the topic: Jim Carrey—sure thing.

STILLER: That's what the money people in Hollywood like about Jim Carrey, that he's a sure thing. Because of Jim, even a dark, strange film like *The Cable Guy* will gross more than $100 million world-wide. Sadly, that's all the money people see him as. They don't see him as what he is, which is an incredibly talented guy who's willing to take chances and who totally commits to what he's doing and really wants to grow.

20

PLAYBOY: Does how you treat your car say something about you? Do you wash yours, take it to a car wash or have it detailed?

STILLER: I made the mistake of taking mine to this car wash in Los Angeles, which I guess is like a big gay hustler pickup type of place. You have to wait 20 minutes for the car to go through and I had nowhere to go. I got trapped there for a while. Don't get me wrong, I'm open to all—it's just not my bag. I care enough to get the car washed, but I just don't think I'll do it at that place anymore.

Seth Green

The pint-size movie star mouths off on short jokes, the casting couch and child stars

Mighty Seth Green has amassed a wildly eclectic filmography that most 26-year-old actors would kill for. A show business veteran of 20 years, he has played the young Woody Allen in Radio Days, the gothed-out slacker son in the two phenomenally successful Austin Powers films and a rock-and-rolling werewolf on the WB Network's cult favorite Buffy the Vampire Slayer.

At six, the son of a West Philly math teacher and an artist was on the road in an RCA/John Denver promotion. At eight, he was working opposite Jodie Foster and Nastassja Kinski in The Hotel New Hampshire. At 12, he played Woody Allen. In his teens, Green pitched Rally's hamburgers and did antismoking ads in a gas mask. There were miniseries such as Stephen King's It, and minor roles in Big Business with Bette Midler and My Stepmother Is an Alien with Kim Basinger. And Green managed to graduate with honors from high school.

Soon he was living in Los Angeles, appearing on Johnny Carson's Tonight Show and co-starring in David Mamet's American Buffalo at the Old Globe in San Diego. Austin Powers: International Man of Mystery landed him on Entertainment Weekly's "it" list. Among Green's 20-plus films appearances are Can't Hardly Wait, playing a wannabe-black kid opposite Jennifer Love Hewitt; Enemy of the State, playing a surveillance operative spying on Will Smith; and the forthcoming Knockaround Guys, opposite John Malkovich. Green also provides voices for animated series such as Fox' Family Guy and Batman Beyond.

Robert Crane caught up with Green in West Hollywood. He reports: "Although Green is only 5'4", he stands huge with his dedicated cadre of fans. Two teens followed him to the office, where he dutifully signed autographs and chatted with them. He is less eclectic than the roles he plays."

1

PLAYBOY: You're a chef creating a new recipe. The ingredients are Sarah Michelle Gellar, Jennifer Love Hewitt, Melissa Joan Hart and Sarah Jessica Parker. What can you come up with?

GREEN: The ultimate empowerment chick flick: *I Know What You Screamed Last Halloween While You Were Having Sex in the City With Sabrina's Teenage Witch Doctor.* Sounds like box-office poison.

2

PLAYBOY: Would there be room for a dash of Pamela Anderson Lee?

GREEN: That would guarantee overseas sales. Put them all in corsets and you have a deal.

3

PLAYBOY: *Entertainment Weekly* put you on its "it" list two years ago. How does one get "it," and when you get "it" what do you do with it?

GREEN: Apparently you have to have a good publicist. And as far as what you do with it, you just cross your fingers that you're still "it" the next year, which I wasn't. Thanks, *EW*. I guess you can only be "it' once. It ain't like tag, right?

4

PLAYBOY: What is Seth short for?

GREEN: It's short for Seth. There are two people in my life who call me Sethy. My sister has been known to call me Sethro. That's as far as it goes. I ran into a White House aide once who dared to refer to me as Sethenopolis. He was quickly corrected.

5

PLAYBOY: Let's pretend Seth is an action verb. What is Seth doing?

GREEN: Seth is doing it and doing it and doing it well. I'm gonna Seth you so good after this interview.

6

PLAYBOY: There are Dana Plato and Gary Coleman, then there's Ron Howard. How do you avoid the shoals of childhood stardom?

GREEN: I'm fortunate that when I was younger I never had one particular project that made me a recognizable celebrity. People have only recently started to know my name. The problem with a lot of child stars who've gotten into trouble is that they had too much too soon—stress, money issues, emotional issues. Suddenly you're not the same person everyone thought was so cute and funny. Ron Howard wisely stopped acting and got into directing and producing.

7

PLAYBOY: You're an aspiring producer. Who would you want on your casting couch?

GREEN: Susan Sarandon keeps calling and saying, "When are we going to make a movie together?" I keep saying, "Sue, just drop the dead weight—a.k.a. Tim Robbins—and we've got a deal." Meryl Streep left a message for me that said, "I'm desperate to have sex with you, and if we can work out a movie deal, that would be great." I'm like, "Mer, baby, wait in line, sister." I was sad when Jessica Tandy passed on, because things between us never worked out. I was getting angry messages from Hume Cronyn, saying, "Stay out of my business, you whippersnapper." Shit like that. What are you going to do? I have too much respect for the institution of marriage.

8

PLAYBOY: Have you had a casting couch experience with a predatory female casting director?

GREEN: Are you kidding me? I don't know if that situation exists. They usually go for the good-looking, buff guys who they think will be a great lay. They never seem to go for the short, stocky character actor who they think can make them laugh afterward.

9

PLAYBOY: You hand a casting agent your business card. What does it say?

GREEN: On the front it says, "He works hard for the money." And then on the back it says, "So hard for it, honey."

10

PLAYBOY: What are the advantages of being vertically challenged?

GREEN: I'm great in a crowd because I can move very quickly. I have a low center of gravity. When I'm playing basketball, the taller players get confused because I can move fast and get inside them. I can't shoot, though. That's the main problem.

11

PLAYBOY: You've heard a lot of them. What is your favorite short joke?

GREEN: When I was in eighth grade this guy belted out, "Seth, you're so short you could sit on the curb and swing your legs." It cracked up the whole room, including me. That image is very funny.

12

PLAYBOY: What do you have against golf?

GREEN: Nothing except I sunburn easily, and to my knowledge there's no indoor golf course. Also, golf clubs are kind of long for me. People look at you funny when you're carrying a sack of mini golf clubs. Besides, those carts don't go faster than six miles an hour, and that doesn't cut it.

13

PLAYBOY: You portray a guitar-wielding, rock-and-roll werewolf on *Buffy*. Ringo has his all-star band. Who would be in yours?

GREEN: Wow. It would be a big band. We'd fill the stage. Tom Morello would be in it, as would Tenacious D. Matthew Sweet would be our songwriter. We'd have some cool, hot chick like Shirley Manson singing. I would love to get Josh Freese, Scott Churilla, Jimmy Chamberlain and Chad Smith to do percussion. That would be brilliant. I'd throw Twiggy Ramirez, Flea and Mike Dirnt and Mark Hoppus from Blink 182 into the bass section. I'm bad with guitars, so I would just sit and watch.

14

PLAYBOY: You have appeared on MTV's *Loveline* many times. What sexual problem stumped you?

GREEN: Pick one that didn't. One guy couldn't control his anal constrictions. I was like, "I've got no advice for you, man." The fact that actors and musicians are deemed appropriate mouthpieces for the sexual problems of a deviate society is stunning to me. It's like, "You liked *Austin Powers*? Thanks, but I don't know what to do about your bleeding nipple. The fantasies you're having about your dog? All I can say is, I think it's unhealthy. You might want to consult someone else."

15

PLAYBOY: Knowing what you know now, how would you go about playing Woody Allen differently? Besides dating girls your own age.

GREEN: I'm pleased that I didn't know then what I know now, because it would have been a different experience. It's like that kid who did the voice in *An American Tail*. They cast him because of the way he sounded, then as soon as he found out that his character was a mouse, he changed the voice and they couldn't get him to go back to what they loved originally. Ignorance is bliss in a situation like that.

16

PLAYBOY: Care to share with us a quintessential Woody moment on or off the set?

GREEN: It was the first time I met him on the set. I shook his hand and said, "I'm so excited to be working with you." He disengaged from my hand, looked at his hand to make sure all his fingers were there, wiped his hand on his shirt and said, "It's not that big a deal!" That gesture indicated to me that I should enjoy myself and do my best work instead of treating it like a huge, reverential situation. Or perhaps he meant my hand was dirty and he didn't trust me.

17

PLAYBOY: In *Can't Hardly Wait*, you portray Kenny Fisher, a wannabe-black kid whose goal is to lose his virginity. Do you suppose the opposite character exists?

GREEN: A black kid who desperately wants to be white and remain celibate? I'm sure he's out there somewhere, in a twisted monasterial cult. I just haven't met him.

18

PLAYBOY: As the son of Dr. Evil you wear black nail polish. What does that tell us about a man?

GREEN: Remember how 15 years ago, people thought it was freaky for a guy to have an earring? Now it's commonplace. It's the same thing with nail polish. I wear it to capitalize on the audience's perception that people who wear nail polish are either weird rock stars or confused and upset kids. Even though I disagree with that option, I wear the nail polish to get that reaction. In *Buffy* the character is a rock star. Rock stars wear nail polish. In *Austin Powers* the kid's fucked up. Fucked-up kids do fucked-up things to their bodies.

19

PLAYBOY: Does one shade work better than another?

GREEN: On film everything looks black. I've had various shades of blue and purple and everyone says, "What's up with the black nail polish?" I've even worn dark greens, though I'm not about to go the sea-foam gold route.

20

PLAYBOY: You've said you have a crush on Geri Halliwell. Are you referring to the pre- or post-Spice Girls Geri?

GREEN: My crush on her has been greatly exaggerated. It was less about Geri as a person and more about what she represented as Ginger Spice. As Ginger, she seemed outspoken and interesting. She seemed to be having a lot of fun. Now she's had a makeover and is trying to prove she's a serious artist. That's far less appealing to me than a trashy tart with a loud mouth who's having a great time.

True Grit

Cowboy, Soldier, Patriot, Superstar—
for More Than Forty Years, John Wayne
Lived the Role of American Hero

In 1938, when legendary film director John Ford was casting his latest western, he handed the short story on which it was based to a young actor named John Wayne. "Who do you think could play it?" Ford asked Wayne, who had been a propman for Ford ten years earlier.

"Well, there's only one actor I can think of who could play it," Wayne replied in his characteristic drawl. "And that's Lloyd Nolan."

"Why, you stupid son of a bitch," said Ford. "I want *you* to play it."

The role was the Ringo Kid, the film *Stagecoach*—a classic that put an end to John Wayne's B movie career (100 films in ten years) and launched the actor onto an unprecedented forty-year-long reign as superstar, cornerstone of machismo and omnipotent defender of America's greatness.

Why was Wayne so successful for so long? According to director Peter Bogdanovich, Wayne was "an extraordinarily effective character actor whose unique qualities and talents brought to each new movie a resonance and a sense of the past—his own and ours—that fills it with reverberations above and beyond its own perhaps limited qualities." In other words, he was the all-American Everyman.

Iowa-born Marion Mitchell Morrison did not aspire to become an actor when he moved with his family to Glendale, California, in the 1920s. Nicknamed "Duke" by local firemen, he attended USC on a football scholarship, then found employment handling props on low-budget serial westerns. When a stuntman was needed, Duke Morrison volunteered. He enjoyed work in front of the camera, and took small roles in silent films until he was chosen by director Raoul Walsh to play the lead in *The Big Trail*. Walsh immediately rechristened his star John Wayne. He also sent him to an acting coach.

Although a new persona had been born, Wayne never forgot his roots. His screen portrayals of levelheaded leaders with high values and definite ideas about right and wrong struck a chord with the American public. Through another hundred films, his characters' take-charge work ethic and no-nonsense attitude showed us that one doesn't have to be brilliant or eccentric to succeed in life. America was the leading world power. It needed strong representatives to embody its mandate. And John Wayne fit the bill perfectly—humble beginnings, pioneer spirit, hard work, sacrifice and success.

Wayne tried to enlist during World War II, but he was turned down because of football injuries and the fact that he was a father of four. Instead, he stepped up production on a succession of war films—including *Flying Tigers, Back to Bataan* and *The Fighting Seabees*—that would successfully boost morale at home. Despite his war films' popularity, it is interesting to note that they represent only 10 percent of Wayne's two-hundred-plus screen appearances.

During the late thirties, forties and fifties, working with directors John Ford and Howard Hawks, Wayne created such masterpieces of Americana as *Stagecoach, Red River, They Were Expendable, She Wore a Yellow Ribbon, Fort Apache, The Quiet Man* and *The Searchers.* During this period, he perfected the swaggering walk that is usually attributed to a fractured ankle during his football days. The slow, halting speech pattern was learned from veteran stuntman Yakima Canutt, who talked like Wayne before Wayne did.

In the 1950s, through the dark days of Senator Joseph McCarthy's blacklist, Wayne remained outspoken and heavily progovernment. He even appeared in a film about the government's investigation into alleged communists—*Big Jim McLain*, which failed to connect with his audience.

As social change gripped the nation in the sixties, Wayne remained steadfast to his ideals and values. The Vietnam War deeply divided the country, and he took it upon himself to speak up for the government's motives and to defend America's fighting men. A record album called *America, Why I Love Her* and the film *The Green Berets* were successful despite being branded by critics as propaganda tools. Wayne was so sincere in his love for the nation—right or wrong—that people young and old, prowar or pacifist, respected his opinions.

Although he was an international star for four decades, John Wayne received only two Academy Award nominations for Best Actor—for *Sands of Iwo Jima* in 1950 and *True Grit*, which finally brought him an Oscar, in 1969. Throughout his career, he won consistently solid reviews from critics—but never wildly enthusiastic ones. Yet today many of his films are studied by cinema students and are in museum collections.

John Wayne has become an American icon to many people—the hard worker, the idealist, the outspoken patriot, the macho war buddy, the pioneering cowboy. He remained unflappable in his vision of America through wars, social change, paranoia, defeat and victory. He beat cancer once, and received 50,000 letters from other cancer sufferers—though he eventually lost his life to the disease. The generally fickle public placed its confidence in him for over forty years, and the Duke always came through with his best.

THE QUOTABLE DUKE

On acting:

"Always tell it like it is, because then tomorrow you won't be wondering what you were lying about yesterday."

-to character actor Hank Worden

On seeking political office:

"I can't afford the cut in salary, and who would vote for an actor anyway."

-to Republicans trying to convince him to run

On Indian rights and socialism:

"The terrible thing we all did was to put them on reservations. It takes a man's dignity away from him. Takes his desire to better himself away from him. That's what they want to do with that cradle-to-grave socialism. They'll have our whole country like that if we keep paying all our taxes for these minorities that you're provoking."

On cancer:

"I've prayed more than once in my life, but I felt a little closer to that man upstairs at that time. I wished he'd give me a hand. If it worked out in his plan for things, and luckily it did. I don't know that smoking gave me cancer. Lots of people have been killed stepping off a curb. I didn't stop stepping off a curb."

-to talk show host Mike Douglas

On winning the Oscar for True Grit:

"Wow! If I'd known that, I'd have put that patch on thirty-five years earlier. Ladies and gentlemen, I'm no stranger to this podium. I've come up here and picked up these beautiful golden men before, but always for friends. One night, I picked up two: one for Admiral John Ford and one for our beloved Gary Cooper. I was very clever and witty that night—the envy of, even, Bob Hope. But tonight I don't feel very clever, very witty. I feel very grateful, very humble, and I owe thanks to many, many people. I want to thank the members of the Academy. To all you people who are watching on television, thank you for taking such a warm interest in our glorious industry. Good night."

-Best Actor acceptance speech, 42nd Academy Awards

On the war in Vietnam:

"If I'm gonna send some neighbor's kid out to be killed, I'll be willing to risk my life to save a few of those boys. I think we should have won it about four years ago and about a quarter of the loss of men and had the respect of the world. Instead of that, we pussyfoot around and now we're trying to get out of it without being a disgrace."

On freedom of speech:

"I shoot off my mouth once in awhile, more than I should probably. Everybody has that right in this country."

On the American West:

"No man who ever entered the West was the same again. Neither was the land and neither were we. It's our heritage. It's your land and it's mine. It's the only land we'll ever have and it's good enough for me."

On his name:

"I never really have become accustomed to the name John. Nobody ever calls me John. No, I've always been either Duke, Marion, or John Wayne. It's a name that goes well together and it's like one word, John Wayne. But if they say, 'John,' Christ, I don't look around today. And when they say 'Jack,' boy, you know they don't know me."

On his toupee:

"It's not phony. It's *real* hair. It's not *my* hair, but it's real."

-at a 1974 screening of McQ by the Harvard Lampoon

THE COMPLETE JOHN WAYNE

Many of John Wayne's films have been released on home video, and some of his earlier work has been included in omnibus collections. Here's the most up-to-the-minute lineup of what's available for purchase or rental.

The Alamo	*The Green Berets*
Allegheny Uprising	*Hatari!*
Angel and the Badman	*Hellfighters*
Back to Bataan	*The Horse Soldiers*
The Barbarian and the Geisha	*In Old California*
The Big Trail	John Wayne Collector's Limited Edition
Blue Steel	John Wayne—Matinee Double Feature, Vol. 1
Brannigan	John Wayne—Matinee Double Feature, Vol. 2
Cahill: United States Marshal	John Wayne—Matinee Double Feature, Vol. 3
Cast a Giant Shadow	John Wayne—Matinee Double Feature, Vol. 4
Chisum	*Lady for a Night*
The Conqueror	*Lady from Louisiana*
Cowboys of the Saturday Matinee	*A Lady Takes a Chance*
The Cowboys	*The Lawless Frontier*
Dakota	*The Lawless Range*
The Dark Command	*The Long Voyage Home*
The Dawn Rider	*The Longest Day*
The Desert Trail	*The Lucky Texan*
Donovan's Reef	*The Man from Utah*
El Dorado	*The Man Who Shot Liberty Valance*
The Fighting Kentuckian	*McQ*
The Fighting Seabees	*'Neath Arizona Skies*
Flame of the Barbary Coast	*Paradise Canyon*
Flying Leathernecks	*The Quiet Man*
Flying Tigers	*Randy Rides Alone*
Fort Apache	*Red River*
Frontier Horizon	*Riders of Destiny*

Rio Bravo

Rio Grande

Rooster Cogburn

Sagebrush Trail

Sands of Iwo Jima

The Searchers

She Wore a Yellow Ribbon

The Shootist

The Sons of Katie Elder

The Spoilers

Stagecoach

The Star Packer

They Were Expendable

Three Faces West

The Trail Beyond

The Trail Robbers

True Grit

Tycoon

Wake of the Red Witch

War of the Wildcats

The War Wagon

West of the Divide

Wheel of Fortune

Wild West

Winds of the Wasteland

Greg Kinnear

The star of auto focus on leaving Indiana, dodging bullets in Beirut and talking dirty in Greek

Greg Kinnear, a native of Logansport, Indiana, likes to keep his distance from the film community. Some of that may have to do with his itinerant upbringing. His father's work with the State Department turned the family into nomads who lived in Washington, D.C., Beirut and Athens. While attending high school in Athens, Kinnear enjoyed his first broadcast experience, hosting School Daze With Greg Kinnear on Armed Forces Radio. After graduating, he moved back to the U.S. and earned a broadcast journalism degree from the University of Arizona.

E! Entertainment Television received one of Kinnear's audition tapes and signed him to host Talk Soup, where he provided caustic commentary on talk-show clips. The series earned Kinnear an Emmy Award and a cult following. NBC was intrigued with his hosting abilities and, upon Bob Costas' departure, moved Kinnear into the late-night show Later With Greg Kinnear. His stint lasted a few seasons before director Sydney Pollack cast Kinnear in his feature-film debut opposite Harrison Ford and Julia Ormond in the remake of Sabrina.

Kinnear established himself with his Academy Award-nominated supporting role opposite Jack Nicholson and Helen Hunt in James L. Brooks' As Good As It Gets. He then co-starred in the Tom Hanks-Meg Ryan success You've Got Mail. Kinnear starred opposite Cate Blanchett in the supernatural thriller The Gift, and with Renee Zellweger in Neil LaBute's Nurse Betty. Further diversifying his resume, Kinnear took a co-starring role opposite Mel Gibson in the Vietnam war film We Were Soldiers. The actor rounds out 2002 starring in Paul Schrader's male sexuality study Auto Focus, playing Bob Crane, the star of Hogan's Heroes.

Robert Crane (who is, in fact, Bob Crane's son) caught up with the life-embracing Kinnear at Shutters on the Beach in Santa Monica. He reports: "Kinnear is sitting atop the world. He has fame, money, looks, a beautiful English wife and good press buzz on his performance in Auto Focus. Damn. This is as good as it gets."

1

PLAYBOY: One of the top FAQs at Indiana tourist information booths is "How do I get the hell out of here?" Does one ever return?

KINNEAR: This one likely will not, but some do. I have great memories of it. I was there until I was nine. It's a great place to grow up. It is beautiful country, a little on the flat side. There seems to be an excess of corn, but I felt safe there. That's quite a commodity these days.

2

PLAYBOY: When was the last time you were back?

KINNEAR: I took my wife recently. We were flying from the East Coast back to Los Angeles and the plane stopped in Chicago for a changeover. I said, "Let's grab our bags and hang for a few days." An advantage of being an actor is when you're not working, you can do stuff like that. We rented a Ford Taurus and drove down to a lake I used to go to when I was a kid, Lake Wawasee. I took her to my old house, which was actually for sale. It probably still is. I signed the register, trying to encourage people to buy it, but the last that I heard it was still on the market. It is a small town. A lot of my old neighbors came out of their houses. "Oh, you're the Kinnear kid. How are Susie and Ed?" They picked right up from when I left in 1972.

3

PLAYBOY: Define Hoosier.

KINNEAR: I think the word was some sort of term meaning hillbilly many years ago, but I would like to think that we've grown out of using that definition and are employing something more appreciative. It's strange for me to talk like I'm the spokesman for the state of Indiana. I was there for all of nine years, and for the first five of them I was drooling. It's not necessarily my place, but the people there are very passionate about sports and keeping life simple. Basketball and keeping life simple define a Hoosier effectively. I'm thinking of all the horrible letters I'll be getting. "What the hell do you mean, simple? You left when you were nine." People love to kill the Midwest. It can be a fairly cynical country when you get on the coasts. Anywhere on the left or right, they tend to look on that middle portion as an odd place that conjures up images of the movie *Children of the Corn*. It's not like that. Today, people are reassessing that small-town-America thing we used to smirk at. Maybe I *should* be a spokesman for Indiana.

4

PLAYBOY: Bobby Knight, Dan Quayle, John Mellencamp, David Letterman. Name the other proud sons of Indiana.

KINNEAR: James Dean. Letterman asked me that question one time on his show. It was the most horrifying moment of my life. He asked, "Now, who else? What other great historical figures are from Indiana?" I still have the tape. You can see little beads of sweat forming on my brow. I didn't know. I beg anyone who is reading this to list all of the great figures from their state.

5

PLAYBOY: Describe your childhood in Beirut.

KINNEAR: We arrived in 1975. We were in Virginia for three years before that and were completely unprepared to hop into a taxicab and drive through the PLO camps to get to downtown Beirut. My father kept us in a hotel for a few months until we moved into a residence. It started great, like a storybook. The weather was beautiful. You could ski and surf in the same day. Wonderful, incredible people. The Lebanese are good-spirited, kind, completely the opposite of the general interpretation of anybody from that part of the world. It was an extraordinary place. A short time after we arrived, the acting American ambassador was assassinated. A bullet in the head. He was found in a burlap bag washed up on the beach with his bodyguard. That started a series of kidnappings, including some Americans. Nobody had done that before. The fighting would start in the late afternoon. As soon as the sun went down you would hear the crackle of machine-gun fire. It would move into heavier artillery at night. We would close all the shutters in our house, gather around a candle and listen to the BBC. It sounds horrifying, but at that age, I was like the kid in *Hope and Glory*— "Wow.

These are real bullets. This is the kind of fun." I actually got shot at one day. There was a street fair every Saturday, with guys and their fruit carts. I was walking across the street to see a buddy of mine. By the time I got halfway across, there were apples all over the ground. At one end of the street there were a couple of guys coming with guns, and another group at the other end. Firing started. I saved a few people that day. Just kidding. I ran to the other side like the spineless coward I am, and then it passed and things were OK. It was intense.

6

PLAYBOY: Your father was a State Department trade rep. Spook, right?

KINNEAR: Yes. I will give you my stock answer, which is that my brothers and I get around the table every holiday and badger him endlessly about that. If he was a spook, I will say he was the greatest spook the country has ever had. His office was the regional trade and development office, which was set up to help promote imports and exports from Middle Eastern countries to the U.S. it was kind of a liaison office.

7

PLAYBOY: Some parents argue that travel is disruptive to children. Is this true?

KINNEAR: I guess it is. I know so many actors and people in this business who come from a similar background. I'm convinced that it's the need to fit in and redefine yourself quickly that causes a lot of people to end up in Hollywood, for better or for worse. For me, it was the greatest experience I've ever had. I am convinced I would be in prison by now if I had stayed in Indiana. I don't think I would have fit into the typical American high school experience. I was fortunate to have ended up in Greece for high school. It was phenomenal. All my best friends to this day are from there.

8

PLAYBOY: As a U.S. citizen who has lived abroad, are you less xenophobic?

KINNEAR: No question about it. The best part of that experience was that it gave me the ability to see America as part of the world, as opposed to the world. I am grateful for that because obviously on September 11 it changed for all of us, and a lot of people who ignored international affairs have opened their eyes. Not that I could have foreseen anything that has taken place, but certainly, with my upbringing, I was aware of a lot going on. I have been a CNN junkie since I was 17.

9

PLAYBOY: Druze women are among the most beautiful in the world. Were you old enough to appreciate them while you were in Lebanon?

KINNEAR: I was just trying to land a French kiss for the first few years there, so I don't know how much I was into beauty. You go to any of the Greek islands, particularly at that time, and you get to understand beautiful women very quickly. It was a good place for an adolescent red-blooded American boy to be. It was a good place to become aware, and I appreciated it. We moved there when I was 12 and left when I was 18, so that was my adolescence. Those are the years you get your training for women. I have good stories and bad stories like every other guy. OK, maybe a few more bad stories.

10

PLAYBOY: How did you prepare for the explicit scenes in *Auto Focus?* Was there a Thighmaster in your trailer?

KINNEAR: There should have been, because I put on some weight to play Bob [Crane]. He was a little softer than I am around the face and the sides. Now I'm desperately in need of a Thighmaster. While I was doing the movie it was the opposite. No push-ups before scenes for me. It was basically hit the craft service table about 10 minutes before doing anything questionable.

11

PLAYBOY: You're known as being a nice guy in Hollywood. Have you disqualified yourself from playing a really dark character?

KINNEAR: I'm a prick. Sashimi-ing a guy's stomach? I can't do that. Your opportunities to do those types of roles depend on people's impressions—right or wrong—about you. As an actor, there are few places I'm not interested in exploring. How far audiences will let you go provides limitations. It is just a matter of finding the right thing. I'll give you an example: Jack Nicholson in *The Shining.* You see him in that movie and associate him with a super-dark character. I found his character oddly charming. You put down the ax, and the guy is somebody you want to have dinner with. I would welcome acting opportunities in that vein. A lot of times you see actors playing roles that feel like they are trying to say, "Look where I can go. Look how crazy I am." That is not interesting to me. What is interesting is creating real characters, human characters. I bring up Jack because that was a guy we believed. A really interesting dark character is, above all else, somebody you have to believe. There is just as much charm and inspiration behind a guy with a hatchet as there is in any other character. It's balance.

12

PLAYBOY: In *Auto Focus* you wear the jacket that was worn by Frank Sinatra in *Von Ryan's Express* and by Bob Crane in *Hogan's Heroes*. If that jacket could talk, would it say, "Ring-a-ding-ding" or "Colonel Klink"?

KINNEAR: After *Auto Focus,* it has a few other things it wants to say—some not fit for print. I have to go with Colonel Klink on that one. As you might understand, I am a little partial to the jacket. It fit like a glove and I'll be the first to bid on it when it's put up for auction on eBay. Give me 24 hours' notice.

13

PLAYBOY: You worked with Garry Shandling in *What Planet Are You From?*, *Love Affair* and *Town and Country*. Should Shandling say no the next time Warren Beatty calls?

KINNEAR: Garry is a really good friend of mine. He is not only an incredible actor, but he's a good person, too. I find Garry to be one of the funniest SOBs—Wait, I have to retract that; it's the wrong term for Garry. He is one of the funniest guys I have ever met. *What Planet Are You From, Part II?* We'll see. Stay tuned.

14

PLAYBOY: We recently declared Arizona State University the number one party school in the country. Care to defend University of Arizona's status?

KINNEAR: Until your *Playboy* editors have lived in the Alpha Pi dorm for six months, I don't want to hear that shit again. I believe the debauchery going on 100 miles south of Tempe is just as impressive as what's happening in the middle of the state, if not more so. I still have the occasional hangover to prove it. Besides, there is a lot of animosity between U of A and ASU whenever you do those *Girls of* features. The women of U of A blow the doors off the parking-lot scene you have up north.

15

PLAYBOY: Please defend for us the rigorous and challenging broadcast-journalism department.

KINNEAR: Shortly after I graduated they closed it down. That's my legacy. Now they call it the communications department or something. When I was there it actually was not a bad school. The journalism department at U of A was one of the best in the country. The radio and television department was OK, though it didn't offer nearly as much help as a film school like USC or UCLA. It got you in and got you out for the hat.

16

PLAYBOY: Are roles denied to Greg that are offered to Gregory?

KINNEAR: If I went by Gregory I would have a different life today. I would be sipping champagne in a hot tub if I were Gregory. Unfortunately, I'm drinking tea, watching the birds fly by. It never even occurred to me to go with Gregory. That name sounds too loud for me. It sounds too imposing and I never was. Although I am legally Gregory, the only time I ever heard the name Gregory was when I was in huge trouble. It usually came from my mom, who would also insert my middle name, which is Buck, and throw in my last name, Kinnear, just so there was no question about who she was addressing.

17

PLAYBOY: Under what circumstances does speaking Greek come in handy?

KINNEAR: When I travel to Greece, and when I go to a Greek restaurant. When I go to Taverna Tony's in Malibu it tends to procure a better table and you don't have to say a lot. Truthfully, I was never that great at it. I was going to take Greek while I was living there. We didn't know how long we were going to be there. My mom said, "You should take French. It is a beautiful language. It is an international language, a language of love." I was easily convinced, so you basically had a displaced American coming from Lebanon, living in Greece, studying French. How screwed was I? I never even had a chance. At the end of the day, I got six words from 14 different languages.

18

PLAYBOY: What can be said in all its fullness only in Greek—and to whom do you say it?

KINNEAR: There is a phrase you would say to someone you truly despise and are very angry with in a moment of passion. It is a nice little run of bad words. Truthfully I am not even sure what it means, but I know it will get you into a good fistfight. I know *malaka* means masturbator. I don't know beyond that.

19

PLAYBOY: Describe the challenges of being a *Later* talk-show host.

KINNEAR: The frustrating part of it is there are nights when you hit it out of the park and it doesn't make a blip on the ratings screen. And on nights when you might as well run color bars, you get a bump in the ratings. By the time you get to 1:35 in the morning, as Tom Snyder put it, "You get your smokers and your tokers."

20

PLAYBOY: Which forms of music are not conducive to a romantic evening?

KINNEAR: I stay away from Twisted Sister if I'm trying to get down. Loverboy is something you want to stay away from if you're talking about romance: *Working for the Weekend* will kill you on a Friday night if you're trying to get hot and heavy. I saw Loverboy in concert in college. I don't know how I got roped into that. Let me go on record saying I did not buy tickets to a Loverboy concert. I got free tickets to a Journey concert—and Journey was happening. Loverboy opened for Journey. I thought those guys were going to be taken out and beaten senseless before they got through the first song. I don't know who booked this, but it was one of the great mistakes in the history of concerts.

Robert Crane

Bruce Dern

IT TOOK TWENTY YEARS OF HARD work for Bruce Dern to get Ann-Margret and Maud Adams into bed. In the movies, that is—Ann-Margret in *Middle Age Crazy* and Adams in his latest pictures, *Tattoo*. Until recent years Dern had a problem: typecasting. He started out his career playing delightfully demented characters who taunted old ladies, twisted heads off babies, and ingested strange drugs in such classics as Alfred Hitchcock's *Marnie (1964)*, *Hush...Hush, Sweet Charlotte (1965)*, *The Wild Angels (1966)*, *Rebel Rousers (1967)*, and *Psych-Out (1968)*. After Dern played a rustler who murders the John Wayne character two-thirds of the way through *The Cowboys (1972)*, even the Duke had to remark, "He's gonna be hated everywhere in the world for this one." Darryl Zanuck, former head of Twentieth Century-fox, was quoted as saying, "Dern's not a leading man. He's a psychotic." Fortunately, Dern didn't believe a word of it.

Enough was enough. Dern wanted to do other things on film, such as get the girl or get some laughs. With the help of another B-movie alumnus, Jack Nicholson, he got the role of the basketball coach in Nicholson's *Drive, He Said (1971)* and won the National Society of Film Critics Award for Best Supporting Actor. He followed that with the starring role in Douglas Trumbull's futuristic, science fact/fiction film, *Silent Running* (1972), playing opposite two three-foot robots named Dewey and Louie. Then Dern teamed up with Nicholson again in Bob Rafelson's haunting *The Kind of Marvin Gardens* (1972), which unfortunately played to empty houses. But the roles were getting better, and Dern held his own with Walter Matthau in *The Laughing Policeman* (1974), Robert Redford in *The Great Gatsby* (1974), and Kirk Douglas in *Posse* (1975). Alfred Hitchcock directed Dern again in what turned out to be the master of suspense's last film, *Family Plot* (1976), calling him "the most off-the-wall-actor I've ever worked with." And in 1977's *Black Sunday*, Dern was memorable as the ex-Vietnam POW whose target is the Goodyear blimp—he was psychologically off-center, for sure, but also sympathetic for a change. Somehow, we cared about this man.

Some people refuse Academy Awards. Others use them as doorstops. Dern's nomination as Best Supporting Actor for his role as a traumatized Vietnam vet in 1978's *Coming Home* symbolized, for him, acceptance by the film community in Hollywood as being not only one of the screen's great character actors, but also a star.

Despite Dern's down-home manner and his history of playing crazies, his background, ironically, is close to that of the character he played in *Gatsby*—the Jazz Age Tom Buchanan. He grew up in the wealthy Chicago suburb of Winnetka. His father was a law partner of Adlai Stevenson; his grandfather was a governor of Utah and a member of FDR's cabinet. On his mother's side of the family are department stores and the poet Archibald MacLeish. His parents expected him to go to law school after Choate and the University of Pennsylvania. Instead he joined the Actors' Studio. He struggled along with bit parts in movies and more than 100 television shows before he began to establish himself.

Dern looks younger than his actual age, which is in the forties. That's probably because he takes good care of himself and is a fanatic about his hobby—running. I first met him in 1972, when I was writing a book about Jack Nicholson; we got together at BBS Productions in Hollywood to chat about his experiences with Nicholson. Dern was constantly "on" – a manic delight for three hours.

He had something to prove—that he was more than a screen hatchet man. He had a personality that the studios hadn't seen yet.

Three years later when we talked again at the Harold Lloyd estate in Beverly Hills, he was depressed because of the way filming was progressing on *Won Ton Ton, the Dog Who Saved Hollywood* (1976). He knew he was better than the material that was being offered to him.

This latest conversation took place at his comfortable office/apartment in the heart of Beverly Hills (he also has homes in Malibu and at Lake Tahoe). Dern seemed more confident and relaxed than ever before. Part of this is due to an upswing in his personal life; part is due to the momentum of his career. In last year's *Middle Age Crazy*, his penchant for comedy and his ability to touch an audience were apparent; now *Tattoo*, which was written by Joyce Bunuel, directed by Bob Brooks, and co-stars ex-fashion model Maud Adams, promises to break additional ground for Dern— as his first venture into erotica. Whatever the box-office results of this latest Dern picture, his career continues to progress and unfold. If it is a long-distance run already, we hope we can look forward to a marathon.

PLAYGIRL: A few years ago you told me that you felt pornography was a threat to the film industry. How do you feel now?

DERN: I don't feel that way anymore. Since home video cassettes have come in, the threat has been erased. Every city now has a porno theater. In those days, they didn't. I was afraid that people would convert legitimate movie houses into porno theaters, which is fine, but if they do that to a whole chain of theaters in every city, they take away a marketplace for regular films. That's not going to happen now. On Ventura Boulevard [in Los Angeles] they have a porno theater. On Santa Monica Boulevard they have a porno theater. So each community now has its "A" theater, its porno theater, its revival house. Now making porno movies is a viable industry, actually. But I'm not about to do one. Aldo Ray did one. I never saw it and I don't know what he did in it, whether he was hard-core in it or not, but he was in one. I remember reading about it in magazines.

I look at a lot of porno films, but I'd never pay to see one in a movie theater. I buy them in cassette.

PLAYGIRL: Isn't that a double standard?

DERN: No, it has nothing to do with a double standard. When I watch a porno film, I watch it to get turned on. I don't want to get turned on in front of 500 people. That's not a double standard, is it? I'm not a wanker, you know. I watch films and cassettes at home with my wife so we don't have to leave the house. It's available, and I'm sexually motivated.

PLAYGIRL: What kind of porno do you watch?

DERN: Anything Serena's in, I buy. I buy the standard films that you see advertised in the paper. I go into the porno store— I have a couple of regular stores that I go to—and I just see what they have and I buy some films; then later I trade those in on others. I'm not a critic of porno films, but I do see a lot of them—the regular ninety-minute movies, the video ones. I don't have any particular favorites, but they really do a pretty good job now on a lot of them, you know.

PLAYGIRL: Did you see *Misty Beethoven*?

DERN: Yes, that was cute. I enjoy them when they're a little more hard-core than humorous, if you want to know the truth. The humorous ones are cute. *Misty Beethoven* was cute and had hard-core, too, but the harder core the better—with a story too, you know. There are certain directors, and I don't know their names because I'm not scanning the credits very carefully, who go for humor. I've never met any of the actors or actresses, but I know their names.

PLAYGIRL: Do you think nudity is acceptable for a major motion-picture star?

DERN: Nudity is always a commitment of some sort, because we'll be nude in front of some people but we won't be nude in front of others, even in our own homes. There are certain friends that you put your clothes on for and there are certain ones that you don't care about. Nudity will always be in movies as long as it works. I remember the fight between the two guys in front of the fireplace in *Women in Love*. They were completely nude, I think. That was excellent. It was a movie you wouldn't think of as having nudity in it, but it did.

PLAYGIRL: So, as long as it's an integral part of the story—

DERN: It does not bother me. I am frontally nude in *Tattoo* as is Maud Adams: frontally nude, "rearally" nude, orally nude—you know, I mean I'm *nude*. *Tattoo* is the most erotic motion picture anybody has ever seen or will ever see in the United States in terms of high eroticism, in terms of nudity and sexuality and love—deep, meaningful love as well as erotic love. It is extremely erotic, and that's just a part of it. If it's part of the story, it's part of the story. I was nude at the end of *Coming Home*, you know.

There's only one love scene in *Tattoo*, at the end of the movie. It is the most explicit love scene we will ever make in America because it *happens*. It was done and the camera recorded it; what can I tell you? It's done in such a way that it's acceptable and not X. You see my pubic hair and you see her pubic hair together; then you see my butt rise and start to drive and you see her stomach thrust to meet me, and that's what you see. You see the claws tattooed on my butt embracing the back feathers of the neck of the bird tattooed on her body. You never see pubic hair after that, and you never see my dick go in her cunt, so to speak. It is unbelievable, but it took a long, long time because of all the cuts which had to be put together. Incidentally, our tattoos were engraved, but not beneath the skin. A regular tattoo goes an eighth of an inch underneath the surface of the skin and lasts forever.

PLAYGIRL: During the lovemaking scenes, are you and Maud Adams actually making it?

DERN: Yes. You see what you get. It took a lot of love and understanding among Maud, me, the director, and the crew, as small as it was. The film is not X-rated, but what the crew saw was X-rated. The crew saw everything.

PLAYGIRL: How do you deal with women who come on to you solely because you are a star?

DERN: I thank them. I thank them because they never came on to me before. I don't know if they are thinking of me as a movie star or if they're thinking of me more as the character that they saw in one of my movies. There are two characters that they come on to me for. One is the guy in *Coming Home*, which shocked me, absolutely shocked me. I never realized I would affect females the way I did at the end of *Coming Home*. They want to put their arms around that guy, they want to say, "It's okay, you don't have to go, I'll be there for you, I'll talk to you." And the other is the guy in *Middle Age Crazy*. It's a little different, but there are a lot of women who would like to spend a day with

250

Bobby Lee Burnett [the Dern character]. It's nice. I like it. I appreciate any kind of public adulation as long as it's controlled.

The hardest part is the actor's responsibility to the audience. You must not come at them in garbage. You must not come at them in things you are not proud of yourself. It is not enough anymore for me to just make money as an actor. I mean, it never was. I never got into it. I make a good salary, but I feel that if you're in it just for the money, you're going to eat it somewhere down the road. When you're not in it just for the money, when you're in it for the art and you're successful, then the money comes with it, which is very nice. Then you've got to be careful and honest with yourself as to what you then want to do with success. What's really interesting today is to see what some people have done with success and then what others have done with it, because there is a real abuse of power in this industry.

For example, I really don't have a relationship anymore with Bob Redford, but I admire his choices—I admired his choice when he did *All the President's Men*, his taking that piece of material and feeling that it was absolutely essential that he produce it and be in it. I admire his choice of *Ordinary People*. I feel that regardless of whether the movie's great or not great, that it is the right kind of undertaking for a guy in his position. This is a guy who can do anything. In the position that he's in now, he can make a story about anything and somebody would finance it. He doesn't abuse his power. He goes out and tries to make a contribution, a movie about people trying to connect, and I like that, I admire that. There are people out there who have not done that with the same opportunity.

PLAYGIRL: Are you talking about stars who get paid enormous salaries nowadays, like Burt Reynolds, who has received $5 million for a film?

DERN: Which Burt Reynolds do you want? Do you want the one in *Smokey and the Bandit*, or do you want the one in *Rough Cut*? I happen to be a Burt Reynolds fan when he does his thing. I loved him in *Semi-Tough*. I liked him in *Deliverance*. I did shows with him in television. We did a *Twelve O'Clock High* together and an episode of *Gunsmoke* together. I feel that I've known him from the crib. I like Burt for one big reason: he's very outspoken. He's not afraid to take on people. I appreciate that. I think there should be more people like him. Also, I think he has his own problems. As a matter of fact, I've read interviews where he says that he feels that he's been slotted just as badly as anybody else has been slotted, that they only want him to do a certain kind of thing. He goes out and does *Starting Over*, and though some people really admired him for it, other people kicked his teeth out.

I'll tell you the thing that really pisses me off more than anything else. That is when an actor comes out in a movie and the print media—as well as any kind of critic or reviewer—will not let an actor emerge as anything other than what they expect him to be. I have had, by and large, superb reviews for *Middle Age Crazy*, but I have had a few that do not want me playing Bobby Lee Burnett. They will not accept it, no matter what. There are a few people now who will not accept Donald Sutherland as the father in *Ordinary People*. There are people who will not accept Burt Reynolds in *Starting Over* or in a serious role, and I resent that. What they are saying is, "Hey, you do this. That's what we like you as, that's the way we remember you, that's where you make your strongest impression. We'll get B to do this and C to do that. You do A. You do what you're supposed to do."

What they're saying is that there's no chance for growth. What they're really saying is that they are narrow-minded. Nobody is given the shot they deserve to break into a different kind of thing. There's a big difference between Bobby Lee Burnett and Bob Freelander [the Dern character] from *Smile*. But people say, "Ah, there's Bruce Dern off doing his thing again." It really angers me. It shouldn't, but I'm not a big enough person that it doesn't affect me. I wish I was. You have to continue to be an artist and you have to function in the marketplace. Acting is not something you can do by yourself or knock off in Interlaken in upstate Michigan or up in the Sierras. I mean, people have to see your work, and therefore, you have to remain in the marketplace. You have to keep trying new things, keep trying interesting things, keep trying new challenges, and keep the industry aware that it's okay to use you for different things.

PLAYGIRL: Do you tend to sustain your relationships with other actors, producers, or studio heads?

DERN: I have lasting relationships socially with every single person I've ever worked with except two, in my own mind. I have some friends that I have worked with, people that I consider to be friends, that I see regularly. I wish I saw Nicholson more. We've been friends now about eighteen years, so that's kind of a long time. We haven't worked together enough, which is too bad, I think, certainly too bad for me and I'd like to think it's too bad for him. I think it's really too bad for the audience. We make real good stuff together.

There's a lot of people I've worked for that I would like to work for again. The sad thing is the family effect making a movie creates, and when it's over we go on, the hair-dressers go on, the grips go on, everybody goes on, and it's a different family. But the actor, particularly the emotional actor like myself, leaves something on that film that he can never get back. That's the toughest part of it for me. I left something in *Black Sunday* as vicious and horrible as the character was. I left something there. I left a great deal in *Coming Home*, and I left a little bit in *Middle Age Crazy*, regardless of the type of film it was. I left an enormous amount of myself in *Tattoo*, probably more than most films. It's real different and strange.

I had two conflicts with two directors making two movies. Both times they said I was wrong, and I gave in to them because of my basic premise—which is, it is the director's medium, and therefore, the director must have the ultimate decision when there is a conflict. You've got to rally behind somebody, and I am a team player basically. I got burned by Michael Winner in *Won Ton Ton* when he wanted me to play the role a certain way; the movie turned out not to be good. I got burned very badly in *The Driver* for the same reason by Walter Hill. Those are the two things that bother me. Both movies could have been much better had I been allowed to progress in the area that I felt confident in as to what the character should be.

PLAYGIRL: So you had a choice, at that point, of being a team player or getting into a total conflict with the directors?

DERN: Well, then you would not have a movie. You must be a team player in those situations unless it says "produced by" you. Even as an actor you must fight as long as you can. But then it finally comes to a point of departure. Thank god, I have the ability to do it their way as well as my own way. But, I really suffered for it. I was unhappy making both movies and the results were unhappy for me.

I'm trying to be an artist. Well, I am an artist in that I am practicing my art. I am not a consummate artist yet as an actor. I've got a lot to learn. I watched *Black Sunday* on television last weekend and I cringed. I like the movie, but I've matured a lot and grown a lot since then. I want to keep growing and keep working on a lot of areas.

PLAYGIRL: Does being a star hurt you as an actor?

DERN: No, I think it helps. I think it enables you to have the time to spend the energy, to give the effort that is beyond what you're able to do if you're not a star. I could not have given the performance I gave in *Strangers* [a play that had a brief run on Broadway with Dern playing writer Sinclair Lewis] had I not been a film star because I would not have been able to win certain battles that I had to win. I would not have had the audiences we had for many weeks, because they were there to see me. Some kinds of actors cannot rise to an occasion and are panicked by audiences, maybe more than are not. I have never once had sweat under my arms or panicked in front of a camera or while on stage. I have absolute confidence in myself to put out my best every single take or every single performance.

I think being a star puts more responsibility on you, so you owe more to yourself as an artist, and ultimately, you owe more to the audience. It's a powerful tool. It can be distracting, and it can then distract away from your work and make a performance suffer, there's no question about it, if you have your priorities in the wrong place. I can think of two very big film stars who are affected by their stardom, so much so that they compensate by endearing themselves to the audience. That affects their work—not always, but in certain roles. One I've worked with. One is a man and one is a woman. It's going to be interesting to see what happens to the man's career in the next few years. School's still out on him as far as I'm concerned. He's now directing as well as acting.

The woman is afraid not to be liked. She's Jane Fonda. I think she suffers because of her public image. I don't mean Mrs. Tom Hayden. I just think deep inside she feels it is important to preserve a certain kind of respectability of person, almost a movie-star thing, to maintain a certain level. Whereas, in public life, she follows her commitments to the death. She does not do that as an actress. I wish she would. She'd be a little better and she's already about as good as there is. I'm giving her the ultimate compliment. She is a tremendous actress; I feel she could be even better. It could be my own jaded way of looking at things from the point of view of a guy who usually doesn't win in movies, a guy who usually loses.

PLAYGIRL: Who is the actor you've been referring to?

DERN: Sylvester Stallone. It's tough to tell because he does a tremendous job as Rocky. Tremendous. But when he steps out of Rocky to play other roles, there's almost a desperate clinging to being a certain symbol of a man. Rocky's much more vulnerable than the other characters he plays. Well, what happens to movies where the guy is just a fuckin' heel? We don't make many movies about guys like that, unless they can get me, and then I have to play them. It's real tough to ask an actor to play an asshole with no redeeming virtues. Real tough. I know. I got cast as a jerk or an asshole or a nut case for a long time. It's not that it got to me, but I needed *Coming Home* and I needed *Middle Age Crazy*.

It's not enough to give just one or two sides of a character anymore. I always felt that; even when I began I gave multi-dimensions to all of the characters I played, even if it was only two lines in *Waterhole #3* or *The St. Valentine's Day Massacre*. In the future, audiences are going to demand that movies and plays examine more characters more deeply than they do now. I think ensemble pieces are going to become more the order of the day than they have been, though I enjoy being out there by myself. I enjoy being in every shot in a movie. I like the pressure and the responsibility.

PLAYGIRL: Now that you've been nominated for an Academy Award (*Coming Home*), have you changed your feelings about them?

DERN: I wish the Academy would eliminate them, but if they're going to have them, and they are, I think they should give a dinner for the nominees, televise it, give each nominee a minute to speak, give them their little trophies, and that's it. I think you'll get the same television ratings, maybe even more, because everybody would show up then. No one would be afraid of losing. There wouldn't be any competition, although there is an original competition for the nominations, of course, which is the grim thing. That's the thing I object to. There are people voting. There is a ballot box. In an artistic forum, I can't believe in that. It just doesn't make sense.

I don't believe in the way they select the all-star baseball team either. If you're going to have an all-star team, then go around to each team, and let players vote for guys on other teams but not on their own team. That's the way to do it. Sure, Vida Blue's not going to vote for Steve Carlton, because Blue feels he's a better pitcher, and Carlton's with the Phillies and Blue's with a team with Joe Pettini playing shortstop. How's Blue going to win more than fourteen games with Joe Pettini at shortstop?

I get an Oscar ballot, and on my ballot are five names. I'm not going to put down a vote for Christopher Walken (as Best Supporting Actor in *The Deer Hunter*) if I'm one of the five names. I'm going to vote for myself unless I think he was better than I was, and it is very rare that you will find an actor who thinks that way. When they announced Christopher Walken's name, I was not disappointed or heartbroken. He had one thing that I didn't have. He had more votes than I did. That's all. The Academy, which I'm a member of, should look into how we can make it more efficient. I can't even begin to get into the Emmy situation. I just don't understand it. There's an Emmy for everything. Best interview, best noninterview, best locker-room interview, best pregame interview, best postgame interview, best halftime interview.

PLAYGIRL: You have an upper-middle-class background, you're handsome, intelligent, you run, you seem to be normal. In the past, why have you been so good at playing characters who are psychologically off-center?

DERN: Well, first of all, those were the only roles they offered me, and I was a victim of original exposure. My original exposure in television was in that type of role, because those were always the available parts when I began. The part of the young leading man was always taken. So, if I wanted work, I had to take those roles. I had nobody guiding me to tell me not to take role after role after role like that. My agent, at that time, just said work, work, work, work, and I agreed with him. So I took them. It's not that I related to that type of character or identified with him more than anybody else, it's just that I was very well prepared as an actor, and I was ready to invest a great deal of effort, energy, and life into whoever it was that I played. I got to play guys who did things that made you wonder why they did what they did. In each movie or television show, one little scene was added in which we saw why the guy made the bomb. The disastrous thing was that we only saw that one scene of why he made the bomb or how he made the bomb, and then a scene of the bomb going off, instead of scenes about what made the guy want to make the bomb in the first place.

I never bagged it in a role. I never backed off it. I gave it everything. I think there are people who will tell you very seriously that this was detrimental to my career for a long time and that I should not have done those roles. I should have been much more career-minded in the way I played them, been much more of a sweetheart. But, you know, do we all want to see an interview on *60 Minutes* with Robert Vesco? We do. We want to believe Melvin Dummar. We wonder where D.B. Cooper is. Jesse James is a hero. Billy the Kid is a hero. And he was a horrible little bastard. He killed twenty-one men by the time he was fourteen years old. Shot 'em in the back. He didn't care. I don't even need to get into modern-day people. We've got a lot of people around here that people want to talk to, people want to see, people want to meet. People want to know something about them. Folk heroes. Why are they called folk heroes? Because the folks made them heroes.

PLAYGIRL: You came up through the ranks with Jack Nicholson, both professionally and personally, but at a certain point, there was a separation due to, it seems, political and life-style differences. When and how did that occur?

DERN: Personally, we simply just don't travel in the same circles and haven't, ever. We were never really together. I was never his roommate. We never double-dated. Our wives were never friends. He was a Forty-Niners fan. I was a Rams fan. So, twice a year we were together on Sundays for that. We were both Lakers fans. We were both sports fans. He wrote a movie, *The Trip*; I was in it. I did a bike movie, *Rebel Rousers;* he was in it. We were both in *The King of Marvin Gardens*. We were both around the Actors' Studio. We both admired each other's work. We were good competitors—not as actors but as athletes.

We played in a Hollywood show league together. That was in 1961 and '62. Jerry Lewis had a team. PJ's had a team. The Raincheck had a team. Bobby Darin had a team. Jack Gilardi had a team called the UJIs, United Jewish Italians. I had a team called Dern's Dirty Shirts. Actors Equity had a team. One of the labs had a team; Deluxe or something like that. Most of the studios had teams, but they weren't in our league.

In terms of who was there, I can tell you who played on my team. Ricky Nelson was my catcher. Elliott Gould played first base. David Nelson or Mark Harris played second base. Joey Walsh played shortstop. Dick Bradford played third. I played center or left. John Strasberg, Lee Strasberg's son, played the outfield. Fred Roos played outfield. Everyone imported pitchers. It was windmill fast pitch, and we didn't have any actors who could fast pitch, although Jim Garner was a great pitcher. That was basically my team.

Jack Nicholson had another team. Jack played second base, Jimmy Caan played shortstop. You wouldn't know a lot of the other guys. I quit in '62 and became a runner. I think the league stopped in '67. Jack always appreciated my running, and I always appreciated his unbelievable competitiveness as an athlete. We played in pickup basketball games. He was good. I'm not very good at basketball. He was just all over the place. But, anything that had to do with regular running, basically, nobody else did but me.

But I don't feel separated from him. He doesn't feel separated from me, I'm sure. When we want to get together, we'll get together. He's not a big entertainer; I'm not a big entertainer. He is single which, I would say, is the first answer to your question about why we travel in different circles. I was married all the time I knew Jack. I was married to Diane [Ladd], then met Andrea and was married to her. As a matter of fact, during those years Jack was married—'61 through '67, I never saw him with another woman except his wife [Sandra Knight]. The next time I really caught up with him, he was divorced from her and was on *Drive, He Said* with a girl named Mimi. Now he lives with Angelica [Huston], and I think that they live very happily together. Ever since I've known Jack, he's always had a girl. A girl, for now.

And he lives in Aspen. I live in Tahoe, as the backup home. I spend a lot of time in Tahoe. He spends a lot of time in Aspen. And, on the career side of it, he was in *Easy Rider*. I wasn't. He was in *Five Easy Pieces*. I wasn't. *Five Easy Pieces* put him in a whole different league. That's what happened, career-wise. By league, I don't mean that his work was so great and mine was so shitty or vice versa. I just mean that he starred in a movie that went out and did good business, and it kicked him off into other things. Jack played a lot of other leading-man roles, but the people didn't go to see those movies. I played leading men, too, but people didn't go to see those movies either. I felt I played a leading man in *The Great Gatsby*. Everybody said no, because it was Bruce Dern, and he wasn't a leading man. Well, that's horseshit. Tom Buchanan [the Dern character in *Gatsby*] is a leading-man character.

I guess what really happened was a political separation. Jack is much more motivated politically than I am and was much more in the limelight because of that. I think he's backed off a little bit from that now; I don't think he's as public now as he was five years ago. I think he may enjoy his life a little better because of that. Plus, we're in our forties. We don't get turned on by the same things. And yet, the things that keep us friends still turn us on the same way. I know some Sunday, somewhere, even though he doesn't pull for them openly anymore, he hopes the Forty-niners will stuff the Rams. They won't.

PLAYGIRL: Was the drug scene a separation point? Did you ever get into drugs?

DERN: No. None. *N-O-N-E.* I'm not a drugger. While I was out grinding out three or four hours on the road running, they were relaxing, and they relaxed differently than I did. I think at that time it was much more clandestine, the whole smoking marijuana or taking coke or whatever it is that they did. It was much more private and secretive because it wasn't allowed. Now... are you allowed to smoke marijuana in your own house or not?

PLAYGIRL: I don't know.

DERN: I don't know, but I'm sure that people do it. Whatever, it's much more out in the open now, much more acceptable to society. I guess the easiest thing to say is that I literally ran through the sixties. I would say between 1961 and 1970, I ran 40,000 miles. I was doing 4,000 miles a year. Well, there's just no place for the other.

PLAYGIRL: One gets the impression that you're quite the opposite of many of the roles you've played, that you're in fact conservative and perhaps a Republican.

DERN: I'm apolitical. There's no one to root for. There's no one on a white horse. I want my leader on a white horse.

PLAYGIRL: Having just gone through an election year, are you hopeful or disillusioned? Are things getting better or worse?

DERN: The system's working. It's worked for 200 years, and it'll work for another 200. Some decades you get good candidates, some decades you get guys who aren't so good. None of these guys was a *bad* guy, you know what I mean? There wasn't a *bad* guy running—there were a couple of schtummies, you know, and a yo-yo. I didn't vote for president.

PLAYGIRL: How important is sex to you?

DERN: It's six and a half inches hard, and it's white, and it does still get hard. It still has bullets in it, you know. Sex is extremely important to me. Actually, first is the orgasm, second is sex in importance. I am orgasmically motivated.

PLAYGIRL: If your sex life is bad at a particular time, does it affect your acting and your life in general?

256

DERN: No, nothing interferes with my work. But I think a good sex life stimulates art. I think a good sex life stimulates anything. Obviously, a bad sex life will affect human performance. I think probably sex and motivation are the two biggest things that affect artists and athletes or anybody who's involved with creative energy. Although it's odd in that the ultimate result of good sex is orgasm, which means you are actually spending something that leaves your body. The whole euphoria of it and the obvious relaxation from it create rather than detract. I think it's the only thing in the world like that where something is leaving you; both men and women are actually losing—what is it made up of—blood cells, sperm? I don't know whether it's red blood cells or white, I always had biology classes during the World Series.

PLAYGIRL: How is your third marriage unlike your previous two?

DERN: It's successful. I'm deeply in love with my wife, whom I hope is deeply in love with me. I have a secretary, Donna, who is my best friend and whom I confide a lot of things in. She is more than a secretary. She's like a sister and a girl Friday. She's just become everything. Andrea trusts her implicitly. I trust her implicitly. She handles a lot of responsibility for me. I identify very well with her, and I identify well with Andrea, and we've worked it out where Donna fits very well into our lives. I don't have many friends at all. I have no men friends that I can really relate to. Outside of Andrea, I need somebody to bounce things off of. Having that has helped the marriage, plus I respect Andrea enormously. She's as close to the perfect lady as anyone I've ever known in terms of having her priorities in the right place, in terms of her attractiveness and her durability and her accessibility to me. I would say her ability to bend, not break, is her greatest attribute, and that was essential with me. It's taught me to be the same way—and I'm still too selfish.

PLAYGIRL: How do you relate to women's liberation?

DERN: I like it. I think it belongs. I even think women should be drafted. If they want equal rights, they should be eligible for the draft. But I don't think they should have to fight if they don't want to. We already know that guys crack who don't want to go but are forced to go. So why put women through it? Why put anybody through it?

PLAYGIRL: You have a daughter, Laura, who's now acting in films. What do you tell her about Hollywood, drugs, relationships?

DERN: You mean, what does she tell me? She knows more than I do. Not about sex but about what's available on the street. Although she's very good, she behaves herself very well. We have a few discussions about sex. I tell her she's going to have to learn for herself. She'll be fourteen in February. She's got a great figure, is pretty and real tall. She's going through the craze—learning that people are attracted to her. I tell her that there's only one thing that's taboo: She's not to take hard drugs in any way, shape, or form. When they call to say that she's down at the jail and she's just been busted for smack or something like that, she's just going to have to fight fires at Camp Sixteen 'cause I'm not coming to get her. No hard drugs. I don't want to see a needle hole in her arm or anything like that. And, uh, no babies. Learn about sex. Experiment all you want to, but put a cork in it. Don't let anybody put it in without a raincoat on, you know what I mean? A pregnancy at an early age ruins lives.

PLAYGIRL: What do you know now about relationships that you didn't know during the previous two marriages?

DERN: You've got to get the sex part of the relationship correct the first night. The first night. You've got to say, "I'm into this, this, this, and this. It all ain't gonna happen tonight, but these things could come out at any time. Accept it or we can't make it."

I really believe that. If both people can accept and understand that, then the morals, the intelligence, the downtime, the athletic endeavors, the drive, the emotional capacities, all the other things will fit in. You spend eight hours a day in bed. If there comes a time when the playroom part of the bedroom is not there enough for both people to be relaxed and achieve an orgasm, there is going to be serious trouble in that relationship down the road. There must be mutual orgasms, and a lot of people never know it. They'll grind it out, but they'll *grind* it out.

My first two marriages were ground out. It was more my fault. I was the pig in the relationship. I was the bad guy, no question about it. Without a really "cohabitable" sexual commitment, it's really a grind. It's not a marathon, because a marathon can be finished. A grind is an unfinishable event.

PLAYGIRL: When did you lose your virginity?

DERN: October of 1952 in a whorehouse in Kankakee. I was so excited. You had to walk in and then pick out a girl. There were six girls there, and I picked out a girl and she took me into the back. They had to wash you off then. They brought you over to the sink and washed you off before you could have sex with them. I came in the sink while she was washing me off. I asked her if I could please stay in the room with her for another fifteen minutes so my friends that I went there with wouldn't think something had happened. First load, in the sink. I didn't jerk off or masturbate or anything until after that. That was literally my first orgasm.

PLAYGIRL: What led up to your journey to the whorehouse in Kankakee?

DERN: Pete Stevens and Tommy Gray drove me. We didn't sneak off. We were sixteen; it was our junior year in high school. I mean, you know, it was Saturday afternoon. I didn't go to all the football games. I didn't play football. We didn't run cross-country then. I think we had a night game against Niles, as a matter of fact, so there was nothing to do that afternoon. So, we went down to Kankakee. It was only sixty miles away, and I had never done it before so I figured, hey, give it a try. The girls were not unattractive.

PLAYGIRL: How did your upbringing affect your views on sex, goals, and choice of a career?

DERN: During my upbringing, there was no discussion of sex. I mean, if a woman wanted to get pregnant, you'd squeeze her breasts. That was my upbringing about sex. I didn't have a clue until I went to Kankakee. I figured it was a biology lab experiment, going to Kankakee. As a matter of fact, I figured on Monday morning I'd be the most popular guy in the biology class. I'd tell them a story they wouldn't believe. I could tell them I saw sperm go down a sink.

The only thing my upbringing did, in terms of my career, was that when I finally made a decision to do what I wanted to do, I knew I was going to do it for the rest of my life, even though it greatly disturbed my family. What I decided to do was be an actor. In my family, the regimen was when you made up your mind, you stuck to it. There was no question that I wanted to stick to it. In 1956, I made up my mind to be an actor. That's it. No turning back.

PLAYGIRL: How did you arrive at acting as a career?

DERN: I was desperate to communicate. Desperate. Nobody was listening at home. My friends were listening, and I'm sure I didn't have a lot to say. Suddenly, I realized that people were sitting and watching and were being touched and moved by true characters in movies and plays. I felt that was something I wanted to do. I couldn't write it down. I was very poor at that. So, I felt the best way to do it was to emote it. That's why I'm drawn, as often as I am, to the emotional character. I feel if people can sit in a dark little theater, or in a big theater, hopefully, and be touched and moved by something that my character is doing, then I'm making contact. I've got to do that or I'm not happy.

PLAYGIRL: What were your initial impressions of Hollywood when you arrived from the East?

DERN: I didn't come here until May of '61. I was in New York from '57 on. I drove a cab in New York. That was memorable.

PLAYGIRL: Could you ever envision being out in Hollywood?

DERN: No. I never envisioned being in Hollywood until the day I got here. Memorial Day, 1961. I just never dreamed of Hollywood. When I first became an actor, I never even dreamed of being in the movies—literally, I never did. I just wanted to be as real and as honest an actor as I could be. I wanted to do plays. I didn't even know how you got in a movie or on a TV show, you know. Then I did *Naked City* in New York, then a *Route 66*, and that was it. And I did a movie while I was in New York. Then I came to Hollywood and realized that if you wanted to make a living as an actor, there was much more work here. There was nothing left in New York. *Playhouse 90* moved to California. There was no more *Studio One. The Armstrong Circle Theater* folded. *The U.S. Steel Hour* folded. After a couple of years, all there was in New York was *Naked City*, and then that folded. You had to come to Hollywood unless you were just a die-hard theatre buff, which I wasn't, although I enjoyed the theater.

In the early sixties, I was struggling so hard to maintain my standards as an actor, studying, teaching, and looking for work, that I would say the first seven or eight years of the sixties really just flew by between that and my running. You know, I had a wife, and I had a child who drowned, and I had another child who was born in 1967. It was tough, man. I had a real tough decade. I had a lot of relatives go out in the sixties.

I look at the sports in the sixties, and outside of being a statistics nut, I don't remember the first half, like the Yankees-Cincinnati series in '61. I can't even remember what happened except that the Yankees won, I think, in five. I don't remember much about Koufax and Drysdale. All of that was going on, a bunch of people at the peak of their careers, and I was just about to be thirty, you know, playing "Billy the Clerk." I never thought in terms of rising to a certain kind of stardom. I thought in terms of just being constantly given the opportunity to work in good projects and having better roles. I just pursued that. I was really, literally, working my ass off during the sixties. By 1969, I had done 120 television shows and 22 movies.

PLAYGIRL: Are you content when you're not working? What do you do?

DERN: I am now. I was not up until three or four years ago. When I'm not working, I run. I'm starting to read a little more. For the first time in my life, I'm starting to develop projects that I want to do, which takes time. I spend a lot of time in Tahoe and a lot of time evaluating myself a little more than I used to. I like to have a six-week period to come down from a character and a six-week period to build up to the next character.

PLAYGIRL: Do you always feel that your latest film is your best?

DERN: No, although I feel *Tattoo* is my best. When I finished *Coming Home,* I felt it was good work, but not the best I'd ever done. I'm always disappointed the first couple of times I look at any of my films because it's never what I dreamed it would be. It never is for anybody. We only start feeling good after we get the adulation, the pats on the back, and the encouragement from our friends or our peers or the critics or the audience, whatever; then we start getting behind it. You always look at it with a sneer on your lips the first time you see it.

PLAYGIRL: What is your perception of the way people in Hollywood deal with you?

DERN: I like the way I'm being dealt with. I appreciate the way they deal with me. I do get a little tired of being called "the man who killed John Wayne" eight years later. I mean, that's boring. That pisses me off. I'm a little bigger than that.

PLAYGIRL: Do you think audiences understand you?

DERN: I don't really care. I'm not looking for that— "Do you really understand me, man?" I look for that in the roles. I hope people don't know who I really am. I hope to have a rather low profile in real life. I want to be anonymous in the crowd. I want them to get to know me through my roles. I want to remain unpredictable on the screen. I want to remain unpredictable.

David Schwimmer

The mopey friend—on hair care, private photos and what you should say after sex

A former NYPD Blue semiregular and now co-star of the wildly successful NBC comedy series Friends, David Schwimmer is making his way in films.

Born in Queens, Schwimmer enrolled in a high school drama class on a whim. Schwimmer's instructor encouraged him to attend Northwestern University in Illinois, where he received a degree in speech and theater. Schwimmer and seven other Northwestern graduates co-founded the Lookingglass Theater and have written, directed and performed original plays all over the world, including the Edinburgh Festival in Scotland. The Lookingglass troupe also took roles in the film Since You've Been Gone, directed by and starring Schwimmer. Other Schwimmer film appearances include 6 Days 7 Nights opposite Harrison Ford and Anne Heche, Apt Pupil opposite Ian McKellen, The Pallbearer and Kissing a Fool. Schwimmer also starred in Breast Men for HBO.

Robert Crane caught up with Schwimmer at Du-par's, a 24-hour coffee shop in Los Angeles. Crane reports: "Schwimmer chose to meet at an off-hour and in an unhip locale. Despite his Friends celebrity and the big salary that goes with it, Schwimmer is low-key. His stack of pancakes and cup of black coffee bore no traces of glamour."

1

PLAYBOY: What are the hairstyle options for men with low hairlines?

SCHWIMMER: The pompadour—you know, the big thick greasy look of the Fifties. If you want to, take a marker and draw in the widow's peak. Just make sure the tip doesn't go all the way to the eyebrows. I did that when I was a kid. I thought Dracula was really cool—you know, sexy, dark—and I wanted to be him every Halloween. I'm very lucky with this head of hair. I wash it every day and put whatever product I want in it. You can do just about anything. I had it down to the middle of my back in college, and I had a crew cut for pretty much the first year of *Friends*.

2

PLAYBOY: Should the eyebrows touch or not?

SCHWIMMER: They should definitely not touch. Wax, shave, pluck, do whatever you need to do. Women don't find the unibrow attractive.

3

PLAYBOY: You played a plastic surgeon in HBO's *Breast Men*—a film about breast augmentation. Does that procedure do a favor for a specific woman or does it do all women a disfavor?

SCHWIMMER: So long as there is no health risk, then it's up to each woman to determine what it is she wants to do with her body. Some women may feel they're not as sexual or as womanly as they'd like to be, and if augmentation would help them overcome that, then they have every right to do what they want.

4

PLAYBOY: Break it down: What makes a good stage, TV and film actor.

SCHWIMMER: It's a question of education. My first experience was acting for the stage, and then I gradually learned to act for TV cameras and I'm still learning how to act for film. They're very different. If you come from the stage it's hard to understand the camera and what can be achieved by doing less in film. It's actually a lot harder to go the other way, to be a film actor and then try to do a play. There are very few who can do it, because you really have to train your voice and body and have endurance as an actor to do a scene for more than two or three minutes. Often you're onstage for two or three hours without a break, which is my favorite thing. That's the biggest high there is. I've never understood actors who don't watch the movies they've completed. I watch the things I've done over and over because I feel that's the only way I'm going to improve as a film actor. Gary Sinise and John Malkovich are phenomenal in all three mediums.

5

PLAYBOY: Discuss the tax problems of a successful show.

SCHWIMMER: Look, $100,000 a week is a ridiculous amount of money for anyone. But consider how much the people who create the show and the studio and the network make. Our request that the six of us be paid equally, which we weren't in the beginning, was important to us. We'll be around as long as all of us are happy creatively and are still being challenged as actors, and as long as the writing stays as good as it has been and, of course, as long as the public wants to tune in.

6

PLAYBOY: If a pirated photo of you were to appear on the Internet, what would it show you doing?

SCHWIMMER: I would hope to have a man's body. Someone once did a computer distortion of our faces, all six of us, that made us 60 years old and fat. I got a real kick out of that. But no, I haven't seen myself nude on the Internet yet.

7

PLAYBOY: Just so we can start looking, have you ever lost any photos or tapes?

SCHWIMMER: Do you know something I don't know? You're getting me scared. I'm racking my brain—when I was 18 did I do some kind of video? You know what's really interesting about that? I'd just graduated from college and had been seeing this girl for a year and a half. One day I was taking a shower and I had shampoo in my hair and eyes, and she whipped open the shower curtain and with an Instamatic took a couple of pictures of me, naked. Though we were happy together, something told me to dispose of the film, and I did. Eight years ago I was thinking, One day I want to be an actor. I don't want photos turning up.

8

PLAYBOY: When is it best not to have video   mementos of one's love?

SCHWIMMER: I think it's best not to videotape yourself steering a boat with your genitalia. If you want any serious consideration as an actor, that may hamper it, though in certain cases it may not. It may even elicit more interest in you.

9

PLAYBOY: What combination of the *Friends* cast would create a well-adjusted human being?

SCHWIMMER: The toughest would be finding the best trait for myself. The others are easy: Matt Perry's sense of humor, Matt LeBlanc's big heart—I was going to say big heart for all of them. Courteney's old-fashioned common sense and honesty. Lisa's basic intelligence. Jennifer's generosity. And I guess my loyalty.

10

PLAYBOY: What plotlines will never be explored on *Friends*?

SCHWIMMER: Three guys in the sack. The one in which Ross and Monica do the unspoken deed. The one in which Ross kills someone.

11

PLAYBOY: We understand you're a poker player. Are you a good bluffer?

SCHWIMMER: It's easier to bluff when you're playing with friends. You get to know who you can bluff and who you can't. Strangers are tougher. I've played only once in Vegas with strangers, and I don't think I was that great.

12

PLAYBOY: Give us some telltale signs of tells.

SCHWIMMER: There's a guy I play with sometimes who suddenly gets incredibly serious. He doesn't laugh with everyone else when he's got the hand. He's very quiet, waiting for play. He thinks he's bluffing by not raising, thinking he's going to bag it at the end. But I know he's not bluffing, because he's quiet, he's not raising, and I fold unless I know I can take him down.

13

PLAYBOY: If you needed quick cash, who would be at your poker table?

SCHWIMMER: If I could get them, the girls on the show.

14

PLAYBOY: Your agent gives you a script about a schlub who has a series of erotic adventures with a lot of gorgeous women before finding his true love. Name the actresses you'd cast and the actress you'd wind up with. By the way, there's a lot of nudity in this film.

SCHWIMMER: I'd probably have to encounter Helena Bonham-Carter, Audrey Hepburn, Sophia Loren, Shirley MacLaine. Winona Ryder, of course. I think at one time I would have said Holly Hunter. Maria Grazia Cucinotta, the actress from *Il Postino*. And Maria Conchita Alonso. I would probably end up with her.

Robert Crane

15

PLAYBOY: In one episode of *Friends*, Rachel thinks Ross has suffered a premature ejaculation in a museum. Have you found most women to be as forgiving as she was?

SCHWIMMER: I wouldn't know about that. I'm a lucky man.

16

PLAYBOY: You're in bed and see something for the first time you don't like. What do you do?

SCHWIMMER: I remind her that I have to be up very early and excuse myself.

17

PLAYBOY: Do *Friends* fuck friends?

SCHWIMMER: You're not talking about the show, right? I've never crossed that line. I know right away if I'm physically attracted to someone. Rarely have I been good friends with someone and then at some later point found her suddenly physically attractive enough to sleep with her. So my answer is no. I guess I operate on a primitive kind of behavior—I either want to grab on and not let go for quite a while, or it's just not there.

18

PLAYBOY: What sorts of scripts should your agent look out for?

SCHWIMMER: Anything but black comedies or anything with a really low budget. I've done that. I don't have any interest in big broad comedy. I like more sophisticated comedies, character-driven movies, dramas, action movies, suspense. I'm up for anything. My agent of ten years knows pretty much what I like.

19

PLAYBOY: We understand the entertainment value of female bisexuality in films. Why do you suppose male bisexuality never caught on?

SCHWIMMER: No clue. I've only watched heterosexual adult films. I don't understand guys who are bisexual—it's a mystery to me because I don't know any. I knew some guys who were straight once and are now homosexual, but I don't know any guys who are bi. To each his own, I guess. I can't imagine. All I can think of is watching a guy and a girl together and getting turned on, then suddenly another guy enters the room. Oh, OK, shut that off. Not even fast-forward. Switch to *Letterman*.

20

PLAYBOY: In the moments after sex, what should a man say?

SCHWIMMER: Uncuff me.

264

ARTISTS

Robert Crane

Pool Hall

The Bearable Lightness of Being

Artist D.J. Hall gazes longingly at the shimmering, pearlescent pool water, accented by aqua-colored tile circa 1950s, the centerpiece of the natural setting at her warm and comfortable Palm Desert home.

"I'm a pleasure pig, I admit it," says Hall, a teen-spirited 46, enthusiastically. "The pool is flawless. It needs new tile, but it's perfect. It's like the pool of my childhood."

Renowned for her exquisitely executed hyper-realistic portraits of eternally-youthful beautiful people celebrating the good life by the pool or at the beach, Hall is arguably the art world's ambassador for Southern California. "It's a real visual fantasy that I create," acknowledges Hall, who also maintains a contemporary-designed home in Venice, California. "It's the best of times people can possibly have; the food, the wine, the beautiful clothing, the happy expressions."

Initially, happiness was not an ingredient of Hall's upbringing in Santa Ana. An only child, her parents divorced when she was two years old. The roles of mother and daughter soon reversed and Hall found herself taking care of a young adult wracked with fear, anxiety and phobias. Hall was expected to shine—to be a perfect child amidst all the misfortunes in her life. Then, on a trip to visit her paternal grandparents (orange growers Margaret and Edward M. Hall) at their new vacation home in Palm Desert, she unlocked a creative door which would eventually lead to D.J. Hall becoming an artist. She recalls: "I remember the first day driving through Palm Springs. It was November 1960. I remember seeing light hitting white, pale green and pink walls. I instantly felt a sense of relief."

Happiness arrived in the shape of a swimming pool. Hall, her family temporarily intact, would celebrate birthdays with luxuriously elaborate parties for years to come. The pool's water conveyed a sense of well-being and peace which years later would become important motifs in Hall's work. "My attraction to my work is the desire to have a perpetual summer," says Hall. "I'm always painting summer light and playing out past, wished-for memories and the fantasy life that my mother would have liked to have had for herself."

Hall began sketching and drawing from her grandmother's *Vogue* and *Town and Country* magazines. She wanted to be able to do likenesses. Later, when Hall attended USC (her parents' alma mater), she led a double life; in art class doing abstract work to satisfy her instructors, but, on the sly, painting realist images for her own pleasure. She had found her art.

After graduating magna cum laude in 1973, Hall started to paint large canvases detailing affluent people on vacation. She would use a telephoto lens to photograph her subjects lounging and soaking up the sun at resorts like the Palm Springs Spa. Hall would use the best of the prints (a face here, a hairstyle there, a body over there) to construct her own vision on canvas of the good life. At first, being young and rebellious, Hall made social commentaries against that lifestyle by showing every vein, wrinkle and blemish. Now, twenty-five years later, Hall's friends are her models and art collectors, the former subjects of her wrath.

One notes that except for an occasional swim-by in the background by Hall's architect husband of twenty-four years, Toby Watson, men are no longer part of her artistic landscape. "My main visual reference is women," admits Hall. "There's a lot more expression in women's faces and a greater variety of women's hairstyles. Let's blame it on Madison Avenue. The image of a woman is what's used to sell everything in our society. I learned how to draw from that imagery and Madison Avenue taught me well."

Many of the women Hall paints and draws bear some resemblance to her and her family and friends and are typically blonde and attractive. Still, she admits her true subject matter is light. Hall is constantly traveling to Jamaica, Mexico, Hawaii and the desert in her quest for the perfect illumination. "Light is how we see," explains Hall. "I'm painting the process of vision. Beautiful, warm light is what makes me happy. The desert offers intense light. I'm happy as an artist here and I'm happy as myself here."

Hall believes there was divine intervention in her purchase of the late Mr. and Mrs. Busby Berkeley's Palm Desert home, two blocks from her now-deceased grandmother's home. "As an adult, on my birthday, I would go with my husband to the desert and stay at the former Antaraes resort. My late grandmother, my late father, my cats and Mrs. Berkeley wanted me to have this house," says Hall in a hushed tone, drawing the listener closer. "Mrs. Berkeley passed away the day we closed escrow."

Legendary choreographer-director Busby Berkeley and his wife, Etta Dunn, built their Palm Desert getaway in 1957. According to Hall, who has researched documents and photographs found at the Motion Picture Arts and Sciences library, the Berkeleys loved the home and entertained often. Many years ago, one guest of particular interest would turn out to be the future Secretary of State Madeleine Albright. "If these walls could talk," whispers Hall, a sparkle in her eyes.

The openness of the Fifties-style home has allowed the artist and her husband to invite fellow artists, collectors, models and writers out to the desert for long weekends. The martini shaker that the Berkeleys left behind is often used.

Having made a few aesthetic changes involving painting and rearranging, the couple has decided to let the home remain in its present design. There will be an addition, however. "We'll be adding on a studio," says Hall, smiling like one of the models in her work.

A year-long battle with Lyme Disease nearly ended her career several years ago. In constant pain and facing physically demanding work, Hall was limited to fifteen minutes of painting a day at her lowest point. Now, after a strict regimen of physical therapy and medication, she is producing more work than ever. "I'm back," yells Hall. "I feel so happy here. I call it 'the happy house.' The good memories I have from my childhood and adolescence filter into my current experience." Hall laughs. "My first romantic situations happened in Palm Desert."

Having produced hundreds of paintings, drawings, sketches, boxes and panels, Hall feels fortunate that she is able to turn out the work she loves. "I hope to have my health so I can keep doing my work," says Hall, staring at the swimming pool's glistening water. "I want my work to be successful enough so I can maintain the lifestyle I have at this point. I am my strongest critic but I'm constantly moving forward and doing what comes from the heart. My biggest fear is loss, losing those I love. I'm where I want to be and I don't really need a whole lot more in life now. I feel complete here."

D.J. Hall's work can be seen at The Koplin Gallery in West Hollywood and OK Harris Works of Art in New York City. She is constantly considering attractive women in their 30s-50s who want to be immortalized.

John Cerney

Art from Zontar

Artist John Cerney likes to be noticed. In a big way. Who, for example, traveling along the highways from Salinas to Irvine, from Indio to Phoenix, could miss Cerney's work? These hyper-realist, figurative oil-based wooden cut-outs (generally 18 feet in height) adorn the sides of commercial sites and private properties all over the Southwest. Not to mention along urban buildings, industrial plants and barns. And a minor league baseball stadium in Central California.

Cerney paints and assembles these super-sized, individual pieces at his studio near the Steinbeck Center in Salinas. He then personally delivers and installs the work with associate Dong Sun Kim and the help of a few assistants. We're talking hands-on, 16-hour days. And John wouldn't have it any other way.

Cerney loves to grab people's attention. He remembers years ago when he worked solely on small commission portraits and felt the frustration: When he died, he figured, a retrospective of his life's work could be held in a broom closet. No more. Not even an airplane hangar can contain his artistic output.

Locally, Cerney's galloping polo players can be seen at the Eldorado Polo Club and his soccer stars in action at West Coast Turf, both in Indio. Next time you drive to Phoenix, just west of the city (in Goodyear) on the north side of Interstate 10, look for the humongous baby sitting in a field using a full-scale tractor as a toy. There's a good chance at any of these locations you'll see John Cerney, paintbrush in hand, standing on a ladder, touching up a portion of the piece, under the relentless, desert sun. Luckily, we were able to speak with him in the shade.

111: *What is the relationship between the work and the desert? Is it easier or harder to create pieces for the desert environment?*

Cerney: I love the desert. I'm also fully aware that there's a line you can't cross before you tick off those who take their desert seriously. It would be foolish on my part to place my artwork in a truly spectacular setting as it would defeat the purpose of drawing attention to the art.

My work is closely tied into the American culture. I try to tell a story rather than just paint something pretty. Much like Rockwell had to get his message across on magazine covers, I try to accomplish the same. The difference is my audience is driving 65 miles per hour and their minds are on getting home in time to watch *Fear Factor*.

111: *Please take us through the installation of the Eldorado Polo Club and West Coast Turf pieces.*

Cerney: The Eldorado Polo Club pieces were fun to work on. I hadn't painted a horse in years so I took it on as a challenge. I had to assemble the two cut-outs in a ballroom at a Las Vegas hotel for a Polo America convention first before installing them on their grounds at Eldorado. Randy Russell from Eldorado had seen my large soccer players at West Coast Turf in Indio. Sometimes, I feel like I'm leaving these massive business cards in the ground.

For West Coast Turf, I photographed six rolls of the company-sponsored soccer team in action, making the perfect shot by taking an arm from photo 7 and attaching it to the torso in photo 23. I made a big color copy of it and, using the grid system, I transferred the squares onto sheets of MDO plywood that are screwed onto my giant easel.

My bigger pieces are often five sheets high, so I don't get to see the entire figure together until the day that I install it.

111: *What are the largest and smallest pieces you've worked on?*

Cerney: I painted a false façade of a home for the Irvine Company in Tustin that stands 36 feet tall. I think they spent more for the I-beams to support the painting than for the actual painting.

The smallest piece I recall is a snarling little bulldog that a couple wanted on their front porch to scare away solicitors.

111: *Is bigger better?*

Cerney: I wanted more people to see my work which was the reason for the initial switch from small portraits to murals. I painted on the side of a few barns in Monterey County just for practice and started getting calls from landowners or businesses in the area.

It was a slow transition from painting on walls to free-standing cut-outs. I tell people I started doing the cut-outs because I was too lazy to paint the backgrounds. The figures look striking because I "use" the existing background landscape, be it the desert, a crop field, or a hillside.

It's the body language and the facial expressions of my subjects that people generally connect with. Each subject has to have a distinct purpose, so I try to get the models to "overact" to achieve this.

111: *Which artists have influenced your work?*

Cerney: The biggest was D.J. Hall [*painter of 111's summer 2004 cover*], one of the premier realist painters in the country. She works out of Venice and Palm Desert. Her husband, Toby Watson, is a very talented architect. I learned that D.J. possesses a rare kind of discipline that I would never know, or at least didn't think, was humanly possible.

While I lived and worked in Los Angeles about 10 years ago, I volunteered to work with other art enthusiasts to help Kent Twitchell restore one of his murals. I ended up working in a similar fashion to Twitchell's except for the "wall" thing.

Otherwise, I get a thrill out of Van Gogh, Vermeer, Edward Hopper, Claes Oldenberg and Christo.

111: *We hear Oprah is a client. What is the upside/downside of working with a celebrity?*

Cerney: There's certainly an extra buzz when I'm working for a celebrity. I got a kick out of working with John Candy. He was such a sweet and genuinely good-natured guy to be around. His office in L.A. was like a clubhouse. I did some of my best drawings for John and he gave Wayne Gretzky and Bruce McNall two of them as gifts. I imagine if McNall still had the drawing in his possession in prison, he would have traded it for five packs of cigarettes and lied and said it was a David Hockney

Robert Crane

[McNall, the former owner of the Los Angeles Kings hockey team, served five years in prison for fraud].

I did some work for Reggie Jackson for a diner he was opening in Monterey. Reggie's used to throwing his weight around and he put a little pressure to speed things up. I didn't realize it until later but I had my first anxiety attack. Reggie was actually fun to work with, but I let the perceived magnitude of it get to me.

111: *What do you enjoy about the communities along 111?*

Cerney: Great times. Great memories. I came here as a kid in the Sixties and went to Angel spring training games. I have this soft-focused romantic vision of Gene Autry leading his Angel ballplayers from his resort to the ballpark on bicycles.

111: *What will be your ultimate art piece?*

Cerney: I took a trip to Mount Rushmore last fall to get inspiration for a very large hillside work I'd like to do. I want to get even closer to the landscape and actually place the image on the slope of a hill to create the feeling that it's painted on the terrain. I'm doing two smaller, experimental pieces using ceramic tiles and wood panels.

The large one I want to do, perhaps in the next two to three years, could be as large as 5,000 to 7,000 square feet. I haven't secured the hillside yet. My ideal situation would be for the farmer or rancher who says, "I've got 40 acres just off the interstate. Make something for me."

Kirk Driscoll and Niki Dantine:

Photographers Above/Below

The dictionary definition of an artist includes "a person skilled in one of the fine arts" AND "one who is adept at deception." Underwater photographer Niki Dantine doesn't necessarily want art patrons visiting Orlando Gallery in Tarzana to know she has been an actress (*Princess Daisy, Westwind*), dancer, and model and is a daughter of the late Loew's theatre chain founder and MGM president, Nicholas Schenck. Contemporary-abstract photographer Kirk Driscoll would prefer that supporters of the art of producing images on a sensitized surface not be bothered with the fact that he's a veteran bartender (27 years at Stanley's in Sherman Oaks), co-author of the upcoming tell-all bar book, *Burn the Ice*, and an early television reality star on Fox's *Paradise Hotel*.

Bob Gino and Don Grant, owners of the 50-year-old Orlando Gallery which so happens to have produced the first decent photography show in a public gallery 35 years ago when photographers still showed at furniture stores, shake their heads in amazement. "We've never experienced so many professions and personalities encased in two artists," says the Mr. Clean-look-alike Gino. Grant adds, "They're polar opposites which make for a great show."

Dantine came up with the show title: above/below. Get it? Driscoll shoots above water level – abstract forms including rusted out urban building facades and dilapidated billboards showing parts of their last four advertisements in an interesting juxtaposition. Dantine shoots below water level – Long Nose Hawkfish off the coast of New Guinea and Red Eye Jacks in The Great Barrier Reef to Crinoids in the Galapagos Islands and Napoleon Wrasse in the Red Sea.

The fifty-seven-year-old Driscoll does admit he enjoys shooting real live models occasionally. "I do have to eat so I take on commercial work or actress/model publicity shots. One of my customers at Stanley's, a lawyer who represents Tera Patrick and Jenna Jameson among others, got me contracts and model release forms at no cost. There's a benefit to bartending."

The attractive, red-headed Dantine experienced the uncertain actress/model rollercoaster ride herself for a time, but, after the death of her second husband, famed Century City attorney Greg Bautzer, she took up scuba diving, bought top notch equipment including Nikonos V and Canon F1 cameras with Ikelite strobes and traveled worldwide, often the only woman onboard sailing vessels. Dantine says, "I discovered the underwater world, and photography, fairly late in life on a trip to Sharm El Sheik, Egypt. Unhampered by knowledge, I dropped over the side of the ship and instantly fell in love. Having traveled to places like Borneo and the Solomon Islands, I find travel to be a constant learning experience. I always try to make eye contact with my subjects (Hammerhead Sharks! Giant Manta Rays!) so we develop a relationship. It's a love affair."

Driscoll has made plenty of eye contact with his subjects while tending bar at Stanley's. He says, "I've talked to (Quentin) Tarantino about our favorite films, sung with Dolly Parton in the bathroom, told Rod Stewart his wife called and wants him home, received an autographed 'adult' DVD from Shane, had a beer with (Wayne) Gretzky and signed a Stanley's placemat for Mel Gibson." Driscoll, who had a much shorter acting career than Dantine, played a hunter chasing down the protagonist in the straight-to-video, *Dominion*, written by a Stanley's co-worker, and a serial killer in a short film. He enjoys a certain autonomy found in both photography and bartending. "We're not just the quarterbacks, we're (Tom) Brady, man. Just as Annie Leibovitz controls her shoot, bartenders are given the run of the bar. We're rewarded and not only in tips." Driscoll's co-bartender of twenty years, Steve DeWinter, says there's a downside. "You learn a thousand drinks and then you end up making 12 of them for the rest of your life."

Dantine is working with the patient, bare-footed Grant in the front room of Orlando Gallery on how her half of the above/below show will be hung. She clearly loves what she is doing. All the countless hours spent waiting on film sets, at dance rehearsal halls, and as a model on location for other photographer's shoots, have prepared Dantine for her ultimate role as conduit between the exotic, undersea life of a hundred feet down and the viewer up top who will never experience the intimacy Dantine has experienced with otherworldly aquatic animals. "It requires great patience to find some of the tiny creatures that inhabit the oceans and, more importantly, to get into their comfort zone and be allowed to photograph them, on film, by the way, not digitally. I am not a marine biologist or scientist. I learn by doing," says Dantine.

The lean, tall Driscoll seconds that. "Everyday I learn something new about photography. I'll be doing this until I figure out what I want to be when I grow up. I really want to be a director."

The gallery erupts in laughter. Grant's Irish Setter, Molly, barks with approval.

Kirk Driscoll & Niki Dantine above/below -- March 6 – 31, Tues. – Sat. 9:30-3:30 p.m., Orlando Gallery, 18376 Ventura Blvd., Tarzana, (818) 705-5368

Facing the Facts

L.A.'s Women Artists Look at L.A. Women

Generally speaking, articles about *women* doctors or *women* dockworkers are about as interesting as in-depth studies of Maori dentists or hearing-impaired chess champions. In fact, this kind of ghettoization—so popular with the mid-cult media of the '70s—may do as much harm as surveys of doctors or dock workers that simply ignore the existence of women and other "minorities." Besides, isn't "woman poet" just as degrading as "poetess?"

We could not help but notice, however, that there is a large group of artists working in L.A. who are women, women whose *subject* is women in L.A. and whose iconography explores the position of women within the context of this city at this time—women like painters Georganne Deen, Margaret Garcia and D.J. Hall and photographer Pamela Fong, performance artist Cheri Gaulke and paper-fashion designer Diane Gamboa.

Even a cursory look at the iconography created by these very different women lets us know that there are still issues at hand, positions to be attained, claims to be staked. Otherwise, there would be no need for a Woman's Building. Otherwise, there would be no need to challenge the L.A. art establishment—its museums and galleries—for under-representing artists who are women. Here in the land of cigar-mauling moguls, even the powerful women who own galleries are not necessarily sympathetic, since money traditionally follows male careers. There are, of course, exceptions.

"I like women as artists first," says Kristina Van Kirk, director of the B-1 and Robert Berman galleries in Santa Monica. "I'm not keen on the idea of strictly women's galleries. I suppose the Museum of Women in the Arts in Washington is a necessary evil. When Susan Seidelman was asked what it's like to be a woman director, she said, 'I don't film with my genitals.'"

Nonetheless, there is a kind of insight about women that only women are likely to have. And it is this vision that is finding its way into the imagery of L.A.'s women artists.

In the 19th century, most women artists were still painting with a man's eye. They had no choice. They weren't allowed their own point of view. Today, however, Gaulke, Garcia, Hall, Deen, Fong and Gamboa all have their own take on life. They might appreciate reaching some degree of equality in the art market, but they're not "feminist" artists in a political sense—unless, of course, you'd call the truth political.

—*The Editors*

CHERI GAULKE

Cheri Gaulke, one of the most acclaimed performance artists in L.A., teaches at the Woman's Building in downtown Los Angeles, the oldest independent feminist art institution in the world. Once considered a private club that represented the on-going lack of communication between women and men, the Woman's Building is now a more professional, more public, more career-oriented facility for studying and creating art.

Gaulke is a member of the Sisters of Survival, an anti-nuclear group that has protested on the steps of City Hall. All of Gaulke's work has socio-political content that addresses both women and men.

Gaulke, 33, is going to have a baby by artificial insemination. Her performance piece, "Virgin," grew from that fact and bills itself as an alternative look at conception: Single parents, gay and lesbian parents, no parents.

"Performance is a very natural art form for women because, as women, we grow up learning the skills of performance," says Gaulke. "We learn how to put makeup on, we learn costume, we learn persona, we learn to be chameleons. When performance started as an art form, the shoe fit, so we ran with it like Cinderella."

I mention several minority artists bucking the art system, and Gaulke's face brightens.

"It's interesting that people have difference backgrounds, difference cultural perspectives. It's not my goal that we all become Wonder Bread, a homogenous, boring, everybody's-the-same kind of thing."

DIANE GAMBOA

Deep in the heart of L.A.'s industrial area, Diane Gamboa meticulously creates paper fashions for women. Model Killy Sena looks like a prom queen in a strapless, layered evening gown made out of silky sheets of off-white paper. Tentacles protrude from the back of the dress culminating in paper tulips. Gamboa places a paper tiara on Sena's head and costume jewelry around her wrists and neck. Sena is ready for the Academy Awards. No smoking, *please*.

Gamboa lives and works across the street from Al's Bar on Traction Avenue, a few miles west of her birthplace in Boyle Heights. Her preoccupation with paper may have to do with the fact that her father used to work at a downtown paper mill.

"Paper fashions stem from a fusion of fantasy and reality tied back with childhood and cutting out paper dolls—and dealing with the glamour women of Hollywood—and growing up in the capital of movies and façade, where things aren't really what they appear to be," says 30-year-old Gamboa. "I think the whole image of Southern California women now is based around the beaches and bikinis. That's rather disgusting to me. We can look at TV and say these are Southern California women in their turquoise bikinis this year and in their black bikinis next year. My art is a mockery of fashion and the *disposableness* of fashion."

For the past few years, Gamboa, along with Gronk, Patssi Valdez and studio-mate Daniel Martinez have been members of the East Los Angeles art group, Asco. Unwilling or unable to wholly identify with the Anglo or Latino art communities, Asco creates work out of its own sense of displacement.

"It's great that my work is showing on the Westside, because women are pulling up in their Mercedes and looking at the art, not necessarily buying it, but just being affected by it, having to face it," says Gamboa. "These women are women who will not cross east of the L.A. River."

Gamboa is confident when she says that art is the most important aspect of her life. She considers the fact that she is a Latin woman as secondary. Gamboa is tired of being labeled a Chicana artist and being invited to Chicano/Chicana and women-only art shows.

"Women have, in some senses, come a long way," she says, "and, in other senses, have not stepped far at all. The percentage of women artists represented in major museums is so low, it's insulting. It's not like there aren't women artists out there. A lot of curators and board members of museums tend to be middle-to-upper-class white women. It's a business to them. It could be art, fashion or furniture. They're creating markets for themselves. They know if they buy now, this particular white male artist is who's going to be successful over the next ten years."

Gamboa's studio has no windows. Artificial light illuminates her paper dolls in exile. We could be in New York or Buenos Aires, the feeling of remoteness is that apparent. Gamboa doubts she'll ever live west of where she lives now.

"The kind of lifestyle we live is have a baby today, give it to the babysitter tomorrow," says Gamboa. "And then you're bored. The media bombards us with, 'This is cool, this is not; this is out of style; this is new Tide; this is the new way to lose weight.' This fabricated truth I see us living in is silly. People go buy it and believe it and it's their reality. It's not *my* reality.

"I'm trying to offer an alternative viewpoint of what Chicana art is, of what female art is. A glamorous Latina doesn't have to wear a rose over her ear or a serape on her back. If something I'm doing right now can make a change over the next hundred years, that's what I'll sacrifice myself now for. It's worth every second, every day to me to do that."

D.J. HALL

The Pacific Ocean is three blocks from Debra Jane Hall's studio/home in Venice. Bright sunlight and water, the two elements in Hall's own environment, are also the two ingredients in every large-scale realist painting she conceives.

"In my early work, I saw women as the enemy," says Hall, 36. "This has to do with the fact that my mother and grandmother were so insecure as women. They saw every woman as being in competition with them. The way to compete was to be physically attractive."

Hall, whose parents are divorced, used to paint men and women. Now, she paints women exclusively because—although she is married—Hall confesses that men have not figured heavily in her life.

"I find women much more intriguing," she says, stroking one of her two cats. "It sounds strange but I can't help but sit and stare at women I consider attractive. That can be a variety of types of people. It doesn't have to be your standard Bo Derek kind of face."

Hall attributes her obsession with pretense to growing up with a mother who was a borderline psychotic. With her mother in a private, unreal world, Hall developed her own mask: a happy child.

"I was brought up with this façade, this idea that you have to be forever beautiful and young," says Hall. "I have these crazy moments when I really believe it's my responsibility to get my thighs back down to the thighs of a fourteen-year-old. If there wasn't the possibility of getting cancer, I'd probably get that suction procedure done."

Hall feels the worst promise ever made to women is that they can have it "all." "It's really unfair what has been put on us. It's partly because we're in Hollywood. We're looking at fourteen-year-old models in magazines and trying to compete with them.

"I'm an artist first, but I have to work more on becoming a woman. The woman in me is just beginning to emerge. It's sort of frightening, but it's part of growing up. Fifteen years ago, my husband suggested I keep the initials in my name because, at that time, it was a man's world in painting. It was probably better not to be overtly woman. Plus Debby, which is how I'd always thought of myself, sounded pretty unprofessional. It never occurred to me that I could be Debra."

GEORGANNE DEEN

"Bitches Lament" is the title of a piece of wickedly satirical computer art by Georganne Deen, 36, who works out of a sprawling 40-year-old Westwood apartment. Her savagely painted scenes of women in uncomfortable situations attract a loyal following, consisting of women from teeny-boppers to blue-haired matriarchs. The slightly built Deen moved to Los Angeles seven years ago.

"It really has reminded me of going back to high school," she says of L.A. "I've encountered more cat fights and bullshit. Women here are superficial and shallow. For the record, there have been some wonderful exceptions."

A large oil painting of an agitated woman applying makeup in a gas station bathroom looms over Deen's studio. The painting, one of her favorites, reminds her of Los Angeles women.

"The façade is so fucking important here," says Deen. "Women make such a big fucking deal out of it. It's the thing that's so despicable about them. They tend to put too much emphasis on their image. They spend a lot of money at their beauty parlor and getting facials and nose jobs. It's like a building that might have a jillion cracks and leaks and bad plumbing in it, and you just keep putting more flowers and another paint job on it. It's just falling apart on the inside and it's tragic."

Through painting, Deen has come face to face with personal issues she didn't want to confront. In her first year in L.A., Deen was waging wars. She started to paint trashy women as a way of exorcising negative thoughts and emotions. She could even the score without having to get into a fight.

"Women always seem to be assessing themselves in relationship to how they *look*. Some women have nothing else going for them except for the fact they have pretty hands and maybe they can do jewelry ads. They've always got themselves marketed. They're figuring which parts of themselves they can sell.

"There's going to be a plastic surgeon coming along," Deen confides over coffee, "whose name will be linked with Michelangelo. This will be a guy who you can't go to, he alone selects his clients. Women will want his signature nose, his signature tits, his signature chin. There will be a lot of imitators."

PAMELA FONG

Photographer Pamela Fong, 34, pulls up in her Volkswagen convertible. She's meeting me at a shopping center up the road from her studio/home because she feels uneasy with men she doesn't know.

"The reason why I mostly photograph women is that I feel safer," says Fong (daughter of the late Benson Fong). "It's a very intimate thing, to photograph someone. I've had confrontations that were not too pleasant while photographing men. My work is not about sex, but an awful lot of it comes through the photographs, from the people, from me. That intimate, very sexual setting lends itself to some potentially dangerous confrontations."

Fong's most impressive work consists of 11x14 black-and-white photographs of mothers and daughters. The photographs fire into the secret society of women and the total mystery of mother and daughter relationships: miscommunications, chasms, unhappiness, bonding, love.

Despite having been assaulted several times, the diminutive Fong refuses to give up her freedom just because she's a woman. She frequently cycles alone into Venice at night and has been known to cruise Watts. She considers getting home at three in the morning an early night, much to the consternation of her boyfriend. Although she is fiercely independent, Fong still believes in male-female relationships.

"My development and blossoming include pursuing a career, following a path and creating a wonderful relationship with someone to share that path," says Fong. "Everyone is finally, rightfully, allowed to follow their own path and breathe their own oxygen instead of sharing someone's tank. Most of our parents had traditional marriages. I think the husband finds the wife much more interesting if she's involved with her own life instead of becoming a vacuum where she's waiting at the door like a dog for him to come in so she can start feeding off him, which is a burden on both of them."

Fong, who spends one week a month in New York, thinks Los Angeles women are more open and freer than other American women. "Los Angeles women love to reveal themselves," says Fong. "They are very healthy, and there is a modicum of narcissism. It's very difficult for women to compete with models in magazines. Men develop character, women develop wrinkles. I know Asian women who have had nose jobs to make them larger. All models now have 34B breasts. There's something too homogenized about it. When women are too perfect-looking, they lose a lot of what makes them interesting.

"It might be biological," she says, "but women still tend to seek males who can provide protection, and, in some ways, financial security is protection. I don't think I know any woman who would not admit that she feels much more feminine—and it's much more attractive—when a man pays for things. I've always evened it out by giving great presents or paying for a trip."

MARGARET GARCIA

Cross over the L.A. River, heading east—downtown behind you. Take an off-ramp called Downey Avenue, double back to Brooklyn and Gage and try to find artist Margaret Garcia.

You'll probably find her painting portraits in her studio behind a storefront at Self-Help Graphics. Most of Garcia's women are strong individuals: In her work, the artist is trying to fashion positive images, instead of underlining negative perceptions.

"I *have* to keep painting," says 35-year-old Garcia. "I used to hold my daughter on my lap while I was painting. I lost custody because they said I didn't have enough money to support her, which is true. If I had been digging ditches or been a secretary, I'd have had enough money."

Her former husband got physically abusive with her twice—once when she wanted to go paint.

"Women sabotage themselves a lot," she reflects, a smile breaking through occasionally. "Especially married women. Instead of saying, 'Honey, I'm going to such-and-such,' it's, 'Honey, *can* I go?' We're trained that way as little girls. Ask your daddy. Ask. We do that with our husbands. We put them in that position. I'm a very strong, assertive woman and, still, in a relationship, I found I was doing that... [It] was a sacrifice for me to continue doing my art. You don't choose to be an artist."

Direct, like her paintings, Garcia wears no makeup, carries no lies.

"Women from the Woman's Building say, 'Why don't we see more Latinas out there? Chicano men are so macho.' They don't understand that women raised these men. They're talking about our entire culture. It makes Chicanas back up a little bit. It's difficult to deal with the so-called feministic fashions of that aspect. For Chicanas, there are other issues. As much as you want to make advancements in terms of women, *mujeres,* you also have to take into consideration other issues that seem much more vital—like Nicaragua and El Salvador and immigration."

ATHLETES AND FANS

Robert Crane

Oscar De La Hoya

The Crooning Boxer Takes a Few Jabs at Prefight Sex and Explains Why He's Squeamish About Blood

The second son of Mexican immigrants, Oscar De La Hoya grew up in East Los Angeles. He was originally attracted to baseball, but he followed his older brother to the neighborhood gym and took part in boxing workouts. Discovering he had a powerful left hand, De La Hoya began winning local tournaments. At 19, he won a spot on the U.S. Olympic Boxing Team at the 1992 Barcelona Summer Games. He won a gold medal in his weight division.

He made his professional boxing debut in November 1992, leveling Lamar Williams in the first round. Eleven matches later, in 1994, De La Hoya won his first title, the World Boxing Organization junior lightweight belt, beating Denmark's Jimmi Bredahl. De La Hoya continued his climb, winning the lightweight title from Jorge Paez later in 1994, defeating Julio Cesar Chavez to capture the WBC super lightweight title in 1996 and besting Pernell Whitaker in 1997 for the WBC welterweight championship—his fourth weight-class crown. In 1999, after 31 straight victories, De La Hoya was dealt his first defeat when he lost a split decision to unbeaten IBF champion Felix Trinidad. In early 2000, De La Hoya won his sixth title—the IBF world championship that had been vacated when Trinidad moved up a weight class—by knocking out Derrell Coley in the seventh round. Later that year, De La Hoya dropped another split decision, to undefeated Shane Mosley in Los Angeles. His image tarnished for the first time, De La Hoya reevaluated his professional and personal lives, dropping Bob Arum, his promoter, and leaving his fiancée, Playmate Shanna Moakler.

At the age of 27, De La Hoya seemed to reach a crossroads. Having grossed $125 million in the ring and millions more in endorsements, he decided to take a break from boxing. In the fall of 2000, De La Hoya, inspired by his mother's love of music, released his first album of love songs in English and Spanish for EMI Latin, Oscar De La Hoya, which included the hit single Run to Me, a cover of the Bee Gees hit. He continued to donate millions of dollars to the children of East Los Angeles via the Oscar De La Hoya Foundation. He also helped a local hospital open a unit dedicated to the awareness of breast cancer. He climbed back into the ring and defeated Arturo Gatti in Las Vegas in March 2001. After the fight, De La Hoya kept his promise to move up to the 154-pound weight class. A rematch with Shane Mosley on hold, De La Hoya rejoined Bob Arum's fold and announced he would fight Fernando Vargas for the WBA junior middleweight crown on May 4, 2002 in Las Vegas. Currently the WBC 154-pound champion, De La Hoya is guaranteed $14 million for the match.

Robert Crane caught up with the confident De La Hoya at the Four Seasons Hotel in Los Angeles. Crane reports: "Damn, he is so rich, so good-looking, such a great athlete, a fine singer, he's got babes, a posse, a $230,000 Ferrari, the love of an entire city. I wanted to hurt him bad, but I thought better of it. Instead, I punched the record button on my tape recorder."

1

PLAYBOY: What is a Hoya?

DE LA HOYA: A Hoya is a jewel. It's basically a diamond, it's an emerald. It's pretty special.

2

PLAYBOY: Are you first among them?

DE LA HOYA: Well, I think everybody in my family has had their little success stories. Mine is the one that's more visible, I guess. It runs in the family.

3

PLAYBOY: Since you're a Hoya, do you get good seats at Georgetown games?

DE LA HOYA: Do you know what? They sit me way in the back. I get a nosebleed. I've never had so many nosebleeds in my life. When I first went, I said, "Why are they giving me binoculars? What's the deal? Do they come with the ticket?"

4

PLAYBOY: What kind of roadwork enhances your singing?

DE LA HOYA: Running hilly roads. As I'm going up the hill, I'm trying to sing a high note, and then as I'm going down I'm trying to sing a low note. Once I get into the studio, I remember the hill, and I can belt out the highest note I have. It kind of helps.

5

PLAYBOY: What are some examples of the expressions you see when you hit someone hard in the face?

DE LA HOYA: I've seen an opponent freeze. I hit them, and they don't know what to do. I've seen an opponent cry. I've seen them get angry. That's pretty scary. It's also scary when I hit them with my hardest shot and they laugh. I think, Oh no, it's going to be a long night.

6

PLAYBOY: Is your fighting based on reflex or intentionality on offense and defense?

DE LA HOYA: It's based on reflex. When I'm training up in the mountains for three months before the fight, we work on certain moves we think will present themselves in the ring, and everything just falls in place when we're fighting. I'm not thinking of that certain move in the ring. It just happens instinctively. It's incredible because this person might be throwing a combination of three punches, and automatically I'll know how to block them. Sometimes I'll go back to the corner and say, "Oh my God. How did I do that?" Then you start thinking about the training. The three months of hard work just falls in place. I've found myself sometimes throwing a hard right hand to my opponent's face and he's also throwing one at the same time to my face, and he misses and I hit. I say to myself, How did that happen? We threw the same punch and we're making the same movement. We train to move, let's say, one inch to the left to miss that right hand and it just happens instinctively. If I didn't move that one inch I would get hit, but instincts take over.

7

PLAYBOY: We hear there's a vulnerable spot between the fourth and fifth ribs. If you hit that area, it just blows the wind out of you. True?

DE LA HOYA: There's a certain spot that maybe I shouldn't reveal because my next opponent may be reading this. But, yes, there is a certain spot that every fighter has that is weak, and it's the rib cage. Right in the middle, near the stomach, if you connect there at perfect speed and timing the guy won't stand up. It would be impossible for him to continue to fight. It's right below the solar plexus. You get hit there and it's over. It's a body part you cannot protect. We train to have an armored shield all around us. We hit our forearms on walls, we hit the punching bag with our fists, we do neck exercises, we do shoulder exercises. We train every part of the body, but you just cannot build up that spot. You cannot train it. It's always weak.

8

PLAYBOY: Did anyone ever come to the ring dressed preposterously and you laughed?

DE LA HOYA: Jorge Paez, he's the clown of boxing. That's what he's known for. His shorts are past his knees and they have 30 different colors. When I was looking at him across the ring, I couldn't help but laugh. You don't want to laugh right in his face or you don't want him to notice that you're laughing, so you're laughing inside and you're thinking, Oh my gosh. I'm going to fight this clown. That fight was funny because he came out like a clown and was joking and bouncing around. I knocked him out in the first few seconds of round two. It was funny because the way I knocked him out, he landed forward and did a whole turn. It was like a somersault. I was thinking, Is he joking around? He's dressed as a clown. Is he trying to be a clown, doing a somersault? But when I saw that he didn't get up for five minutes, I knew he was seriously hurt.

9

PLAYBOY: Outside the ring, what kinds of robes and shorts do you wear?

DE LA HOYA: Well, I actually go to the place where Hugh Hefner gets his robes. I love putting on my silk pajamas and slippers. A smoker's jacket. It's pretty cool. There's a shot of me in a smoking jacket at a pajama party at the Playboy Mansion.

10

PLAYBOY: Do you have any advice for someone in a bar fight?

DE LA HOYA: Run. Just run. You've got beer bottles flying around, you got the chairs. Just keep your hands up and if you can, run. I'm sure those bottles over the head hurt. I've never experienced one, but I'm pretty sure they hurt.

11

PLAYBOY: Layer by layer, what's in your trunks?

DE LA HOYA: In my trunks I wear a protective cup. You've got to protect the jewels. The Hoyas. That's it. You want to be as light as possible inside that ring. No secrets, none whatsoever.

12

PLAYBOY: How good do you feel going into the ring?

DE LA HOYA: I actually don't feel good at all going into the ring. I'm so nervous. I'm never scared, but I have butterflies in my stomach, and I have this feeling of getting cold and I start shaking. You have to feel good, because if you don't, then you start thinking, Did I train for the fight? Did I do enough rounds for the fight? Did I run enough miles? I've seen fighters postpone fights on the night of the fight—actually postpone or cancel them. You have to feel good. It's your life in the ring.

13

PLAYBOY: Is there a place you don't like to get hit?

DE LA HOYA: My face. I try to take care of my face as much as possible, especially my nose. You touch my nose and it's all over for you.

14

PLAYBOY: When someone lands a great punch, do you get pissed?

DE LA HOYA: Yeah. I start feeling fire all over my body. My eyes get red. I get angry, but you have to control that anger. Because if you're angry in the ring you won't win. As much as I want to be angry because they hit me, you have to keep your calm. You have to be collected, you have to be cool inside the ring. Anger works against you in the ring. You just start whaling away, and you throw your whole game plan away, and that's when it gets dangerous.

15

PLAYBOY: We're told fighters shouldn't have sex before a fight. Do you?

DE LA HOYA: I had a girlfriend a long time ago who I had sex with the night before a fight. Must have been my best performance ever—in the ring that is. And to this day my trainer doesn't believe it, my father doesn't believe it. She was there and I couldn't help it. And it was my best performance. I proved a lot of people wrong.

16

PLAYBOY: Should Mike Tyson be allowed to box?

DE LA HOYA: That's a toughie. I don't want him coming after me, because he would. Mike Tyson gives boxing a bad name. We all know that, but since we're in the land of opportunity you cannot take away a person's livelihood. But then again, you think of Tyson and you think of biting ears and eating children. So he's in such a tough position because people don't watch him now for his talent in the ring. They watch him because they want to see what crazy thing he'll do with his opponent. It's really sad because we grew up watching Mike Tyson as the destroyer, the champ. Over the years he has changed.

17

PLAYBOY: In the age of AIDS, is the sight of blood cause for concern?

DE LA HOYA: It's scary, because you worry about all the diseases out there. We have to get checked all the time—before a fight and after—but it still worries me. You never know what's out there. It also actually helps when you have somebody bleeding. You're so eager to have the fight stopped that it makes you throw more punches, and it makes you more aware. It makes you want to get away from the opponent so you won't get blood on yourself. I've found myself wanting to knock my opponent out very early or using the best defense of my life because I don't want that blood on me.

18

PLAYBOY: Ever had your knees buckle outside the ring?

DE LA HOYA: Many times. That one night before my fight, my knees were buckling. Yeah, many times. I can't elaborate on that. I think that's the reason why all trainers say it's bad to have sex before a fight, because your knees buckle. They're right. They do buckle after you do the deed. I've never been in a street fight in my life. I've never had anybody punch me in the chin and my knees buckle or anything like that. Other than that night before the fight, my knees have been all right.

19

PLAYBOY: Place Don King in the pantheon of boxing personalities. Is he a savior of the oppressed or a sewer rat?

DE LA HOYA: Don King is a smart man for what he's doing. Every single fight of his, if you notice, is controversial. Yet he gets away with it. People still tune in to his fights. As he says, "only in America." Well, America has given him the opportunity and he's taken advantage of it. If it's in a corrupt way or an honest way, he still takes advantage. I don't praise what he's doing, but he's a smart businessman. That's all he is and that's all it is to him—a business.

20

PLAYBOY: Can you be both a lover and a fighter?

DE LA HOYA: I've always been. I've always balanced it out.

Jan Stephenson

America's First Jiggle Jock

Before the 1981 season, the press—and probably her peers—treated Australian golfer Jan Stephenson like the tour's resident floozy. Despite her consistent play, Jan's curvy form and Hollywood-caliber face were constantly stealing the spotlight from the LPGA's trophy-winning gorillettes.

To make matters worse, Jan's seemingly low-key forays into self-exploitation were brilliantly successful. Since the mid-Seventies she has been part of a fashion layout in the LPGA's annual house organ, Fairways. The series started with bathing suits and progressed to thigh-exposing cheesecake by 1980.

The 1980 shot, showing just about every inch of Jan's right leg, provided the last straw for veteran Janie Blalock, who publicly blasted Stephenson for her before-the-lens antics.

This only created more of a storm, resulting in several low-cleavage shots in the sport magazines (noticeably an Inside Sports cover with Jim Palmer) and sexpot appearances on the major talk shows.

The Fairways fashion feature, apparently designed by the LPGA to put some girls back into their butchy breed and get some more green from the galleries, reached a pinnacle this year when the chosen quartet of lady duffers mimicked the Hollywood pin-up sensations of the past. Stephenson, quite naturally, impersonated Marilyn Monroe.

But a funny thing happened on the way to the Meat Factory. Jan's game, pretty much a forgotten factor since she Came Up from Down Under, suddenly awoke. During one stretch, she captured three tournaments and finished high on the leader board in several others. Now she could no longer be dismissed as just another piece of ass in the Laura Baugh-Colgate mold. She had to be reckoned with on the greens as well as in print.

This interview with Robert Crane was recorded just before her amazing hot streak began. The reason we are only running it now is simple. A few months ago, Jan's agent called us and told us that Jan had been coerced into granting the interview by the Ladies Professional Golf Association. We laughed at that one, but stopped laughing when the people at Fairways told us they wouldn't supply us with any of the photos Jan had posed for during the last six years. Shortly afterwards, Jan herself called Editorial Director Peter Wolff and begged him to not use the interview because she feared it would hurt her status as a golfer and her ability to get commercial endorsements. Wolff told her that he wouldn't run it if she did, indeed, change her image. But, after seeing her on TV immediately before Game 5 of the World Series, posing in a south-of–the-clavicle dress for a cheesecake photographer, he decided that she was hardly holding back on the T&A factor.

Stephenson told Howard Cosell that she wanted to be the most famous woman athlete of her day, that she was interested in Hollywood, and that self-exploitation was a necessary game to play. She is a bright, lively, still-innocent celebrity with a real talent for sports and a glowing physical presence that emanates the truest form of charisma. She is the shiniest jewel on the women's tour. She is going places. And here's a look at the original Jan Stephenson, pre-Superstar, before the hype drowned the reality.

OUI: You could have gone into a number of things, modeling, acting. Why are you golfing?

STEPHENSON: I think it's the most challenging. Anyone can act and anyone can model to a certain extent but, gold is such a difficult sport, you never can master it. I would like to go into acting but not until I can do my best at golf. It is so difficult and it's something I really enjoy. When something good happens or if you win, it is worth everything.

OUI: Is winning the attraction?

STEPHENSON: Yeah, winning is. It happens so rarely for me. The game is kind of failing all the time because, even if you win, you may have beaten everyone you played against, but you didn't, probably, do as best you could do or there was some shot you weren't happy with. Basically, every week, you're trying to handle failure. There's something you didn't do right. That's really hard for me to accept. I kinda like it.

OUI: Playing doesn't get easier?

STEPHENSON: Oh, no. It gets tougher because, once you know you can do it, it's even worse because you don't do it more often.

OUI: You've been on the circuit eight years?

STEPHENSON: Yeah, since '74. I haven't reached my peak yet, that's the thing. When I reach my peak and I haven't done as well, maybe I'll kind of peter off a little bit. My coach tells me I'm two years away from being my best.

OUI: Does the commotion amongst fellow golfers over your photographs bother you?

STEPHENSON: No, it doesn't bother me, it surprises me that those girls can't see the reason for it, you know, those girls against it. It really benefits them, too, to get the exposure because of the pictures to show that we're feminine and to get the attention whether it's by selling it through sex or whatever. The fact that we get the exposure or the attention means that we get bigger galleries and better media coverage and that brings bigger purses. So, it does benefit everybody.

OUI: Is there a lot of jealousy?

STEPHENSON: No, I think it's a total misunderstanding or not being able to understand or comprehend the reason for the LPGA selling that way. I don't think it's jealousy. I just don't think they can see the reason for it. We tend to get carried away with the fact that we're golf pros. We're so good at doing one thing that people tend to listen to you as though you're an authority and that's why we've hired such a big staff of marketing and PR people because that's where they're pro's. We should really listen to them and be behind them more than we are.

Robert Crane

OUI: Where did the idea originate for the photograph?

STEPHENSON: I've done it every year and usually in some kind of risqué pose. I've done swim suits, too. We're trying to show that we can look like something other than jocks. I would do it again. Probably start it all over again and I probably will have to do it again for the LPGA. I do it because I've been asked to do it by these PR pro's and they do know what they're doing.

OUI: Where does Women's Lib figure in?

STEPHENSON: I've had a lot of bad comments, a lot of bad mail, female and male, saying they thought I was sexist or against women's lib and the feminist movement. It's really not the case. I just believe when you open any magazine everything is sold with sex, men or women. That is life— whether we like it or not. There are beautiful women on every page of every magazine. That's just the way it is. I've had a lot of people really down on me saying, "You know it's really hard to get along in a man's world and you do this and put us right back." People forget I'm very independent. I mean, this is my career. I don't have any man looking after me and paying my bills. So, I'm as much a woman's libber as anyone. But, I don't think that there's anything wrong in looking like a girl. I'm not ashamed of my body and if I feel like flaunting it, I'm going to.

OUI: Are there golf groupies?

STEPHENSON: Yeah.

OUI: Do you have a flock following you around?

STEPHENSON: As a matter of fact, they show up tournament to tournament. Sometimes, it may only be from one year to the next. But, you recognize a certain amount of people that you've had in your galleries over the years. In some of them, you even get to say "hi" even though you've never met but you just recognize them because they're there every other week and you may even strike up some kind of friendship over a period of years. People say it's impossible to have dates or strike up friendships because we are only in town from Monday to Sunday. It may be a long time before you do but you eventually do in some cases. And by mail, I recognize a lot of people I've never even met and, yet, I know them by their signatures and their addresses. I get birthday cards from people I've never even met. They know when my birthday is and every year I get a birthday card and all these kind of funny things.

OUI: Beyond birthday cards, do you get guys calling you or notes passed to you down on the golf course during a tournament?

STEPHENSON: Oh, sure. Depending on how I've played, my caddie will know whether to give them to me or not because sometimes I'll be really mad and start tearing them up and sometimes I take it as a compliment. I don't ever go out with any of them. I've had a lot of obscene phone calls lately where they've found out where I'm staying and say pretty bad things in the middle of the night. I guess that's part of it, too.

OUI: Does that get scary?

STEPHENSON: I've been staying with friends in each of the towns to keep away from that so they can't find out where I'm staying because it's easy to find out the major places where the girls stay. I'm thinking of having to check in under an assumed name because I'm having such a problem with that.

OUI: Is there much partying on the LPGA circuit?

STEPHENSON: We have parties every week because of the tournament. If you want to, you can go to one every night of the week. I don't go to any of them.

OUI: I mean "party" parties.

STEPHENSON: You mean personal parties? Not really. It's very hard to know a lot of close friends that have parties when you're in town because when I'm in town and I have friends around, they know not to put a party on because I'm not going to come when I'm trying to play. So, it's not as glamourous as everybody thinks.

OUI: It's not like the stories we've heard about football, baseball and tennis players, for that matter?

STEPHENSON: I think it's a little more difficult in golf because, you know, you have a team to pull you through if you had a bad night or something happened, but, in golf, you've just got yourself. So, you have to really be at your best all the time. If I go out, I usually get punished for it.

OUI: How do men approach you off the golf course?

STEPHENSON: I guess they all have a wrong image of me. Sometimes, I think that they must think I'm cheap; some of the comments and the way they approach and some of the things they ask you to do. It disappoints me. They put you in a different category than their own wife. Most of them are married. They flirt like crazy with you. It surprises me. I guess it shouldn't. I think the fact is that they think they only have one week so they move twice as fast as they probably normally would and it comes on so strong that it turns me off.

OUI: How do you approach men?

STEPHENSON: I don't know. It hasn't really happened. It's so easy because everybody approaches me. A lot of them don't because they think that there wouldn't be any chance. The ones that usually do are so brash that they're not the type of person that I would like. The ones that wouldn't say anything are usually the ones I would like but they wouldn't say anything because of who I am or what I am.

OUI: What kinds of men turn you on?

STEPHENSON: I think their actual appearance is not as important to me as what they've done in their lives. I'm really into people who are into their career or have made something of themselves. I guess because I have and I realize what they've had to sacrifice to get there. If I had a relationship with a man and he didn't have a career, it would be hard for him to stay home and be faithful while I'm out on mine. He has to be very secure. He has to take the back seat and he has to understand that and that's very difficult to find—someone that can sit back there when we go to dinner, have everyone be really nice to me and fall all over them and even have men coming up and flirting and just sit back and understand. I love to flirt. I love people. That's the way I am. They have to understand that.

OUI: The Mister Stephenson syndrome.

STEPHENSON: Yeah, which even in this day and age it's still hard to find. I like men to be into some sports, not necessarily golf. I like them to be athletic.

OUI: A jock?

STEPHENSON: Not a professional jock but one who likes to play racquetball or tennis. I love to play so many sports that it wouldn't be much fun if I couldn't play racquetball or tennis with someone that I care about when I can do all those things.

OUI: How about much-older guys?

STEPHENSON: Well, the reason I think I like older guys is if I had a relationship, I would feel like if I had to share him with his career and my career, I wouldn't like the fact that I was sharing him with a bunch of other girls. I know that's really old-fashioned. I shouldn't even expect some one to be that way if I'm never home.

OUI: It's the double-standard.

STEPHENSON: Yeah, but, um—

OUI: You're a female chauvinist.

STEPHENSON: No, I'm not saying I mess around on tour. I feel like a younger guy would have a problem with that. He still has to do his conquering and proving himself and an older guy has already done that. I would like to feel like I'm special to an older guy. I love to be pampered and spoiled. I guess we all do.

OUI: Where do you place the importance of work versus a relationship?

STEPHENSON: At this stage, obviously, a relationship is going to suffer. I keep saying there's plenty of time. Even though it may not be a party every night, it is an exciting life. Right now, I couldn't turn it down and compromise to be a housewife or give up being normal, whatever that means. Over the last few years, I've changed my mind up and down about that. Golf is fun and exciting and it is still in my blood. I'm home for two days and I go crazy. I went to Australia for Christmas, that's where I was born, and I thought the idea of getting a suntan and lying there, I'd spend the whole winter there. I lay on the beach for a week and I had this perfect tan? I've got to get home. I've got to go.

OUI: When do you know you're in love?

STEPHENSON: This is awfully corny, but, you know. You know when it's the right man. Being in love is a very healthy feeling. It makes you feel great. You're happy. When you miss a putt, it's not even any big deal. Mine goes up and down. It goes in stages. It's funny, when I'm playing well, I'm not as in love as when I'm not. When I'm playing badly or I'm sick, I call my boyfriend a bunch, and I want to be in love. I eat bad food and I don't sleep well. When I'm playing well, I eat all the right foods. I don't need to call anybody. I'm just having a great time. It seems like when you're really at your worst, you need someone. I guess that's normal. You'd think when you're playing really well is when you'd want to be in love. But, it's not. I guess it's when you need something else, when your golf's not doing well, you need a crutch. I'm not saying that love is a crutch, but, in a way, I think it's a need. I think, if I'm playing well, and I am in love, love's gonna suffer. My game is not gonna suffer if I'm in love because I think I'm in love after my game has suffered.

OUI: What is your favorite physical feature of yourself?

STEPHENSON: I guess my eyes. That's what everybody says so I guess that's why.

OUI: Do most people think less of your athletic abilities because you're so attractive?

STEPHENSON: I think that happens a lot with men. Men don't appreciate what you can do if they meet you off the golf course. If they've seen me perform, then it usually opens their eyes. I've had a lot of people that have really flirted and been cheap with me, they've met me the night before I've gone and played somewhere, and the next day they've really changed their minds and it's kind of quieted them down. So, off the golf course, that may be the case. Out here you don't get any recognition unless you are good because there are a lot of good-looking girls around. You still have to be able to perform and get the galleries and have your name on the leader board.

I've had a lot of younger men in my galleries because of (Johnny) Carson and "Today" and because of the articles. I come off on the golf course almost mean because I'm trying to concentrate and keep my emotions in some kind of order. I appear a lot colder than I really am. So, when people see me on TV shows and in these photos, they realize that maybe I'm normal and fun to be around and they come on a little differently which is nice, a little more friendly.

OUI: Now that you've appeared on some of the talk-shows, how do you rate the talk-show hosts?

STEPHENSON: Carson's the greatest. He still is good. I'll tell you who I was really surprised with— Regis Philbin. He had me cracking up the whole time. He was great. I think the men try to put you more at ease. I don't know whether it's because I feel more comfortable that way or because I work with the girls all the time under a competitive situation. I thought Jane Pauley on the "Today" show was very good but the questions were tough and she was all business.

OUI: Who turns you on in terms of talk-show hosts?

STEPHENSON: I never even think about that but I have to admit that there's been people that have really attracted me when I'm doing interviews. It's almost like you're having a relationship. But, nothing has ever come of them. What happens is—maybe it's the way my mind works, it's almost like it's dirty—when they ask a question, I feel like I get two meanings from it, and then I answer back and I think, God, that sounds like two meanings to that, too. The reporter thinks I'm really dirty. It's kind of like you're flirting and sharing with everybody, the whole public. I think that's exciting. It feels good.

OUI: What is the most outrageous outfit you've worn to turn a man's head?

STEPHENSON: When I'm on the golf course, I'm all business and usually dress like that in golf clothes. Sometimes, depending on my moods, I will really feel like flaunting it or just being a real girl. Most of the time, I'll just wear jeans but, sometimes, I'll feel like dressing up. I've noticed that it intimidates a lot of people. They know me on the golf course and suddenly they realize that I'm a girl. I've seen it change a lot of people. On the golf course, they feel fine because I'm wearing pants and I'm an athlete. When I, sometimes, act like a real woman, it scares a lot of them away.

I bought a lot of outfits that I've never even worn. I always get in these moods where I really think, Boy, I'd love to just shock everybody. I have a million of them in my closet that still have the tags on. If you looked at my closet, you'd think, God, this girl's a whore. I never wear them. When I travel, I put my jeans in and some silk shirts and that's about it. If I go out, maybe I'll wear a shirt and a pair of pants or a dress.

OUI: What kinds of outfits are in your closet?

STEPHENSON: They're all probably slashed up one side, at least. They've either got no back or no front in them, or they're so skin-tight, I can barely breathe. This is typical, when I was going on Carson, I thought, Okay, I'm gonna do one of those actresses and wear something really sleazy. So I went down to Rodeo Drive and went into one store and said, "Okay, I want to see all of your sleazy dresses" and the lady said, "What?" and I said, "Anything that shows something. I want to see them all." Eventually we found a dress. I wear a size six and I bought a size four so I would bulge out of it. It had a big slit up the side and it was black. I took it home and I still have the label on it. I could not wear it on Carson's show. I choked when it got right down to it.

OUI: Which golfers are sexy?

STEPHENSON: I think (Nancy) Lopez is sexy. I think she enjoys men. Even though she's married, I mean she just enjoys men and she has a way with the press. She kind of wraps them around her little finger. Obviously, she has a good feeling with the men in the press. Who else? It's hard for me to remember all the girls.

OUI: What about men?

STEPHENSON: You should see the men's tournaments. All these little girls in their short shorts and their little tube tops and their little—they're obviously out there to get everyone's attention and the men pro's all think it's great. They can't wait until the spring tournaments because everybody really comes out in their short shorts and stuff. It's who can show the most. Everybody comes out to look at the girls and the cute guys playing golf.

One thing, I certainly don't think Arnold Palmer is sexy. Everybody says he is. I guess the older women think he was because of the way he pulled his pants up. He used to always be flirting with all the girls and all the women in the gallery. I think he still does. I don't like anyone that flaunts it.

OUI: What do you think of Johnny Miller and Tom Watson?

STEPHENSON: I don't think Johnny Miller is sexy because he's pushing religion. Tom Watson's a cute guy. There's something about him that's appealing but I don't think it's sex. I think it's his great putting stroke. I'd love to have his putting stroke.

To me, once they're married, they're not appealing anymore. I guess it's one of those things where even though you know you would never do anything with them, the fact that they're married has some little thing about it.

OUI: Does the relationship between golf and the fact that it's considered a rich person's game make it sexy?

STEPHENSON: Absolutely. Golf is high class and it's a very different society; even more so than tennis. Basically, it's not your average person that is watching golf. They are high class. You can tell by the cars that are parked and by the commercials played during a tournament on TV. That is the way it is. It's expensive to belong to country clubs. It's expensive to play.

I think it's kind of fun that anybody can play with anybody in golf. In tennis, you have to be all one standard to have a good game. I can go out and play with any guy, no matter what his speed is on the golf course, and have a good time.

OUI: Do you think golf is classier than tennis?

STEPHENSON: Oh, without a doubt. It has to be because it's more expensive.

OUI: Do you ever forget which town you're in?

STEPHENSON: Yeah.

OUI: Why do golfers make better lovers?

STEPHENSON: Obviously, their touch is better. Golf is not all power like in tennis or baseball. There is a certain amount of finesse needed to excel in golf. Another point is you have to control your emotions in golf. Normally, you'd think that that wouldn't be the case when you're making love but I always feel like if you can control your emotions, you can prolong an experience or shorten it.

OUI: While you're making love, do you ever think about what kind of a day you had on the golf course?

STEPHENSON: Never. Never. Never, never, never.

OUI: You can totally divorce yourself—

STEPHENSON: Absolutely. It's great. I think maybe that's why I feel like I like to be in love when I'm playing bad. It's great to get away from it. When I play bad, it's usually when I'm feeling sick and when you're feeling sick, you never notice you're feeling sick when you're making love. You don't notice anything but how good it feels. I don't, anyway.

OUI: A bad day on the golf course doesn't carry over into the bedroom or wherever?

STEPHENSON: In fact, I think it makes it better. You're so down that it's like an extra high. Whereas, when I'm feeling good, I'm already up there somewhere so it's just a little lift.

OUI: If female reporters can come into men's dressing rooms, should male reporters be allowed into women's dressing rooms?

STEPHENSON: It wouldn't be as much a big deal in golf as it would be in tennis or something else because we don't change clothes. When you're in your golf clothes, you don't really do too much sweating and you usually go home and change. We're not allowed to wear jeans on the premises otherwise I'd wear jeans to the golf course, change into my golf clothes and wear jeans home. All we're ever doing is changing our shoes or putting an extra sweater on or off.

I don't approve of women or men in the locker room. It is, probably, your only time of privacy. Normally, I'll go in there and shed a few tears and get myself together and go out and practice. The fact that it is a male or female reporter makes no difference.

OUI: Have you gone to the other emotion extremity like throwing golf clubs?

STEPHENSON: Sure. We have fines for all of that stuff. In the Colgate-Dinah Shore one year, I blew a putt that cost me $7,000. Most of the people who do really well in golf are unemotional. Sometimes, they even seem boring. There should be no highs and lows. So, someone like myself has a lot of problems with the mental. Cool, calm and collected is not my best asset.

OUI: Is there life after golf?

STEPHENSON: Golf is gonna be part of my life for a long time. When I do officially retire from the tour, there's still gonna be things in the golf world that I'm gonna do. There are so many things that I have put down on my list and I think we all do. I always say I'd love to be normal.

OUI: Where do you go to get away from golf?

STEPHENSON: I like my home, Fort Worth. There are a lot of places I'd like to go without my golf clubs and really see the place. We don't get to see anything because you have to be thinking of your tee time and you're tired and you have to work on your game. I love this country and I'd really like to see a lot more of it.

OUI: Do you see differences between East Coast men and West Coast men?

STEPHENSON: Oh yeah. In fact, you can usually tell by the gallery where you are by the way they dress. They're more conservative in the East the way they dress. They're more overweight. They're not as much into health. They look pale. Californians and the West tend to be much more competitive like they're trying to outdo each other or beat everyone and look just right. They're trying to look casual. Everyone's trying to impress with their cars and what they have. In the East, they're much more personally aggressive. They'll come on and talk and move.

OUI: We've heard you're getting into acting.

STEPHENSON: Yeah, I'm doing a "Love Boat." I think I'm gonna play a professional athlete. A lot of people don't want me to do it. There are too many good actresses. It's even more competitive than golf and much more cut-throat. There are a million pretty girls who can act.

John Candy

Yes, the *Real* Great One

Had to happen: Where else—besides at a Lakers game, and everybody's going to those— can you see and be seen, sit in the comfortably hip confines of a state-of-the-art arena and still enjoy the thrill of a big-ticket action game? Which is why the Kings, who are heading into their 25th season at the Forum, have become the town's second-hottest ticket for fast-trackers. A quick camera pan around the rink (except maybe when the lowly Quebec Nordiques are in town) routinely espies the likes of Sylvester Stallone, Tom Hanks, Michael J. Fox, Bruce Springsteen, Chuck Norris and, of course, the team's first honorary captain, John Candy (who, maybe not so coincidentally, is a co-owner— along with Kings owner Bruce McNall and Wayne Gretzky—of the Toronto Argonauts football team). We recently faced off with Candy for a preseason preview of his new duties on—and off—the ice.

Los Angeles: So just what does an honorary captain do, anyway?

Candy: I'm not sure yet, but one thing's certain: I don't play.

Did you ever play?

I played quite a bit while growing up in Toronto. Remember, it's the birthright of Canadians to bear sticks and skate.

If you played now, what position would you want to play?

Owner would be a good position. There's less injuries—and you get a great seat.

Have you ever been hit by a puck?

Yes. Did I bleed? You bet.

As honorary captain will you get to ride the Zamboni?

I get to *repair* the Zamboni.

Will you let Stallone ride it?

Hey, he can do whatever he wants.

What number jersey will you wear as honorary captain?

Whatever number everybody doesn't want. Are you kidding? I'm happy getting any jersey.

Any new sports ventures ahead for you and Bruce and Wayne?

I'll have to check with Bruce. Could be we're getting into arena football or arena lacrosse or arena polo—or maybe even monster trucks.

Would you rather win an Oscar or see the Kings win a Stanley Cup?

Can there be a tie?

Robert Crane

Lady Amid the Sport of Kings

Interview with Caesars' Boxing Fans, Bo and John Derek

SEVEN: We see you and your husband, John, at title fights at Caesars Palace regularly. What is it about the sweet science that attracts you both to watch it ringside?

BO: Boxing isn't something I grew up with. My father was a boxing fan, a Muhammad Ali fan, but it wasn't until I was 17, when John and I started living together, that I began to take an interest, primarily because John is such a big fan. I just inherited it from John, I guess. I'm still not what you'd call a diehard fan; I don't watch a lot of the smaller fights. I'm a major-event fan. I really enjoy them. John is a diehard fan and a very noisy one, too. We have a great time.

JOHN: The major fights are very different from any event in the world. They're big, big, big events. It's like a Super Bowl game with a different crowd.

BO: It's a different group but a wonderful group. Our first one was the Hagler-Duran fight [Caesars Palace, November 10, 1983]. A friend of ours asked if we wanted to go to this fight in Vegas. At first we were reluctant; it seemed like a lot of trouble going into a big crowd, but we were willing to try it. So, we went and had such a good time. The whole town changes. It was very easy for us to be there. We'd eat all our meals in the coffee shop and walk around. People are very, very nice. The excitement is fantastic. Even if you miss the actual bout, I think it's worth going to Las Vegas just to experience the atmosphere before a big fight. We had a wonderful time. The crowd was fantastic. Very nice and fun. People are in a different mood at a boxing match, different from most sporting events. It's not just the high rollers that show up because, I mean, our bulldozer guy, we get him tickets. Even our friend who likes to drink a lot of beer when he goes to football games, when it's the fights, it's this big important thing to him.

JOHN: He gets drunk later. He's sober for the fight because the price of those tickets makes him want to see what he paid for.

BO: It's such a special event. You get a lot of different types of people there. They're all in this great mood. When we saw the Hagler-Duran fight, people came from all over the Latin world and they were there screaming and having a great time. It's a very happy feeling rather than a dangerous one.

SEVEN: Is boxing a sexy sport?

BO: I don't really see it as a sexy sport. The crowd, though, is very good-looking. It's definitely a physically-fit crowd.

JOHN: It's more than just the gambling thing. The males live vicariously, consciously or subconsciously, by watching somebody else being quite marvelous at a very primitive, fundamental, basic thing.

SEVEN: Do you remember the first fight you ever saw?

BO: It was probably the Muhammad Ali fight in Zaire that we watched on television in Germany at 3 in the morning, when we were first married. It was exciting.

Once, we were in a really remote part of New Zealand and it was winter. Nobody was there. We were scouting locations for our *Adam and Eve* film, and we were driving around and John said, 'Gee, the fight is today. Cooney versus somebody outdoors at Caesars Palace.' The man who was driving us around said it was on television. So, we rushed back to his house and we had tea out of these lovely, little cups and watched the fight. It was great. They had good coverage there. It was broadcast live and it was fabulous.

JOHN: Boxing has a certain beauty when somebody evades getting the crap kicked out of him.

SEVEN: What makes a good fight?

BO: One of the best we've seen recently was the Hearns-Hagler fight at Caesars Palace [April 15, 1985]; it was over very quickly but it was fabulous because of the hype beforehand. I guess it's all the speculation. Everyone was saying afterward that it was the second most exciting fight after the Thrilla in Manila.

JOHN: People paid lots of bucks and flew halfway around the world to see this damned fight. You sit down, the bell rings, Hearns swells up like a balloon, comes flying out like Batman and looks like he's going to take Hagler out of there, and a few moments later he's on his ass. The real aficionados saw something magnificent that night.

BO: It was because of all the hype beforehand. For me, that makes a great fight.

JOHN: Everything in society is so complex today, yet here, the basics get it done—courage, the right weight and a modest amount of skill.

SEVEN: Who are your favorite boxers?

BO: Ali is my favorite boxer. I like Frazier a lot, too.

JOHN: No person has ever been accepted on Earth, universally, like Ali. He was like a ballet dancer in the ring. He was truly beautiful in his prime. Ali was unique in a devastating sport. He's been very nice to Bo. The favorites at a Caesars Palace fight are Jack Nicholson, Bo and this guy who dwarfs everyone on earth, Ali. A boxing crowd nowadays could almost pass on the scheduled event and cheer Ali if he were just standing there. It's incredible the things he did, resisting the draft, which wasn't popular then, and coming back to regain the title.

BO: Currently, I like Hagler and Curry.

JOHN: I like people like Ray "Boom Boom" Mancini, the guys who go out there and tear up the ring because they want to be the best so desperately.

SEVEN: Do you think boxers have bigger egos than other athletes?

JOHN: You can't fight without ego. The strongest thing you have in there is your idea of yourself. Leonard had to live out of the ring as a non-champion for a while which is not a good thing. It must have been like a festering sore.

BO: It amazes me that no matter how big the last fight, the next fight is always the biggest, bigger than the last. Caesars manages to do that every single time. When we travel all over the world, someone will come up and say they saw us at a fight.

JOHN: I like it for Bo because she has embraced it. She's not a ghoul who sits there and wants them to beat the hell out of each other, and she's not a little violet that wilts when they get in there and break a sweat. The men in the crowd consider Bo one of them. They treat her with a nice respect.

SEVEN: Should boxing be banned?

BO: No, it's obviously a natural thing. We live in a valley [north of Santa Barbara] where there are a lot of tough guys. For fun, they go down and fight. It's something that's in man. We're an aggressive animal. By banning it, there will just be more barroom things.

JOHN: Boxing is a lot less violent than hockey where the violence is orchestrated. In boxing, you're trying not to get hit. The good thing about boxing is that it's one-on-one. At any time you can sit down on your ass and say thank you, but *no mas*. You don't have to be knocked out.

SEVEN: How do you feel about women boxing?

BO: It upsets me. The breasts should not be hit.

JOHN: Women don't have the same neck muscles as men. The head is a heavy piece of our body and, if you pop that thing around, you have to have the neck muscles to support it.

BO: I don't think women are built for it.

JOHN: They're built for more finessed things like judo.

BO: Even wrestling, where you're using leverage.

SEVEN: Can you recall the most powerful punches you've seen in a fight?

BO: The Hagler-Duran fight was most remarkable to me because when Duran hit, he looked like he was killing Hagler. He wasn't. The punches that went back and forth between those two were frightening. The only real knockout I've seen is the Hagler-Hearns fight. The punches that excited John that night I never even saw. They were small. They're not big like the ones that miss or don't do anything.

JOHN: Some referees are getting in now before the guy has really been hit.

BO: That's a shame but I'd rather have that happen occasionally than the other end of the spectrum where the officials let the fight go too long.

JOHN: But, Bo, that's what boxing is all about. It's part of the game.

Pau Gasol

Off The Court, the L.A. Lakers Superstar Fights Polio And Famine

Between the end of the 2012 London Olympics and the start of the NBA season, Los Angeles Lakers superstar Pau Gasol has some free time. Instead of resting up, he heads to Chad, a landlocked Central African nation where the natural hazards include, in the words of the CIA World Factbook, "hot, dry, dusty harmattan winds; periodic droughts; locust plagues."

While there, Gasol, a UNICEF Spain ambassador, visits schools and feeding centers for children suffering from acute malnutrition. "I'm in Chad to remind people that one million children are at risk in the Sahel because of the nutritional crisis, and that it is possible to end malnutrition," he tells reporters.

When he's off the basketball court, the 32-year-old spends much of his time fundraising and volunteering for charity, with an emphasis on health and education. Pau's Project, which he founded in 2010 to support UNICEF and other humanitarian organizations, rebuilt 80 schools in two years. He has also traveled to Angola, Ethiopia, and South Africa for UNICEF, and he regularly visits patients at Children's Hospital Los Angeles.

Recently, Gasol agreed to join Rotary's This Close public awareness campaign to eradicate polio.

He credits his parents – Marisa, a physician, and Agusti, a nurse, both of whom played second-division basketball in Spain – with inspiring his sports career and his charity work. Gasol almost became a doctor; at 18, he enrolled as a pre-med student at the University of Barcelona but left after a year to play professional basketball in Spain. He joined the Memphis Grizzlies in 2001, finishing the season as NBA Rookie of the Year.

For the past several seasons, Gasol has played forward-center for the Lakers, alongside Kobe Bryant. He is a four-time NBA All-Star and helped lead the Lakers to two NBA championships. Playing for the Spanish national team, he helped win the 2006 FIBA World Championship and earned silver medals at the 2008 and 2012 Olympic Games.

As the Lakers prepare for the 2012-13 season at their training facility at the Toyota Sports Center in El Segundo, Calif., Gasol takes a break from practice to talk with writer (and longtime Lakers fan) Robert Crane. The 7-foot-tall Gasol ducks his head as he enters the Lakers' front office conference room, and smiles when he notices a photo of himself high-fiving Bryant during a championship game.

THE ROTARIAN: Why did you decide to join Rotary's campaign against polio?

GASOL: My family had a close friend who suffered from polio. It was a challenge for him throughout his life. Polio has been around for so long and has taken so many lives. And it is very close to being eradicated.

TR: Rotary's polio awareness campaign features Bill Gates, Desmond Tutu, and Jane Goodall, among others. What's a basketball player from Barcelona doing in this group?

GASOL: It's high-level company, but I'll continue to be humble [smiles]. I am proud to be a part of this initiative with such a great group of people known around the world.

TR: Why have you directed most of your humanitarian work toward health?

GASOL: I've always had a great passion for medicine. I value good health over anything in life. Without that, it's hard to do so many things. We have to emphasize how important it is to be healthy. We must support health care, including preventive measures and treatment.

TR: As a student, why did you choose to be pre-med?

GASOL: When Magic Johnson learned that he was HIV-positive and announced it publicly, that was a pretty big shock for an 11-year-old growing up in a little town outside Barcelona. I loved basketball. That was the moment I decided I wanted to do something special in medicine. When I was in pre-med, my two areas of interest were pediatrics and research. I turned pro and didn't finish. But I have close relationships with Children's Hospital in Los Angeles, St. Jude's in Memphis, and a few hospitals in Barcelona.

TR: Do you ever revisit your first career choice by watching any medical television shows?

GASOL: I love *Grey's Anatomy* because of the medical lingo, which I've heard at home with my mom and dad. And I like to see the different patient cases and surgeries.

TR: Which public figure, outside of the sporting world, has most inspired you?

GASOL: Nelson Mandela, because he's a man of great strength. He's a role model because his values and thoughts are incredible and worth following. I'd love to talk with Bill Gates – he's a remarkable human being – but I don't think he comes to Lakers games. [Gates lives near Seattle.]

TR: You've been a UNICEF Spain ambassador since 2003. Recently you visited Chad, one of several countries in the Sahel, where the food crisis has affected 18.7 million people. That's not an easy trip. Why did you go?

GASOL: The world's support and contributions can make a huge difference. Our visit attracted a lot of attention and raised a lot of money to give these people a better chance.

TR: Combating poverty and hunger is a Sisyphean task. How do you keep going?

GASOL: You have to believe in the work and understand how important it is, and just take it one step at a time. There are going to be setbacks you can't control. In Africa, like in many places, a conflict could start at any time and push you back quickly. You have to focus on the people, especially children, who are in danger. They're worth fighting for. If you or your children were in trouble, you would want somebody to fight for you. I feel fortunate and privileged to have the life I've had, the opportunities I've had, and to enjoy great health. So, to be able to help others less fortunate than myself provides me great joy.

TR: How should people decide which causes to support?

GASOL: I always encourage people to get information and see how they feel. You shouldn't give money just because somebody tells you to. You have to feel it. It has to be personal. It has to be something you believe in.

TR: You've participated in a Basketball Without Borders camp, which promotes the sport and encourages social change. Why are sports so important for young people?

GASOL: Sports are a powerful tool for educating children. Kids can express themselves through sports, and find and develop their own character. It's a healthy activity that creates good habits, and it's therapeutic for kids with struggles in their lives, who have gone through difficult situations. All children need role models, mentors, and positive influences.

TR: What did playing sports teach you when you were growing up?

GASOL: Basketball helped me to be the person I am today. I learned about important values, dynamics, coordination, and communication.

TR: What have you learned about your teammate of six years, Kobe Bryant?

GASOL: We've been through a lot together and have great respect for each other. He's the ultimate hard worker, competitor, and winner. He wants to be remembered as not just one of the best, but as the best. He's got that tremendous will, that inner force and power to do it.

TR: And he keeps leading the U.S. men's basketball team to gold medals in the Olympics. Do you think you'll ever win a gold with Spain, or will you have to switch to the U.S. team?

GASOL: I don't think I'd be able to switch teams. But I don't want to. There still might be a chance for Spain to win in 2016 in Rio. I'd love to be a part of it, because I'm a fighter. But I'm also a person who takes it one day at a time and tries to be as happy as possible on a daily basis. So, maybe it would be good for me to do something else, besides playing basketball.

Robert Crane

Ladies to a Tee

The world of professional sports is filled with he-men and not a few he-women.

The hulk-like body of the tournament leader pushes a twenty-five foot putt toward the eighteenth pin and falls short.

"OOOOOHHHHHHH," the gallery moans.

"Shit," the tournament leader says in the direction of her male caddy.

Fortunately, she turns away from the network television camera as she mutters the obscenity. She removes a few blades of grass from her putter, surveys the six inches between her ball and the hole and taps it in. The tournament is hers. She picks up the ball and throws it intentionally toward three enthusiastically squealing college-age girls.

"EEEEKKK!"

The easily impressed vulture-girls fight over possession of the ball. The most cherubic of the three victoriously reveals the dainty Dunlop.

"I've got one of her balls."

"You can say that again," a resident male golf pro whispers to me as we watch the action at the eighteenth.

"It's disgusting, the bulls going after the lambs and the spectators and reporters having to act like nothing's going on."

I'm playing devil's advocate.

"But, it's only a professional woman athlete playing to her adoring fans."

"Bullshit. It's a seasoned veteran looking for new recruits."

Hmmm. This guy is truly disgusted. Maybe it's the Canadian Club talking.

But, there was Billie Jean King's shocking confession. That even prompted golden-girl Nancy Lopez-Melton to write in the staid Golf Digest – "It never ceases to amaze me how closely the lives of public figures, such as prominent athletes or movie stars, are so closely scrutinized. We virtually live in a fishbowl. This is very much a private matter, and that's the way it should have remained."

Yeah, I guess so. But one will not forget the heavy camaraderie one is witnessing during the 1981 Kemper Open in Costa Mesa, California.

The commissioner of the LPGA, Ray Volpe, is critical of the media's coverage—"The three

304

subjects guaranteed to get the most ink in women's golf are pornography (referring to golfer Jan Stephenson's photos in Fairway magazine), marriages and divorces and homosexuality. Why don't they write about the personalities and good golf?"

Nobody cares about *that*, Ray.

Burch Riber, general chairman of the LPGA Championship and a past member of the LPGA Sponsors Board, acknowledges that homosexuality has been a constant topic in women's sports for over thirty years.

"It exists everywhere in life," he explains. "But I feel strongly that the women on the LPGA Tour have conducted themselves as well as, or better than, any group of athletes I have observed. I see no reason why the statements of Billie Jean King should have any effect on the future of women's golf."

Billie Jean King. That's tennis. Who will be the first professional woman golfer to come out of the caddyshack?

I can name a few who won't have to. They're straight. Jan Stephenson, the Australian sex bomb, who makes Olivia Newton-John look like cream of wheat. Nancy Lopez-Melton. I know what you're thinking. She's married. She could never be a golf bull. Marriage has nothing to do with it. But, I concur, in this case. She's too squeaky-clean wholesome to be butch material. Laura Baugh Cole, the Tour's sexpot before Stephenson, got married because she was uncomfortable fending off the constant advances of the dyke patrol. Myra Van Hoose recently married her caddy. Well, that's four out of seventy.

Jane Blalock, who is among the top five LPGA money-earners of all time, labeled Stephenson's cheesecake spread in Fairway magazine as "quasi-pornographic." If you've ever seen Blalock playing a round of golf in short-shorts, you know what the definition of pornography is. I'm not sure about Janie's sexual preference but her dismal attempt to ace feminine is truly laughable. Other veterans JoAnne Carner, Donna Caponi, Joyce Kazmierski and Marlene Floyd look like washed-up junior high P.E. teachers who did too many laps around the football field. The younger members of the Tour are adapting the same West Point look of the veterans: short-cropped hairdos, chunky bodies and expanding hips wrapped by J.C. Penney sports department clothing. Amy Alcott, Debbie Massey, Vicki Tabor and Vicki Fergon have it. Ten-hut. At ease. Get down on your knees.

I'm telling the resident golf pro about a television show I saw the other night where authors Grace Lichtenstein, Julie Anthony and Marie Brenner were talking about lesbianism in sports. There seems to be a domineering mother behind many of the successful women athletes. Many lesbian athletes have a secret hatred for their mothers. I could never understand mother/daughter relationships anyway. Individualistic sports like golf and tennis seem to promote the safe womb-like world of lesbianism. One hears comments like "It's easier not to go out at night while you're in some strange city on the road." The women are living in a small universe filled with highly competitive women, male executives running the tour and resident golf pros like the one I've been talking to. Not a big choice. Male athletes will go out at night. Women athletes don't or can't. It's easier and safer to get into the Jacuzzi at the hotel with another female body. Jan Stephenson does not stay at the hotels where the golfers stay. She stays at friends' homes in each city.

With team sports, at least, everyone can go out together or have a gang-bang. Golf is solitary confinement. Loneliness is rampant on the LPGA Tour. But, there is a major factor involved in wanting to keep driving and putting the ball better than anyone else on the Tour in exotic places like Hershey, Pennsylvania, and Indianapolis, Indiana. Money. Lots of it.

Money also plays a part in the attraction the young squealing college girls have toward these lady cadet-types and motherly P.E. teachers. It's fun to be around money and winning. It's safe to be with your mommy or big sis. There is an adulation of someone in the center of flashing bulbs, television cameras and reporters' questions; someone momentarily better or different than the rest.

Some of the golfers I talked with imply that Donna Caponi is the father-figure of the Tour at the moment. She's dad, mom and sis to the girls. They ask her for advice just as they ask Nancy Lopez-Melton where they can find the best Mexican food and margaritas in town.

The LPGA front office is trying desperately to make the Tour as feminine as possible. Some of the tournament sponsors include Sarah Coventry, Mary Kay Cosmetics and, of course, Dinah Shore. Colgate-Palmolive pulled out of the latter tournament. How about a vibrator distributor sponsoring a tournament? That's feminine. Or a douche manufacturer. The $150,000 Summer's Eve Invitational from Ball, Ohio. Or the $200,000 Rely Tampon Tournament from Death Valley, California.

Kyle O'Brien is a twenty-two year old rookie on the Tour. She is a graduate of Southern Methodist by way of Indianapolis. Nice, wholesome, pure-bred American stock.

"The best thing I ever did was stay in school," she says. "If you come out here too early and you're not mature, this place will eat you up."

Or someone will.

Unless she is of the bull persuasion, O'Brien will have to say "no" repeatedly and kindly to the bull vets and she will be placed on the "out" list. Uncooperative. She'll have to marry someone—her caddy—to keep from relating the LPGA Tour to a twenty year stay at San Quentin. Or, she can become the new lamb chop and submit to the constant pleas. Tough decision. It's so tempting to jump in the Jacuzzi with someone who's made $900,000 more than you have on tour and can help you with your putting.

Former tennis great Arthur Ashe relates this to the women's tennis tour – "Billie Jean King's affair with Marilyn Barnett aside, I knew all along about the lesbianism on the women's tennis tour. In the men's locker room, we long ago ceased to make jokes about it. If you tell the same joke every day, it quickly loses its humor. Not that there were not new incidents as time went on. We even knew who was currently going with whom. The female-female relationships just became so routine at our joint tournaments that we ceased to find it amusing. But more important, we ceased to find it uncomfortable."

The tournament comes to a close. Some unknowns have crept into the top ten finishers for the seventy-two-hole event. This is the last year for the Kemper Open at Costa Mesa. Next year, it'll be in Hawaii. The country club bar is doing a brisk business. The resident golf pro orders another shot.

"There's a goddamned awards dinner tonight. You should see some of these gals in dresses. Embarrassing. Some of them shave their legs, armpits *and* faces."

I ask who they bring as their dates, males or females?

The pro looks at me and laughs.

Robert Crane

STUDIO EXECUTIVE, NEW RELEASE, DIRECTOR, WRITER

Robert Crane

Dawn Steel

Hollywood's madam mogul on how to win an argument, what the Japanese don't know about movies and what to say when a woman asks, "How do I look?"

Many film industry observers would argue that selling a motion picture to the public is as important as creating one. No one knows that better than studio executive turned independent producer Dawn Steel. After marketing and merchandising novelty items through her own company, Oh Dawn, in the mid-Seventies, Steel came to Hollywood in 1978 and joined Paramount Pictures as director of merchandising. She created the first feature-film commercial tie-in with Klingons eating McDonald's Big Macs to publicize the film "Star Trek." By 1980 Steel was supervising the development and production of such films as "Flashdance," "Top Gun," "Beverly Hills Cop 2," "The Accused" and "Fatal Attraction." Helping to redefine and expand the role of women in Hollywood, in 1987 Steel became the first woman to head a major motion picture studio—Columbia Pictures. During her tenure, she was responsible for the production of "Ghostbusters 2," "Karate Kid 3," "When Harry Met Sally" and "Look Who's Talking," among others. Having survived at Columbia for three years (twice as long as the average studio executive), Steel departed and independently produced the hit films "Sister Act 2" and "Cool Runnings," the latter of which has earned more than $150 million to date. Last year she wrote the best-selling book "They Can Kill You, But They Can't Eat You," which chronicles her journey through the Hollywood maze. Recently, Steel formed Atlas Entertainment in alliance with Turner Pictures and is currently releasing their first feature, "Angus."

Robert Crane caught up with the diminutive Steel at her production office in West Hollywood. Crane reports: "Dawn Steel is small, pretty, sexy, funny—and definitely in charge. You wouldn't want her to be pissed off at you."

1

PLAYBOY: Your autobiography is called *They Can Kill You, But They Can't Eat You.* How did the title come to you?

STEEL: I was in labor and 24 hours later gave birth to my daughter on March 17, 1987. I had been having some difficult times at my job, and I was at odds with my boss. I knew he didn't like me, but I didn't know how much he didn't like me. In the hospital, my husband had gone down to the coffee shop to get a newspaper. He came back and I was feeding my child and blissed out. He looked at me with the newspaper under his arm and said, "I don't know how to tell you this, babe, but you got fired while you were in labor." I remember thinking, I will not cry, I will not let them make me cry. I have my daughter in my arms. I looked up at my husband and said, "You know what? They can kill you, but they can't eat you." I had heard that years before. Someone smarter than me had said it. But at that moment I realized that's how it felt. I'm still here.

Robert Crane

2

PLAYBOY: Remember the film *The Player*? Is the real story more complicated or less complicated than that?

STEEL: I hate that movie because it makes all of us in the movie business look like schmucks, and we're not. We don't murder people. I can't name one studio executive who's killed anybody. That movie makes really intelligent people believe that we are all immoral, amoral—and jerks, which is worse.

3

PLAYBOY: How do you get your way? Whom do you sweet-talk and whom do you bully?

STEEL: I don't give up. I just annoy people until they give me what I want. I badger them.

I hope I don't bully anybody. It's not something I would be proud of. I want what I want when I want it and I'm very straightforward about it. One of my mentors used to call me "the tank." He said, "You put your head down and you just keep rolling forward until you get what you want." That's basically what I do. I just keep going forward. Jeffrey Katzenberg used to go to the front door. If they didn't let him in the front door, he'd go to the back door. If they didn't let him in the back door, he'd go to the side door. If they didn't let him in the side door, he'd go to the basement. You keep going in different orifices until you get where you want to go. You never give up. That's how I get what I want.

4

PLAYBOY: How do you know you've won an argument?

STEEL: They hang up. They can't take it anymore. They want to go home and take a nap.

5

PLAYBOY: How would you define the word bitch? Are there other things you can call a woman?

STEEL: I won't define it. In fact, it's a word I particularly loathe and don't think we should use. There's no equivalent for men. If I cut somebody off, he calls me a bitch. If I offend someone, he calls me a bitch. I strap on my balls, he calls me a bitch. I find it offensive. I am not a female dog. I don't understand how it came to mean what it means today. In my office, we don't use the bitch word. The C word is unacceptable. If you absolutely need to call a woman a name, you can call her a shithead.

6

PLAYBOY: Men are born with balls, but most don't use them. Women acquire balls and use them. Give us rules for wielding balls in a postfeminist society.

STEEL: Always do it with humor. Men don't like having balls wielded seriously. Men don't like having balls wielded by women, period. Girls, I suggest you always have a gleam in your eyes when

312

you're wearing your balls.

7

PLAYBOY: What can a woman tell a man about balls?

STEEL: I once heard a pop psychiatrist say, "Ladies, leave your balls at home," which was weird because I would say wear your balls to the office and then take them off when you're going out.

8

PLAYBOY: Do men take their balls for granted?

STEEL: Yes, completely. We're dealing with the image of balls as opposed to the psychological advantage of knowing you were born with balls. But, in some way, I always knew I was born with balls. It's much more comfortable for me than it is for you. Mine are figurative and yours are literal.

9

PLAYBOY: You make stars. Which star makes you weak in the knees?

STEEL: Brad Pitt. I've had nothing to do with his career, though I hope to. I just want to be his friend.

10

PLAYBOY: Have you ever used a casting couch to your advantage?

STEEL: Before I was married, I thought it worked only for men. It took me a long time to figure out that I could use it. That's a really different thing between men and women. I've heard specific references to it and, in fact, heard recently that a studio executive was caught giving head to a writer she wanted for a particular project. Whatever it takes, honey.

11

PLAYBOY: Please tell us three lies of Hollywood.

STEEL: "I'll read the script tonight." "I'll get back to you tomorrow." "I loved your movie." No one sets out to make a bad movie, but it happens. If you're in a position where you get to see a movie before it's finished, you have an obligation to be completely honest. But if you see a movie after it's finished, and it's somebody you care about, you're not going to walk up to them and say, "I hate it." You're going to say, "Good for you. Congratulations. I really enjoyed it." I don't want to be too tongue-in-cheek about that answer.

12

PLAYBOY: Describe three danger signs of becoming "too Hollywood."

STEEL: Number one is when you begin to think that you're different and, of course, you're not. Number two is when you get really angry if you (a) can't get a favorite table at a restaurant, (b) are made to wait in line at a movie theater rather than be rushed in ahead of the line, or (c) have to fly,

313

God forbid, commercial. There's the car thing, which is mainly a male issue, when the cars get fancier and fancier and you look around and wonder, Can't they think of something else to do with their money? Finally, you have, legitimately, people who lose their temper way too easily because the stress level is way too high. When you finally get to that place, and I've certainly been there, it's time to go. People who don't know they're there don't know it's time to go. But I promise you, it's time to go.

13

PLAYBOY: What does Hollywood have too much and too little of?

STEEL: It has too much money and too little integrity. In every business you find people who have honor and people who don't. There are only two kinds of people in the world, honest ones and dishonest ones. We have our share of dishonest people here. I think the problem is that we're all— and I mean all of us—paid way too much money, more money than we would be paid in any other business at our career levels. The union people who are just starting their careers are being paid so much more than minimum wage. So kids coming out of college are making $50,000 a year. That's a fortune. I'm not talking about the tens of millions of dollars that people like Tom Hanks or Bruce Willis make. I'm not talking about movie stars. I'm talking about regular people. Every day I thank the universe for putting all of this on my plate. The minefield for me is trying to avoid the people who are dishonest.

14

PLAYBOY: What have the Japanese learned from their incursion into the U.S. film industry? Should they have stuck to Godzilla?

STEEL: They've learned to stay home. I think the Japanese have been ill-advised and they've made a mistake that is common in Hollywood, which is thinking that anyone can make an American movie. It's not true. Only Americans can make American movies. It is the most exportable product we have. It is the thing we're most noted for. An American movie is a calling card anywhere in the world. The Japanese can make Japanese movies, but they can't make American movies.

15

PLAYBOY: We never hear about your husband. How do you balance work and your relationship?

STEEL: Chuck is incredibly solid and doesn't really give a shit. Work doesn't come anywhere near the importance of my relationship with my husband and my daughter. It became clear when I was at Columbia Pictures that I needed to figure out a way to do everything. There was this myth about Superwoman. She doesn't exist. Some days I was a great mother and some days I was a great studio executive or a great producer. But not every day. I can't be great every day. There were times I didn't get my legs waxed for months. It's an awful image, I know. Something had to go and it was my legs.

16

PLAYBOY: Who wears the pants in your relationship?

STEEL: We both wear pants. My eight-year-old daughter wears pants, too.

17

PLAYBOY: What is the oddest file in your PowerBook?

STEEL: My daughter's games. She's on my computer all the time and she's really annoying about it. We have all these games like Math Blaster and Spelling Buster and Shanghai Shuffle Puck. Do you know how annoying the sound is when the puck gets hit? I also have all sorts of bizarre letters because I have figured out how to fax from my computer. I have all sorts of weird correspondence. I'm not going to tell you with whom.

18

PLAYBOY: When a woman asks, "How do I look?" is it an invitation to be truthful?

STEEL: For me it is. My husband doesn't miss anything. On one hand, I want to say to him, "Could you put on a blindfold?" He sees every zit on my face. On the other hand, I absolutely want him to be truthful with me because I don't want him to let me go out if I look ridiculous. If there's something I can do about it, then it's really helpful. But if he says, "Your nose is gigantic," there's nothing I can do. So I don't want to be told that. I'm a finished product, basically, give or take a couple of pounds and wrinkles. I want to be told the truth except for the things I can't change. Only certain responses are permitted, on things I can change. If he doesn't like my nose, what can I do about it?

19

PLAYBOY: What happened to tan lines?

STEEL: The ozone layer. Gone. Skin cancer wiped out tan lines. Can we talk about sunspots? In the Sixties, I was lying out there on Jones Beach plastered with baby oil and iodine with a sun reflector surrounding me. I was really tan. Flash forward a couple of decades and now I have sunspots all over my legs from where I was sunburned. That's what happened to tan lines. No more sun. Sunspots and skin cancer—that's what you get from tan lines. I'm very neurotic about my sunspots, too.

20

PLAYBOY: With whom will you never have lunch again?

STEEL: I recently read a book called *The Tibetan Book of Living and Dying*. One of its great insights is that we should have compassion for every human being because we're all dying. I have compassion for everyone because everyone's dying, and I'll eat lunch with anybody because they're going to die. We're all going to die.

Robert Crane

Auto Focus

Like John Belushi in WIRED, my dad, actor Bob Crane, in AUTO FOCUS is a driven, meteoric show business phenomenon whose lack of self-respect and naiveté lead to an early demise. We read about or watched Belushi because he was an uncontrollable fireball who was hilarious and did things we fantasized about doing. We watched Bob Crane because he was an in control leader who said and did funny things always at the right time. Many HOGAN'S HEROES viewers wanted to be him. Belushi and Crane – fueled by the need to make people laugh. Unfortunately, because of time limitations, writer/filmmaker point of view and arc of story, the humor, the driving force behind Belushi and Crane, is left behind. Drugs, sex, and death take center stage. People slow down on the highway to view the accident. Some want blood, some want survivors, everyone must ease up on the gas pedal to take a look.

Sense of timing, razor sharp wit, better than average drummer, handsome, man's man, take charge, work your ass off, non-stop, do it better next time, are some of the adjectives that come to mind regarding my father. Also, love of jazz (Buddy Rich, Louie Bellson, Stan Kenton, Glenn Miller), photography, electronics, yes, and women. My dad was the sort of male who probably should never have been married. Yet, my dad, mother Anne, sisters Karen and Debbie and I had a blast. We made 8mm (film striped for sound) movie epics like I WAS A TEENAGER FOR THE FBI. My dad and I had the POOL LEAGUE, where we played a full schedule of baseball games against each other in our swimming pool in Tarzana, California. My father videotaped my rock power trio with Dave Arnoff and Ron Heck playing live in 1967, long before MTV videos. Okay, it was in black and white. We went on what we called Fellini Excursions like attending a celebrity bocce ball tournament at Caesar's Palace in Las Vegas. We got to meet a very crabby Joe DiMaggio. At the end of the evening, my dad and I turned toward each other and said, "What the hell are we doing here?" AUTO FOCUS doesn't pretend to be a biopic. It isn't interested in showing how much time Bob Crane spent with his kids. My dad was a big kid. He loved to have fun. My mother was the rock, the glue that kept our family together as long as it did. Although my mother only met Paul Schrader and Rita Wilson once, Schrader and Wilson capture her perfectly. She is a small-town, east coast product, who put family and sanity first. She is Ingrid Bergman, Grace Kelly and Donna Reed. Although she has been happily remarried for almost thirty years to Chuck Sloan, she still speaks of my dad with love and affection. We had great times.

AUTO FOCUS is among Paul Schrader's best films. My dad and I saw Schrader's TAXI DRIVER together in Westwood, California, in 1976. I compare AUTO FOCUS to Mike Nichols' CARNAL KNOWLEDGE with Jack Nicholson and Art Garfunkel. If there were double features today, AUTO FOCUS would be the darker second half only this time with Greg Kinnear and Willem Dafoe stepping in. Both films are brilliant and disturbing looks at male sexuality and the sexual revolution. They both capture the time periods in painstaking detail. Kinnear nails the essence of my father, non-stop pleasing of the world at large, the laugh, the beat, the timing, the small town thinking in the big bad world of L.A. Dafoe is the too-loyal sidekick, the Tonto to Kinnear's Lone Ranger. Dafoe captures the eternal hanger-on, the second tier, the pathetic. Rita Wilson is my mother, Anne

Crane. Too sweet, too trusting for her own good. Maria Bello is the second wife, Patti. Ron Leibman (my longtime friend Chris Fryer and I have loved Leibman since WHERE'S POPPA?) behaves, speaks and breathes as THE Hollywood agent. Kurt Fuller IS Werner Klemperer/Col. Klink. It's a great film but, guys, don't expect to get laid after you and your female companion see this film. It's not a date movie. In fact, you'll probably want to hang out with some of your buds and get drunk. My dad would have seen this film and headed directly to a strip club. If you want the biopic treatment on Bob Crane, read the book or watch El True Hollywood Story or A&E Biography. Or, keep supporting Sumner Redstone's (Viacom) lifestyle by watching HOGAN'S HEROES via syndication. For you Belushi fans, SATURDAY NIGHT LIVE is all over basic cable. Keep laughing.

Paul Schrader: Guest Shot

Paul Schrader wrote *Taxi Driver* and *Raging Bull,* both directed by Martin Scorsese. Not bad for a former Calvinist who saw his first film at the age of 16. Director Schrader's disc library contains an eclectic collection of masterpieces (*American Gigolo, Affliction, Auto Focus*). His American short list includes *Vertigo, The Lady Eve, The Searchers* ("John Ford and John Wayne's best"), Sam Peckinpah's *The Wild Bunch* and Orson Welles' ("overlooked") *Touch of Evil.* "Among my foreign favorites," says Schrader, "are *The Rules of the Game, Pickpocket, The Conformist, Tokyo Story* and *Masculin-Féminin.*"

Kevin Williamson

The Man Behind *Scream* and *Dawson's Creek* Talks About Teenage Sex, Bad Dreams and Scary Lingerie

It took the son of a fisherman to resurrect the dormant horror film genre. Writer-director Kevin Williamson drew on his childhood love of scary movies to create the highest-grossing horror film franchise in movie history—"Scream" and its sequel, "Scream 2." Along with director Wes Craven and a cast of young TV stars, Williamson has parlayed his "unconditional love of Jamie Lee Curtis and director John Carpenter" into a cottage industry.

Williamson was born and raised in the fishing town of New Bern, North Carolina. Influenced by his storytelling mother, he originally considered a career as an actor, studying theater and film at East Carolina University. He moved to New York, where he landed bit parts on stage and TV, then relocated to Los Angeles, where he worked as an assistant to a music-video director and took screenwriting classes at UCLA. His first screenplay, "Killing Mrs. Tingle," will serve as his directorial debut this year. Williamson's second sale, "Scream," made horror film box-office history and was followed by an adaptation of the novel "I Know What You Did Last Summer." After that, Miramax secured Williamson's services for $20 million. "Scream 3" and "The Faculty" are forthcoming, and Williamson wrote the story for "Halloween: H2O," starring one of his idols, Jamie Lee Curtis. Williamson has also found time to create the provocative TV series "Dawson's Creek" for the Warner Bros. Network and is developing another series, "Pamlico," for ABC.

Robert Crane caught up with the indefatigable screenwriter and director at his West Hollywood office. Crane reports: "The smell of success permeates Williamson's office—assistants and publicists scurry about the comfortable surroundings, which are laden with 'Scream' merchandise and posters. Williamson is young, handsome and rich. It's enough to make anyone scream."

1

PLAYBOY: Which involuntary bodily response serves as a standing ovation for the horror film auteur?

WILLIAMSON: A scream? I like to hear the gasp. I like that lull, when your mouth is dry and you hear the gurgle of not being able to swallow. You hear the gasp, followed by laughter, because the viewers are laughing at themselves for getting so worked up. And then you realize that they are really enjoying themselves.

2

PLAYBOY: Would you be better or worse at what you do had you gone through therapy?

WILLIAMSON: I have gone through a lot of therapy, and I'm a much better writer for it. I mean, my entire career is based on my therapy. The kids on *Dawson's Creek* all speak psychobabble. The fact that I sat down to write at all was a result of some huge breakthrough I had in therapy, working through my demons in order to have the confidence to put pen to paper.

3

PLAYBOY: We read about your Uncle Phil holding you by the ankles and dangling you over a school of sharks. Do you two still hang out?

WILLIAMSON: We do hang out, actually. He is the coolest guy. There was a long period of time when I was traumatized by that experience. I had nightmares about it. My uncle was 18 years old at the time, a kid himself. Now we have a big laugh about it. We sit back and smoke cigars and laugh about the whole thing. But he gets harassed—it has reached a point now where every time he walks into the local grocery store, the local diner, people just look at him and go, "I can't believe you did that to your nephew." I guess I should give him ten percent of my earnings because it was experiences like that that led my brain down a dark path, which has ultimately been fruitful. So I'm very grateful for that shark experience. In fact, I just signed a book for my uncle with the message "Thank you for what was possibly the best experience of my life."

4

PLAYBOY: Is a partially clad woman more fearful than a fully clad woman?

WILLIAMSON: What is scarier for the viewer will not necessarily be scarier for the woman. But seeing skin is definitely scarier for the viewer because there's a vulnerability factor. Our clothing is our armor a lot of the time, so, yes, a scantily clad woman is probably more scared than someone who has an armor of clothing around her. There's something vulnerable about visible skin—seeing the surface that can so easily be punctured. When you cover it up with clothing, you put a whole layer between the audience and the character.

5

PLAYBOY: You're directing your script *Killing Mrs. Tingle*. Is this an opportunity for revenge?

WILLIAMSON: Yes, it's my revenge movie. My high school English teacher said to me, "You can't spell, your diction is terrible, you come from the sticks. You'll never be a writer." I wrote this story about a girl who is raped by her boyfriend, and it was a little too graphic. When I stood up to read it out loud, the teacher stopped me in the middle of it and told me to sit down. She said, "Your voice is one that should never be heard, and you should give up any idea of becoming a writer, because it will never, ever happen." And I believed her for a long time. The story was a little ahead of its time, because date rape wasn't a big issue then. It struck a chord and the teacher certainly didn't want to hear it and she wanted to shut me out. And she did shut me up, for a dozen years.

6

PLAYBOY: Why are horror films excellent date movies?

WILLIAMSON: They're a roller-coaster ride. You're sitting in a dark room clutching each other. It's great foreplay.

7

PLAYBOY: Neve Campbell said in *Scream,* "All scary movies are the same. Some stupid killer is stalking some big-breasted girl who can't act and who's always running up the stairs when she should be going out the front door." Would the horror be diminished if the character had smaller breasts?

WILLIAMSON: I guess it would depend on what she looks like. Most horror films are so plot driven, you don't really have enough time to develop character. So breasts replace character. A young guy—the core audience for these films—responds to young, bouncing breasts. That's supposed to take the place of character development. So in a sense those breasts are the character. It's all about breasts. Oh God, I'm going to get killed for this.

8

PLAYBOY: Which actors make good horror film heroines?

WILLIAMSON: Jamie Lee Curtis is the end-all. I have had an unconditional love for Jamie Lee Curtis since I was 12 years old and saw *Halloween* for the first time. That's the reason I participated in *Halloween: H2O*—just for the opportunity to sit in a room with her and gawk at her, which I did a lot. And getting back to the breast thing, you know. I wrote the story for *Halloween: H2O.* The screenplay was written by others. I sat down with Jamie—and her breasts—and we discussed where Laurie Strode would be 20 years later.

9

PLAYBOY: What more can you do to Laurie, this poor woman?

WILLIAMSON: That's what we asked. This movie is played very real. We play it straight in the sense that we do know it's *Halloween,* part seven, and we don't shy away from it. One thing we try to do is go back to the original. We try not so much to send up the first one, but to honor it, you know, and to pay homage to it, pay tribute to this wonderful, groundbreaking film. So there are all sorts of little inside jokes—all the true fans of *Halloween* will get them. We left in dialogue and scenes and beats, so you almost have to be a *Halloween* expert to get the movie. I would urge everyone to see the first movie again before going to see *Halloween: H2O* because then you'll truly enjoy it.

10

PLAYBOY: There's a strange cross-wiring in horror films. The killer wants to kill the woman, and the straight guy sitting in the audience wants to fuck her.

WILLIAMSON: You just want to thump that killer on the forehead, don't you? Since there's no character development, there is no way to relate that character to the viewer except to show someone who is beautiful and desirable. We want her, so we root for her. We want her to live. We want her to persevere. That too takes the place of character development, which is unfortunate, but it's typical for a plot-driven movie.

11

PLAYBOY: What are some of the new variations on horror film stereotypes?

WILLIAMSON: What I'm dying to do is kill the heroine. It's time to see Jamie Lee Curtis die, or to have Neve Campbell get it at the end of the movie and then begin *Scream 3* with the surprise revelation that she's alive. Traditional filmmaking dictates that you can bend the rules only so far. In horror movies, the stereotype is that if you do something bad, you will be punished. I try to dispel that in a lot of instances, particularly in *Scream*. Neve's character loses her virginity and doesn't die. The horror genre has set up this plot that rules that if you have sex you die. So I knew immediately upon sitting down to write it I was going to let her lose her virginity and still live. I would have fun with the idea that sex doesn't always equal death. When you are drinking and doing drugs, that is an extension of the sex-equals-death idea, because drinking and doing drugs usually lead to sex and in a teenager's world, sex always leads to lots of judgment. That's the big stereotype.

12

PLAYBOY: Dawson's Creek is a real place. Did the Williamson Realty and Development Corp. buy creekfront property in anticipation of the show's becoming a hit?

WILLIAMSON: Kind of like the baseball diamond in *Field of Dreams* that everyone is going to come to? No. I come from a family of fishermen, and we don't deal in real estate at all. But Dawson's Creek really exists. It's where I lost my virginity.

13

PLAYBOY: Describe the Dawson's Creek theme park. Would a high school teacher be one of the rides?

WILLIAMSON: Oh God, I hope so. You know, I'm new to all this TV and movie stuff, but it's my understanding that marketing is where it's at. So, sure, *Dawson's Creek* lunch boxes and action figures. We could have a lot of fun with teacher and student action figures. You have set my mind racing. I hadn't really thought of any of this until now, but I'm going to make a few phone calls as soon as this interview is over.

14

PLAYBOY: For a teenager, is there such a thing as too much sex?

WILLIAMSON: No. When you're a teenager, it's all about sex. There's no such thing as too much sex because when you're a teenager you're getting very little sex. I remember a point when I was having sex all the time, but until I hit that point it was never happening, and all I could do was talk about it. Or I'd have sex once, and then it wouldn't happen again for months. All I could do was talk about that one experience until I forgot about it. *Dawson's Creek* has been criticized for dealing too much with sex, but the show is about romance. It's about passion. And it's about sex. *Dawson's Creek* goes beyond sex, but the characters talk about it because that's what kids talk about. I've sat down with them and listened to them. That's what I talked about when I was a teenager.

Ultimately, though, the show is about romance. How romance doesn't equal sex. For instance, the teacher-student relationship started out as sex but has become a nonjudgmental romantic relationship, whether people want to realize it or not. That relationship is based on romance, and I think that's why people have a hard time with it and why the Moral Majority has gone after it. It's probably not the most responsible relationship on television in terms of right-wing philosophy. But it certainly is a nonjudgmental relationship that I find very endearing.

15

PLAYBOY: What is the set like? Is it as hyperactive as the stories?

WILLIAMSON: It's a little *Peyton Place* down there, because we shoot in North Carolina. The cast will kill me if I reveal too much, but I will say that, yes, you could write an exposé, a *Behind-the-Scenes of Dawson's Creek*, believe me. I'll leave it at that, because I have to answer to these kids. They would never forgive me, and they are a great bunch of kids.

16

PLAYBOY: Can you describe where the characters will be five years from now?

WILLIAMSON: We're going to treat the first two seasons as one year, and then by the third season I'm sure we'll move into summer, and they will all get summer jobs, and Dawson's dad's restaurant will have opened, so they can all wait tables there. Then we'll push it all the way up to when they're seniors in high school, then they'll go off to college, maybe a nice little liberal arts school nearby with the same picturesque environment. I don't want to do the *90210* thing. I haven't really even thought about it other than to say God, I hope I get to the point of having to figure it all out.

17

PLAYBOY: Is there anything you won't write about?

WILLIAMSON: You'll probably never get some huge war drama or period piece out of me. I'm not interested. I'm more into a contemporary vibe. I've studied Steven Spielberg. I've studied James Brooks. I've studied *Terms of Endearment*. I learned dialogue from Quentin Tarantino and James Brooks. They have an ear for unique dialogue. I saw *As Good As It Gets*, and I'm amazed at how the dialogue flows from the characters' lips. I get so jealous when I see someone so talented at writing dialogue. I'm dying to explore as many genres as I can, and you can pretty much guess the stuff I won't be writing about. I'm just not interested in the past.

18

PLAYBOY: You sleep four hours a night. Do you ever have really bad dreams?

WILLIAMSON: I have really bad dreams. I scratched myself last night in my sleep while I was dreaming. I don't know what I dreamed, but I clawed myself in the face. It was really bizarre. I am a big dreamer, but I can barely remember my dreams. It's scary, isn't it? I am most alert at four A.M., when I wake up. I'm alert, I'm alive, I'm headstrong. So I get my best work done then. I can get done in two hours what it would take me ten hours to do in the afternoon. I move fast, and my brain is sharp at that time of day. It's a shame no one else is up with me to experience it, because I'd probably be great in bed. Actually, I've been sleeping a little later these days. I get up about five A.M. now. I have been pushing it, because I've been exhausted. I am running on empty at the moment. I need to go away and rejuice for a while. Then I can get back to that four o'clock schedule. It used to be three A.M. I don't sleep that much—it's really bizarre. Maybe there's something psychological there that I haven't broken through yet in therapy, but I'm not interested.

19

PLAYBOY: Is it ever a good idea to taunt a monster?

WILLIAMSON: Oh sure. That's the most fun. For instance, in *Halloween: H2O*, there's a point where Jamie Lee Curtis' character goes after Michael Myers. She gets an axe and goes after him. She's like, "You want a piece of me? Let's go." She drops to his level instead of running from him. It's great. It's the cheering moment. Ripley did it in *Aliens*. The reason it works so well is that it's all about character. What type of character when facing death would choose to talk? You have to be driven to that point by that monster, and that's what leads you to the moment of madness, when you don't care about your life anymore. It's a character-defining moment. It's hard to get there, and it's hard to make it believable. If you can get there, what a great place to take the audience.

20

PLAYBOY: Being scared and having sex: Describe the connection.

WILLIAMSON: For me, the emotions involved in sex and in being scared are the same. When blood rushes and things get engorged, it's a sign of the same emotion. When you're scared, your face gets flushed. You turn red. Your forehead throbs. Blood rushing is always a wonderful thing.

DEAD ICONS and ODDBALLS

Frank Sinatra

10 Stupid Questions: Robert Crane rudely interrupts the afterlife of the Chairman of the Board, on the eve of Frank Sinatra's golf tournament and release of a boxed set of film recordings.

1

STUPID: The Rat Pack is almost totally reunited. Are you all waiting for Joey Bishop?

FRANK SINATRA: I don't give a #!@ about Joey Bishop. We're getting our chops. Dino sounds great. Sammy is my main man. He has two eyes now, by the way. Throws off his dancing. Lawford is swingin'. We did a show with Count Basie as a surprise for Shirley MacLaine – who visited us a few months ago.

2

STUPID: What did you think of the *Ocean's Eleven* remake?

SINATRA: Ca-ca. Soderbergh is a putz. Clooney could never swing like us. Damon and Pitt look like two broads in suits. We screened *our* version recently. It slayed the audience.

3

STUPID: That was easy. Years ago, you reunited Dean and Jerry at Jerry's telethon. Any regrets?

SINATRA: Dino was drunk. Jerry stank. I did it as a goof. What's with Jerry's face, anyway? They raise a billion dollars and they can't fix the poor schmuck? By the way, Dino say no on their reunion. I'm steppin' aside, daddy.

4

STUPID: Is there a Mob in heaven? Have you seen John Gotti?

SINATRA: No comment. Gotti ain't here. And, if I did see him, I wouldn't tell you, putz. What do you think I am... stupid?

5

STUPID: No, we are. What's your favorite recording?

SINATRA: "Something," by those English fags, Lennon and McCartney. "Something Stupid," is my second favorite. Nancy couldn't sing worth a damn, though. I carried her.

6

STUPID: You do know that George Harrison, who wrote "Something," died a year ago?

SINATRA: Eh, who cares? The English screwed over music. Bono, the Beatles, Englebert Humperdork. It all went in the tank. The only thing the English can do right is sex scandals and bubbles 'n' squeak. The rest of that island is a bunch of drunk fairies.

7

STUPID: You have a golf tournament this month. Do you still play golf?

SINATRA: I hate golf. That's another thing the English do well. I play cards. Craps. The ponies. On Thursday afternoons, Jilly Rizzo and I play dominoes. Golf is for guys like Crosby and Hope.

8

STUPID: You were romantically involved with a wide range of actresses. Who was your favorite lover?

SINATRA: Truth? Ethel Merman. I had her once on a soundstage at MGM. She hit a note that shattered a camera lens. We were young. Man, she had pipes.

9

STUPID: Do you miss your children?

SINATRA: Of course I do. What kind of a half-assed question is that? Do *you* have children? I can't believe I'm in heaven and still getting bugged by friggin' journalists.

I never should have named my son Frank Jr. What a weight that put on him! But now he's doing well. He's finally *me*. Nancy shouldn't have done *Playboy*. I almost had a heart attack. Tina is my gorgeous baby. She dated Dino's son a long time ago. The one who died in the plane crash. I won't talk to him.

10

STUPID: What do you think of Las Vegas now?

SINATRA: It's friggin' Disneyland. Even Disney says that. It doesn't swing. There are no lounges, no broads. Roller coasters and Wolfgang Puck? Gimme a break. Pretty soon, you won't even be able to smoke there. I got out at the right time. And, you're getting out right now, you putz. Capeesh?

Jayne Mansfield and Marilyn Monroe

Interview to Die For - Robert Crane interrupts the afterlife of two of the 20th century's bombshells and discovers we might have overlooked something.

HWY 111: *Norma Jean Baker and Vera Jayne Palmer. We're talking with an icon… and the poor man's Marilyn Monroe.*

JAYNE MANSFIELD: How kind of you to call me an icon. Just kidding. Norman Mailer never wrote about me. *Juggs Magazine,* on the other hand…

MARILYN MONROE: Believe me, Robert, the only part of Jayne that's not frivolous are her breasts. My God, I'm looking at them right now and I feel like Sophia Loren in that famous photograph. Cleavage, Ohio.

HWY 111: *You're in heaven. Are you guys nude? Please say yes.*

MONROE: No, silly, I'm wearing a white terrycloth robe and chipped-red toenail polish. My hair is short and I never wear makeup.

MANSFIELD: I'm squeezed into a leopard-skin bikini, a size too small, and a mink stole. I still make Mr. Blackwell's worst-dressed list.

HWY 111: *Many fans consider you perfect females. What do you think of each other?*

MANSFIELD: Miss Monroe has a tummy pooch, a horrible singing voice and thunder thighs.

MONROE: Jayne can't act her way out of a paper bag and claims to have an IQ of 163. That's 82 per breast.

HWY 111: *You both died in your prime: Marilyn, 36, of an alleged sleeping pill overdose… Anything you want to clear up?*

MONROE: I'd had a fight with Bobby [Kennedy]. I don't remember taking those sleeping pills… I had too much wine. I've tried to ask Jack and Bobby if they know anything but they avoid me like the plague. So does Joe Sr., Jackie, Sam Giancana and Sinatra. Rose Kennedy gives me the evil eye. I still see Joe [DiMaggio] who's very sweet to me but has me followed everywhere I go.

HWY 111: *Outside of the Beatles, no one has been written about more than Marilyn. Why is that?*

MONROE: I don't have a clue. Arthur Miller called me a shiksa with no talent.

HWY 111: *You were the prototypes for sex symbols of the Fifties. What do you think of today's sex kittens like Pamela Anderson, Anna Nicole Smith and Madonna?*

MANSFIELD: Pamela Anderson is a nine-year-old with two globes on her chest. I have a Chihuahua who's smarter than Anna Nicole. Madonna is a terrible actress.

MONROE: Carl Sandburg says Madonna could be a poet, though, or a really fine gossip columnist like Louella Parsons. I like to have a glass of wine in the late afternoon and dance alone to Madonna's early music. She has been compared to me, especially after stealing my *Gentlemen Prefer Blondes* number for one of her videos. Overall, I'm better at what I do.

HWY 111: *You both appeared in* Playboy *numerous times as part of the sexual revolution of the Fifties and Sixties. What are your impressions now of that movement?*

MONROE: In the Fifties, men were men and women were women. Now, with liberation, women and men are confused. There is no raw sexuality, no spontaneity. Emotions are packaged. Instead of a man asking a woman out for a date, both sexes are watching a TV show where a woman picks the sexiest man from 100 men she doesn't know anything about and --

MANSFIELD (INTERRUPTING): Sexual revolution? Who won? I wasn't paying attention.

O.J. Simpson – No Stone Unturned:
An Independent Search for New Evidence in
The O.J. Simpson Case (Excerpt)

Prior to the investigation documented in this magazine serial, we (Carl Spihek and B.J. Wilkom) had been serving the Loogootee, Indiana, area by publishing *The Loogootee Ledger* on a bi-weekly basis.

At the time we acquired *The Ledger* in 1993 (for $900 and a set of snow tires), its primary function was to serve the classified needs of the community. Our aspirations of turning *The Loogootee Ledger* into a more newsworthy publication began with the addition of two columns—Carl's "Automotive Alley" and B.J.'s movie review, "Wilkom to the Movies."

Our first hard-hitting news story came with the big manure-truck overturn on Interstate 50 just outside of town. The first and only paper on the scene, we provided full coverage, as well as photos in the following week's *Ledger*.

Having gotten our journalistic feet wet at the manure spill, it was a natural progression for us to cover the 1993 visit of a famous figure—Kato Kaelin. Never in our wildest dreams did we imagine a personality from the "Trial of the Century" making it to our corner of the world. His personal appearance at the Honey Creek Square Mall in nearby Terre Haute was front-page news. More than 5,000 Indianans showed up to chant, "Ka-to, Ka-to," and *The Ledger* was there to cover the story (*Loogootee Ledger*, Volume 9, Week 16).

We normally published the paper out of the break room of Shirley Finkle's Century 21 office. However, the Kato story proved immense and our operation temporarily spread over into Shirley's office, forcing us to enlist the help of Shirley, Ben Posey (Shirley's Century 21 partner) and Carl's wife, Mary Jo.

The stacks of *Loogootee Ledgers* covering the Kato appearance disappeared in record time and we did an extra press run of 250 copies. We had gotten a taste of the whole O.J. Simpson phenomenon.

One afternoon we sat rehashing the case, eventually fixating on one aspect, evidence. Shirley wondered: With so many teams of investigators that worked on the criminal case, could it be possible that some ambiguous (yet crucial) piece or pieces of evidence were overlooked? Carl uttered the old saying, "Can't see the forest for the trees."

Ben recalled the time the real estate office three a baby shower for Greta, the UPS driver. Shirley thought for sure one of her Hoosier basketball hoop earrings had dropped off into one of the potluck dishes on the break room table. We all helped dig through the three-bean salad, onion dip and Chex mix—with no sign of the bauble. Only when Shirley had given up and decided to go on with her life did Ben discover that her earring was, in fact, caught on the collar of her blouse. It was right there the entire time.

Robert Crane

What if the investigators working the case only turned over the bigger more obvious stones? And what if someone unrelated to the case were to conduct their own investigation, taking on the task of looking under the smaller, less obvious stones?

With Mr. Simpson having been found "not guilty" in the criminal trial, the real killer or killers could still be at large. We recalled Mr. Simpson's personal investigation into the homicides and wondered how it was progressing.

It wasn't long after opening this can of worms that we realized the task of conducting an independent investigation must ultimately fall on our own shoulders.

One would be hard-pressed to find two people further removed from the case than ourselves—two small town journalists hailing from Loogootee, Indiana, the heartland of America. Truth and justice were our mandate (although Mr. Simpson's $500,000 reward for information leading to the real killer[s] could make B.J.'s dream of a Copy Master 20000 with collating and multi-color capabilities a reality).

Soon folks in and around town were lending their support and doing what they could to help out financially. Shirley got things started by placing an empty Folger's can on her desk in order to collect funds for our journey. Around the can she taped a piece of paper explaining our objective. Seeing that there was not enough room to spell "Investigation Team," she simply wrote I Team. The name stuck and the I Team was born.

After months of intense fundraising and tub-thumping, we were ready to go. With support and encouragement of friends and family, we closed up shop on the paper one week and made the trip to Los Angeles to conduct our own investigation.

During our stay in Los Angeles, we were lucky enough to cross paths with two "Hollywood" writers who had just finished shooting the pilot for a game show version of *Go Fish* with Bob Eubanks. Unfortunately, for them, the show did not get picked up, but, fortunately for us, they were now available and willing to bring their professional writing skills to our story.

No Stone Unturned chronicles the only independent investigation of the O.J. Simpson case. Regardless of your beliefs about his guilt or innocence, what you are about to read will undoubtedly have an impact on the way you view the entire Simpson phenomenon.

There have been numerous articles about the criminal and civil cases involving Mr. Orenthal James Simpson.

This is another one.

- Carl Spihek and B.J. Wilkom

THE ROAD TRIP

Day 1

January 30, 1996

Time: 6:12 a.m.

Climate: 22 degrees, light dusting of snow on the ground

Wind-Chill Factor: 12 below

The frozen ground cracked beneath the feet of the friends and supporters who had gathered in the parking lot of Shirley Finkle's real estate office to bid the I Team farewell.

Carl, wide awake, did not like goodbyes and was already positioned behind the steering wheel checking his gauges and tuning in the all-news station on the AM dial. B.J., though half asleep and still hugging her pillow from home that she planned to take with her, was working the crowd like a politician. Ben Posey and wife Pamey even provided the baby. Unfortunately, Carl's wife, Mary Jo Spihek, was unable to attend the send-off. Being Loogootee's self-appointed Welcome Wagon, she felt obligated to show the gentlemen from the new Zippy Lube around town the previous night and was now resting.

Folks had braved the cold not only to see Carl and B.J. off, but to present them with the Folger's can of funds collected by the community for their journey. Judging by the many coins and bills stuffed in the can, it was apparent the I Team was not alone in its quest for the truth.

B.J. graciously accepted the can and after hugging everyone in the crowd of 14, she took her place in the passenger's seat beside Carl. Carl's Dodge Dart, having been warmed up for a full 25 minutes, was road-ready. In the backseat: two greasy paper sacks of home-fried chicken from Pamey Posey, one large Thermos of black coffee from Gebbhart's Diner, as well as a fruitcake to be delivered to Shirley's cousin who lived in the Los Angeles suburb of Pacoima.

Carl and B.J. waved their goodbyes and began pulling out of the parking lot when Rory Champus of Rory's Bar and Pool Hall ran alongside the Dart, tapping on the glass. Carl braked but did not come to a complete stop. He wanted to get the show on the road. B.J. rolled down her window and Rory handed her a matchbook that someone had left behind in the bar. Though he had never been to L.A. himself, judging by the matchbook cover, Rory recommended that the I Team stay at the Bamboo Motor Lodge on Lincoln Boulevard in Venice. The rates, printed inside the cover, would accommodate their budget.

Amped on caffeine and nicotine, Carl drove the Dart hard through the varied terrain; it maxed at 85. It's possible they were going faster but had no way of gauging as the speedometer had been broken since '87. The I Team drove straight through, with Carl at the wheel for most of the trek. It was better that way. The one time Carl took a two-hour nap, B.J. had nearly derailed the trip to attend a k.d. lang concert in Albuquerque.

Robert Crane

OPENING THE INVESTIGATION

Day 2

January 31, 1996

Time: 10:55 p.m.

Climate: 55 degrees Dark

Wind-chill factor: N/A

      The I Team arrived in Los Angeles—a tangled mess of humanity. Tired, hungry and in need of a shower, they were anxious to find that motel from the matchbook cover. The freeways in Los Angeles were rarely referred to by name, like the Eisenhower Expressway or the Merritt Parkway, for example. Instead, they are referred to by number, "Take the 10 all the way into downtown L.A., go past the 110 to the 10 West, stay off the 405, it's a nightmare. Take the 10 all the way to the ocean," a trucker had schooled them outside of Palm Springs.

      Carl had to push the Dart to its limit in order to stay even with the flow of traffic. Wedged between two 18-wheelers, he unintentionally took the 605 to the 405, turned north to the 110 which led into the 105, back to the 405 eventually to the 10, which theoretically pointed at the Pacific Ocean, although they couldn't see it. Fortunately, what they did see was the Lincoln Boulevard exit. They turned right at the top of the exit ramp (later discovering that they should have turned left toward Venice).

      The L.A.P.D. had set up a sobriety checkpoint. While one officer wrote up a speeding ticket for an irate Porsche driver, a second officer, who bore an uncanny resemblance to Lyle Waggoner of *The Carol Burnett Show,* approached Carl's driver side window.

"Evenin'. Have you been drinking?" asked the officer.

"No sir," replied Carl.

"From out-of-state, I see."

"Indiana, sir."

"Do you have any drugs in your possession?"

"Absolutely not, sir."

"Welcome to L.A. Proceed with caution." He waved them through the roadblock.

      After a couple of gas station stops for directions, they finally spied the Bamboo Motor Lodge, which appeared to be cleaner and possess fewer prostitutes than most of the other motels in the vicinity.

"Not bad," said Carl, commenting on Rory's matchbook referral.

Pulling into the parking lot of the Bamboo Motor Lodge, Carl and B.J. witnessed an altercation between the motel manager and a vagrant. Apparently, there was an ongoing disagreement between the two regarding public access to the motel's private dumpster. As the street person disappeared into the night with his small cache of aluminum cans, the motel manager, a slight, wiry Asian gentleman, returned to his office, slamming the door on Carl and B.J. A string of bells hanging from the bulletproof glass door jangled as the I Team entered. From the two photos hanging above the check-in desk, Carl and B.J. concluded that the Bamboo Motor Lodge was a family-owned and operated business. Mr. Tran Nguyen held the position of night manager, his wife, Maylee Nguyen, took the day shift.

"What you want? You want room?" demanded Mr. Nguyen.

"Ah, yes," replied Carl.

"You want rent by hour?" asked the man, giving Carl and B.J. the once-over.

"By the hour? No, we'll be needing it for about a week," said Carl, then adding, "One room with two beds," as if to clarify the situation for Mr. Nguyen.

The night manager turned to look over the remaining room keys hanging from hooks below a small altar. Apparently, the Nguyens were people who worshipped citrus fruit.

"Got best room in whole place. You got credit card?"

"We'll be paying with cash," said Carl.

"Still need credit card deposit."

B.J. gave Mr. Nguyen one of her cards to imprint. Carl preferred to deal in cash for personal reasons. He'd only recently managed to whittle Mary Jo down to one major bankcard and her well-worn Sears charge.

Mr. Nguyen handed B.J. the key but did not release it until he impressed a few of the Bamboo Motor Lodge rules on his new guests. "No funny stuff. I no care what you into but no hang harness from ceiling. And no meth lab! Last month I have twenty-five rooms, then rent to crazy long hair white guy. One night, boom boom! Now only got twenty and half rooms."

Harness and meth labs? Carl hoped the person who left the matchbook behind at Rory's was just passing through and was now far, far away from Loogootee.

As Carl and B.J. were leaving the motel office, a late-night news promo on Mr. Nguyen's 13-inch black-and-white TV reiterated that the verdict in the Simpson civil trial had gone to the jury late that afternoon. The team was unaware of this development, having given up on radio just outside of Barstow, opting instead for B.J.'s Melissa Etheridge tape collection.

Inside Room 102, the antiseptic smell of Pine-Sol attempted to cover up the sins of a thousand people. Heavy stainage covered the gold shag carpet and upholstery but the room suited their needs, with two double beds and a table to serve as a writing desk.

While B.J. emptied a bladder that had been holding a Big Gulp since just outside of Riverside, Carl picked up the black 1960s model phone to call home to his wife, Mary Jo. Even though it was now 12:55 a.m. in Indiana, he wanted to let her know he had arrived safely.

Carl was always embarrassed to phone his wife when he was in the presence of B.J. He knew B.J. didn't care for Mary Jo, in fact despised her. The situation was aggravated when Mary Jo answered the phone drunk or hung over. Obviously disappointed it was B.J. on the line, Mary Jo would drop the receiver on the floor, then scream for Carl to "Pick up the damned phone! It's that broad you work with!"

Staring at a dark blob of chewing gum ground into the carpet, Carl sighed. At the end of 13 rings, he heard B.J. flush and quickly hung up.

Wasting no time, the I Team set up shop. They wanted to get the word out on the street that no piece of information would be dismissed—no matter how small or insignificant it may appear.

What they needed was a simple, yet effective, way to solicit any and all leads. Being a huge fan of The X-Files, B.J. came up with a plan. Pulling a roll of masking tape from the I Team kit (a gym bag loaded with enough stuff to stump even Monty Hall), B.J. taped the letters "O" and "J" to the motel window. Now it was just a matter of waiting.

By one a.m., they could no longer fight the exhaustion and took to their beds. B.J. forced herself to stay awake long enough to write the I Team's first journal entry. Tomorrow was the first day of the investigation here in Los Angeles and they would need to be sharp.

IT'S TAPIOCA DAY

February 1, 1996

Time: 7:10 a.m.

Climate: 65°, sunny

Windchill Factor: N/A

Carl tried his wife Mary Jo again before the I Team began its day. Again, no answer. He was not terribly concerned at this point as she had a very full social calendar. Besides, they had an investigation to conduct.

Where to begin? B.J., having nine (9) units of Telecommunications at the local J.C., recalled what she had learned years ago in Professor Fliggum's Beginning Journalism class: "Start with what you know about the story and go from there to uncover what you don't know about the story."

What did they know about the Simpson case that they could have ready access to? The murder scene, Mr. Simpson's house, and the route between the two (and if they were lucky, the Santa Monica courthouse where the civil trial was currently in progress).

According to the prosecutors in the criminal case, Mr. Simpson's Rockingham Road home was supposed to be a short five minute drive from the condo on Bundy Drive, so they should be able to hit both of these locations in short order.

The team decided the Bundy condo would be the first stop. They pulled out of the motel parking lot and onto Lincoln Boulevard with Carl at the wheel, already consuming his morning ritual of a Carlton and a lukewarm cup of bitter black coffee from the motel vending machine. In a matter of blocks, a set of golden arches appeared. Where Carl could subsist on cigarettes and coffee till noon, B.J. needed a substantial start to the day. A breakfast sandwich or two was in order.

The drive-thru lane at this particular McDonald's was a labyrinth that snaked its way through the parking lot before arriving at the food window and depositing customers back out onto Lincoln. B.J.'s attention, now fully on her two Sausage McBiscuits with Egg, three bags of flat hash browns and a large orange juice, left Carl to his own directional devices as he juggled his second cup o' joe. Due to an ill-placed speed bump and subsequent coffee spill, Carl made an unscheduled left at the end of the drive-thru.

Passing the motel they realized they were now heading south instead of the intended north. In order to correct the situation, they headed west on Venice Boulevard and in a matter of blocks found themselves face-to-face with the Pacific Ocean.

The runoff pond from the Crane Naval Weapons Depot back home could be beautiful—if the wind was blowing the right way—but this was breathtaking. It was hard for B.J. to take her eyes off the ocean in order to consult the map and call out directions.

Glancing over Carl's shoulder at the great blue sea, B.J. spied a battalion of 18-wheel trucks, orange Ford Rangers, Mercedes two-seaters and several limousines in a parking lot near a large pier cluttered with amusement park rides. Beautiful extras in bikinis and Speedos dotted the beach.

"*Baywatch!*" screamed B.J., Carl's right ear bearing the brunt of the audio assault. "Turn! Turn here!" she shouted.

Carl made an impossible left and drove down a two-lane ramp and onto the Pacific Coast Highway. They were now heading up the coast away from the pier, the limos and the *Baywatch* shoot.

"Turn around!" demanded B.J.

Suddenly, without warning, the car began to shake violently. Carl checked the instrument panel which was lighting up like a pin ball machine. The Dart bucked like a newborn Dik Dik finding its legs.

"Maybe we got a bad batch of gas," commented Carl.

But there was no response from B.J.—she had left her body and was running in slow motion alongside Yasmine Bleeth, down the pristinely beautiful sands of the Southern California beach.

"Damn. There's nowhere to turn around," said Carl, keenly observing the unbroken yellow lines running down the middle of the four-lane highway.

The whining engine interrupted B.J.'s daydream and Carl made a radical turn across the double yellows, cutting off oncoming traffic and shooting the car into a parking lot on the beach side of the highway. The synchronized blasts from irate drivers sounded like the "Chicago" horn section.

The near-death experience snapped B.J. back to reality and Carl, having used up a week's worth of adrenaline, was in need of a cigarette. As he pushed in the lighter, the Dart shook and stalled.

"That was some fancy driving, son," an elderly man commented as he religiously worked a metal detector over the ground beside Carl's open window. "You from out of town?"

"Yeah. I guess it shows."

"Beautiful day out. Alfred T. Sewald, Hughes Aircraft, retired. You can call me Al." The elderly gentleman stooped to reject a beer tab. "Picked up nearly $12 a few weeks back," beamed Sewald, proudly displaying his mini minesweeper for Carl to admire.

"Is there an exit for the Pier off this highway?" asked Carl.

"The Santa Monica Pier? Lord, I used to take my wife to the merry-go-round there back in the Forties, when I first went to work for Hughes. Helped design the first armrest ashtray for aircraft. Course, nowadays, they're all soldered shut. Smokers don't stand a chance in this world." Carl nodded in agreement as Mr. Sewald politely raised his eyebrows requesting a hit off the Carlton smoldering between Carl's fingers. Mr. Sewald inhaled lightly and exhaled with a slight rattle to the lungs.

"Don't get to have these anymore. Tommy Boles—God rest his soul, got sucked into a jet engine—used to smoke four packs of Camels a day. And that was before they invented filters. Always said he'd outlive us all. Poor bastard. What a mess. Knock on wood. I'm in good health, except for the skin cancer. Scientists are right—ozone's shot to hell. Chlorofluorocarbons—too many of the damned things. Keeps your beer cold in the fridge but gives you skin cancer when you're out looking for change at the beach. Beautiful day though. Where'd you say you were from?"

"Indiana," replied Carl who was now under the open hood, casting his eyes over the various aspects of the engine. Mr. Sewald continued with his monologue as Carl focused on the carburetor and loosened its cover.

"God Bless America, but I'd never own a Dodge," said Sewald passing his metal detector over the engine with no audible reading.

B.J. joined the two beneath the open hood. "Excuse me, Mr. Sewald, but do you by any chance know how to get to O.J.'s house?" she asked deciding it might be easier to backtrack starting with the Rockingham estate.

"Who?"

"O.J. Simpson," said B.J.

"Oh yeah, that young football fella everybody's making such a fuss over. Now let me think. I think he lives over there on that street off... Oh, I'd recognize it once I saw it. Take you there if you like."

The I Team considered this for a moment. The old boy seemed to go on forever but he might just save them valuable time in the long run. Carl signaled for B.J. to get in and turn the ignition key. The Dart started up like a bomb. A huge pyrotechnic cloud of dark smoke escaped from the exhaust system. They were ready to roll. Carl took the wheel, Mr. Sewald rode shotgun and B.J. squeezed herself into the back seat. She looked back longingly as the Dart headed away from the *Baywatch* location, under the direction of Mr. Alfred T. Sewald, Hughes Aircraft, retired.

Though he started out strong, Mr. Sewald quickly became disoriented and after 20 minutes of improbable directions, Carl decided to invest in a Star Map from one of the many lounge-chair vendors on Sunset Boulevard. Consulting the map, they found their present location to be a stone's throw from Mr. Simpson's Rockingham estate.

On Bristol Circle, not more than a couple blocks away from Mr. Simpson's house, they noticed an open (though fenced off) field on the righthand side of the street. The words left Carl and B.J.'s lips at the same time, "What if..."

Carl pulled the Dart over to the side of the road and they all got out to take a look. If Mr. Simpson had committed the murders, the open field would have been an ideal location to discard any...anything, on his way back home. The field was an amazing find—a potential hotbed of evidence.

"Well kids, it's a damn good thing I brought along the metal detector," said Mr. Sewald as he surveyed the approximately 80' x 120' patch of land with large homes on either side.

B.J. retrieved the I Team Kit from the car, which included among other things, evidence collection supplies. ("Baggies do more than just keep foods fresh," Mary Jo used to say.) Meanwhile, Carl pulled back a section of chain link to allow Mr. Sewald and his metal detector into the area.

Mr. Sewald began scouring the field with intent and the detector started whining almost immediately. Wearing bright yellow Playtex Living Gloves, Carl and B.J. followed directly behind the elderly gentleman. The I Team retrieved, bagged and marked into evidence every item (metal and otherwise) that might prove to be vital to the investigation. Combing the field they discovered a multitude of items: wooden stakes, a hair clip, a chewed up Frisbee, dozens of beer and soda cans, an empty Marlboro carton, broken glass, several types of nails, a nearly deflated party balloon, to name a few.

With each new squeal of the metal detector they wondered, Didn't the L.A.P.D. bother to look in this field? They were amazed what a fresh perspective can bring to an investigation. Without warning, the detector started giving Mr. Sewald trouble. It seemed to be shorting out.

"Kids, I'm gonna have to do a visual on it," said Mr. Sewald referring to the earth at his feet. His eyes were amazingly sharp for a man of his age and he continued to point out things that might otherwise have been missed. He stopped before an unopened condom.

"A Trojan! The mighty Trojans of USC!" proclaimed Mr. Sewald picking up the item with the ungloved haste of Andrea Mazzola before Carl could intercept him. Hadn't Mr. Simpson attended the University of Southern California? The I Team bagged this new kind of glove that looked like it might fit.

Suddenly the detector, with sensor now pointing skyward, became stuck, emitting an extremely painful high pitch. As Mr. Sewald fiddled with the thing, neighborhood dogs began howling and soon a couple from an adjacent house appeared on their upstairs deck to see what was producing the horrific sound. Try as he might, Mr. Sewald could not get the detector to cease its screeching.

The man on the nearby sun deck began to shout. "Shut that thing up and get the hell out of here! You're on private property!" He turned to his wife (who seemed used to this sort of occurrence) and continued his tirade. "I'm sick of these goddamn lookie-loos. Call the cops, Belinda!"

Mr. Sewald calmly continued fussing with the malfunctioning detector. Theoretically, the old boy could sit there all day tinkering with the thing while those around him were losing their minds.

Carl attempted to instill the urgency of the situation. "We're gonna have the cops all over us if you can't shut that thing off, Mr. Sewald."

Finding a nearby eucalyptus, Mr. Sewald reluctantly choked up on the detector and took a full swing at the unforgiving Australian import. The detector fell silent, except for the clanging of its battered frame hitting the ground.

"We're moving the investigation!" announced B.J.

"Let's roll," said Carl as he picked up the shattered body of the detector and took Mr. Sewald by the arm. Not only did they not want the attention of the L.A.P.D. focused on their independent investigation—they didn't want the competition. Fortunately, they had covered the bulk of the field and Carl and B.J. were satisfied that they had pretty much gathered everything at the scene with the exception of weeds. The trio hustled back toward the Dart, stopping only to assist Mr. Sewald back through the hole in the chain link fence.

After a few anxious moments the Dart turned over, emitting another dark cloud of exhaust.

"Well kids, I'd better get home. I missed my noon meds," announced Mr. Sewald.

Obviously disappointed they would not be viewing Mr. Simpson's house today, Carl turned to Mr. Sewald, "Okay, where's home?"

"Seventeenth and Broadway."

B.J. instinctively consulted the map rather than the passenger. En route, Mr. Sewald's face lit up upon sighting Tommy's in Santa Monica—his medication need apparently forgotten, he hinted at a pit stop.

"You kids hungry? All that excitement gave me an appetite."

For his time and effort, the I Team bought Mr. Sewald a chili cheeseburger with everything on it, onion rings and a large root beer. Everything he said they wouldn't let him eat at home.

Turning onto Arizona Avenue, B.J. asked Mr. Sewald for an exact address.

"Oh, I can't remember dear, it's that big pink thing on the corner," said Mr. Sewald, now sporting a large quantity of chili down the front of his shirt.

Carl stopped the car in front of The Ocean View (it didn't have one) Retirement Home. A mini bus was picking up a load of seniors for an outing. Mr. Sewald seemed nervous and apprehensive.

"Oh crap," he muttered under his breath. "There she is—Frau Kommandant."

A stout woman in a blue suit, comfort shoes and hair pulled tightly into a bun, was assisting seniors onto the bus. She turned and approached the car. "Are you here for the..." Suddenly, the woman spied Mr. Sewald attempting to hide in the back seat. *"Mister Sewald!"* she bellowed. "Where have you been? I've already called the police and reported you missing."

"I've been with my friends here," said Mr. Sewald defiantly. "They're just out from Indiana and they wanted me to show them around. Isn't that right kids?"

Before Carl or B.J. could come to Mr. Sewald's defense, the woman began scolding again. "You never, never leave this facility without the staff knowing your whereabouts." She then turned her focus to the front seat. "Mr. Sewald is known as 'The Escape Artist of Ocean View,' but I've vowed to break him of his little adventures."

With that, B.J. felt compelled to come to Mr. Sewald's defense. "Excuse me, but I didn't catch your name," said B.J.

"Trudy Hufnagel, Facility Director. And just who might you be?" asked Hufnagel with feigned sweetness.

"I'm B.J. Wilkom and this is my partner Carl Spihek. We're investigative reporters. I'm very sorry we failed to check Mr. Sewald out through the proper channels but we're working on a very sensitive case and it was imperative that we have Mr. Sewald's expertise on the matter."

"Mr. Sewald's *expertise*?" Ms. Hufnagel asked sarcastically.

"Yes," added Carl. "Mr. Sewald was helping us with some very delicate evidence gathering for our investigation."

"*Mr. Sewald*?" scoffed Ms. Hufnagel. "That's correct. Mr. Sewald's expert handling of a metal detector was invaluable," replied Carl.

"That old thing? He found it in a dumpster behind the facility."

"Then you can see what we mean regarding his honing skills," said Carl.

"And what exactly are you investigating?" asked Ms. Hufnagel.

"Two murders," said B.J.

"The Crime of the Century," added Carl before being tapped hard on the leg by B.J.

"As in O.J. Simpson? As far as I'm concerned, that matter is over and done with."

"It's not over until someone is behind bars for committing the murders. It's possible our investigation will lead to that person or persons," said B.J.

"I see. Well, Mr. Sewald, are you planning to stay on investigating the Crime of the Century or would you care to join us inside for Tapioca Day?"

"Tapioca Day! I almost forgot. Well kids, I guess this is good-bye."

As Carl helped Ms. Hufnagel extract Mr. Sewald from the back seat, they were hit with a powerful odor. Obviously, there was a reason why the senior was denied easy access to Tommy's chili cheeseburgers.

"A bath smells like a good idea, don't you think Mr. Sewald?" suggested Ms. Hufnagel.

"I'd consider a bath after two servings of tapioca," bartered Mr. Sewald as they headed up the walkway arm in arm. The old boy seemed almost eager to be back at the pink stucco facility he now called home.

"Wait!" called Carl, grabbing the remains of Mr. Sewald's metal detector from the back seat. "Your equipment!" Carl jogged up to Mr. Sewald who was now fully entangled in the stern but affectionate web of Ms. Hufnagel.

"You keep it, son," replied Mr. Sewald, putting an arm around Carl's shoulder. "Might help you find the truth. The truth is out there." Carl smiled at the familiarity of the phrase.

"X-Files. Damn good show!" exclaimed the octogenarian as he turned and entered the double glass doors of the Ocean View Retirement Home.

Carl tossed the metal detector in the back seat. The unit crackled for a moment, then fell silent.

Big John Wayne

Interview to Die For - Robert Crane rudely interrupts the afterlife of our greatest western hero to get some foreign policy advice.

ROBERT CRANE: You've got an interesting perspective nowadays on the Middle East. Tell me, how would you handle Saddam and Iraq?

JOHN WAYNE: Wellllll, pilgrim, I'll tell ya.

CRANE: Wait, wait a minute. What is that pilgrim stuff?

WAYNE: Sorry, John Ford bet me I'd never utter that phrase again. Pay up, you son of a...

CRANE: But back to the subject. How would you handle Saddam?

WAYNE: I would turn over 11 of Hollywood's crack stuntmen to USC's football coach Pete Carroll, give them a month to train using the Viet Cong codebook as back-up and parachute them into Baghdad. End around, quarterback sneak, the old Statue of Liberty, Saddam would quickly fall in his own end zone. Safety. America 2, Iraq 0.

CRANE: You were a big Republican while you were alive. Tell me, how do you rate George W.'s performance so far?

WAYNE: Sure beats Gore to hell. After 9/11, America needed a larger-than-life character like Bush to pick them up and dust them off. Howard Hawks always tells me he thinks little Georgie would have made a fine actor in Westerns.

Dick Nixon, General Eisenhower, Napoleon and I had some drinks the other day. Nixon's still upset with Oliver Stone's picture about him. Oh, and Napoleon doesn't like brandy. Don't serve it to him. Gets mad.

CRANE: The world's a different place since you passed on in 1979, isn't it?

WAYNE: America hasn't changed. The rest of the world's gone to hell in a hand basket. Our hardworking men and women still have more smarts than the Ruskies, Chinese and Mexicans all put together. Little Akbar in Afghanistan or Swing Lo in Cambodia look to us to show them the way. That hasn't changed, partner.

CRANE: What is your opinion of today's liberal Hollywood?

WAYNE: They wouldn't know a rifle butt from Jennifer Lopez' butt. Don't get me wrong. I do admire Miss Lopez' talents. I would have gladly cast her in *The Alamo*. This Ben Aykroyd fella isn't right for her, though. Doesn't appreciate her.

Robert Crane

CRANE: You were nominated only twice for Academy Awards for Best Actor—*Sands of Iwo Jima* in 1950 and *True Grit* in 1969 for which you won the statue. Who's going to win Oscars this year?

WAYNE: Nicholson and some British actress. Same as every year.

CRANE: Bing Crosby and Carl Reiner always wore great hairpieces. You and Sinatra had more money than Fort Knox but between the two of you, you managed to find the worst looking rugs in show business. What was up with that?

WAYNE: I always hated hair, makeup, and wardrobe. That's for sissies. I'd rather be playin' cards with the boys or talkin' up a sweet Chiquita on the set in Durango. Same with Mr. Sinatra. We're all topless up here—Bing, Bogie, Mr. Sinatra, Ray Milland. And John Ford doesn't have to wear that eye patch, either. Makes him look different.

CRANE: What do you miss most about Earth?

WAYNE: Craft service on movie sets. My family. Wives. Football. Lesley Ann Warren.

CRANE: After you got lung cancer, it convinced a lot of people to give up the coffin nails. Are you proud that you've helped people live longer?

WAYNE: Still miss 'em. Especially after sex, which up here, as you can guess, is pure heaven.

CRANE: The world is overpopulated, ravaged by war, hunger, poverty and pollution. Give us some encouraging words so we can go on.

WAYNE: Courage is being scared to death and saddlin' up anyway. I believe tomorrow is the most important thing in life. It comes to us at midnight very clean. It's perfect when it arrives, and it puts itself in our hands and hopes we've learned something from yesterday.

CRANE: Any other advice?

WAYNE: Yeah, find a good sports bar. Get out of your casa, away from the little lady, watch a football game and drink. Drink a lot.

CRANE: There's the John Wayne Airport, the John Wayne Cancer Institute and the John Wayne Marina. What's next?

WAYNE: My son, Michael, who oversees the maintenance of my legacy, is talking about the John Wayne Channel. Well over 200 movies and television shows. The Duke, 24 hours a day, seven days a week. By the way, if you see Michael, tell him those Coors ads were embarrassing. Cheap.

Kid, don't do it again.

Cheech and Chong's Comedy Film Festival Magazine

The Doobie Awards

As with anything else, excellence in comedy is not judged solely on its own merit. It's also judged on the size of the donation. Cheech and Chong realize that awards are generally doled out only to the superstars. But now there's a forum for the underrecognized, undersized and undernourished. Finally the little guy gets his time under the bright lights. But why Amsterdam and not Hollywood or New York for the site of the awards? None of your business. The writers, producers, directors, stars, agents, extras, executives, caterers, makeup people—they're all here and so are you. Aren't you? Smile and have fun. This is going to be on pay-TV. Oh, that's the other point of why we're doing this thing. You thought only for fun? Come on, this production is costing us a lot of bucks. We've got to recoup it somehow. And then there are the plane tickets. Air transportation is not cheap. There's fuel costs, not to mention the wonderful food served on board. And the stewardesses' uniforms have to be dry-cleaned. OK, the Doobie Awards. This year's beautifully constructed Doobie Award statue, L'Award, features the world's largest joint glued atop a magnificent wood base. The winners' names are engraved in expensive brass glued on to the front of the award. It looks like it cost a lot of money. That's what we want you to think.

Generals Robert E. Lee and Ulysses S. Grant

Interview to Die For - Robert Crane rudely interrupts the afterlife of two of the great military minds from the War Between The States.

HWY 111: What do the colors red, white and blue mean to you?

ROBERT E. LEE: France...(Pause) Sir, that off-handed comment was meant to be nothing more than a bit of merrymaking. Those colors mean, of course, the great Confederate, um, United States of America.

ULYSSES S. GRANT: (laughing) General Lee has amused me since he was cornered like a rat at Appomattox in his proud state of Virginia. No, the colors remind me of leading this land for eight prosperous years... And, may I add, since the whiskey seems to be kicking in, those colors also remind me of a rather distasteful but amusing joke involving a Union soldier getting hit with buckshot.

HWY 111: What do you think of President Bush?

LEE: Mediocre student. Could have been a great general. Enjoys his libations. Less than adequate president. Come to think of it, he's reminiscent of my dear Mister Grant.

GRANT: When in doubt, fight. The president has Colin Powell, I had Secretary of State Hamilton Fish. Saved my Yankee ass. Mister Bush will enjoy eight years in the White House as General Eisenhower and yours truly did. I wish I had had Karl Rove to help, though. And Condoleezza. She stirs my emancipationist urges.

HWY 111: Civil War, World Wars, Korea, Vietnam, Afghanistan, now Iraq. Has this country been involved in enough war?

LEE: Sir, you sound like a Yankee turncoat. I lost hundreds of thousands of good men fighting for what they believed in. Unfortunately, there will always be war.

GRANT: And that's why the only presidency General Lee ever assumed was at Washington College in Virginia after the war. I recently shared a draft with two free-thinkers named Gandhi and T.E. Lawrence. Slight men like myself but persuasive speakers. They pointed out that on my Hudson River tomb are the words, "Let Us Have Peace." When we're finished with this Iraq skirmish, we should obey those words.

HWY 111: How do two old warhorses spend their days?

GRANT: I bowl with Dick Nixon two days a week. Play chess with a fascinating thespian named George C. Scott. Share meals with soldiers and statesmen—Churchill, MacArthur, Napoleon. Drink. One never gets drunk here. Pull General Lee's leg a lot. By the way, why does every Chinatown in the United States have a restaurant named General Lee's?

LEE: I still meet with Stonewall Jackson to discuss where we went wrong. I've met most of the Presidents. I particularly enjoy the company of Kennedy and Roosevelt. They're not bad for a couple of Yankees.

HWY 111: You had such great names back then: "Stonewall," "Ulysses," "Zachary," "Thaddeus," "Tecumseh." Where are those great monikers today?

LEE: Son, you're joshin' me. Go to the east and then go south. Go to South Central L.A. "Dr. Dre," "Snoop Dogg," "50 Cent," "Ludicris," "Ja Rule." No northerner ever devised monikers resembling these.

GRANT: I beg to differ, General. "Eminem" represents the proud state of Michigan. "DMX," "P. Diddy," "Jay-Z." All northern boys. Forgive me. Men.

HWY 111: The War Between The States lasted five long years. Two-and-a-half-million men enlisted. More soldiers were killed or wounded than in Vietnam, Korea, and WWII combined. Were you pleased to see the war end and the country reunited?

LEE: This would have been a far better country if the Grays had won. I am eternally grateful to my ragamuffins. Of course, events could have taken a drastic turn. We could be ruled by Tony Blair or Jacques Chirac right now. Instead of rap and football, we'd be obsessed with Gilbert & Sullivan and cricket. Or, Marcel Marceau and frog's legs.

GRANT: We had one-and-a-half million men in blue. The South didn't have a chance. When the general surrendered in Virginia—his home state, I might add—I respected him and his men as brave soldiers. I allowed them to keep their horses for spring plowing. Though critics called me 'Grant the Butcher,' upon war's end, I proclaimed, 'The war is over, the rebels are our countrymen again.'

HWY 111: A new book, *Redneck Nation,* argues that the South has risen again. Considering that our last six Presidents have either hailed from the South or played "The Southern Strategy" to win, do you think, perhaps, the Grays won after all, General Grant?

GRANT: What a coincidence: Abe and I were just talking about that the other day. Abe was saying, 'What was it all for, anyway?'

LEE: What a name-dropper.

HWY 111: Are you aware that you both died at age 63?

LEE: You're really digging now for questions, young man. What an unqualified, loafing, mediocre, Northern dunderhead posing as a journalist! You must have studied at some Yankee school.

GRANT: Well, at least the young man can speak without sounding like he's drawing a longstocking out of his mouth. You Dixie gentlemen never could talk; no wonder you lost. You couldn't make out each other's commands!

HWY 111: Give it up, guys. General Grant, you hailed from Illinois. What do you miss most about the Midwest?

GRANT: Beef. Lots of beef. Honest folks. Large windows. Kielbasa. Big porches. Amateur crafts. Baseball. Oh, and Second City. Improvisational humor has always been a real favorite of mine.

HWY 111: General Lee, your turn: What do you miss most about the South?

LEE: Chicken fried steak. Red eyed gravy. Grits. Hush puppies. Mint juleps. Young Negro women.

GRANT: *Black*. Young *black* women.

LEE: Once a Reconstructionist, always a Reconstructionist.

Ya Gotta Have a Gimmick!

Radical solutions to a problem that doesn't even exist

Visitors to the Coachella Valley consistently remark on how tastefully understated our casinos are. Although our local gameries offer much the same action as found in Las Vegas (with the travel time from L.A. cut in half), people can't help but notice that our local venues haven't yet gone for the ersatz "themes" of our friendly gaming capital to the east.

There's the faux Roman Empire motif with its naked statuary at Caesars. The indoor chlorined waterways plowed by gondoliers at The Venetian. Pirates' plunder at Treasure Island. And some misplaced love of the French at the Paris.

What's next? We've been noodling with some of the following ideas.

World's End Survivalist Compound and Casino

Once you've made your reservation, you receive coordinates to our secret location via ham radio transmission. Upon arrival, enjoy the challenge of infiltrating our compound surrounded by heavily armed federal agents.

Next, negotiate through the Ho Chi Minh Obstacle Course of barbed wire, snake pits and booby traps, to arrive at the World's End Check-in point where our hard-ass staff will assign you your accommodations. Bivouac in your 8 x 10, cramped, windowless, cement-lined cell complete with functional cots—one latrine on every floor.

After you've slipped into camo fatigues and face-paint, belly-crawl down to the casino where the action is. Agent Orange couldn't penetrate the dense foliage of our Jungle Casino where you and your family will enjoy an arsenal of paramilitary entertainment. Imagine the excitement of playing slots as a surface-to-air missile whizzes by, barely grazing your helmet. And everyone loves our Live Ammo Shooting Gallery. Best of all—we never tax your winnings!

We haven't forgotten about your little soldiers of fortune, either—the kids will love Punji World where life and death is served up on a stick.

Hungry? Turn in your voucher at our adequate dining facility, MESS, where you'll chow down on chipped beef on toast, C-rations, gorp and freeze-dried ice cream.

Feel like a swim? Wade in up to your neck in our water moccasin-infested Survival Swamp. You may want to burn the leeches off your body with a complimentary still-lit cigarette before heading off to our spectacular midnight show, *Incoming 3-D! A Celebration of the Independent Spirit* (flack jackets optional).

Our Koresh and Weaver Ballrooms are perfect for weddings, baptisms and anti-government meetings.

Before you pack up the Hummer in the Schwarzenegger Garage—don't forget to visit the NRA gift shop and stockpile provisions for your cache back home.

FanDome Hotel and Casino

You've punched a clock for 50 weeks. Now, you've abandoned your boss, your wife and your kids. It's just you and your buddies about to experience the Super Bowl of vacations: FanDome.

Your adventure begins in the world's largest parking lot where hundreds of tailgate parties beckon. After slamming down a hot link and a cold one, jump aboard our power-tram to the Players Gate.

A bellman in referee stripes escorts you and your posse to a luxury box suite complete with balcony overlooking the sporting event of your choice. Teams are playing 24 hours a day in our four concourses: Pigskin Palace, Boys of Summer Yard, Hoop Heaven and Puck Pavilion.

Betting on live action sports is never illegal at FanDome. In fact, our resident oddsmaker, colorful Joey Eight Fingers, will be happy to drop by your room to distribute winnings—or, ahem, encourage you to make good on your wager. (He can be very convincing, we understand.)

Room service? No need to pick up the phone, simply holler out your door to one of the many vendors working the hotel. "Hey, peanut!" "Yo, beer man!"

Tired of hanging out with the guys? Call our 24-hour Personal Cheerleader service— guaranteed to get you up for any game.

Now hit the showers before weaving your way down to the Main Event Casino where you can bet on every sport across the globe. We wouldn't want you to miss a minute of televised action either—with monitors attached to all our slot machines, you can access every sports channel in the world via satellite.

Stop in at the Hock A Lugie Bar and Grill and gauge your velocity in the Robbie Alomar Interactive Spit Zone. Then wash down a dog, nachos and pretzels with one of our four thousand beers on tap.

Speaking of beer, the FanDome offers our world famous two-mile-long urinoir—you don't even have to leave the casino floor.

Next, take Antacid Alley to the Coliseum where every seat is a LazyBoy Lounger. Sit back and enjoy our live stage extravaganza starring Joe Namath and hundreds of former *Sports Illustrated* swimsuit models covered mostly in face paint. Eating, drinking and flash photography are encouraged.

After the show, visit the Hall of Shame where you can heckle wax figures of the most controversial sports personalities. Boo Mike Tyson, Marv Albert, Frank Gifford, Pete Rose, George Steinbrenner, John Rocker and may more.

Then, be there at midnight when the FanDome's retractable roof is opened, releasing trillions of cubic yards of accumulated methane gas into the atmosphere. With the assistance of the world's largest flame thrower, FanDome creates its own Aurora Borealis.

The Good Life Casino and Trailer Park

Pull off the I-15 at Access Road and drive till you see the giant water tower—that's when you know you've arrived at The Good Life Casino and Trailer Park.

Back it on in and park yourself for a spell. Enjoy propane hook-up and fire pit at every site. Ten kids or more stay free. No cheating—they have to be birthed afore ya come in.

Feel the hum as three million volts of pure 'mercan electricity flows through the giant overhead electrical towers. Stay with us during the summer and you might be lucky enough to see the fireworks if a transformer blows during a storm.

Now that yer all settled in, come on over to the only casino in the world shaped like a giant Airstream. That's right, two stories of shiny aluminum siding! It's a sight to behold when the sun hits it just right. Why planes have to be diverted it's so bright!

Ever try an' find a penny slot machine at one a them other casinos? Not a problem at The Good Life—we got row after row o' penny slots and food stamps are as good as gold at all the gaming tables.

Bet on your favorite games like pitchin' pennies, cock fightin', mumbletypeg, checkers (or Chinese checkers for you big-city folk), frog jumpin' and much more.

While you're at the gamblin' hall, ya never gotta worry about the little ones. Let the kids loose on the Pile o' Tires. No smokin' allowed, little Jimmy! And kids love Uncle Carl's Moonshine Ride. And don't you be concerned none—all them false charges against Uncle Carl never amounted to nothing.

Experience *Dust!* — the only simulated Oklahoma storm this side of the Mississippi.

After a full day at the casino, cool off in the runoff pond located behind the nearby water treatment plant. Piles of stinky clothes takin' up room? Visit the world's largest outdoor laundromat, Laundry Land, where dryers are only a dime.

You won't be confused by too many choices when it comes to eats—we only got one place—that's the Opossum Shack where everything is deep-fried. You won't want to miss our world-famous squirrel on a stick.

After supper, catch the giant nightly show as four water tankers come barreling through the park and wet down the dirt. Not a dry eye in the house.

Bob Crane's Ten Stupid Questions

Robert David Crane, Jr. goes online to interview his late father, Bob Crane, celebrating the occasion of the release of Auto Focus, *the Paul Schrader film that stars Greg Kinnear as his father and Rita (*My Big Fat Greek Wedding's *producer) Wilson as his mother. The film depicts his father's tabloid-worthy life.*

STUPID: What do you think of the movie about your life, *Auto Focus?*

BOB CRANE: Outside of *Hogan's Heroes* and Angel Carter of the Classic Cat, it's the most important project I've ever been affiliated with.

STUPID: Who's a better Hogan, you or Greg Kinnear?

CRANE: Me. Kinnear's too pretty and too small. The Hogan jacket fit me better. Werner (Klemperer, who played Colonel Klink in the hit series) told me, however, that he prefers Kinnear.

STUPID: I understand Frank Sinatra wore the jacket before you did in his movie *Von Ryan's Express?*

CRANE: The jacket still had the Western Costume label. It was an honor. I recently met Frank and Dean up here, incidentally. They don't live with the rest of us, however. They share a Neutra-designed house on a hill.

STUPID: Because of your second wife and her X-rated web site, you're now more known as an amateur pornographer than the star of a hit TV series.

CRANE: She needs the money. The *Hogan's* residual checks apparently ran out. Her acting career stalled after she played Hilda, Klink's secretary on *Hogan's.* It doesn't matter to me because here we're all naked all the time. I'm staring at Ava Gardner right now as we speak.

STUPID: You've been the subject of a book (*Murder of Bob Crane*), television documentaries (*The E! True Hollywood Story, Biography*), numerous magazine and newspaper articles and now a Paul Schrader film. Your career has more buzz now than when you were living. What's next?

CRANE: Stanley Kubrick was disappointed that his career ended with a Cruise-Kidman film. He's here filming another take on sex: *Eyes Automatically Focused.* I'm doing a cameo as a strip club drummer.

STUPID: You were a better-than-average drummer. You appeared on variety shows and even released an album on Epic Records. How often do you play now?

CRANE: That was sad how Michael Jackson turned on Tommy Mottola, don't you think?

I play everyday. My teacher is Buddy Rich, for God's sake. Yesterday, I jammed with Lennon, Harrison, Morrison, Entwistle and Keith Moon. I was the oldest one there. That Moon—what a nut.

STUPID: You were brutally murdered, bludgeoned to death. Who did it?

CRANE: I don't know. I was asleep. John Carpenter's here now. He swears he didn't do it.

STUPID: Hogan, Klink, Schultz and your producer Edward H. Feldman are together again. Are you thinking of a reunion film?

CRANE: No. We have great crews available but we want to shoot film, not digital. Everything's digital here. And there's no SAG contract yet.

STUPID: You were killed in 1978. You loved technology. *Rolling Stone* called you a cool video sex pioneer. Yet you missed cell phones, CDs, DVDs, and PCs.

CRANE: More important, I missed Pamela Anderson, Anna Nicole Smith and the real Erin Brockovich. Talk about equipment!

STUPID: Last question. Are you happy with the way you're being remembered?

CRANE: I don't mind. It's not important up here. We're all equal—except for Sinatra and Dino. I would like to say to my first wife Anne, Rita Wilson played you magnificently in *Auto Focus*. There's an Oscar buzz around here.

And by the way, Anne, Donna Reed says "Hi," and thinks you did a great job rearing our three children, particularly Robert David, who, up here, is considered a brilliant writer.

And to Sumner Redstone, CEO of Viacom, which syndicates *Hogan's Heroes:* We shot 168 episodes at $90,000 per. Viacom has grossed $90 million off *Hogan's* reruns that play internationally. How about sharing some of the wealth with the surviving members of the cast, writers and directors who've made you a billionaire? I'm a volunteer gatekeeper here twice a week. Good luck getting in!

Made in the USA
San Bernardino, CA
19 May 2018